TEACHING GERMAN:
A Practical Guide

TEACHING GERMAN:
A Practical Guide

SECOND EDITION

WILGA M. RIVERS
KATHLEEN MITCHELL DELL'ORTO
VINCENT J. DELL'ORTO

National Textbook Company
NTC a division of *NTC Publishing Group* • Lincolnwood, Illinois USA

THE AUTHORS

Wilga M. Rivers is Professor of Romance Languages and Literatures and Co-ordinator of Language Instruction at Harvard University. She has her *Licence ès Lettres* from the University of Montpellier and a Ph.D. from the University of Illinois at Urbana-Champaign. She has taught language and courses on language teaching and learning previously at the University of Illinois at Urbana-Champaign, Northern Illinois University, Columbia University, and Monash University in Melbourne, Australia. Professor Rivers is the author of *The Psychologist and the Foreign-Language Teacher* (1964), *Teaching Foreign-Language Skills* (1968 and 1981), *Speaking in Many Tongues* (1972, 1975, 1983), and *Communicating Naturally in a Second Language* (1983). She is co-editor of *Changing Patterns in Foreign-Language Programs* (1972), and co-author of *A Practical Guide to the Teaching of English as a Second or Foreign Language* (1978), *Teaching French: A Practical Guide* (1988), *Teaching Spanish: A Practical Guide* (1988), and a book on teaching Hebrew now on press. She has lectured in 30 countries, and her work has been translated into 9 languages.

Kathleen Mitchell Dell'Orto is a scholar and translator. She taught previously at the University of California, Riverside, and at Johns Hopkins University, and was Lecturer at Georg August Universität, Göttingen, West Germany. She received her Ph.D. in German from Johns Hopkins University.

Vincent J. Dell'Orto taught as Assistant Professor of German at the University of Illinois, Urbana-Champaign. He received his Ph.D. in German from Johns Hopkins University.

1991 Printing

Published by National Textbook Company, a division of NTC Publishing Group.
© 1988 by NTC Publishing Group, 4255 West Touhy Avenue,
Lincolnwood (Chicago), Illinois 60646-1975 U.S.A.

1 2 3 4 5 6 7 8 9 ML 9 8 7 6 5 4 3 2

Preface

We hear a great deal about communication these days, particularly about communication in foreign- or second-language classes. It is easy to talk about communication, but much harder to realize it. Communication becomes a possibility when people are in an interactive relationship where they have messages to share — when people are at ease with each other or are affectively driven to say what they have to say because of some situational imperative. It is not enough to learn grammar or to accumulate vocabulary or even to make native-sounding noises with the appropriate stress and melodic contour. Language learners must be able to understand others when they speak the language and to frame utterances to express their point of view; they should also be able to invite others to communicate with them. The continual use of language in interaction with others is basic to successful language learning and teaching.

For effective language learning in the classroom, we need an *interactive approach,* where emphasis is placed on the whole fabric of language and on ways to use it to express meaning. Continual efforts to find the "best" way for all to learn, or the "best" way for all to teach, have never been successful. We must leave room for individuality in learning *and* in teaching. Human beings continue to elude all efforts to cage them, shape them, or restrict them in any way. They "break out all over," whether as students or teachers — both of whom are learners. Theory can suggest ideas to teachers and to learners, but not impose them. Students continue to learn languages in all kinds of ways — with teachers, without teachers, and despite teachers (or theoreticians, for that matter).

The essential element of a language class is interaction. Without it, the most sophisticated techniques are not enough. If we examine successful ways of learning and teaching, we find, at the heart of that success, interaction: people interacting with people (face-to-face or directly with authors through the intermediary of the written word). Teachers interact with students, students with teachers, students with students, students with the community of speakers of the language (wherever possible). Interaction is two-way, three-way, or four-way, but never one-way.

Teacher-dominated classrooms are not interactive classrooms. Interaction in a classroom setting requires that individuals understand other individuals and appreciate their uniqueness and their particular needs — not manipulating or directing them or deciding how they can or will learn, but encouraging and drawing them out (educating them in the true sense of the word), while building up their confidence and their enjoyment of language learning and use.

Interaction is not just shallow discussion: talking back and forth to each other in artificially stimulated exchanges, where no participant really shares, but instead waits for an opportunity to take over. Students should be involved together in activities that require use of the language they are learning. From a simple Show and Tell to a full-scale simulation game, an extemporized skit, a vigorous argument on a point of cultural misunderstanding, or a group recasting of the ending to a story or novel, students interact and develop each other's facility in comprehension and production. Drama, songs, music, games, even dance, draw out uninhibited student participation and make them wish to communicate, using what they have learned in its most elastic and flexible form.

An interactive approach requires the highest degree of indirect leadership and emotional maturity. Teachers are persons, and excellent teachers are persons with emotional control, imagination, and a high degree of perceptiveness and sensitivity. These are the qualities needed for success in language teaching, not a particular collection of techniques or tricks. We teach and interact most effectively according to our own personality. The interactive approach encourages such teacher individuality. Whatever promotes student participation in a relaxed and enthusiastic atmosphere stimulates the interaction that is essential to successful language learning. The interaction may be quiet; it may be noisy; it may be assured and vigorous; it may be indirect, providing almost imperceptible encouragement for self-expression.

As teachers venturing into the profession, readers of this book must actively seek a well-rounded approach to language teaching with which they feel comfortable. Then their students will feel comfortable with them. Courses and books can suggest and provide ideas. It is for each teacher to choose among them, developing his or her personal approach to the task at hand.

With this in mind, foreign-language teaching becomes an interesting and exciting occupation. Since the nature of language and its complex operations is still a matter of controversy and since the psychologists have still much to learn about how language is acquired (the native language as well as a second or third language), teachers of language have an open field. They are free to experiment and innovate. They can appropriate what has proved successful in other times and other places. They can repeat and refine what they have found to be effective in their own circumstances with their own students. They can share successes and explore failures with their colleagues, learning much from each other.

Learning to use a language freely and fully is a long and effortful process. Teachers cannot learn the language for their students. They can set their students on the road by creating situations in which they can use the language, thus helping them to develop confidence in their own learning powers. Then they must wait on the sidelines, ready to encourage and assist, while each student struggles and perseveres to convey meaning in interaction. Some students learn the language well, even while the teacher observes. For those who find the task more difficult, we should at least make every effort to ensure that their language-learning is an enjoyable and educational experience — something to which they will be willing to return when changed circumstances and inner needs draw them to it.

As foreign-language teachers we must remain optimistic. Rarely will we see the fully developed product (the autonomous, confident language-user), although we will often be stimulated by the enthusiasm of those we have started along that path. Let us not be discouraged by the jeremiads of those who tell us our task is an impossible one in the time at our disposal. Our colleagues in mathematics and physics do not produce Einsteins after three or four years of study, and Stravinskys are rare in the music room. Students who are interested in language and are uninhibited in using the little they have assimilated will have a foundation to build upon when the opportunity presents itself. Surely all true education is beginnings. It is the hope of the authors that this book and its companion volumes will play some part in stimulating imaginative and resourceful teaching that will arouse and sustain effective self-motivated learning.

In this book we do not provide final answers. What we have written is intended to provoke lively discussion. This is clearly an age when flexibility is a crucial attribute for the young teacher who will need, as time goes on, to develop language courses to meet a variety of student and community objectives. As prospective and practicing teachers consider the many techniques we have described and understand the rationale behind them (recognizing their strengths and weaknesses), they will establish a solid basis for choice when faced with students of different ages, abilities, interests, and styles of learning. Ultimately, their selection will accord with their educational ideals, the resources of their own personality, and the needs and learning preferences of their students. The one all-sufficient answer for the classroom teacher in all circumstances may be an alluring panacea, but it is as illusory and unattainable as the philosopher's stone.

Method books for the preparation of foreign-language teachers abound. Some students using this book may have a background in general methodology, such as is provided in *Teaching Foreign-Language Skills** and books of a similar nature. The range of material in that book, however, is not covered in detail in this one. Rather, many ideas implicit and explicit in *Teaching Foreign-Language Skills* have been developed here in practical detail, so that theory comes alive in actual activities. Teachers are thus provided with a great deal of information without the obstacles created by overly technical language. The use of language from the earliest stages for normal purposes of interaction is stressed throughout.

For all of the *Practical Guides* in this series, the basic theoretical discussion and the elaboration of techniques remain parallel. However, for all exercises, activities, and study materials discussed, examples are supplied in the language the teacher trainee will be teaching. Proper attention is also paid to contemporary developments in that language, so that the teacher may learn while preparing to teach. Since they are parallel, the books are appropriate for simultaneous use in multiple-language methods classes, as well as for language-specific courses in foreign-language departments. The material they present is applicable to future high-school or elementary-school teachers or to those who will teach at the undergraduate level. The material will also be useful for in-service training courses and institutes, enabling teachers of different languages to consider general problems together, as they penetrate to the heart of the matter through the language of concentration. The books also provide a treasury of ideas useful to practicing teachers: suggestions for developing supplementary learning packets, for conducting small-group activities, as well as for stimulating learning in a conventional classroom.

A few additional explanations may facilitate the use of the book. Although there is some detailed discussion of points of syntax and phonology, these are subordinate to the discussion of preparation of teaching and testing materials and to the elaboration of techniques. No attempt has been made to treat syntax and phonology systematically or exhaustively. Other books are available to meet this need, and these are listed in the notes and bibliographies. On the other hand, material used in the examples has been selected with a view to opening up discussion of areas of language about which the non-native speaker may not be quite clear. Particular emphasis has been put on the differences between spoken and written language. Examples are not intended

*Wilga M. Rivers, 2d ed. 1981. Chicago: The University of Chicago Press.

to be complete, but rather to illustrate technique. The suggested exercises (indicated by ✱) then extend the application into other areas of possible confusion or difficulty. One cannot teach what one does not fully understand oneself. Teachers in training will thus have a further opportunity to clarify matters that have worried them in the past.

It should be noted, at this point, that the asterisked activities are to be assigned, so that students actively participate in creation of new materials and in the adaptation and refinement of those provided in current textbooks. The close examination and judicious adaptation of text, test, and taped materials should be part of every trainee teacher's experience, along with the trying out, in actual teaching situations, of what has been developed (whether in microlessons or in practice teaching with a class). Students should be encouraged during their training period to begin a permanent file of personally collected teaching materials, along with ideas for activities and projects. In that file, they should keep reading passages, cultural information, poems, scenes from plays, songs, and games appropriate for various ages and levels, as well as informal visual aids, interesting and amusing variations of techniques, practical activities to help students use language informally and spontaneously, useful pictures and handouts, and sources of information and supplementary assistance. If students share what they gather during this important period of preparation, they will not approach their first year of full-time teaching empty-handed.

The artificiality of dealing with various aspects of language use in separate chapters is apparent (e.g., the separation of listening and acceptable production of sounds from communicative interaction—and both of these from internalization of the structure of the language). Students will need to hold certain questions in abeyance until they can see the whole picture. For those who wish to consider aspects of language in a different order, numerous cross-references are included in the text, in addition to the comprehensive information found in the Contents and the Index. To facilitate the finding of examples dealing with particular aspects of language use, initial-letter classifications have been used throughout different sections, that is, *C:* Communicating (both speaking and listening); *G:* Grammar; *S:* Sounds; *R:* Reading; and *W:* Writing.

Examples go beyond the elementary course. Although it is difficult to establish a level of difficulty in the abstract, *E* has been used to indicate the elementary level (first or second year of high school, first or second semester of beginning college study), *I* for intermediate level (second or third year of high school, third semester of college), and *A* for advanced level (fourth or fifth year of high school, fourth semester or above in college). This classification is non-scientific and intended only as a rough guide. It will be for the instructor, the student, or the practicing teacher to adjust those levels of difficulty to particular situations.

In conclusion, the authors wish to thank most warmly the numerous persons, scholars and teachers in the field, who have contributed to the development of their thinking through discussion, demonstration, or published work. Special thanks must, however, go to our colleagues, U. Henry Gerlach, Philip Grundlehner, Karl-Heinz Schoeps, Rainer Sell, and Virginia Coombs, who so graciously read through various parts of the manuscript and whose suggestions we sought to incorporate into the book. We owe a debt of gratitude to Arlene VanderWerff for her tactful and incisive assistance in coordinating the work on this book with its parent volume in the series, and to Carol Mussey, Claire Riley, and Thérèse Chevallier, whose diligence and patience in preparing the manuscript greatly facilitated the realization of this project.

Cambridge, Massachusetts   W.M.R.
Washington, D.C.   K.M.D.
Washington, D.C.   V.J.D.

Contents

II THE WRITTEN WORD

6. *Reading I: purposes and procedures,* 167

7. *Reading II: from dependence to independence,* 199

TEACHING GERMAN:
A Practical Guide

I
COMMUNICATING

Communication acts

In Part I, speaking and listening are discussed in separate chapters, although in a communication act one clearly complements the other. The reader will bear in mind that being able to speak a language without understanding what is being said by native speakers is of limited use, while being able to understand a language but not speak it can have specialized utility (for the enjoyment of foreign-language films, broadcasts, plays, and songs, or for professional monitoring purposes) but is very frustrating in normal communication situations. Being able to speak comprehensibly does not necessarily ensure ability to comprehend normal native speech; on the other hand, many people develop a very high level of aural comprehension without being able to express themselves freely. Both areas require serious attention.

In a well-rounded program, success in each will be recognized as a separate achievement and given equal importance in the eyes of the students. Nevertheless, practice of each should normally be in relation to the other if communicating is the ultimate goal.

Developing skill and confidence in communication

When selecting learning activities, we must always remember that our goal is for the students to be able to interact freely with others: to understand what others wish to communicate in the broadest sense, and to be able to what others wish to communicate in the broadest sense, and to be able to convey to others what they themselves wish to share (whether as a reaction to a communication or as an original contribution to the exchange). To do this effectively, however, the students must understand how the German language works and be able to make the interrelated changes for which the system of the language provides mechanisms.

The following schema will help us to see the essential processes involved in learning to communicate.

C1   Processes involved in learning to communicate

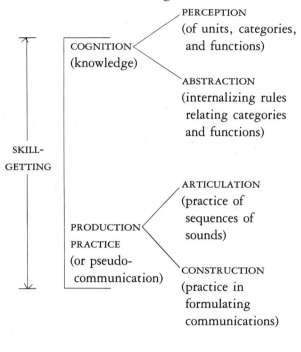

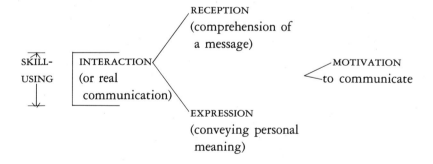

Commentary

1. This is not a sequential but a parallel schema, in the sense that skill-getting and skill-using[1] are continually proceeding hand in hand. Both have some place in every lesson. There is genuine *interaction from the beginning,* with students exploring the full scope of what is being learned.

2. *Bridging the gap* between skill-getting and skill-using is not automatic. Skill-getting activities must be so designed as to be already *pseudo-communication,* thus leading naturally into spontaneous communication activities.

3. The terminology of this schema will be used in discussing appropriate activities for skill-getting and skill-using.

Knowledge and intensive practice (skill-getting) are not enough to ensure confident interaction. The latter requires practice in actual, purposeful conversational exchange with others. In Chapter 1 we shall discuss linguistic aspects of the spoken language with which the students need to be familiar if their communication is not to be stilted and various types of bridging activities (e.g., the many uses of dialogues, Cummings devices, and action chains); in Chapter 2 we shall turn our attention to ways of involving students in real interaction.[2] In Chapter 3 the problems of understanding the spoken language are considered in depth. Chapters 4 and 5 give the rationale for techniques and activities for perception, abstraction, articulation, and construction.

1
Structured interaction

According to the *progressive development* view, ability to speak the language derives from the systematic study of grammar, phonology, and lexicon. This is the approach of grammar-translation texts, where it is assumed that accuracy in expressing oneself orally is dependent on prior study of language forms through reading and written exercises; of audio-lingual or aural-oral texts, where oral imitation, memorization, and drilling techniques precede attempts to speak spontaneously (although in this case the latter is attempted much sooner than in traditional grammar-translation texts); and of texts which begin with narrative and conversational reading passages.

The *immediate communication* view holds that speaking skill is developed from the first contact with the language. The student may be encouraged to express himself in simple ways under the guidance of the teacher (*Was ist das? Das ist ein Buch; Wo ist das Buch? Das Buch liegt auf dem Tisch*). Alternatively, in a simulation of the total immersion experience of the foreigner in another culture, he may be expected to use for the expression of his own message anything he has acquired of the language from hearing it, supplemented by gestures, pantomime, or the showing of objects, with the teacher suggesting words and expressions only when the student falters.

This chapter takes a *middle position* between these two approaches, advocating that students be encouraged to express themselves freely in the language from the beginning through carefully presented experiences and games which provide them with a framework for spontaneous communicative creation, while presupposing they will use what they have been learning through an orderly progression of study and practice. The Type B exercises described in Chapter 4 prepare students to use the language for expressing their own meanings[1] and are paralleled from the beginning with extensive opportunities for autonomous interaction of the type discussed in Chapter 2. If students are to develop as uninhibited communicators who seize opportunities to use the language with native speakers, they must early overcome their timidity and the fear of being embarrassed when they express themselves simplistically or awkwardly, as they will often do when their knowledge of the language is at an elementary stage.

Differences between spoken and written German

Much of any foreign language learned at school is acquired from books. Even where conversations and dialogues appear, they are often unrepresentative of authentic speech. Tapes and records attempt to bring the oral language into the classroom, but some of these are no more than stilted oral recitations of written forms of the language. If students are to learn to use authentic speech, their teachers must be aware of the features which differentiate the spoken language from the conventional written forms, and particularly from the literary usages to which they have become accustomed in their own advanced studies.

For conciseness and precision of meaning the Germans usually employ in written material more complicated structures and a wider vocabulary than in speech. This is one reason why learning to write German well is an advanced art. Generally, written German is *less redundant* than the spoken form of the language (that is, it contains fewer signals of the same aspect of meaning) in that repetitions and duplications are avoided and the additional clues provided by such things as rising and falling intonation and tone of voice are absent. But in another sense written language may be more redundant. There are a few signals of meaning which are completely lost when the written form is presented orally, such as the capitalization which marks nouns. Furthermore, while written language must provide a complete context, spoken language is often influenced by the response of the listener (if there is one), i.e., the speaker may communicate his meaning with very few words and little background information if he sees the listener has caught on immediately.

C2 Analysis of two sentences from a modern short story highlights a number of differences between the written and spoken codes in German.

Ich hatte in diesem Winter angefangen, an die Kinder aus der Nachbarschaft Bücher auszuleihen, die sie an einem bestimmten Wochentag holen und zurückbringen sollten. Natürlich kannte ich die meisten dieser Kinder, aber es kamen auch manchmal Fremde, die nicht in unserer Straße wohnten.

MARIE LUISE KASCHNITZ, "Das dicke Kind."[2]

If recounted orally this incident might have been expressed as follows:

In dem Winter hatte ich einen Einfall. Ich wollte was für die Kinder tun, weißt du. Ich habe ihnen also Bücher geliehen. Die konnten sie einmal in der Woche abholen, sagen wir am Mittwoch, und mit nach Hause nehmen. Sie sollten die Bücher dann am gleichen Wochentag zurückbringen. Die meisten waren Nachbarkinder, deswegen kannte ich sie ja. Manchmal sind aber auch andere gekommen. Das waren fremde, die haben nicht in unserer Straße gewohnt.

Commentary

1. Not only would the second version when spoken contain more clues to meaning (that is, be more redundant) because of the prosodic features of intonation and pitch, and the expressive features of tone of voice, gesture, and facial expression with which it would be accompanied, but it is expressed in simple declarative sentences, with considerable repetition of semantic detail *Ich wollte was für die Kinder tun—Ich habe ihnen Bücher geliehen; einmal in der Woche, sagen wir am Mittwoch—am gleichen Wochentag*); with grammatical substitutions with the same referent (*andere—die—fremde*); and with expletives and conversational tags and clichés like *sagen wir, ja, weißt du,* which establish contact with the listener as well as giving the speaker time to organize the succeeding segment of production.

2. *Assimilation:* The verbal ending *-en* tends to be reduced to some degree in the oral version of the text; e.g., *abholen* becomes [apho:l̩n]; *haben,* [habm̩]; *sagen,* [sagŋ]; and *ihnen,* [i:nʌ̃]. The *-e* in the first person singular of verbs frequently disappears entirely; *kannte ich* would be pronounced [kantIç]. *Andere* becomes [andRə] in the spoken language. Assimilation also takes place in the case of *weißt du,* which may be given the form [vaIstu] or even [vaIstə]. The article *einen,* on the other hand, may be reduced to the ending alone, i.e., simply *'n.*

3. *Bindung:* Certain sounds while remaining separate run together in the flow of speech, for example [n] (or [ŋ]) and [v] in *sagen wir* [sagŋvi:ʁ].

* Be sure that you are familiar with the most important usages regarding assimilation and *Bindung*. (Carl and Peter Martens describe a number of the most common cases with examples in *Phonetik der deutschen Sprache*.[3])

Syntax and stress
POSITIONAL EMPHASIS

C3 Many of the characteristics of spoken German are demonstrated by Luise Rinser in her description of postwar experiences seen from the point of view of a child:

> Wie ich auf die Hauptstraße komm, steht da ein amerikanisches Auto, so ein großer Wagen, ein Buick, glaub ich, und da fragt mich der Fahrer nach dem Rathaus. Auf englisch hat er gefragt, und ich kann doch ein bißchen Englisch. "The next street", hab ich gesagt, "and then left and then" —geradeaus hab ich nicht gewußt auf englisch, das hab ich mit dem Arm gezeigt, und er hat mich schon verstanden. —"And behind the Church is the marketplace with the Rathaus." Ich glaub, das war ein ganz gutes Amerikanisch, und die Frau im Auto hat mir ein paar Schnitten Weißbrot gegeben, ganz weißes, und wie ich's aufklapp, ist Wurst dazwischen, ganz dick. L. RINSER, "Die rote Katze."[4]

Commentary

Syntax and stress are closely interrelated both in spoken and in written German. Usually if a word or phrase other than the subject is to be stressed, it is placed at the beginning of the sentence. In *Auf englisch hat er gefragt,* the element transposed to the beginning, *auf englisch,* is in the position of greatest stress. The same pattern applies in the sentence:

Geradeaus hab ich nicht gewußt auf englisch.

This example illustrates not only how an element may be stressed at the beginning of the sentence in both spoken and written German, but how in spoken German elements may also be stressed when added as an afterthought in an end field beyond the normal range of the sentence.

Notice the difference in effect between the following forms:

Die Frau im Auto hat mir ein paar Schnitten ganz weißes *Weißbrot* gegeben.

Die Frau im Auto hat mir ein paar Schnitten *Weißbrot* gegeben, *ganz weißes.*

Und wie ich's aufklapp, ist ganz dicke *Wurst* dazwischen.
Und wie ich's aufklapp, ist *Wurst* dazwischen, *ganz dick.*

der, die, das AS STRESSED ELEMENTS

While *der, die,* and *das* may simply serve as articles or informally as pronouns replacing *er, sie,* and *es,* in stressed position their demonstrative meaning may be intensified.

C4 Compare:

Kennen Sie Herrn Fichte?
Ja, den kenne ich. (Wir haben uns irgendwann kennen gelernt.)
Ja, *den* kenne ich! (Wer kennt ihn nicht?! or: Diesen einen kenne ich, die anderen aber nicht.)
or even further intensified: Ja, *den* kenne ich, den *Fichte.*

Den Brief habe ich geschrieben. (Aber meine Schuhe habe ich noch nicht geputzt.)
Den Brief habe ich geschrieben. (Die anderen Briefe aber nicht.)

✻ Consider various manners of emphasizing the different elements of an utterance, noting which alternatives would be most likely to occur primarily in spoken language, e.g., *Ich habe mit meinem Taschengeld ein neues Buch gekauft.*

Even though we would not normally teach our students to express themselves in quite such a familiar register as is used by Rinser's young girl, writing such as this dramatically illustrates certain basic tendencies of spoken German which spring from the prosodic features that do not appear in writing. The mere inclusion of expletives and clichés does not transform formal language into conversational language. The teacher must be aware of these basic patterns and encourage students to use them when expressing themselves orally in German.

Style of language (register or level of discourse)

In addition to dialects of various regions and to specialized jargons of particular fields, there are various styles of language which we use in diverse situations. The standard language or *Hochsprache* has traditionally been differentiated from *Alltagssprache* (or *Umgangssprache*), but in practice these two broad categories include a much greater number of language levels or styles. While it is true that a certain group or class of people may use one level of language far more than another level, any individual will adjust his speech to the circumstances at hand. Students should be made aware of these facts and learn to recognize, and eventually to use, a range of styles in German. Even some knowledge of *vulgäre Sprache,* which the students should be encouraged to understand rather than to use, can help one to discern an author's intent in presenting a particular type of conversational material in written German. Wahrig's *Deutsches Wörterbuch* is useful in determining what lexical usages are acceptable at various levels of language, and the *Duden Grammatik* can be of some assistance when investigating the level of a particular syntactical structure.[5]

If students are to develop a feeling for different styles of language they must learn to associate the styles with specific sets of circumstances. A point of departure is provided by Joos, who in *The Five Clocks*[6] distinguishes five styles: intimate, casual, consultative, formal, and frozen. By adapting his criteria we may develop a similar sequence for German. Each style of speech is used under different conditions for a similar situation, and one speaker might resort to any or all of the styles on one day.

C5 In an *intimate* situation, a parent might say to a child who is embarrassingly present and has shown some reluctance to leave: *Husch, hinaus mit dir!* (According to Joos, in intimate style no information is given which is known to the participants.) This is *intime Sprache.*

In a *casual* style the parent may say: *Laß uns ja!* (Once again complete information is not supplied and this style involves the use of well-known formulas.) This is *familiäre Sprache* and employs *duzen.*

Consultative style, the style of standard exchange between strangers, would require rather: *Verlassen Sie das Zimmer, bitte.* (Since consultative style is used for persons outside the intimate circle, the *du* form would not be used. Consultative style supplies all necessary background information.) In such a situation one would use *Verkehrssprache.*

A *formal* situation, on the other hand, may require: *Würden Sie so freundlich sein und sich fünf Minuten lang zurückziehen.* (In formal style, the speaker often does not refer to himself and he does not anticipate any immediate participation on the part of the person addressed.) Here *formale Sprache* is used.

Frozen or printed style of one type may be observed outside a door: *Es wird gebeten, das Zimmer nicht zu betreten.* This sort of frozen language is *Amtssprache.*

Compare the following:

Salz, bitte; reich mir bitte das Salz; darf ich um das Salz bitten; würden Sie so freundlich sein und mir das Salz reichen; es wird gebeten, das Salz nicht zu monopolisieren.

✱ Try constructing a similar series on the themes: "Please do not talk" and "Write to me about it."

C6 In the light of the above discussion on styles of language, examine the following passage from "Reusenheben" by Wolfdietrich Schnurre:[7]

Sie liefen ein paar Waldwege entlang zur Chaussee. Gerade als sie raustraten, kamen zwei Radfahrer an.

"Was ich dich noch fragen wollte", sagte der Mann laut, "magst du eigentlich Meerschweinchen gern?"

"Hör mal", sagte Willi, "wo ich doch selber drei hab."

Sie liefen ein Stück die Chaussee entlang. In den Birkenblättern am Rand glänzte die Sonne; eine Elster zuckte scheckernd vor ihnen her. Einmal tauchte ein Fußgänger auf.

Der Mann blieb stehen und sah auf die Uhr. "Hui, hui."

"Spät—?"

"Vier gleich."

"Mensch! Ich werd verrückt." Willi gab dem Mann die Hand. "Oder rennst du noch'n Stück mit."

"Laß man."

"Dann mach's gut."

"Du auch."

Vor der Kurve drehte Willi sich noch mal um.

Der Mann stand immer noch auf der Chaussee. "Wie ist'n los!" rief er.

"Verrätst du's auch *wirklich* nicht?"

"Was?"

"Na, daß ich geschwänzt hab."

"Bestimmt nicht."

"Dann ist's gut. Servus!"

Der Mann hob den Arm.

✱ Discuss in the above passage: structures commonly used in *intime Sprache* or *familiäre Sprache;* words and idioms which are particularly indicative of familiar language levels; any allusions which reflect typically German customs. (In some cases it may be helpful to consult Wahrig's *Deutsches Wörterbuch.*)

C7 The style of language in dialogues of the sort found in textbooks may not always be used consistently.

Frau Müller trifft eine Freundin in der Stadt.

FRAU MÜLLER   Guten Tag, gnädige Frau. Wie geht es Ihnen?

FRAU ZIEGLER   Es geht mir gut, danke.
FRAU MÜLLER   Und Ihrem Gatten?
FRAU ZIEGLER   Nicht schlecht.

Commentary

1. If Frau Ziegler were really a *Freundin* of Frau Müller, she would normally say: *"Guten Tag, Dorothea"* and probably (although not necessarily) use the *du* form. By the tone of Frau Müller's address, Frau Ziegler is probably a *Bekannte* and a distant one at that.

2. The response of Frau Ziegler to Frau Müller's very polite greeting and inquiries is brusque and out of keeping with the general tone of the exchange. In response to Frau Müller's greeting Frau Ziegler would normally add to her reply an inquiry about Frau Müller's health. Given the tone set by Frau Müller, Frau Ziegler's abrupt *"nicht schlecht"* would best be replaced with a more polite reply, e.g., *"Es geht ihm ganz gut, danke."*

* Examine dialogues in current textbooks to see if they use different levels of discourse appropriately and consistently.

Bridging activities

All that we can teach students in a foreign language is how to construct the appropriate framework, in all its detail, for the expression of meaning. We cannot teach students to express their own meaning; we can provide opportunities which stimulate motivation for this personal activity to take place and we can help the student to improve the framework so that it can really convey the message intended. We can develop activities where the student constructs various types of frameworks and help him try them out to see if they will carry effectively the meanings he intends. Searle calls language "rule-governed intentional behavior."[8] We can help the student internalize the rules; we cannot supply the intention, although we can stimulate it by contriving situations and encounters. One way in which we help students try out frameworks of varying degrees of complexity and subtlety (that is, to perform "speech acts"[9]) is by providing practice in *pseudo-communication*. This is communication in which the content is structured by the learning situation rather than by ideas springing autonomously from the mind and emotions of the student. *We bridge the gap to true communication by encouraging the student to use these structured practices for autonomous purposes from the early stages.* In this way, the average student acquires confidence in his ability to function on his own. (Linguistically gifted students will always develop confidence in their own way, with or without special guidance.)

The concept of *individualization of instruction* has to be very carefully analyzed in relation to the development of communication skills: it can mean small-group practice and interaction, but not independent study, because communication by definition involves someone other than the communicator. Students also learn a great deal from listening to the way other people formulate their communications. At the other extreme, communication cannot be efficiently practiced in large groups. For a discussion of suitable groupings of students for communication practice, see Wilga M. Rivers *et al.*, "Techniques for the Development of Proficiency in the Spoken Language" in H. B. Altman and R. L. Politzer, eds., *Individualizing Foreign Language Instruction* (Rowley, Mass.: Newbury House, 1971), pp. 165–74.

RULE-GOVERNED BEHAVIOR

In language use, we fit our meaning into a framework which conforms to many types of rules, or recurring regularities: not only syntactic, morphological, and phonological, but also semantic and cultural. Once we have an intention to express, not only do we have to select the "right words" for our purpose, but these choices entail other lexical selections within the sentence which we must respect, but which function according to rules at present only vaguely understood. Semantics also dictates our choices in syntax,[10] and syntactic selection forces certain morphological adjustments. We cannot operate effectively in speech or writing until we have understood the possibilities the rules afford and are able to put into operation the sheer mechanics of the language at the level of verb endings for person and tense, required agreements, conventional word order, and so on.[11] Cultural expectations come into play as well, that is, rules of relationships and obligations in interpersonal communication within a society, expressed in part through registers or levels of discourse, but also through expected and implied questions and reactions, social taboos, and the mutually understood references of words used in certain associations.

C8 Er hat mich daran gehindert, das zu tun, was ich wollte.
Er hat mein Unternehmen vereitelt.

The decision to express this intention at a more formal level in the second sentence motivated the choice of *vereiteln* instead of *hindern* and this lexical choice entailed other lexical choices and a different syntactic framework from that in the first sentence.

Es tut mir leid, daß ich Sie nicht begleiten kann, aber meine Patin hat an dem Tag Geburtstag.

Comprehension of this sentence is dependent on comprehension not merely of the individual words but of certain extra-family relationships and obligations of German society.

Supplying the student with a basic corpus

The first problem we face in teaching students to speak a foreign language is how to plunge them into using natural language when they know little or nothing of the new tongue. Proponents of the grammar-translation approach have usually maintained that conversing in the language should not be attempted until students control the essentials of the syntactic and morphological systems intellectually and in graphic form and have acquired through reading and memorization an extensive vocabulary, at which stage they can learn to express themselves orally quite rapidly by drawing on what they have learned. But with the modern emphasis on the importance of oral communication and the present generation's greater familiarity with aural-oral rather than graphic presentations of information, this approach can be discouraging for many students.

A number of approaches have been proposed at different times for plunging the student into active language use. All have proved effective in the early stages when intelligently and imaginatively implemented. We need some way of supplying the student with a basic corpus with which to work. We can identify four main approaches to this problem: the object centered, the melody and rhythm centered, the verb centered, and the situation centered.

OBJECT CENTERED

In this approach, students begin by discussing objects in the classroom in imitation of the teacher. The grammatical structures introduced are demonstrable in relation to these objects, so that students hear and practice them in a realistic setting.

C9 Hier ist das Buch. Das ist das Fenster . . . Was ist das? Das ist ein Buch. Das ist ein Fenster . . . Wo liegt das Buch? Das Buch liegt auf dem Tisch . . . Das Buch ist grün . . . Es ist das Buch von Peter . . .

The class then goes on to discuss persons in the classroom in much the same terms:

Peter ist ein Schüler. Er ist groß.
Ursula ist eine Schülerin. Sie ist klein.
Sie ist die Schwester von Peter.

Variant: Teachers sometimes use the contents of a handbag or shopping basket instead of classroom objects. Later, pictures of houses, gardens, airports, farms are used to expand the environment for purposes of description and discussion. Sometimes these pictures are in the textbook. Otherwise, use is made of commercially available wall-pictures, full- or double-page scenes cut from magazines, or projected slides. Students often construct posters, with items labeled in German, to illustrate these environments and these are posted on the bulletin board so that students can assimilate the vocabulary casually through frequent contact. (This approach can lead to an overemphasis on acquiring names for a multiplicity of objects.)

This approach sometimes limits students to accurate production of very trite sentences which they would not conceivably wish to use in spontaneous conversation: *Das ist ein Buch. Es ist grün. Es ist im Büro des Lehrers. Es ist das Buch des Lehrers.* Modern students find this approach boring and trivial. It is well to remember that in real conversation we rarely comment on things which are visible unless the situation is exceptional: *Der Hund ist im Büro des Lehrers. Warum denn das*?! A little whimsy will help to enliven the exchanges and keep the students alert.

MELODY AND RHYTHM CENTERED

In a quite different approach, only one noun is used for quite a long time: *ein Stäbchen* (a rod). Called "the silent way" by Gattegno, its originator,[12] this method concentrates at the beginning on developing sensitivity to the melody and flow of the language. Students listen to tapes of a number of languages trying to recognize which of the speeches they hear is in the language they have been studying.[13] Gattegno considers that

since babies learn to talk their mother tongue first by yielding to its "music," we can . . . trace the first elements of the spirit of a language to the unconscious surrender of our sensitivity to what is conveyed by the background of noise in each language. This background obviously includes the silences, the pauses, the flow, the linkages of words, the duration of each breath required to utter connected chunks of the language, the overtones and undertones, the stresses as well as the special vowels or consonants belonging to that language.[14]

The teacher works with only about thirty words in the initial lessons, mainly the neuter articles *das* and *ein* for use with *Stäbchen*, pronouns in the direct and indirect object forms (*es, sie, mir, ihm*), some color adjectives with neuter endings, possessives (*mein, unser, Ihr*), a few numerals, some forms of *haben* and *sein* (*habe, haben; ist, sind*), the imperative forms of *geben* and *nehmen*, the conjunction *und, ja, nein,* and a few adverbs like *auch, da, hier.* Using a box of colored rods, the teacher induces the student to utter fluent sentences with native-like facility, while talking as little as possible himself. There is a minimum of imitation of the teacher and a maximum of concentration by the student on constructing sentences with the help of the rods. The teacher does not explain grammatical features but encourages the students to think about what they hear and to try to construct utterances which conform to the rules they have discovered for themselves.

C10 Types of sentences practiced with the rods:

Nehmen Sie ein blaues Stäbchen (rotes, grünes).
Geben Sie es mir.
Nehmen Sie ein gelbes Stäbchen und geben Sie es Richard.
Nehmen Sie zwei grüne Stäbchen und geben Sie sie mir.

The rods continue to be used for learning such things as comparatives, temporal relationships, and tenses.

Later, through the technique of *visual dictation*,[15] students are given practice in recognizing the printed equivalents of the words they have been using orally as they created situations with the rods and also in the fluent construction of sentences using these words. Here the teacher points silently and rapidly, but only once, to a succession of words on a chart of scrambled words with phonic color coding, and in a short time students are able to produce with acceptable diction long sentences like: *Nehmen Sie ein blaues Stäbchen und ein grünes Stäbchen und geben Sie Richard das blaue Stäbchen und geben Sie mir das grüne Stäbchen* and to demonstrate through action that they have understood what they are saying.

Gattegno claims to be "rejecting the learning of vocabularies and grammar . . . and replacing it with as thorough a penetration of the spirit of a language as possible."[16]

VERB CENTERED

One of the best-known devices under this head is the *Gouin series*.[17] Gouin had observed the way his child commented on his own actions, and he developed from this the idea of an *action series* or *action chain*. He divided common events into five general series: the home, man in society, life in nature, science, and occupations. These were subdivided and resubdivided into shorter series centering around the verb, which, according to Gouin, is "the generating element of the sentence."[18] The language was then taught by means of a series of commonly performed actions, first orally, then in writing. A different verb was used in each statement, and students were expected to acquire the situational vocabulary along with the verb through performing or miming the actions while they described what they were doing. The teacher first demonstrated the series in the native language and then, when the students had understood it clearly, in the foreign language. The students next repeated the actions under the guidance of the teacher or of other students, describing what they were doing in the foreign language as they were doing it. (Gouin advocated peer teaching, saying that "in Nature, one child can and does teach another child to talk."[19]) While the students were trying to reproduce the series the teacher would make encouraging remarks in the language. After this aural-oral phase, the series would be read and then written out by the students.

C11   The example Gouin himself gives[20] is the following (the verb is emphasized orally in the initial demonstration):

schreite zu	Ich schreite auf die Thür zu.
nähere mich	Ich nähere mich der Thür.
komme an	Ich komme bei der Thür an.
bleibe stehen	Ich bleibe bei der Thür stehen.
strecke aus	Ich strecke den Arm aus.
fasse an	Ich fasse den Griff an.
drehe um	Ich drehe den Griff um.
mache auf	Ich mache die Thür auf.
ziehe an	Ich ziehe die Thür heran.
gibt nach	Die Thür gibt nach.
dreht sich	Die Thür dreht sich auf den Angeln.
lasse los	Ich lasse den Griff los.

We may be surprised at the amount of specialized vocabulary this method entailed. Gouin considered that general terms were infrequently used in comparison with specific vocabulary. His emphasis was, of course, on the verb, but the verb in complete sentences.

This approach can be extended to provide practice in all persons and in different tenses.

C12   STUDENT A   Was mache ich?
             STUDENT B   Du öffnest die Tür.

        STUDENTS A & B   Wir schreiben an die Tafel.
             TEACHER   Was machen sie?
             STUDENT C   Sie schreiben an die Tafel.

        STUDENTS A & B   Was machen wir?
             STUDENT C   Ihr schreibt an die Tafel.

TEACHER   Was haben sie gemacht?
STUDENT C   Sie haben an die Tafel geschrieben.

STUDENT A   Schauen Sie, was ich heute abend machen werde. (miming action)
STUDENT B   Du wirst einen Spaziergang machen.
STUDENT C   Sie wird einen Spaziergang machen.

Through mime the variety of the actions can be expanded considerably, and the activity becomes a competitive game with students describing each movement and then guessing what is being mimed. In an individualized or group work program this may be a completely student-to-student activity.

C13 (1) In another variation, the student is given an order or a series of orders (of increasing complexity) by the teacher or another student:

Gehen Sie[21] an die Tür; öffnen Sie die Tür; legen Sie das Buch in die Schublade; nehmen Sie das Buch aus der Schublade; öffnen Sie das Buch auf Seite zwanzig und lesen Sie den ersten Satz vor.

The student obeys the order saying what he is doing, or if he is learning the present perfect, what he has done. If he makes a mistake another student can describe what he actually did and what he should have done. (*Er hat das Buch auf den Tisch gelegt. Er hätte das Buch aus der Schublade nehmen sollen.*) This provides a useful situational context for learning difficult expressions like *hätte . . . machen sollen* and *statt . . . zu machen.*

Recent revivals of this type of activity learning have been called the *strategy of the total physical response*[22] (in which students respond physically to commands in the foreign language of increasing morphological and syntactical complexity) and *Situational Reinforcement*[23] (which uses the techniques of C12).

The Gouin approach can be developed in considerable detail beyond these simple examples and can be the basis for factual learning about the geography of Germany, the monuments of various cities, activities at festivals, matters of etiquette, and so on.

C14 (1) A map of Germany is drawn, as a cooperative project, on the floor of the classroom, and students are asked to undertake journeys. (A posted map and pointer may be substituted, but this reduces the physical response to a symbolic one.)

TEACHER OR ANOTHER STUDENT   Nachdem Sie Bonn verlassen, fahren

Sie am Rhein entlang. Sie kommen in Koblenz an und bleiben dort einige Stunden. Dann fahren Sie von Koblenz mit dem Dampfer nach Bonn zurück.

The student addressed then describes his journey in the present perfect tense with personal embellishments.

STUDENT   Ich bin um acht Uhr morgens von Bonn weggefahren. Das Wetter war schön aber noch kühl. Als ich am Rhein entlang gefahren bin, ist es wärmer geworden. Am sonnigen Hang habe ich viele Weintrauben gesehen. Ich bin in Koblenz angekommen, und nach einem Stadtbummel habe ich dort zu Mittag gegessen. Nachher habe ich am Flußufer auf den Rheindampfer gewartet.

Recognizing its debt to Gouin and to the subsequent work of Emile de Sauzé of Cleveland, whose influence can still be perceived in many a modern textbook, the *verbal-active approach* has also been called "a rationalist direct method."[24] Yvone Lenard says, "The sentence arranges itself around the verb" and "it is, therefore, imperative that the student learn to listen for the verb in the sentence, recognize its form, and answer immediately with the appropriate form."[25] In essence, this echoes Gouin, although Lenard's method adds a question-answer sequence to the action series. Since this is a direct method, unlike the Gouin approach it excludes the native language from the classroom and the textbook.

In this approach grammar is learned inductively and through action rather than through deductive grammar rules. Diller says, "Knowing a rule and being able to act on it is quite independent of being able to formulate the rule adequately. The rule can be psychologically real without any formulation of it. . . . Rules for action are best learned in conjunction with demonstration and practice of the action."[26] Both Diller and Lenard emphasize the necessity for the learning stage to develop into opportunities for innovative sentence creation on the part of the student. Quoting de Sauzé's viewpoint, Lenard says, " 'Language is invention.' It has no existence apart from the speaker or the writer who recreates, reinvents the language for his own needs each time he uses it."[27] She lays great stress on the daily oral composition as "the most important exercise of the verbal-active method in building the elements of which fluency is composed."[28] In these oral compositions, prepared in advance in writing but delivered orally in front of their fellows, students try to use only what everyone else is learning, thus cultivating "originality, free invention, and personal expression within a strictly controlled structural framework."[29] (Note that the verbal-active method moves from listening and speaking to writing before reading, another deviation from Gouin which is traceable to de Sauzé.)

C15 *Verbal-active action series*

Frage	*Antwort*
Ich wasche das Kind und lege es ins Bett. Was machst du, Fred?	Ich wasche *mich* und lege *mich* ins Bett.
Musik interessiert Sie, Herr Hipper, nicht wahr?	Ja, ich interessiere *mich* für Musik.
Die Kinder bewegen die Hände. Was macht das kleine Kind?	Es bewegt *sich* im Bett.
Fritz, wir müssen *uns* beeilen, wir müssen schneller gehen, die Schule beginnt um 8 Uhr. Warum gehst du so langsam?	Ja, ich beeile *mich,* ich gehe schneller.
Guten Morgen, Günther Hipper, wie geht's? Wie fühlst du *dich* heute?	Danke, Herr Schmidt, mir geht es gut; ich fühle *mich* ausgezeichnet.[30]

SITUATION CENTERED

For many centuries, situationally based dialogues have been in and out of fashion for providing students with a corpus of foreign-language words and expressions with which to work.[31] They are very frequently found in present-day textbooks. The situations chosen may be experiences common to both the native and the foreign culture, or may introduce the student to typically German ways of interacting and reacting. Sometimes they are printed with a parallel idiomatic translation; at other times students are expected to comprehend the meaning through action or through simple German explanations.

Dialogue construction can be indicative of diverse philosophies. Some dialogues are designed to *demonstrate grammatical rules,* and examples of rules in use, and the variations of paradigms are introduced systematically in the exchanges.

C16

DORLA   Wirst du schon müde?

JUTTA   Nein, aber mir wird kalt.

DORLA   Macht nichts. Wenn wir einmal zu Hause sind, werde ich einen heißen Tee kochen.

JUTTA   Werden wir von deinen Eltern erwartet?

DORLA   Ja, sie werden wohl wissen, daß wir gleich kommen.

The aim of grammar-demonstration dialogues is to lead students to inductive recognition of the rule or the paradigm. These dialogues need not be memorized: they can be studied and discussed in German, dramatized, and used as a basis for recombinations. They lead naturally to grammatical explanations and intensive practice exercises through which the operation of the rule, or paradigm, becomes clear to the student, enters his active repertoire, and is then used by him in a genuinely communicative interchange.

Other dialogues, which we shall call *conversation-facilitation dialogues,* are intended primarily to provide students with a stock of useful expressions (clichés of conversation, frequently used expressions, conventional greetings, expletives, and rejoinders) with which to practice conversing, while the teaching of the grammar proceeds as a parallel but distinct activity.

C17   FRANZ   Tag, Theo. Wie geht's?
        THEO   Gut, danke. Und dir?
        FRANZ   Prächtig! Willst du mit in die Stadt?
        THEO   Gerne. Jetzt gleich?

Students memorize the segments, which have been selected because of their potential usefulness, and then practice using them in recombinations to form new dialogues involving different personalities.

Many dialogues combine both of these functions: grammar-demonstration and conversation-facilitation. It is important to recognize the type of dialogue with which you are dealing so that it may be used for the purpose for which it was constructed.

A third type of dialogue we may call *recreational*: the familiar skit. This activity has always been popular with students and teachers in an orally oriented approach.[32] It is a true bridging activity which provides for spontaneous creation within the limits of what is being learned. It is discussed under *Dialogue Exploitation*, p. 35.

Dialogue construction and adaptation

You should be able to recognize the good and bad features of dialogues for several reasons:

—so that you can select well-written materials for use in classroom teaching or in individualized learning packets;

—so that you can rewrite poorly constructed dialogues when you are forced to use materials selected by others;

—so that you can write dialogues yourself, if you wish to supplement available materials (e.g., you may decide to prepare a dialogue based on a story which has been read).

C18

1. HILDE   Wohin fuhren Sie in der vorigen Woche?
2. VRENI   Ich fuhr zu meiner Freundin Elke, die in einem kleinen Dorf wohnt.
3. HILDE   Was unternahmen Sie da?
4. VRENI   Wir besichtigten die berühmte Burg und wir gingen täglich im Walde spazieren.
5. HILDE   Was gibt es zu sehen in diesem kleinen Dorf?
6. VRENI   Vieles—die alten Fachwerkhäuser, das renovierte Rathaus, die neue Schule, und auch den schönen Schwarzwald.
7. HILDE   Blieben Sie längere Zeit?
8. VRENI   Ja, selbstverständlich. Ich kam erst gestern abend zurück.
9. HILDE   Ziehen Sie ein kleines Dorf oder eine Großstadt vor?
10. VRENI   Ich ziehe ein kleines Dorf vor.
11. HILDE   Ich persönlich habe eine Großstadt lieber.

Commentary

1. As a sustained exchange between two friends, this dialogue is very artificial and stilted. It has been laboriously constructed to include various persons of the simple past tense of regular and of certain common irregular verbs.

2. *Contemporary usage.* Certain features of authentic modern speech have been completely ignored.

a. Two friends of school age would use the *du* form. There is some controversy about the usefulness of the *du* form for foreign students. Some say that foreigners rarely reach a stage of intimacy where the use of *du* is acceptable and may offend by using it too freely. It is, of course, frequently used among students in Germany and it is becoming much more acceptable in many situations of contemporary German life, especially among the younger generation. Offense can be caused by the person who is insensitive to the right moment for using *du* as well as by the person who uses it inappropriately. Furthermore, students who have not experienced through use the different relationships *du* and *Sie* imply in various situations will miss many nuances in their later reading. It is the teacher's role to train students in correct use of the two forms.

b. *Tenses.* The dialogue uses only the simple past tense throughout in order to illustrate the use of this one tense. But in German, unlike English, the present perfect not only has the same value as the simple past tense, but it is also generally employed in conversational German. (In fact, dialects of Southern Germany, Austria, and Switzerland no longer even have a simple past tense.) Unless the conversation becomes a one-sided narrative, which is not the case here, the simple past is not appropriate and sounds awkward, particularly in 3: *Was unternahmen Sie da,* and in 4: *Wir besichtigten die Burg und wir gingen täglich spazieren . . .*

c. The inversion form of the question used throughout the dialogue in 7: *Blieben Sie . . . ?* is the most common form. But there are other possibilities in use which should be practiced and which could have been included to give the passage a more authentic flavor: *Sie sind längere Zeit geblieben, nicht wahr?* or merely *Sie sind . . . geblieben?* with rising intonation. (Practice in the latter form is often neglected in the classroom.)

3. *Weaknesses in the construction of the dialogue.*

a. In sentence 4 *Wir besichtigten* is not only awkward because of tense; it is also difficult to pronounce. *Wir haben . . . besichtigt* is preferable on both counts.

b. Sentence 6 is incredibly trite, constructed with the obvious intent of introducing vocabulary items and certain adjective endings.

c. Certain questions which seem clearly to have been introduced into the dialogue because of their usefulness for an unimaginative question-answer period in class add to the artificiality of the dialogue: *Ziehen Sie ein kleines Dorf oder eine Großstadt vor? Ich ziehe . . . vor. Ziehen Sie das Leben auf dem Lande oder das Stadtleben vor? Ziehen Sie Sommerferien oder Winterferien vor?* (Similarly: *Was gibt es zu sehen . . . ?*)

C19 *Rewritten,* with sentences shortened and language and usage modernized, this dialogue might read as follows:

INGE   Wo warst du letzte Woche?

GISELA   Ich bin zu meiner Freundin Elke gefahren. Sie wohnt in einem kleinen Dorf nicht weit von hier.

INGE   Was habt ihr dort gemacht?

GISELA   Wir haben die Burg besichtigt. Wir haben ja auch jeden Tag einen Spaziergang im Walde gemacht.

INGE   Du bist lange geblieben?

GISELA   Aber natürlich. Ich bin erst seit gestern wieder zu Hause.

Commentary

This short dialogue demonstrates the use of various tenses expressing past time in the matrix of a possible conversation which could be exploited in various ways apart from its grammatical purpose. Clearly the morphology of all past tenses cannot be appropriately taught through a dialogue, but this short version, which includes one person of the simple past, four persons of the present perfect (two with *sein* and two with *haben*), and one case of the present tense expressing past time, provides a basis for the discussion of the contemporary uses of these tenses. In C18 the simple past forms of regular and irregular verbs appear in a very unrealistic dialogue, with no use of either the present perfect or the present expressing the past tense. Not only is there no clear demonstration of appropriate use, but the student is given a false view of conversational possibilities.

* Find some grammar-demonstration dialogues in textbooks in current use, comment on their good and bad features, and practice rewriting the least effective of them.

CONVERSATION-FACILITATION DIALOGUES

Many textbooks include dialogues purely for the purpose of providing students in the early stages with *useful utterances and exclamations* which, with variations of vocabulary, can be recombined in all kinds of personal ways to make possible active classroom conversation and creative skits. Well written and presented, such dialogues can provide the student with a fund of very authentic expressions for use at a stage when his overall knowledge of the language is still quite minimal. This ability to put together something meaningful encourages him with a sense of progress.

C20 1. JÜRGEN   Tag, Heinz.
     2. HEINZ   Tag, Jürgen. Wo gehst du hin? Ins Kino?
     3. JÜRGEN   Nein. Ich habe Hunger. Ich gehe essen.
     4. HEINZ   So. Ich habe auch Hunger.
     5. JÜRGEN   Komm mit, wenn du willst.
     6. HEINZ   Gut! Wo gehen wir hin?
     7. JÜRGEN   Es gibt ein kleines, gutes Restaurant nicht weit vom Bahnhof.
     8. HEINZ   Ach, dahin. Aber los! Hier kommt Meta! Die will ich nicht sehen.
     9. JÜRGEN   Ich auch nicht. Schnell, zum Restaurant!

Commentary

1. With this type of dialogue, students are expected to memorize the sentences (through active role-playing) so that they can produce them quickly in new situations. This provides practice in the rhythm of the phrase and in specific intonation patterns.

2. The dialogue would be learned and practiced in sections (1-3, 1-7, 1-9). In other words, the dialogue is open-ended.

3. Utterances are short or are easily divided into short, meaningful segments (*ich habe Hunger, nicht weit vom Bahnhof, wo gehst du hin*). The aim of the memorizing is for the students to be able to use these segments freely in new combinations, and to learn to vary segments semantically, not to know the sixteen utterances by heart so that they can produce them parrot-fashion in the original sequence.

4. Students will learn short utterances like these easily by acting out the dialogue in small groups. Memorization and recall processes are aided by visuals: flashcards, stick figures, flannel board, puppets, vanishing techniques (where the dialogue is written on the chalkboard with major elements of the phrase being obliterated one by one until students know the complete utterance thoroughly).

5. Small groups will perform their version of the dialogue for the others. Meaningful deviations from the original wording and paraphrases will be welcomed as indications that the students have indeed assimilated the material in a more than superficial way. The students will be encouraged to develop new situations, including as often as possible material learned in other dialogues or in other classwork. (See *Dialogue Exploitation,* below.)

6. Conversation-facilitation dialogues do not follow a question-answer, question-answer sequence. This is not the natural mode of ordinary conversation. C20 consists of greeting, greeting returned, question, question, answer, explanation, statement, exclamation, statement, suggestion, acceptance, question, oblique answer, exclamation, exclamation, statement, statement, statement, suggestion.

7. Items are not exploited grammatically or paradigmatically as they would tend to be in a grammar-demonstration dialogue. Here students are familiarized, in a meaningful context, with constructions which they may not study systematically for some time (e.g., *Die will ich nicht sehen*) but which are immediately useable in their present form and in semantic variants (*Den will ich nicht besuchen, Ich will es nicht lesen*).

8. Many modern textbook writers would consider C20 too long for an early dialogue. The material in it can easily be rewritten as a spiral series.

SPIRAL SERIES OF DIALOGUES

Short dialogues are usually more useful than longer dialogues. The interrelated content of two response pairs is more easily remembered than the development of thought in six response pairs. One response pair (A to B) allows little scope for an interesting mini-situation, although it is used as the basic unit in the Cummings device illustrated in C29.

Sometimes several short dialogues develop a continuing theme, each in succession using some of the linguistic material from the one preceding. Such a succession of dialogues is called a spiral series. As students exploit each section, they are consolidating material already learned, and the now-familiar material makes the learning of the new material more meaningful. Dialogue C19 could be developed spirally as follows:

C21   1.   INGE   Wo warst du letzte Woche, Gisela?
             GISELA   Ich bin zu meiner Freundin Elke gefahren.
             INGE   Wo wohnt sie?
             GISELA   Sie wohnt in einem kleinen Dorf nicht weit von hier.

      2.   INGE   Wen hast du letzte Woche besucht?
             GISELA   Meine Freundin Elke, die in einem kleinen Dorf wohnt.
             INGE   Es ist weit von hier?
             GISELA   Eigentlich nicht. Es ist das kleine Dorf mit der berühmten Burg.

      3.   INGE   Wann hast du deine Freundin Elke besucht?
             GISELA   Letzte Woche war ich bei ihr. Ich bin erst seit gestern wieder zu Hause.
             INGE   Sie wohnt in einem kleinen Dorf am Schwarzwald, nicht wahr?
             GISELA   Richtig. Wunderschöne Gegend. Wir konnten jeden Tag einen Spaziergang machen.

      4.   INGE   Hast du mit deiner Freundin Elke einen Spaziergang gemacht?
             GISELA   Aber natürlich, jeden Tag. Ich war bis gestern noch bei ihr.
             INGE   Habt ihr auch die berühmte Burg besichtigt?
             GISELA   Ja. Am ersten Tag hatten wir keine Zeit, aber später sind wir dann doch mal hingekommen.

Commentary

Practice with expanding dialogues gives students the confidence for making up their own recombinations and original skits and provides a useful link with writing. The spiral sequence above gives experience with various past tenses, different types of questions, and the varied possibilities of use of simple adverbial phrases.

✳ Rewrite C20 as a spiral series.

Many textbook writers are criticized for writing dialogues which are culturally neutral, that is, which deal with situations as in C20 that could take place in any culture.

They feel that C20 would convey a feeling for German culture if its content were more like the following:

C22 1. JÜRGEN   Tag, Heinz.

2.   HEINZ   Tag, Jürgen. Wo gehst du hin?

3. JÜRGEN   Ich muß Geld von meinem Postsparkonto holen, um eine Rechnung zu bezahlen.

4.   HEINZ   Die Post liegt um die Ecke, nicht? Soll ich mitkommen?

This dialogue conveys the useful piece of information for a visitor to Germany that he can take care of numerous financial transactions, e.g., savings accounts and paying bills, through the postal system rather than having to go to the bank as in many other countries. This kind of superficial difference in social organization has no deep significance and, if such snippets of information are over-emphasized by repetition and exploitation in dialogues, students may well develop the attitude that the Germans persist in doing things in odd ways for no apparent reason. This type of factual information can also become outdated overnight as a result of a shift in social organization or habits. (Note, for instance, the recent introduction of personal checks or the radical changes in the German educational system, and the influence of the increasing number of refrigerators and supermarkets on the German housewife's traditional routine.)

True cultural understanding means an appreciation of basically different attitudes and values which are reflected in the things people do, but not necessarily explicitly stated. It is difficult to work such concepts into short situational exchanges without oversimplifying and stereotyping social behavior.

The following dialogue,[33] obviously for students with some experience in reading, does convey a basic German value which is reflected in many aspects of individual and social life.

C23 LKW-FAHRER   Ganz schön warm heute?

ANDREAS   Ja, ich habe hier fünf Stunden gestanden. Da merkt man das erst richtig.

LKW-FAHRER   Ich bin immer froh über Wärme. Einmal im Jahr will ich Sonne haben. Urlaub mache ich nur im Süden.

ANDREAS   Da wird es aber oft sehr heiß.

LKW-FAHRER   Mir ist es nie zu heiß.

ANDREAS   Fahren Sie allein in Urlaub?

LKW-FAHRER   Nein, nein. Mit Frau und Kindern. Mein Ältester wollte letztes Jahr nicht mehr mit. 'Ich bin jetzt achtzehn. Ich verdiene selbst. Da kann ich auch allein in Urlaub fahren.' Na, dem habe ich aber die Meinung gesagt.

ANDREAS   Und? Ist er mitgefahren?

LKW-FAHRER   Aber sicher. Am Schluß hat es ihm sehr gut gefallen. Er hat sich sogar bedankt.

ANDREAS   Aber mit achtzehn ist er doch schon alt genug zu wählen. Wie soll Ihr Sohn selbständig werden?

LKW-FAHRER   Solange er bei uns im Haus wohnt, fährt er auch mit in den Urlaub. Familie ist schließlich Familie.

✳ Examine some textbook dialogues which purport to convey some understanding of German culture. Analyze the cultural content in the following terms: Is the cultural content of a superficial nature, reflecting interesting but insignificant aspects of behavior or social organization, or are the features portrayed surface indicators of deeper attitudes and values?

CHECKLIST FOR ORIGINAL OR REWRITTEN DIALOGUES

1. Do I intend this to be a grammar-demonstration, a conversation-facilitation, or a recreational dialogue?

2. Is the conversation interesting and natural? Do the participants say something worthwhile? Have I avoided the question-answer-question-answer format?

3. What points of grammar (or conversational items) do I wish students to assimilate?

4. Is my list so ambitious that it has made the dialogue stilted and unnatural? (What can I omit while still achieving my purpose? See C18.)

5. Can I increase the redundancy to make the conversation more natural? (See C2.)

6. Can I include more expletives and rejoinders to make it sound more spontaneous? (See Chapter 4: G44.)

7. Are the levels of language I have used appropriate and consistent? (See C5.)

8. Is the dialogue of a reasonable length for classroom use and exploitation? (Is it open-ended? Should I rewrite it as a spiral series?)

9. Are individual utterances short enough to be assimilated or, alternatively, do they break naturally into useful segments?

10. Have I re-entered lexical items, idioms, and grammatical structures from previous dialogues to refresh the student's memory?

11. In how many ways can this dialogue be exploited? (See below.)

12. Does the situation lend itself naturally to interesting or amusing recombinations? Is it likely to stimulate students to produce their own recreational dialogues or skits?

Dialogue exploitation

The dialogue as a teaching technique has come in for much criticism because it has been used unimaginatively and its full potential ignored. There is more than one way to use a dialogue. In fact, the possibilities are so extensive that one could actually exploit each dialogue differently for a whole semester, if one wished.

DIALOGUE MEMORIZATION

The most criticized way of teaching through dialogues has required of each student that he memorize every dialogue completely and thoroughly (and this often for dialogues of fifteen or twenty sentences) and that he be able to recite the whole sequence on demand. This type of activity is time-consuming and tedious and gives indefensible importance to a particular sequence of utterances. As a result, students are at a loss when they do not hear the precise cue they are expecting. They become discouraged and exasperated by the mistakes they make in recalling memorized materials— mistakes which have nothing to do with their comprehension and assimilation of the material.

As has been noted earlier, there is no need for memorization of *grammar-demonstration dialogues*. A certain amount of repetition to ensure correct, fluent production is sufficient. Thorough exploitation with variety, in the ways suggested below, paralleled by as much grammatical explanation as the students need, will ensure understanding of the principles behind the structures used, while judicious practice in their meaningful use in all kinds of variations of their original setting will prepare students to use them perceptively in utterances of their own creation. Similarly, vocabulary will be retained more thoroughly if used frequently in various contexts.

Conversation-facilitation dialogues, which are short and full of expressions of wide applicability, may be memorized to the point where the useful segments, rather than the original sequence, are immediately available for use. Meaningful variations of the sequence will be welcomed as signs of real assimilation of the material. Recall may be aided by the use of a series of pictures on film, flashcards, or transparencies for overhead projection. Some teachers in the early stages like to have an English translation readily available when the student momentarily forgets the sequence of the dialogue; others reject this aid, preferring to concentrate on direct association of utterance and action.

With imagination the teacher can vary ways of presenting the dialogue. There are *five aspects* of the dialogue activity which need to be provided for if the energy expended is to yield any fruit in terms of the students' growing ability to function freely in the language.

1. Some *setting of the scene* to arouse student interest in the content of the dialogue and facilitate comprehension of the language used.

For example: acting out of the conversation first of all in English, or in mime, with appropriate props; discussion of the content of the dialogue with the help of pictures, slides, flashcards, projected diagrams, maps, plans; discussion of some aspect of life or some social situation for which the dialogue will supply a cultural contrast; some classroom language activity of the direct method or Gouin type (C11-13) which relates to the content of the dialogue; some preparing of the semantic area through discussion or through a competition or game; the recounting in the foreign language of an incident or anecdote of related interest, or the showing and discussion in English of a cartoon or a series of stick figures related to the theme. For a *grammar-demonstration* dialogue: raising some questions about the grammatical problem to arouse interest in its manifestations in the script and as a stimulus to the students to find out for themselves how the rule works.

2. Some technique for *focusing student attention* on the meaning of the interchange.

For example: students may be asked to listen to the whole dialogue on tape several times as a listening comprehension exercise, with opportunity between each hearing for group piecing together of the meaning; students may listen to the dialogue as they watch a series of slides, or look at a series of sketches illustrating the content of the interchange; students may be supplied ahead of time with a set of questions for which they should find answers as they listen to the dialogue; sometimes, for variety, students may be given the written script of the dialogue to peruse and ask questions about before listening to it without the script.

3. Some *familiarization* of students with the actual utterances in the dialogue through an activity which makes cognitive demands on them.[34]

For example: as students in the initial stage repeat the lines of the dialogue to develop fluency in their production, they take roles, group speaking to group or class to teacher, until they can handle the material with reasonable efficiency; after hearing an utterance two or three times, students try to reconstruct it as a group endeavor; the teacher writes the material on the board and gradually erases sections to see if students are repeating meaningfully and can supply the erased portions (erasures increase in length). For a *conversation-facilitation* dialogue: some students mime the dialogue while the class supplies the words; students go off in pairs and practice taking roles, testing each other on knowledge of the material; students act out the roles on an individual basis or as group presentations.

4. Some *formal manipulation* of the material in the dialogue, exploiting the useful expressions in a *conversation-facilitation* dialogue or the morphological and syntactic items in a *grammar-demonstration* dialogue.

For example: directed dialogue or guided conversation (see C24); group recombinations for similar but slightly different situations; chain dialogue (see C25). For *grammar-demonstration* dialogues: analysis of rules demonstrated in the material, leading into intensive practice through the various kinds of oral exercises described in Chapter 4. For *conversation-facilitation* dialogues: items of the dialogue may be used as personal questions to students who either answer for themselves or pretend through their answers to be someone else (the teacher or other students guess who they are); the teacher, or a student, establishes a situation by a remark and another student responds with a suitable expletive or rejoinder:

A   Ich kann nicht mit dir essen. Ich habe kein Geld.
B   Schade! (*or* Im Ernst?);

for a given expletive, the student creates an utterance:

A   *Vorsicht!*
B   Vorsicht! Hier kommt ein Auto.
A   *Entschuldigung*
B   Entschuldigung, wo ist die Keplerstraße?

5. Some ways in which the dialogue material can be used in the *creation of new utterances and new dialogues* expressing the students' own whims, feelings, and imaginings. The suggestions below encourage students to draw on anything they know from previous dialogues, from group conversation, or from reading, in preparing their versions. (They should be discouraged from seeking extra vocabulary in dictionaries at this stage.)

For example: the creation of a similar situation in another setting (the irate shopper demanding money back for a faulty appliance becomes the irate air traveler demanding a refund for a ticket, or a householder trying to get rid of a door-to-door salesman becomes a television viewer trying to cut off a telephone advertiser); group preparation, using a series of pictures of a different setting and a climactic utterance (*Aber es ist kaputt!*), of a dialogue with a similar dénouement to the one already studied. See also suggestions for *Recreational Dialogues,* below.

DIRECTED DIALOGUE OR GUIDED CONVERSATION

The teacher prompts pairs of students to reproduce sections of the dialogue. Directed dialogue may be conducted in several ways.

C24 (Working from C20)

1. TEACHER TO STUDENT A
   Ask B where he's going.
   STUDENT A   Wo gehst du hin, Heinz?
   TEACHER TO STUDENT B
   Tell him you're going out to eat.
   STUDENT B   Ich gehe essen.

2. TEACHER TO STUDENTS A AND B
   You meet each other in the corridor and one of you asks the other where he's going. The other replies he's going out to eat.
   STUDENT A   Wo gehst du hin, Heinz?
   STUDENT B   Ich gehe essen.

3. TEACHER TO STUDENT A
   Frage(n Sie) Heinz, wo er hingeht.
   STUDENT A   Wo gehst du hin, Heinz?
   TEACHER TO STUDENT B
   Antworte(n Sie) Jürgen, daß du (Sie) essen gehst (gehen).
   STUDENT B   Ich gehe essen.

Commentary

Directed dialogue is more difficult than most teachers realize because it involves a transformation of the teacher's cue for which students must be well prepared. Any potential usefulness is often negated by the amount of time devoted to the pure mechanics of the performance. *It is sometimes helpful to perform the operation several times in English to accustom the students to the procedure before using any of the approaches suggested.*

4. TEACHER TO STUDENTS A AND B
   Sie treffen sich im Gang. Einer von Ihnen fragt den

anderen, wo er hingeht, und der andere antwortet, daß
er essen geht.

STUDENT A   Wo gehst du hin, Heinz?
STUDENT B   Ich gehe essen.

Commentary

Here the language of the directions is more complex than the language,
possibly memorized, of the response. This can make the exercise confusing
and difficult for an elementary-level student.

CHAIN DIALOGUE

This is a challenging and amusing way for students to practice retrieval of
many expressions and structures they have learned. It can begin with very
recent material (for instance, a response pair from C20), but should soon
develop into a competition to think up questions and answers of all kinds.

C25 TEACHER TO A   Wo gehst du hin, Heinz?
              A   Ich gehe essen.
         A TO B   Komm mit, wenn du willst.
              B   Prima!
         B TO C   Wohin gehen wir?
              C   Ins Kino.
         C TO D   Interessierst du dich für Filme?
              D   Nein, ich sehe lieber fern.
         D TO E   Wie alt bist du?
              E   Ich bin vierzehn Jahre alt.
         E TO F   Und du?

RUBBISHING THE DIALOGUE

As a variation of the chain dialogue, but with a similar aim of developing
flexibility by drawing on all kinds of expressions which the students have
acquired, one team of students (Karl) undertakes to keep to the utterances
in the dialogue recently studied, and the other team (Peter) thinks up
possible responses other than those learned. (Later the teams exchange
roles.) Students try to remain within the bounds of what they have learned
but may ask the teacher occasionally for a few new expressions, thus adding to their repertoire things they would like to say. (Since this is a satirical
approach there is no need for the resulting sequence to be semantically
probable.)   •

C26 (Based on C20)

KARL   Tag, Peter.

PETER   Guten Tag, mein Herr. Kennen wir uns? (*or* Ich verstehe nicht, mein Herr; *or* Entschuldigung, haben Sie mich angesprochen?)

KARL   Wo gehst du hin? Ins Kino?

PETER   Nein, ich bleibe hier. (*or* Nein, ich gehe ins Bett; *or* Das ist nicht Ihre Sache; *or* Was ist ein Kino?)

KARL   Komm mit, wenn du willst.

PETER   Ja, gerne. (*or* Nein, ich habe keine Zeit; *or* Schön, aber nur, wenn du mir die Karte bezahlst.)

THE DIALOGUE AS A CULMINATING ACTIVITY

It has become customary to think of the dialogue as an introductory teaching technique, but it can also come at the end of a unit of study, whether dialogues are or are not used as a technique in the body of the lesson. In this case, it demonstrates in operation in a realistic situation what has been studied analytically. It is then enjoyed as an opportunity to express oneself in language and structures which are now familiar. This is the place for the *recreational dialogue,* or skit.

As a bridging activity, the *recreational dialogue* should have as its starting point a situation for which the student has some vocabulary and expressions available to him. "Situation" here is used in its broadest sense: a person alone in a house who hears a strange noise outside the window experiences a similar nervous reaction to a person watching a spider weave its web from the ceiling to a shelf of his bookcase and may very well exclaim in the same fashion: *"Meine Güte! Was mache ich!"*

Most students need the stimulus of seminal ideas such as the following, which take them from the shelter of the cove further and further into the open sea.

1. Skits may be based on an adaptation of this type of situation in a dialogue just studied: two people discussing their meal in a restaurant become the seven dwarfs grumbling about the meal Snow-White has prepared; two people meeting in a supermarket become a boy meeting a girl at the school dance.

2. Students are given one side of a conversation which is not explicit and are asked to create a dialogue. Different groups act out their versions.

C27 A   Entschuldigung, was haben Sie da?

B   . . . .

A   Aber so etwas habe ich noch nie gesehen.

B   . . . .

A   Es gefällt Ihnen aber doch?

B   . . . .

A   Auf Wiedersehen. Leider muß ich jetzt arbeiten.

3. Students are given a response-pair beginning: A: *Wer hat das dir gesagt? Deine Schwester?* B: *Nein! Sie war nicht zu Hause.* They extemporize a response-pair completion (or prepare a longer completion). Students should not strive each time for wit, which requires fairly sophisticated manipulation of language, but rather for a sensible conclusion.

C28   ROBERT   Wer hat das dir gesagt? Deine Schwester?
       PAUL   Nein! Sie war nicht zu Hause.
       ROBERT   Aber ich habe sie auf dem Balkon gesehen.
       PAUL   Das war meine Mutter. Sie sehen sich ähnlich.

4. Students are given a punch line and different groups work out short skits leading up to it. (*Aber er ist schon weggegangen!* or *Nein, nein! Mich nicht!*)

5. Skits are based on a list of words providing basic elements (*Zug, alte Dame, zwei Studenten in den Ferien, Grenze, Zollbeamter, kleiner Briefumschlag, am nächsten Tag*).

6. Students prepare puppet plays using the particular settings of recent dialogues (*Restaurant; Bank; bei der Großmutter*). Timid or reticent students will often express themselves in the voice of a puppet.

7. Students create original dialogues arising from an ambiguous picture, or a cartoon without caption. The pictures chosen should show an obviously emotional situation, or a predicament involving two or more people, or some incongruity.

8. Students invent dialogues based on problems caused by differences in everyday living in Germany; e.g., a foreign visitor invited to a German home for *Abendbrot* must face the decision of whether to put *Harzerkäse* or *Gänseschmalz* on his bread, or two tourists try to find a German acquaintance in an apartment building (*Namenschild, Klingel, Lichtknopf, Lift, erster Stock*).

The Cummings device[35]

One attempt to link structural practice and lexical exploration to communication is Stevick's Cummings device, based on the two-utterance communication. Stevick says, "The shorter a dialog, the less unexplained, confusing clutter it contains."[36] As a technique for moving from manipulation of structures to communication at each learning step, the Cummings device merits a place in this section on bridging activities.

"Cummings device" is Stevick's preferred term for what he earlier called his "microwave cycle." He describes the device as follows:

The ... format itself, in what we may a little wryly call its "classical form," contained a basic utterance (usually but not always a question) and from four to eight potential answers or other appropriate rejoinders. If the basic utterance and the rejoinders are well chosen, they can lead to almost immediate real or realistic ... conversation in class, and are also likely to find use in real life outside of class. At the same time, new structures and new vocabulary can be kept to a minimum.

A ... "cycle" was divided into an M-phase and a C-phase. *M* stood for *mimicry, manipulation, mechanics* and *memorization,* and *C* for *communication, conversation,* and *continuity.* Within the M-phase, the first section usually introduced the answers or rejoinders, often in the form of a substitution drill with a separate column for cue words. The second section contained the question(s) or other basic utterance(s). The C-phase combined the elements of the M-phase with each other and, ideally, with material from earlier lessons, to form a short sample conversation.[37]

The C series is so designed that lexical items are easily substitutable (substitutable items being placed in parentheses as a guide). As Stevick explains,

it is only through this kind of "delexicalization" that one can get away from content words chosen either at the whim of the textbook writer, or for their high frequency in the language as a whole, and that one can insure the use of the content words that are of high frequency in the student's immediate surroundings. In this way, through localization and personalization of vocabulary, we improve the likelihood that language *study* will be replaced by language *use,* and that language *use* will become a part of the group life of the students.[38]

The usefulness of this technique is that the teacher who has mastered the principle can derive Cummings devices, as need and interest suggest, from any materials—lessons in books, newspaper articles, material heard on tape, radio, or film track, or ongoing communicative activities. As with any device, it is intended, not as the whole of the course, but as one among the many possible activities which provide variety for student learning.

C29 *The Cummings device*

M-1		Hans arbeitet in der Stadt.
	Wir	Wir arbeiten in der Stadt.
	Heidi und Fritz	Heidi und Fritz arbeiten in der Stadt.
	jeden Tag	Heidi und Fritz arbeiten jeden Tag.
	acht Stunden am Tag	Heidi und Fritz arbeiten acht Stunden am Tag.
	ihr	Ihr arbeitet acht Stunden am Tag.
	Ursula	Ursula arbeitet acht Stunden am Tag.

in einer Bank   Ursula arbeitet in einer Bank.
heute   Ursula arbeitet heute.
Sie   Sie arbeiten heute.

M-2 Arbeiten Sie jeden Tag?
Nein, ich arbeite nicht jeden Tag.

M-3 Wo arbeiten Sie?
Wann arbeiten Sie?
Wie lange arbeiten Sie schon?

C-1 A   Arbeiten Sie in (einer Bank)?
     B   Nein, ich arbeite nicht in einer Bank.

     A   Arbeitet Marianne in (einer Bank)?
     B   Nein, sie arbeitet in (einer Buchhandlung).

     A   Arbeiten Sie (heute)?
     B   Ja, ich arbeite (jeden Tag) . . .

C-2 A   Wo (arbeiten) Sie?
     B   Ich arbeite (in der Stadt).

     A   Arbeiten Sie (in Chicago)?
     B   Ja, ich arbeite (dort).

     A   Wann (arbeiten) Sie?
     B   Ich arbeite (jeden Tag).

     A   Wieviele (Stunden) (am Tag) arbeitet Hannelore?
     B   Sie arbeitet (acht) (Stunden) (am Tag).

     A   Wieviele (Tage) (in der Woche) arbeiten Sie?
     B   (Fünf) (Tage) (in der Woche).

C-3 A   (Sie) arbeiten (in Chicago)?
     B   Ja, (ich) arbeite dort.

     B   (Man) arbeitet hier (acht) (Stunden) (am Tag)?
     C   Nein, (wir) arbeiten (sieben) (Stunden) (am Tag).

Note that in the C (Communication) phases the questions will be personalized: names and activities used will be those of members of the class.

Stevick warns his readers that the device "is not a theory, nor a method, but only a format,"[39] that there are a number of pitfalls to be avoided in writing individual cycles (these are discussed in Chapter 6 of Stevick, 1971), and that no course should consist of just one format. "Procedures and systems and approaches," he says, "supplement one another more than they supersede one another."[40]

THE CUMMINGS DEVICE AND CULTURAL INFORMATION

In C29, questions and answers refer to general activities of daily life in any society. The device can also be used to interest students in differences between daily activities in their own country and in Germany. The following types of information could be incorporated in a Cummings device based on question forms.

C30 In Deutschland ißt man mit dem Messer in der rechten Hand.
Ißt man in Deutschland Spiegeleier und Schinken zum Frühstück?
Wann ißt man Kuchen? (um vier Uhr nachmittags)

✻ Try to construct a Cummings device incorporating the type of information in C30.

Oral reports

Up to this point most of the bridging activities discussed have involved questions and answers, short statements and comments, requests, and exclamations. Another important facet of communicating includes describing, narrating, and explaining, all of which involve more sustained speech. Very early in the language course, students should have opportunities to practice these skills, taking as topics whatever suggests itself in the course of their reading or classroom activities. Reading passages, dialogues, sets of pictures, films, magazines, or class discussions of aspects of the country, its achievements, and the people who live in it provide basic vocabulary and ideas from which the students fan out in a creative way.

1. Reports at first are *short* (four or five sentences), later expanding as the students gain in confidence and experience. Students are always encouraged to ask the presenter questions about details of the report.

2. Initial efforts may be combined ones. Students in small groups construct their reports orally, with one student writing the group production on a chalkboard while the others criticize and improve on it until all are satisfied. When the class is next reassembled, a spokesman for the group gives the description or narration orally, without referring to a script, and

students from other groups ask questions. (The role of presenter is taken by different members of the group on successive occasions.)

3. In Lenard's verbal-active method, oral compositions play an important role.[41] She reiterates to her students the slogan: *"Ein hervorragender Aufsatz ist originell, phantasievoll, fehlerfrei. Wörterbuch? Nein, nein, auf keinen Fall."*[42] After the composition has been thoroughly discussed and worked over orally in class, it is written out and corrected by the teacher. "There is no point," Lenard says, ". . . in permanently recording . . . anything that has not reached its best possible form."[43]

We may add that, at least by the intermediate level, teachers need to give students help in the effective use of the dictionary, and some oral reports can then be devised as demonstrations of successful dictionary search. (See Chapter 9: *Exploring the Dictionary*.) In these cases, presenters explain in simple German paraphrases any specialized vocabulary they have used, thus developing another useful skill.

4. Early reports may be guided in a number of ways.

a. A sequential series of questions is provided on what has been read, viewed, or discussed, or on a similar, but personalized, situation.

C31 (Based on R38)

Günther und Jochen sind Freunde. Was machen sie zusammen? Warum besuchen sie sich gern zu Hause? Günther gibt der Schwester von Jochen Nachhilfe. In welchem Fach braucht Uschi Nachhilfe? Warum? Warum hilft Jochen nicht? Wieviel bekommt Günther für die Nachhilfe? Welche Fächer hat man in der Schule?

With an undefined series such as this, the students' answers become very diverse: they may be drawn directly from the text or may deviate considerably from it; e.g., instead of going to school together, Günther and Jochen may be sent by the student on a train trip to Berlin or to a party with Jochen's sister Uschi.

b. The student is given a series of pictures with no questions attached, the interpretation being left entirely to his imagination or invention.

c. A framework of key words from a skeleton outline.

C32 Sie machen bald eine Reise mit dem Flugzeug.
Vorbereitungen — Wagen — Parkplatz — Gepäck — Flugkarte — Gepäckaufgabe — Wartesaal — Zeitung — zwei junge Geliebte — ein Junge, der dauernd stört — zwei Matrosen — Meldung — Einschiffung — Abflug

d. Persons, places, or things in the students' own environment lead to mystery descriptions for which the other students guess the referent.

5. A simple form of oral report is a regular *Show and Tell* session, where students of their own volition share with their classmates things they have discovered about West Germany, East Germany, Switzerland, or Austria, and show objects imported from these countries, stamps, postcards, maps, menus, objets d'art, and bric-á-brac brought back by touring relatives.

6. Oral reports are an essential part of learning about the great figures and artistic, scientific, and social achievements of the people as well as their pleasures and aspirations in daily living; students prepare individual and group presentations as a culmination to their research on specific topics.

7. At more advanced stages, many opportunities arise for students to explain and discuss what they have been reading, hearing, or seeing in films, or to discuss topics of general interest arising from these or from current events in the news.

Situation tapes

Cartier[44] reports experimentation with situational conversations on tape for individual practice. The student hears the voices of two or more persons who are ostensibly conversing with him; spaces are left for him to record his parts of the interchange. The conversations are so designed that the student is led to make replies consistent with their drift, although what he actually says and how he says it are his own choice. The interlocutors call each other by their names and soon the student feels that he knows them and that they are actually speaking to him. After he has recorded his responses, he listens to the completed conversation and then re-records it as often as he wishes until he is satisfied with his part. (After all, we always think of that clever response after the crucial moment has passed.) The context can also be filled in with visuals. No monitoring or correction is supplied, the student being perfectly free to express himself to the best of his ability. In this way, the less confident student is able to practice real communication without the embarrassment of expressing himself inadequately in front of others.

C33 Jürgen und Heinz treffen Sie vor dem Kino.

The student is shown a picture of the cinema, with the name of the film being shown and a notice stating the times at which it will be shown. Italicized speeches are on the tape. A blip (shown here as an asterisk) indicates when the student is expected to reply.

JÜRGEN   *Abend, Alter. Willst du auch diesen Film sehen?* *
SCHÜLER   Ja, der Film soll gut sein.
   or   Ja, ich habe sonst nichts zu tun.

or	Nein, ich bin nur zufällig vorbeigekommen.
HEINZ	*Meine Schwester hat mir gesagt, daß der Film ausgezeichnet ist.*
JÜRGEN	*Ich persönlich weiß nichts darüber. Und du?* *
SCHÜLER	Ein Freund von mir hat ihn gesehen.
or	Ich weiß auch nichts.
or	Nein, mir hat man gar nichts davon gesagt . . .
JÜRGEN	*Was machst du jetzt, Heinz?*
HEINZ	*Nichts. Ich mache einen Stadtbummel.*
JÜRGEN	*Wir kommen mit, wenn du willst. Wartest du auf jemand?* *
SCHÜLER	Ja, ich warte auf meinen Freund.
or	Nein, ich bin allein hier.
HEINZ	*Wir haben noch Zeit. Hast du Durst? Ob wir schnell einen Kaffee trinken?*
JÜRGEN	*Eine gute Idee. Um wieviel Uhr fängt der Film an?* *
SCHÜLER	In zehn Minuten, glaube ich.
or	Um zwanzig Uhr, so steht es auf dem Schild.
or	Er fängt gleich an . . .

* Imagine that you are at a ski resort in St. Moritz. Try to make up a series of taped utterances for a situation tape. Then see whether different kinds of responses can be inserted without destroying the coherence of the sequence.

2
Autonomous interaction

Returning to the schema C1, we observe the gap between skill-getting and skill-using. Some indications have been given of ways in which production or pseudo-communication activities can become bridging activities, facilitating and stimulating autonomous interaction. (See also Chapter 4: *Oral Practice,* Type B exercise, p. 126.)

The crossing from bridge to shore, however, will not necessarily take place without encouragement. Many students will remain on the bridge, rather than face the unprotected autonomy of real communication, unless they are given opportunities very early to develop confidence and self-reliance through frequent, pleasant incursions into autonomous territory. In other words, the student will prefer the safety of the structured exercise and develop a nervous attitude toward the unstructured exercise which will be hard to change. He must learn early to express his personal intentions through all kinds of familiar and unfamiliar recombinations of the language elements at his disposal. "The more daring he is in . . . linguistic innovation, the more rapidly he progresses."[1] This means that priority must be given to the development of an adventurous spirit in trying to convey one's meaning to others in the foreign language.

How can we develop this necessary confidence and self-reliance? We must create, and allow to develop naturally, opportunities for our students to use the foreign language for the normal purposes of language in relations with others—as Birkmaier puts it, "to use language in a natural, useful way, in a significant social setting."[2] Such activities link listening and speaking, since, without ability to comprehend the speech of others, "communication" becomes an uninteresting and frustrating one-way street. In some approaches, activities such as those described in this section are the chief preoccupation. Even where this is not so, they must be given time and place if students are to communicate in uninhibited freedom.

Categories of language use

The student needs situations where he is on his own (that is, not supported by teacher or structured exercise), trying to use the foreign language to exchange with others messages of real interest to him. Yet we cannot send students off in groups or pairs and tell them to interact. *Motivation to communicate* must be aroused in some way. We must propose, or encourage students to develop, activities which have an intrinsic interest for them —activities in such natural interactional contexts as the following: (1) establishing and maintaining social relations, (2) expressing one's reactions, (3) hiding one's intentions, (4) talking one's way out of trouble, (5) seeking and giving information, (6) learning or teaching others to do or make something, (7) conversing over the telephone, (8) solving problems, (9) discussing ideas, (10) playing with language, (11) acting out social roles, (12) entertaining others, (13) displaying one's achievements, (14) sharing leisure activities.

These types of interactional activity lend themselves to various patterns of individualization, with students naturally seeking out partners with whom they feel at ease. Maslow[3] has shown that each individual has a hierarchy of needs to be satisfied, rising from physiological needs through the needs for feelings of security, belonging, esteem (of others and for oneself), and self-realization. These are reflected in complex interrelationships within any group. Since genuine interaction springs from the depths of the individual personality, all of these needs affect student reactions in a truly autonomous situation. For these reasons, only the student himself knows whether he feels more at ease with a fluent speaker who can help him along, a less fluent speaker whose lesser ability encourages him in his own efforts, or a good listener who inspires him with confidence. Some students, by their nature, interact very fully with few words. Students thus form their own small, natural-affinity interactional groups which select or generate activities as the group becomes a compatible unit.

An imaginative teacher and involved students will think of many absorbing and exciting interactional activities. Listed below are some expansions, by no means exhaustive, of the possibilities for language use within each category and some sample activities which would lead to the use of language in the terms of the category. Naturally, once an activity becomes truly autonomous the student automatically draws on elements from other categories; e.g., while making something (category 6), he overturns a container of paint and apologizes (category 1), then solves a problem by suggesting how such a situation could be avoided by a different arrangement of working space (category 8).

All of the activities suggested will obviously not be possible for all students from the earliest stage of learning. The teacher will *select and graduate activities to present* from these categories, so that the attitude of seeking to communicate is developed early in an activity which is within the student's growing capacity. An impossible task, which bewilders and discourages the student too early in his language learning, is just as inhibiting of ultimate fluency as lack of opportunity to try what he can do with what he knows. The sample activities within each category are broadly labeled E (Elementary), I (Intermediate), and A (Advanced). This is obviously not a hard-and-fast guide since the maturity, capabilities, and goals of groups are so diverse.

1. ESTABLISHING AND MAINTAINING SOCIAL RELATIONS

(E) Greetings between persons of the same and different age and status, introductions, wishes for special occasions, polite enquiries (with attention to the permissible and the expected questions in the culture), making arrangements, giving directions, apologies, refusals; (I) excuses, mild rebukes, conventional expressions of agreement and polite disagreement, encouraging, discouraging, and persuading others; (A) expressing impatience, surprise, dismay, making promises, hedging (the gentle art of non-communication), teasing.

Conversation capsules or *mini-incidents* can be developed by interaction groups to demonstrate how to handle various situations. These need not be lengthy. Students learn appropriate gestures as they enact the situations.

(E) Answering the door and politely getting rid of an unwanted caller; calling on the phone with birthday greetings, congratulations on a successful achievement, an enquiry about the health of a friend, or to make some arrangements; enacting urgent situations (fire, drowning, street attack) which require quick vocal responses with set phrases; (I) welcoming visitors at home, customers in a shop, or clients in an office.

(A) These uses become inextricably interwoven within other activities. Reality is achieved when students are able to greet, escort, and entertain a German-speaking visitor to the school or the town, interact in German with an exchange student, or participate in a visit abroad or an informal activity of category 14.

2. EXPRESSING ONE'S REACTIONS

The student can be put in real or simulated situations where he has to react verbally throughout a television show, at an exhibition of pictures or photographs, during a friendly sharing of slides, or at a student fashion show. (In these cases the clever or amusing remark, instead of being frowned upon as presumptuous, is welcomed, as long as it is in German.)

3. HIDING ONE'S INTENTIONS

(I) Each student may be given a mission which he must not reveal under any provocation, but which he tries to carry out within a given period of time. This activity carries purposeful use of the language beyond course hours as students try to discover each other's missions. (E) Selekman[4] has developed for this category a game called *Super Spy* (*Superspion*). One group forms a team of spies who decide on a mission. Each spy goes to a different group, the members of which try to find out his mission through astute questioning. The group which is successful first then explains how their spy's mission was discovered. This activity also involves (5), (8), and (13).

4. TALKING ONE'S WAY OUT OF TROUBLE

Simulated or real situations of increasing verbal difficulty should be set up, where the student must use his wits to extract himself from his dilemma: e.g., giving non-answers to an inquisitive neighbor anxious to know the origin of a loud noise he heard in the middle of the night; redirecting the course of an awkward or embarrassing conversation; answering the complaint: *"Ich habe dich gestern abend angerufen, wie verabredet, aber niemand hat geantwortet"* without revealing where one was or what one was doing.

5. SEEKING AND GIVING INFORMATION

a. *Seeking information* on subjects for which students have some basic vocabulary. (A) Finding out specialized vocabulary for a special interest can be part of this type of interaction, particularly in connection with (6). (I) Students may be sent to find out specific information from a monolingual German speaker or an informant who pretends to be monolingual, or the students seek the information from other German speakers outside of the course or the school. The information may be useful for activities in categories (1), (6), (8), or (12).

b. *Giving information* (E and I) about oneself, one's family background, the area where one lives, one's career aspirations, vacation preferences, pet peeves; (I and A) about some subject in which one is proficient (the student may be giving information to other students learning to do or make something, perhaps explaining what he is doing while he is doing it).

Combining (a) and (b). (E and I) All kinds of classroom opportunities arise for students to wonder why and ask the teacher or each other. Students should be encouraged to ask questions in German about what they are to do and to seek information about German customs and institutions. If a new student has joined the class, if there is a new baby in the family, if some student has returned from a vacation or a summer job, or if someone saw an accident on the way to school, other activities should be suspended while students ask about it in German. *Simulated settings* like bank or airline counters, customs desks, workshops, or restaurants may be used to expand the school setting. Advertisements from magazines can give an initial fillip to the interaction, with students enquiring about advertised services. Students may use German air schedules, customs forms, menus, or maps (often brought home by traveling relatives or the teacher) as a basis for asking and answering questions or giving directions. The *interview technique* also combines these two aspects of information-sharing. (A) The interview may be based on social roles adopted by the participants, thus linking (5) with (11). The results of the interview may be written up for a wall newspaper, as a link with writing practice.

6. LEARNING OR TEACHING HOW TO DO OR MAKE SOMETHING

Here, language is associated with action. The possibilities for increasing the interest and motivation of students of all kinds of abilities and interests are limitless. It is the basic technique of foreign-language camps and should be incorporated automatically into the programs of foreign-language clubs. On a smaller scale it can become part of a regular course. The pressure of intensive courses is certainly relieved by sessions in the foreign language where students actually work with real-life materials and activities (sports, hobbies, crafts, physical exercise, dances).

7. CONVERSING OVER THE TELEPHONE

This is always difficult in a foreign language because of the distortions of sound, interference, and lack of situational, facial, and body language clues to meaning. It should, therefore, be practiced early. The students should learn to use a phone book from the country where the language is spoken, and, where this is possible, make actual calls enquiring about goods, services, or timetables for transport.

The help of monolingual, or presumed monolingual, contacts outside the course should be enlisted. Some incapacitated persons, older persons living alone, and retired teachers would enjoy participating in this type of activity. They should be instructed to act strictly as monolinguals[5] and should be informed of the specific nature of the student's assignment.

Where none of these are available, teachers will act as informants for A students from their colleagues' classes, and A students will act as informants for E and I students.

The telephone practice is usually associated with (6) or (8).

8. PROBLEM SOLVING

The problem should require verbal activity for its solution. It may involve (5) or (6), even (3), (4), (9), or (10).

a. (E) Such well-known games as *Einundzwanzig Fragen, Identität, Tierreich-Steinreich-Pflanzenreich,* and their derivatives are popular. One student thinks of something (or someone, or an historical incident . . .), the others try to guess what it is with the fewest possible yes-no questions. (See G43.) (I and A) These games can become very sophisticated as versions of television panel series like *Was ist mein Geheimnis?, Wer sagt die Wahrheit?* (where three people pretend to be the person who performed some particular acts, and the students try to decide which one is telling the truth), and *Erraten Sie meinen Beruf* (where the questioners try to decide the occupation of the one being questioned).

b. (E and I) Selekman has experimented with a game called *Guilty Party*[6] (*Der Angeklagte*), where one student is accused by the group of an unspecified crime which he must discover through a series of questions (When did I do this? Where did I do it? Why did I do it? Did anyone help me? . . .). After he has discovered his crime, the accused must attempt to defend himself to seek an acquittal. (A) This game can follow a study of the German legal system and incorporate relevant features of German justice.

c. (E and I) Lipson,[7] in an attempt to focus the students' attention on the *content* of the sentences they are producing, has worked out materials which take up the principle of this well-known type of puzzle:

A, B, and C live on X, Y, Z streets.
A works in an office.
B is a lawyer.
C stays home while his wife goes to work.
The people on X street all work in factories.
The people on Y street are all single.
The people on Z street all own their own businesses downtown.

On which streets do A, B, and C live?

Lipson's materials are about hooligans who steal in factories, conduct themselves badly in parks, like to smoke on trolley buses, and are often uncultured people (uncultured people never wash). Later we find out that hooligans are of two types: those who conduct themselves badly in parks never wash, while those who steal in factories like to smoke on trolley buses. The plot thickens when we find out that there are two gangs of hooligans, Borodin's and Gladkov's: Borodin steals at Gladkov's factory and Gladkov at Borodin's. This complicated background leads to questions such as the following:

Which hooligans often wash?	Hooligans who steal in factories OR hooligans who don't conduct themselves badly in parks . . .
When does Borodin steal at his own factory?	He never steals at his own factory.
Why not?	Borodin steals at Gladkov's factory.
What does Gladkov do when Borodin is not stealing?	As far as I know, Gladkov steals at Borodin's factory.

Both Selekman[8] and Lipson[9] report that students become so involved in these problem-solving activities that their verbal participation becomes really creative and personally meaningful. As Lipson puts it: "What often happens is that members of the class start arguing with each other, and the teacher steps aside and lets the argument run."

d. (A) Problem-solving activities may be associated with some project for another course. Students may want to find answers to such questions as the following:

i. What is the significance of the recently altered relationship between East Germany (*Die Deutsche Demokratische Republik*) and West Germany (*Die Bundesrepublik Deutschland*)? What economic and cultural changes might be expected to result?

ii. Why do my *Rotkohl* and my *Sauerkraut* not taste German?

The answer to (i) may be sought through library research, listening to speeches, interviews with German visitors, reading of newspapers and magazines, and finally classroom discussion of what each student has gleaned, thus interweaving (5), (8), (9), and (13). Question (ii) may require some of the same procedures, along with experimentation in the kitchen (6).

9. DISCUSSING IDEAS

(E and I) Factual details of things read, seen, or heard provide a basis for discussion. Mystery stories are useful. Cultural differences are most likely to provoke lively discussion. Since students at the E and I stages are at a disadvantage in such discussions because of the teacher's wider command of the language, the teacher must refrain from taking over and doing all the talking. At these levels, topics for discussion are normally kept to areas for which the students know some vocabulary and expressions. Otherwise, they come after a project of research into the area; or students are provided with some written or recorded materials from which they can acquire the necessary German terms for use in the discussion.

(A) Students decide on controversial subjects they wish to discuss, prepare their points for discussion, but make their remarks without a written script; two groups prepare the same topic and discuss it with each other while students from other groups ask questions; one student takes a viewpoint and tries to convince other students that this viewpoint is tenable.

Stevick's *microtexts*[10] are useful as starters. A short text in German on any subject may be selected by teacher or students. This text is distributed, shown on the overhead projector, or written on the chalkboard; students then discuss and elaborate on the details of the text and any implications of it. The text should not be more than fifty words in length, or, if delivered orally, should not take longer than thirty seconds to relate. With experience, teachers and students can draw an astonishing amount of interesting discussion from almost any text. Possible microtexts are: (E) a menu, a concert program, an airline timetable, selections from letters from German correspondents, or a paragraph from a newspaper about the official activities of the *Bundeskanzler;* (I) newspaper accounts of the dog that saved its master during a fire, a bank robbery, two children lost in the mountains, a recent German, Swiss or Austrian Nobel Prize winner, a swing in fashions for dress or hair styles, or selected ads from the *Ehewünsche* section of a newspaper. (A) Accounts of recent decisions on German domestic or foreign policy (editorial comments from two different German newspapers or from a German- and an English-language newspaper may be compared), new developments in the German educational system, the latest approaches to the drug problem in Europe, letters to the editor raising interesting questions.

10. PLAYING WITH LANGUAGE

Newspapers and magazines have for years published regularly all kinds of word games (crossword puzzles, acrostics and double-crostics, vocabulary expansion quizzes). Books on language enjoy a perennial popularity, and magic and esoteric words continue to mesmerize devotees. From early childhood people are fascinated by language. This natural love of language can be exploited in the foreign-language class.

(E, I, A) *Scrabble* games geared to the letter frequencies of different languages are obtainable.

(E) Nonsense and counting rhymes may be learned by heart and recited for fun. Songs with repetitive refrains are popular. Students like to learn onomatopoeic expressions (animal cries, rain dripping, doors banging) and these can be used in games and classroom drama.

(I) Oral construction, in groups, of crossword and other language puzzles can stimulate much discussion in the language, particularly when the construction becomes complicated in the final stages. *Scharaden* provide amusing themes for classroom dramatization. Students take a two-syllable word (*haltbar*) and for each syllable they improvise a short episode which brings in the word it represents (*Halt/Bar*). They then act out an episode which brings in the complete word (*haltbar*) and their classmates guess which word it is. (Other possibilities are: *Bäcker/Ei/Bäckerei; Block/Ade/ Blockade; an/Kern/ankern;* or three syllables *er/zäh* or *Zeh/Lungen/ Erzählungen.*)

(A) Students may seek out and discuss word origins, word histories, and borrowings. They may examine German popular magazines like *Der Spiegel* or *Stern* to see the extent of contemporary German borrowings from English. At this level too, students may begin to take an interest in regional differences in the German language (e.g., the accent and common expressions of Berlin or München as contrasted with standard High German).

11. ACTING OUT SOCIAL ROLES

Psychologists point out that we are constantly taking on different roles and the style of language which goes with them.

Dramatic improvisation is an excellent technique for eliciting autonomous interaction. Situations and participating characters are suggested in a very sketchy fashion. Students are allowed a short time to plan what they will do before they enact the scene, improvising the dialogue as they proceed. Several groups or pairs may improvise the same situation with very different results. Even inhibited students feel free to express themselves when they are being someone else in a recreational activity.

(E) Students act out roles in which they can use expressions learned in (1).

(I and A) Situations are proposed which represent various social settings, with characters of different occupations, relationships, and levels of authority.

a. The job interview with a timid (or over-confident) applicant.

b. The overbearing bureaucrat and the applicant for a visa extension.

c. The *Wirtin* trying to find out all about the reticent new *Mieter* on the fourth floor.

d. The hippie son asking his very proper father for money.

e. The cocktail party at the *Deutsche Botschaft:* the vapid female talking about nothing at great length or echoing what other people say (*Das ist das erste Mal, daß ich hier in der Botschaft bin. / So, wie interessant. Sie sind zum ersten Mal hier?*); the boastful type (*Mein neuer Roman—der zwanzigste—ist schon wieder ausverkauft. Sie haben doch* Frühstück in Venedig *gelesen?*); the parallel monologue (A: *Meine Tochter heiratet nächste Woche.* B: *Wirklich? Ich habe nur Söhne.* A: *Sie heiratet einen Oberstudienrat aus Tübingen.* B: *So? Mein ältester Sohn studiert Zahnheilkunde*); the ignoramus talking to the Nobel Prize winner . . .

f. Situations based on proverbs.

g. Well-known political figures or characters in films or television programs may be mimicked in familiar situations.

12. ENTERTAINING OTHERS

The student should be given the opportunity to use his natural talents for singing, making music, or acting as host for a radio call-in program or a TV talk show. Groups of students may prepare and present radio or TV commercials. (These may involve more or less talking interspersed with mime, and are, therefore, very suitable for the early stages of a course.) A complete radio or TV program with news, situation comedy, commercials, weather report, interview, give-away show, sports, song and dance routine, and *Lieder* may be prepared for presentation to another class, for an Open Day, or for a school assembly.

13. DISPLAYING ONE'S ACHIEVEMENTS

(E, I, and A) Students may tell the group about what they did in (3), (4), (5), (6), or (8), or present and explain special projects, which will often be interdisciplinary (e.g., the study of an aspect of German art, music, architecture, or history). (A) As a climax to (9), groups may present their different viewpoints in a full-scale debate.

Some kind of public presentation can become a regular culminating activity to draw together many individualized interaction projects.

14. SHARING LEISURE ACTIVITIES

Students should have the opportunity to learn, and become proficient in, the games and diversions of the German people. They should be able to participate in verbal competitions. Where there are special activities traditionally associated with festivals or national holidays, students should be able to engage in them at the appropriate time (*Nikolaustag, Heiliger Abend, Silvesterabend, Fasching, Karfreitag, Ostern, Tag der Arbeit, der erste August* [*Schweiz*], *Oktoberfest, Martini* . . .).

Much autonomous interaction takes place at German clubs, German tables, class picnics, or at German camps. Visits are arranged to see exhibitions of German paintings, eat at German restaurants, see German films, or attend performances by visiting theatrical companies. Groups within a class may take turns preparing a German meal and inviting the others. Schools should investigate possibilities for inviting German exchange students. German-speaking residents of the district, or visitors passing through, should be invited to talk with German classes on a formal or informal basis. Students should undertake to show their town or their school to German-speaking visitors or tourists on a regular basis.

At the advanced level students often opt for *purely oral courses* to perfect their ability to communicate. For these courses, activities such as those described above which plunge students into normal uses of language are essential.

✳ Take three of the categories listed and for each try to think of three more activities which would lead to these particular normal uses of language. If you are studying this book in a class group, have a brain-storming session to see what you can add to the suggestions given.

Verbesserung, *nicht Vervollkommnung*
CORRECTION OF ERRORS IN AUTONOMOUS INTERACTION

It is during intensive practice exercises, or construction practice, that immediate corrections may be made. Even then, we should not jump in before our students have had time to think and often to correct themselves. Our task is to make our students conscious of possible errors and to familiarize them to such a degree with acceptable, rule-governed sequences that they are able to monitor their own production and work toward its improvement in spontaneous interaction. In interaction practice we are trying to develop an attitude of innovation and experimentation with the new language. Nothing dampens enthusiasm and effort more than constant correction when the student is trying to express his ideas within the limitations of his newly acquired knowledge of the language. Teachers who are non-native speakers of the language know that they are very often fully conscious of a mistake they have just made, even mortified by it, but unable to take it back. We should be happy when our students have reached the same level of awareness of acceptable usage, since it means they are becoming autonomous learners as well as autonomous speakers.

The best approach during interaction activities is for the instructor silently to note consistent, systematic errors (not slips of the tongue and occasional lapses in areas where the student usually acquits himself well). These errors will then be discussed with the student at a time when the instructor is helping him evaluate his success in interaction, with particular attention to the types of errors which hinder communication. The instructor will then use his knowledge of the areas of weakness of a number of students as a basis for his emphasis in instruction and in review. In this way, we help students focus on what are problem areas for them as they learn from their mistakes. Steady improvement will come only from individual motivation and purpose—that personal desire to perfect one's communicative effectiveness which is stimulated by genuine interest in what one is doing.

WHAT LEVEL OF CORRECT SPEECH CAN WE EXPECT FROM OUR STUDENTS?

The first question we must ask ourselves is: How does a native speaker frame his utterances when he is thinking only of expressing his meaning?

C34 Ich glaube, daß der Rhein in seiner Anzahl der Schiffe über—, wie sagt man, über–, überlegt ist, also zu, zu—. Der Rhein ist für die Gesamtschiffahrt zu klein geworden, und wenn man überlegt, daß in dem Krieg die Hälfte der Flotte versenkt wurde und nach dem Krieg durch Neubauten, Umbauten, Zusatzbauten heute ein Schiffspark, also internationaler Schiffspark dort steht, der den Rhein bevölkert, so muß man sagen, daß die Schiffahrt gegenüber dem Rhein, also die Anzahl der Schiffe auf dem Rhein gegenüber vor dem Krieg sich ungefähr verdoppelt hat.[11]

This passage, transcribed from a taped interview with a Rhine river pilot, shows clearly how we feel our way toward the most effective framework for expressing our meaning, leaning heavily on hesitation and transition expressions (*ich glaube, wenn man überlegt, so muß man sagen*) and repetitions (*über–, wie sagt man, über–, überlegt*), changing our minds in mid-stream about choice of words (*ein Schiffspark, also internationaler Schiffspark*) and about the type of sentence which will best express our meaning (*die Schiffahrt gegenüber dem Rhein, also die Anzahl der Schiffe auf dem Rhein gegenüber vor dem Krieg*). Note that we do not make basic errors in morphology or syntax, and that we frequently eliminate lesser errors by correction or rephrasing. (The first sentence in the passage is awkward and the choice of the word *überlegt* inaccurate. The speaker himself immediately gropes for another word and subsequently reformulates the whole sentence: *Der Rhein ist für die Gesamtschiffahrt zu klein geworden.*) The repetitions also help the listener to process each segment at the speed of utterance by providing redundancy to reinforce the meaning he is extracting.

It is clear that we cannot expect our students to speak German always in well-formed sentences in the heat of personal expression, when they do not do so in their native language. We must also expect students to hesitate, restructure sentences, and make sudden changes of lexical choice which may temporarily affect agreements of person and gender in the immediate vicinity. These imperfections are important only if they affect comprehensibility.

THE SI LINE

Stevick draws to our attention an interesting fact about simultaneous interpreters. "These remarkable individuals," he observes, "perceive both lexical meaning and grammatical form, and come out with their own reformulations in the other language after only a few seconds delay. Even as they speak, they are taking in new data for interpretation. . . . But if they are to continue, there is a line that they dare not cross: they must not become personally involved in what they are saying. Once the content of the message begins to make a difference to them, they lose the power of speaking and listening at the same time."[12] Stevick calls this boundary the SI (simultaneous interpretation) line: "Above it," he says, "lie grammatical form and dictionary meaning; below it lies everything that matters to speaker and listener."[13]

In view of this psychological phenomenon we have no reason to be surprised that students engaging in genuine interaction make many slips which we know they would not make in structured activities. Correcting them immediately and frequently will force students, for self-protection, to keep their attention above the SI line and will result in speech which is more carefully correct but which never goes beyond the banal and the obvious. This is surely not our goal.

INDIVIDUAL DIFFERENCES

Because of the personal nature of autonomous interaction, the participation of a particular student will naturally be consistent with his personality. Some people are temperamentally incapable of interacting by means of a babble of words; to expect them to do so is to force them back into pseudo-communication and into mouthing memorized phrases. The quality of the interaction will be judged by other criteria: ability to receive and express meaning, to understand and convey intentions, to perform acceptably in all kinds of situations in his relations with others. The means by which the student attains these desirable goals will be a function of his personal learning strategies. We can allow these full play through the provision of a wide choice of activity options, but we cannot determine for him what they shall be.

THE INDIVIDUAL TEACHER

Some non-native teachers feel inadequate to the demands of autonomous interaction activities because of insufficiencies of training or a long period of time away from foreign-language teaching. Just like their students, such teachers grow in skill and confidence as they participate. In a nonauthoritarian approach, the teacher accepts and acknowledges his weaknesses, drawing on his strengths as an *Anreger* to compensate. The students then accept him as a member of a group which is learning together. From year to year his control of the language improves, especially if he uses tapes of authentic native speech regularly to supplement his teaching and seizes every opportunity to listen to the language on the radio or on the sound tracks of films and to speak it in his contacts with colleagues in the school, at professional meetings, and *especially in his own classroom.* He also reads for pleasure modern books and plays in the language to keep him in contact with its contemporary spoken form. What he does not know, he encourages his students to find out, or, better still, he and his students find it out together. He also makes every effort to join in professional visits to German-speaking areas, or he goes on his own. If finances are the problem here, he organizes a group of students for such a visit and covers his expenses by accompanying them as guide and host. Many a poorly prepared teacher has overcome his inadequacies. The essential is the determination to do so.

3
Listening

Essential to all interaction is the ability to understand what others are saying. Even in the native language many people are poor listeners, whether through weak powers of concentration, egocentricity, or short auditory memory. Yet it has been estimated that, of the time adults spend in communication activities, 45 per cent is devoted to listening, only 30 per cent to speaking, 16 per cent to reading, and a mere 9 per cent to writing (and these data are from a pre-television, pre-talking-picture, pre-dictaphone era).[1] Apart from communicative interaction, much of the enjoyment in foreign-language use comes from listening activities—watching films and plays or listening to radio broadcasts, songs, or talks by native speakers. Even in class students learn a great deal from listening to their teacher, to tapes or records, or to each other.

It is noteworthy that some students who do not excel in other areas of foreign-language use achieve a very high level of success in understanding spoken messages. It has been suggested by some researchers that there is a special listening comprehension factor,[2] but this has not yet been fully characterized. Even in life situations many people become skilled, in their own or a foreign language, in understanding registers, dialectal variations, and complexities of structure which they cannot produce in their own speech. Troike[3] has called this a difference between receptive and productive competence. Students with special skill in listening comprehension should be encouraged and given opportunities to go beyond others in this area, which is especially suitable for individualized work. They should also be rewarded in final grading with full consideration for this skill in which they excel.

Listening is a complex operation, integrating the distinct components of perception and linguistic knowledge in ways which are at present poorly understood.[4] Psychologists have tried to explain this phenomenon from several viewpoints, each of which can give us some clues to our students' problems in listening to a foreign language and suggest ways of structuring effective materials for practice and enjoyment.

The schema C1 brings out the cognitive nature of listening, which involves *perception* based on *internalized knowledge* of the rules of the language. Students have to learn to abstract from a stream of sound units which machines cannot as yet be programmed to identify, to assign these to categories, and to attribute to them functions in relation to other units, so that an intelligible message may be constructed from what they are hearing. While they are doing this, they are anticipating the import of the message, holding segments already identified in their immediate memory, and readjusting their interpretation of earlier segments in accordance with the final message *as they understand it.*

In this context, the phrase "as they understand it" is basic, because listening is not a passive but an *active process of constructing a message* from a stream of sound with what one knows of the phonological, semantic, and syntactic potentialities of the language. Even in our own language we often "hear" what was never said. This becomes an even more frequent occurrence in a language we are still learning. It is this active process of message construction which has been labeled *reception* (or comprehension of the message) in C1. The two terms *perception* and *reception* represent the two levels[5] of practice required to improve systematically the student's skill in interpreting messages intended by speakers.

Models of listening processes

Some linguists[6] maintain that knowledge of the same system of grammatical rules of a language is basic to both listening and speaking. Some psychologists, on the other hand, believe the rules we apply are different and that we employ perceptual strategies[7] for surface scanning of what we are hearing, stopping to penetrate to underlying relations only to resolve ambiguities or untangle complexities. Despite their theoretical divergence, interesting insights can be derived from various linguistic and psychological schools of thought, each of which emphasizes a different facet of the complicated processes of listening and receiving messages.

In this section, we will discuss in detail (A) the role of uncertainty and redundancy in Cherry's theory of communication, (B) Neisser's active processing of a message, and (C) Bever's strategies of perceptual segmentation (with which we will link Schlesinger's semantic-syntactic decoding).

The uncertainties of a spoken message

Cherry[8] says, "Communication proceeds in the face of a number of uncertainties and has the character of . . . numerous inductive inferences being carried out concurrently." He lists these uncertainties as:

1. Uncertainties of speech sounds, or acoustic patterning. Accents, tones, loudness may be varied; speakers may shout, sing, whisper, or talk with their mouths full.
2. Uncertainties of language and syntax. Sentence constructions differ; conversational language may be bound by few rules of syntax. Vocabularies vary; words have many near-synonyms, popular usages, special usages, et cetera.
3. Environmental uncertainties. Conversations are disturbed by street noises, by telephone bells, and background chatter.
4. Recognition uncertainties. Recognition depends upon the peculiar past experiences of the listener, upon his familiarity with the speaker's speech habits, knowledge of language, subject matter, et cetera.

Here we have in a nutshell many of the problems our students face in the comprehension of speech, each of these being compounded where a foreign language is involved. "Yet," Cherry continues, "speech communication works. It is so structured as to possess redundancy at a variety of levels, to assist in overcoming these uncertainties."[9] In C2 we examined some of the redundancies of spoken, as opposed to written, German. It is time now to examine a specimen of unedited, authentic speech, uttered in an informal interview by a person who was not aware that what he said would ever serve any pedagogical purpose. (This passage will reinforce the impressions gained from C34.)

EDITED AND UNEDITED LISTENING COMPREHENSION MATERIALS

In preparing materials and activities for listening comprehension we do not give enough consideration to the differences between edited, or artificially constructed, messages and an authentic output of speech in natural interaction. As a result we make the listening comprehension materials we record, or present to the students orally in class, much more difficult to comprehend than we realize. The difference is like that between listening to a prepared and polished scholarly paper read verbatim and the free interchange of unprepared discussion which follows the paper and usually makes the speaker's ideas seem much clearer.

C35-37

The following edited and unedited discussions of the same subject will illustrate this difference. The unedited version is taken from a tape transcribed in *Texte gesprochener deutscher Standardsprache I.*[10]

C35 Edited description

Wir sitzen hier vor der Krakau, eine Hochebene, die sehr reich gegliedert ist, und die für unsere Begriffe viele Bauernhäuser hat. Dieses ist also die klassische Landschaft des Faschingrennens, eine Faschingveranstaltung, die noch sehr an der Grenze eines auch bei den Zuhörern und Mitwirkenden Ehrfurcht erweckenden Brauchtums steht. Es ist nicht das fröhliche, lärmende, und vor allem nicht das bunte und verkleidete Treiben, das wir aus Imst und anderen Gegenden kennen, wo der Fasching öffentlich gefeiert wird, sondern der Faschinglauf gehört heute fast noch zu den kultischen Notwendigkeiten dieser Landschaft. Es ist noch gar nicht lange her, daß die alten Bauern den größten Wert darauf legten, daß der Faschinglauf über ihre Felder und Wiesen ging, weil er ihnen vergewisserte, daß ihr Grund entsprechend gut tragen würde. Der Hafer würde reicher sein, der Leinsamen würde höher wachsen, und alles würde gut gedeihen.

C36 The following passage, transcribed from the original tape, shows how the same ideas were expressed in authentic interaction. Periods indicate segments that correspond to complete sentences, but incomplete utterances remain as part of these sentences.[11]

Wir sitzen jetzt vor der Krakau. die ganze Landschaft, die Sie hier sehen, heißt zum großen ganzen die die Krakau eine Hochebene sehr reich gegliedert viele für unsrige Begriff viele Bauernhäuser. und das ist die (ich möchte fast sagen) klassische Landschaft des Faschingrennens. das Faschingrennen ist ein eine Faschingveranstaltung, die noch sehr an der Grenze eines noch fast Ehrfurcht auch bei den Zuhörern Mitwirkenden Ehrfurcht erweckenden Brauchtums steht, es ist nicht das fröhliche und nicht das lärmende und vor allem nicht das bunte und verkleidete Treiben, was wir aus Imst kennen und aus anderen Gegenden, wo der Fasching öffentlich gefeiert wird. sondern der Faschinglauf gehört heute fast noch zu den kultischen Notwendigkeiten dieser Landschaft. es ist noch gar nicht lange her (ich hab das noch selber erleben können), daß die alten Bauern zumindest den größten Wert darauf gelegt haben, daß der Faschinglauf (er läuft jeden Faschingmontag) daß der Faschinglauf auf jeden Fall über ihre Felder über ihre Wiesen geht, weil er ihnen vergewissert, daß ihr Grund entsprechend gut tragen wird. der Hafer wird reicher sein. der Leinsamen wird höher wachsen. und alles wird gut gedeihen.

C37   If we set these passages out in parallel columns we see much more strikingly how much verbal redundancy has been eliminated even in such a colloquially expressed version as C35. For C36 each sentence has been listed separately.

C36	C35
Wir sitzen jetzt vor der Krakau.	Wir sitzen hier vor der Krakau,
die ganze Landschaft, die Sie hier sehen, heißt zum großen ganzen die die Krakau eine Hochebene sehr reich gegliedert viele für unsrige Begriff viele Bauernhäuser.	eine Hochebene, die sehr reich gegliedert ist, und die für unsere Begriffe viele Bauernhäuser hat.
und das ist die (ich möchte fast sagen) klassische Landschaft des Faschingrennens.	Dieses ist also die klassische Landschaft des Faschingrennens,
das Faschingrennen ist ein eine Faschingveranstaltung, die noch sehr an der Grenze eines noch fast Ehrfurcht auch bei den Zuhörern Mitwirkenden Ehrfurcht erweckenden Brauchtums steht.	eine Faschingveranstaltung, die noch sehr an der Grenze eines auch bei den Zuhörern und Mitwirkenden Ehrfurcht erweckenden Brauchtums steht.
es ist nicht das fröhliche und nicht das lärmende und vor allem nicht das bunte und verkleidete Treiben, was wir aus Imst kennen und aus anderen Gegenden, wo der Fasching öffentlich gefeiert wird.	Es ist nicht das fröhliche, lärmende, und vor allem nicht das bunte und verkleidete Treiben, das wir aus Imst und anderen Gegenden kennen, wo der Fasching öffentlich gefeiert wird,
sondern der Faschinglauf gehört heute fast noch zu den kultischen Notwendigkeiten dieser Landschaft.	sondern der Faschinglauf gehört heute fast noch zu den kultischen Notwendigkeiten dieser Landschaft.
es ist noch gar nicht lange her (ich hab das noch selber erleben können), daß die alten Bauern zumindest den größten Wert darauf gelegt haben, daß der Faschinglauf (er	Es ist noch gar nicht lange her, daß die alten Bauern den größten Wert darauf legten, daß der Faschinglauf über ihre Felder und Wiesen ging, weil er ihnen vergewisserte, daß ihr

läuft jeden Faschingmontag) daß der Faschinglauf auf jeden Fall über ihre Felder über ihre Wiesen geht, weil er ihnen vergewissert, daß der Grund entsprechend gut tragen wird.

Grund entsprechend gut tragen würde.

der Hafer wird reicher sein.

der Leinsamen wird höher wachsen.

und alles wird gut gedeihen.

Der Hafer würde reicher sein, der Leinsamen würde höher wachsen,

und alles würde gut gedeihen.

Commentary

Although the edited version C35 retains the colloquial flavor of C36, it eliminates synonymous expressions which merely repeat the thought content or elaborate it in minor ways (*die ganze Landschaft/die Sie hier sehen/heißt zum großen ganzen die die Krakau*); function words indicating a direction of sentence structure which is not followed through [*daß der Faschinglauf (er läuft jeden Faschingmontag) daß der Faschinglauf...*]; conversational tags and formulas (*ich möchte fast sagen*), and false starts (*ein/eine Faschingveranstaltung*). It also regularizes syntax which does not observe the accepted constraints (*was wir aus Imst kennen und aus anderen Gegenden, wo der Fasching öffentlich gefeiert wird*); the present tense used in colloquial narration is replaced with the simple past. Thus, in a well-meaning attempt at "improving" the disorderly output of C36, the editor has provided in C35 a version which would demand much more concentrated effort in listening than the authentic speech of C36. *As with speaking, we may well be demanding more of our foreign-language listeners in the exercises we present than is demanded in native-language listening.*

Authentic materials of the type illustrated are unfortunately not easy for classroom teachers to obtain. The following suggestions should be implemented:

1. When visiting German speakers and German exchange students are temporarily at hand, teachers should seize the opportunity to tape-record general conversation with the visitors. Suitable excerpts from the tapes should then be shared among groups of schools.

2. German cultural services should be bombarded with requests for tapes of radio discussions, informal chats, and film sound tracks, until an awareness is created that these are the types of materials our students need.

3. Exchanges of tapes should be encouraged between twinned classes in German- and English-speaking schools. Both classes should be encouraged to send unedited tapes—not of prepared talks, but of free discussion among members of the class on aspects of their daily lives and their likes and dislikes. To obtain such tapes requires a change of attitude on the part of teachers who often expect a class exchange tape to be a perfectly orchestrated performance.

4. Individual students should be encouraged to begin tape exchanges with correspondents in German-speaking countries, along the lines of the more conventional letter exchanges.

Listening to authentic tapes recorded by native speakers who are not teachers provides one of the best opportunities for students to have real contact with the life and thought of German-speaking people, whether from West Germany, East Germany, Austria or Switzerland. Through these tapes, they encounter the normal and the natural, even the trivial, much more than in the reading of newspapers, magazines, novels, plays, and short stories, all of which tend to choose as subjects the exceptional, the sensational, the idealized, or the eccentric in order to arouse and maintain interest.

RECOGNITION UNCERTAINTIES

The listener constructs a message from what he is hearing according to certain expectations[12] based on:

—what he knows of the language, not only syntax and lexicon, but usage in these areas for different styles of language (see C5);

—his familiarity with the subject under discussion;

—the knowledge of the real world that he shares with the speaker (through which he can assume certain things which have not been expressed);

—his acquaintance with or assumptions about the personal attitudes and interests of the speaker;

—his observation and interpretation of the circumstances of the utterance, including what has preceded it;

—his understanding of the cultural context in which it occurs;

—his reading of paralinguistic cues (speed of speech, length of pauses, loudness, pitch, facial expressions), gestures and other body language which differ from culture to culture.[13]

The listener imposes a syntactic structure on what he is hearing and this arouses further expectations about what is to come. Sometimes a succeeding segment proves to be incongruous with his syntactic expectations and this forces him to reconsider and project a different syntactic structure, in other words, to resolve the ambiguity.

For these reasons ability to receive messages aurally becomes more refined as knowledge of the potentialities of the grammatical system increases.

C38

1. *Welche Truppen führen diese Offiziere?*

2. *Welches Kind haßt deine Katze?*

Commentary

a. On hearing the interrogative adjective (*welche*) + noun of the first sentence, the listener anticipates the order subject-verb-object, as in the question: *Welche Soldaten haben die Stadt angegriffen?*

b. His experience of the real world (normally, officers are in charge of soldiers) makes him restructure the message he is extracting. His knowledge of German syntax confirms this restructuring: since the inflected verb is always in the second position, the subject will come after the verb when the question centers on the object.

c. The second sentence is truly ambiguous because either *Kind* or *Katze* could be the spontaneous enemy in the real world.

In these cases, the listener must hold the utterance in his immediate memory while comparing it with the context or the circumstances of the utterance before assigning it a disambiguating structure.

✱ Discuss the two possible syntactic structures of the following:

C39

Das Buch habe ich leicht gefunden.
Ich habe den Brief von Hans bekommen.
Inge liebt Hans mehr als Jochen.
Dumpf und verworren hörte er die Alte sprechen.

Find other examples of ambiguities of structure in German.

Ignorance of the cultural context can be an impediment.

C40

(A) Hans-Peter und Else treffen sich vor der Mensa der Freien Universität.

HANS-PETER   Die Reaktion in die Enge treiben! Wo warst du heute? Wir haben dich vor dem Springer Haus vermißt.

ELSE   Und? Man sollte dich vielleicht für einen Achtundvierziger halten? Ich habe zu viel zu tun.

Commentary

A student could well understand every word of this interchange without having any real idea of its meaning and its emotional or ironic overtones. Full comprehension of it requires knowledge in various domains:

1. *The setting.* The *Mensa* of the *Freie Universität* is a popular meeting place in Berlin for students interested in discussing current political topics. In addition the very name of this Berlin university conjures up a picture of student activism and unrest, since it remains the focus of student protests against national and international political developments as well as university policies.[14]

2. *The subject matter.* Ever since the student demonstrations in 1968 which led to an attempt to establish a counter-university to the *Freie Universität,* Berlin has witnessed demonstrations before the *Schöneberger Rathaus,* the *Amerika-Haus* and, as mentioned here, the *Springer Haus,* the headquarters of Germany's largest publisher of newspapers and magazines. Springer has been the object of attack because he controls such a substantial part of the German press.

3. *The historical allusion* is clear to all Germans. *Die Achtundvierziger* refers to the participants in the revolution of 1848 and the naiveté of the liberals who gathered in the *Paulskirche* in Frankfurt to establish a constitutional government. Else's remark draws a parallel between the enthusiastic modern activists and the intellectuals of 1848 whose ideals were left unfulfilled.

4. *Syntax.* One use of the subjunctive in the main clause (*man sollte*) is to express skepticism.[15] She is saying: you act as if you were a forty-eighter, but your behavior seems silly to me. In spoken form, tone of voice would convey some of this significance. If the person speaking were visible (on film, for instance) facial expression and movements would help in the interpretation, which is supported by her declaration that she has more important things to do than spend her time demonstrating.

C41 (A) *Deutsche Welle: Blickpunkt*[16]

Für die Freidemokratische Partei, so stellte der Chefprogrammierer der FDP, Professor Maihofer, fest, seien die deutschen Jungdemokraten ohne jegliche Relevanz. Dieses ziemlich vernichtende Urteil des Mannes, den man gemeinsam als den Vertreter des linken Flügels der FDP zu bezeichnen pflegt, über die Nachwuchsliberalen sagt mehr aus, als vieles andere, was über das Wochenende aus Bad Honnef bei Bonn das Ohr der Öffentlichkeit erreichte. Dort hatten sich 100 Delegierte der rund 30.000 Mitglieder der deutschen Jungdemokraten zu ihrem diesjährigen Bundeskongreß versammelt. Die Tagung stand von vorneherein in Zeiten einer Standortsuche, einer Kursbestimmung, die der Organisation wieder Profil und Einfluß auf die Politik der sogenannten Mutterpartei, der FDP eben, verleihen konnte. Beides nämlich war dem Jugendverband in den letzten Monaten mehr und mehr abhanden gekommen. Das Profil in gleichem Masse, in dem sich die Jungliberalen ideologisch den Jungsozialisten annähern, der Nachwuchsorganisation der Sozialdemokratie. Und der Einfluß auf die FDP sank kontinuierlich je mehr die Judos sich in ideologische Systemkritik vergassen. . .

Commentary

1. News commentaries of this type are more difficult to follow than conversational style material. If we compare this broadcast with C36 we find that many of the redundancies and rephrasings of natural, informal speech have been eliminated. The announcer does, however, reduce the strain on the listener by providing redefinitions (*einer Standortsuche, einer Kursbestimmung; der sogenannten Mutterpartei, der FDP eben*). In addition, radio essays are generally delivered in a more deliberate tone, with clearer enunciation, and distinct pauses at major syntactic boundaries.

2. Radio commentaries are often easier to follow than newscasts because they pursue a single subject for some time, whereas a complete newscast moves rapidly from one context to another.

3. While a broadcast about current conditions in Germany introduces the student to the problems and conflicts in contemporary German society, it also requires some background. Here the student will want to know who the *Jungdemokraten* are, he will need some basic political vocabulary (*FDP, Nachwuchsorganisation*) and some acquaintance with contemporary jargon (*ideologische Systemkritik*). The teacher may want to keep a file of relevant newspaper and magazine clippings from *Die Zeit* or *Der Spiegel* and make these available to students or ask students to give reports on the necessary background information in German.

4. *Place names and personal names* given orally can hinder recognition. Students should be given instruction in the recognition of names in the news. [zɔlʃeniːtsɪn] is not easily recognized by an American as Solzhenitsyn. In the combination [bɑt hɔnɛf baɪ bɔn] the student may miss the more familiar *Bonn* which tells him that the meeting was held in the vicinity of the West German capital. If newscasts are made available within the week in which they were broadcast, familiarity with recent

events of international significance will provide conceptual background for recognition of many of the names of people and places.

World geography lessons with German wall maps and guessing games with names of famous persons in the accepted German oral form are helpful as associated activities when newscasts are being used as listening comprehension material.[17]

5. The difficulties faced by the students on first hearing a newscast can be diminished by encouraging them to relisten to the recording of the broadcast until they have comprehended the gist of the discussion.

* What additional knowledge of current political trends and divisions in Germany would a student need to have in order to comprehend fully the import of the C41 broadcast?

Equally important for the comprehension of radio broadcasts is *recognition of numbers,* as in the following:

C42 (A) *Die deutsche Welle*[18]

Noch weniger positiv war das Umfrageergebnis bei der jüngeren Generation, vor allem bei Oberschülern und Studenten. Wer von der Wehrpflicht unmittelbar betroffen ist, zeigt die geringste persönliche Dienstbereitschaft. In der wichtigen Gruppe der Sechzehn- bis Neunzehnjährigen hielten 23 Prozent den Wehrdienst für eine notwendige Pflicht. 25 Prozent wollten nur sehr ungern Soldat werden und 34 Prozent am liebsten gar nicht.

Rapid recognition of numbers, and dates as well, is indispensable to modern communication. One has only to think of common situations like asking the operator for telephone numbers, requesting airline and train schedules, changing travel plans, and understanding prices, rates for service, final accounts, bank balances, exchange rates, current dates, dates of birth, times for performances, or document numbers. With the multiplication of computerized services, more and longer numbers are becoming a part of everyday life, the latter often involving also rapid recognition of the *names of letters of the alphabet.*

Practice in attentive listening to numbers is provided in games like Bingo, in dictation of series of numbers of increasing complexity, and in competitions where events must be selected from lists of multiple-choice items to correspond with dates given orally. The alphabet should be learned early, and students should become adept at recognizing the oral spelling of new words and names letter by letter—a skill which is also useful for a foreigner in many communication situations.

1. Activities to *prepare the learner conceptually* for the type of content in a listening exercise are valuable in helping students develop expectations and project possible meanings.

2. Listening comprehension materials should preferably be well *integrated thematically* with the rest of the learning program; otherwise, *discussions of a related subject* may be necessary to stimulate the student's thinking. For example, discussion of German holidays and the celebrations connected with them would prepare students for listening to C36; a study of student life and attitudes in contemporary Germany would bring to life a listening tape of which C40 was a part; discussion of some aspects of the German educational system makes comprehensible a conversation among students waiting for the *mündliche Prüfung* of the *Abitur;* at a more elementary level, practice in telling the time in German prepares for a tape where several prospective travelers are making enquiries at an airline counter.

3. Students may be encouraged to project, to think ahead to reasonable completions, by games which test their alertness in detecting tricks in the completion of sentences.

Verbessern Sie den Erzähler is a team game which forces the student to think of the meaningful use of learned phrases or facts by dislodging them from their familiar settings. It may be given orally or on tape.

At the elementary stage, simple narratives may capitalize on common errors in meaning which students are making in everyday phrases they have learned in dialogues or classroom conversation. (For instance, elementary students often confuse *Wo ist er?* and *Wer ist er?* or *er will* and *er wird.*) Groups of students can prepare these narratives to try out on other groups. The team preparing the narrative gets points for each item missed by the opposing team.

One, or two, narrators read the prepared narrative expressively, not pausing or indicating in any other way where there are anomalies. When a student interrupts to point out an anomaly and is able to give an appropriate replacement, his team scores a point.

C43 (E) With anomalies italicized:

Heute früh gehe ich allein weg. Mein Bruder, *der mit mir kommt,* fragt mich:

—*Fräulein,* wo ist *Ihre* Freundin?
—*Sie heißt* Emma. Wie geht's, du?
—*Ich bleibe heute zu Hause,* antwortet er.

Commentary

If each utterance begins, as in the last three utterances, with an inappropriate segment, the position of the error becomes predictable. Students preparing narratives should be alerted to avoid clues such as positional regularity, alternation of correct/incorrect, and so on.

(I) Attention to detail to overcome the lulling effects of expectation can also be encouraged in listening to factual material. In C44 below, some of the facts will be known to the students from a lesson in German geography; the effect of this lesson will be to create expectations which may make it difficult for him to "hear" some of the discrepancies. Once again a point is awarded to the team of the student who detects a fantastic or incorrect fact and can supply a suitable replacement for the offending segment.

C44 (I)

Statements read	*Replacements*
Hamburg ist eine wichtige Hafenstadt *ungefähr fünf Kilometer* von München.	ungefähr fünfhundert Kilometer *or:* weit nördlich *or:* fern
Einige Schiffe kommen jeden Tag in den Hafen von Hamburg.	viele
Jeden Tag fahren auch große Schiffe aus dem *Hafer.*	Hafen
Sie *verpassen* Hamburg, um in alle Teile der *Wälder* zu fahren.	verlassen Welt

Commentary

The narrator must be careful not to accentuate slightly the incorrect word or look for a response. Because of the phonetic similarity in some cases (*verpassen/verlassen*) and the fact that other words belong to the same semantic field (*viele/einige*), student expectations will often result in their thinking they have heard what makes sense in the context.

The active process of constructing a message: stages in perception[19]

1. PERCEIVING A SYSTEMATIC MESSAGE

In listening comprehension *we first learn to perceive that there is a systematic message rather than accidental noise in a continuous stream of sound.* We learn to recognize a characteristic rise and fall of the voice, varying pitch levels, recurrences of certain sound sequences which may seem somewhat like those of our own language, yet strangely different. At this stage, we make an elementary segmentation of what we hear in order to retain it in our memory. Even with gibberish or an utterance in a completely unknown tongue, we must segment in some way in order to repeat or memorize it. Many of the amusing things little children say result from their idiosyncratic segmentation of what they do not fully understand. (This is the stage called *Identification* in the chart of activities for listening comprehension, C67.)

Prolonged listening as an introduction to language study

Students are often plunged into trying to produce utterances in a new language too soon. As a result, they approximate these to the phonological system of their own language without having any feeling for the distinctiveness of the new language.

It has been suggested by some that foreign-language learning should begin with a prolonged period of listening to the language without attempting to produce it. Prolonged listening to a strange language which is not associated with visuals, action, writing, or some intellectual exercise to help in identification of meaning, can become boring and will not necessarily lead to advantageous results. A baby hears a great deal of language around him for a long time before he speaks, but always associated with persons, places, objects, and bodily needs, so that he gradually focuses on segments of it which are functional in his living space.

The *total physical response* approach encourages early attentive listening with physical action to demonstrate comprehension, but with no attempt at production.[20]

C45 (E) In the form of the game Simon Says (*Jakob sagt*), this approach to teaching has always been with us:

TEACHER OR STUDENT   Heben Sie die Hand!
Students do not react.
TEACHER OR STUDENT   Stehen Sie auf!
Students do not react.
TEACHER OR STUDENT   Jakob sagt: Stehen Sie auf!
Students stand up . . .

C46 In the game's more developed form, students learn to perform progressively more complicated series of actions, still without any attempt at production. This has been shown to produce a high rate of retention.[21]

Students move from simple imperatives (*Schreiben Sie; Stehen Sie auf*) to short directions (*Gehen Sie an die Tür; Schreiben Sie an die Tafel*), then to more complex directions (*Gehen Sie an den Schreibtisch des Lehrers und legen Sie die Kreide darauf*), and finally to novel directions combining utterances already heard (*Gehen Sie an das Fenster, nehmen Sie das Buch mit, legen Sie das Buch auf den Schreibtisch des Lehrers, und dann setzen Sie sich*).

Some practice of this type should be included in all early lessons, no matter what approach is being used.

Discriminating sounds which change meaning

1. Gattegno, it will be remembered, encourages early listening to tapes and disks of different languages, so that the student gradually comes to *recognize characteristics of the language he is learning*. This is useful practice in identification. The classroom teacher can introduce this element without much difficulty by playing tapes of German songs and readings of poetry as background in the elementary classroom—in intervals before classes begin, while students are engaged on projects, over amplifiers to set the atmosphere for the beginning of a language laboratory session, or in a listening room or a listening corner of the classroom. This strategy encourages individual students to listen for the pleasure of the sounds. Some students will pick up parts of the songs, particularly refrains, purely by imitation as some opera singers do, thus learning to segment what they are hearing. This is pure perception, not reception of a message. Documentary films may be shown with the original German sound track, even before students can be expected to understand it, to familiarize the ear with the sound-aura of the language. After hearing a great deal of the language in this way, students will be far less inhibited about pronouncing words so that they really sound German.

2. Various types of *aural discrimination* exercises are given in Chapter 5. Some of these exercises can be worked into aural discrimination games and into competitions which involve listening practice. They should be continued at the intermediate level to keep students alert to sound distinctions which affect meaning.

C47 *Verbessern Sie mich*

Groups of students, or the teacher, prepare stories into which they work words which are inappropriate in the context but could be confused with the appropriate word if the listeners were not paying careful attention to sound distinctions. The student who has the best pronunciation, or the teacher, tells the story orally. A point is awarded to each student who notices an inappropriate word and is able to give the appropriate substitute with correct pronunciation.

In the sample text below, incorrect words are italicized and correct words are given in parentheses.

(I) Es war zehn Uhr abends, und der *Mund* (Mond) schien hell. Ich war *schön* (schon) dreizehn Stunden auf der Autobahn. Ich hatte Hunger. Zu *messen* (essen) und zu trinken hatte ich nichts. Ich mußte noch weiter *reiten* (fahren). Ich war aber so müde. Wer könnte mir aus dieser *Note* (Not) helfen, dachte ich. Da hörte ich, "Du sollst nicht *schaffen* (schlafen)." Ich erinnerte mich *denn* (dann) an meinen Freund, der neben mir saß. "Es ist zu dunkel," sagte er, "wir können fast nichts *sehnen* (sehen). Gottseidank, da vorne ist eine Gaststätte." Wir hielten da an. Der *Keller* (Kellner) war unfreundlich, und das Essen hatte uns überhaupt nicht *geschmückt* (geschmeckt), aber wir haben uns ausgeruht.

2. IMPOSING A STRUCTURE

In the second stage of perception, we identify in what we are hearing segments with distinctive structure—segments which seem to cohere. These segments may not be distinguishable by machine, because it is at this stage that *we impose a structure on what we are hearing according to our knowledge of the grammatical system of the language*. The more we know of a language the more easily we can detect meaningful segments, such as noun phrases, verb phrases, or adverbial phrases. Our experience with our own language makes us expect such structural segmentation. For this reason, we may segment incorrectly at first in a language with a very different structure. (It is interesting to note that in psychological experiments subjects rarely report hearing ungrammatical sentences, and when asked to repeat ungrammatical utterances they correct them, which indicates that they are imposing known structures in constructing a message from the sound signal.)

This early segmentation determines what we will remember of the actual sound signal. It is a process of *selection*. The identification of "chunks,"[22] or syntactic groupings, reduces the load on our memory. Just as it is easier to remember nine numbers in three groups (382 965 421), so it is easier to remember *Mein Bruder möchte/schon nächstes Jahr/nach Deutschland fahren* as three syntactic groupings, or meaningful chunks, rather than as nine separate words, even if we are not sure of the lexical meanings of some of the words.

If we have segmented incorrectly or heard inaccurately, we will retain what we think we have heard, because we will have no further access to the sound signal after echoic memory has faded. (Echoic memory is estimated to last a few seconds only. It is during this interval that we can still readjust our segmentation, as discussed in C38.)

Practical application

Except in specialized courses, listening comprehension is not usually practiced in isolation from other language-learning activities. Some common classroom techniques help students develop their ability to hear language in organized chunks (or to segment according to syntactic groupings).

1. The *backward buildup* technique is frequently used in the memorization of conversation-facilitation dialogues. Each utterance to be memorized is divided into syntactically coherent segments. Students learn the last segment with correct end-of-utterance intonation, then the second-last followed by the last, and so on.

C48 Utterance 7 of C20 would be memorized in imitation of the model as follows:

nicht weit vom Bahnhof.
ein kleines, gutes Restaurant nicht weit vom Bahnhof.
Es gibt ein kleines, gutes Restaurant nicht weit vom Bahnhof.

In this way students move from a new segment to a segment they already know, making for more confident recitation.[23]

2. *Dictation* is useful when well integrated with other learning activities. Dictation also involves listening to language segmented in meaningful chunks. Students in the early stages should be encouraged to repeat the segments to themselves before trying to write what they think they have heard. This gives the student practice in imposing a construction on the segment before he writes it, thus increasing his short-term retention of the segment.

3. Oral exercises which require students to vary syntactic segments purposefully provide practice in "hearing" language in syntactically coherent chunks. (See Chapter 4: G9-G21.)

4. *Information Search* (*Nur das Treffende!*), a kind of spot dictation, gives practice in detecting syntactic cues to segmentation. In this activity, students are asked to listen to a sequence of sentences, writing down only the segments which answer certain questions with which they are supplied beforehand. The passage is given orally several times, and students write down the segments which answer particular questions as they comprehend them, that is, after the first, the second, or the third hearing. This encourages attentive listening for specific segments that fulfill certain syntactic functions, e.g., who? where? what?

C49 (E)

Es ist der erste April. Um fünf Minuten vor acht ist Inge in der Schule. Sie sitzt schon an ihrem Platz in der dritten Reihe. Vor ihr sitzt ihre Freundin Christa. Die Stunde fängt bald an. Inge nimmt aus ihrer Mappe einen kleinen Fisch. Schnell legt sie ihn auf Christas Schreibtisch.

Questions supplied	*Segments to be written*
1. Welcher Tag ist es?	der erste April
2. Wie spät ist es?	fünf Minuten vor acht
3. Wo ist Inge?	in der Schule
4. Wo ist ihr Platz?	in der dritten Reihe
5. Wer sitzt vor ihr?	ihre Freundin Christa
6. Fängt die Stunde schon an?	Nein, die Stunde fängt bald an.
7. Was nimmt Inge aus ihrer Mappe?	einen kleinen Fisch
8. Wo legt sie ihn hin?	auf Christas Schreibtisch

5. *Subjekt oder Anderes.* Inexperienced students need practice in listening for certain *syntactic signals* which must be recognized automatically in rapid speech in order to understand the meaning of another's remarks. One such signal is the marker for the nominative and the corresponding ending on the verb. Students need to recognize that in German the subject does not have to stand in first position, but can follow the verb whenever another element precedes the verb in the sentence.

In this game, which can be devised at quite an elementary level, students listen to a narrative and mime or do not mime actions according to whether the subject stands first or not. The narration is given at normal speed. Students who make the wrong movements are progressively eliminated until only one student remains.

C50 (E and I)

Meine Eltern stehen morgens früh auf.

Das Frühstück macht mein Vater.

Die Zeitung liest meine Mutter vor dem Frühstück.

Die Kinder weckt meine Mutter später auf.

Wir waschen uns sofort.

Nach dem Frühstück putzen sich die Kinder die Zähne.

Die Post holt mein Bruder, bevor er weggeht.

Seine Freunde trifft mein Bruder an der Ecke.

Sie erwarten ihn da.

A variation of this game, *Ich oder von mir?*, draws attention to *signals of voice.* Students mime an action in the future tense active, but clap or tap with a pencil when they hear the past participle indicating the passive voice. Students making wrong reactions are progressively eliminated.

C51 (E and I)

Morgen werde ich früh aufstehen.
Ich werde mich zuerst waschen.
Dann wird der Brief geschrieben.
Er wird aber erst später abgeschickt.
Um elf werden wir von Peter and seinem Freund abgeholt.
Wir werden alle zum Park fahren.
Dort wird es dann zu Mittag gegessen.

* Work out a game to train the student to distinguish between the past tense, indicative, of the modals and the present tense, subjunctive II, of the modals.[24]

3. RECIRCULATING, SELECTING, RECODING FOR STORAGE

At the third stage of perception we recirculate material we are hearing through our cognitive system to relate earlier to later segments and *make the final selection* of what we will retain as the message. In this way, we follow a "line of thought." We then *recode what we have selected for storage in long-term memory.*

Rehearsal or recirculation of material perceived

1. Unfamiliar language elements which are being held in suspension and recirculated while decisions are being made as to the composition of the entire message impose a *heavy load on the short-term memory.* Sometimes the short-term memory becomes overloaded and some of these segments have to be discarded in order to leave room for the absorption of new segments. It should not surprise us, therefore, if inexperienced listeners, at an elementary or even intermediate stage, declare that they understood everything as they were listening but are unable to recall what they understood. At this stage students may be able to recognize from multiple-choice items or true-false questions details of what they heard, whereas they would not be able to give a full account of the message without this help.

2. *Many different aspects of a listening text may be retained* by students, and these may not always be those elements the teacher expected. Students often need some guidance as to the facets of a message on which they should concentrate for the purpose of the exercise. This guidance in selection, which relieves the memory of some of the burden of detail, can be supplied by preliminary discussion or questions (given orally, or in writing).

3. At the elementary stage, students may be provided with questions with multiple-choice items *before* they begin listening. They should be encouraged to mark a tentative choice during the first hearing and confirm this on the second or third hearing. Teachers should remember that this method combines listening with reading. They should take care to see that the multiple-choice items supplied are short and expressed in language simple enough for the level of the students concerned. The items should not reproduce verbatim any sections of the material for listening practice, since this makes the task merely one of recognition, not comprehension.

4. Although some people consider that providing written questions is a *mixing of modalities* which raises doubts as to whether one is testing listening comprehension only, several other facts must be kept in mind.

a. *Oral questions* cannot be absorbed during the process of listening to other material. (Psychological studies show that we filter out competing oral stimuli when the material to which we are listening demands careful attention.)

b. Oral questions given before or after the listening material add a further aural exercise to the one being evaluated. (Students may have understood the exercise, but not the questions on it.)

c. Oral questions asked *after* a listening exercise of some length require the retention of details over a period of time. They therefore test not only immediate comprehension but long-term retention. The same observation may be made about oral questions asked *before* listening to an oral narrative, or dialogue, as a guide to selection. These will need to be repeated after the material has been heard. Otherwise, we are evaluating not only listening comprehension, but also retention and recall. The use of oral questions is, therefore, more appropriate at the intermediate level. (For the special problems of short listening comprehension items, see *Designing Multiple-Choice Items for Listening Comprehension* below.)

d. At the elementary level, the problem of oral versus written questions is often solved by the *use of pictures*. Students are asked to circle the letter corresponding to the picture which best represents what they are hearing. They may also be asked to complete a diagram or picture according to oral directions or to mime what they are hearing.

5. When the attention of students is directed to particular aspects of the listening task, they will not retain in their memory material they do not require for this specific purpose, except incidentally. With C47, for instance, students may very well comprehend as they proceed and make correct decisions about the inappropriate items and appropriate replacements, yet still not be able to say at the end what the complete narration was about. After the C47 exercise has been completed, the passage should be read as a whole, with the appropriate replacements, as practice in comprehension of a complete narrative.

Note that since *the processes involved in fluent reading and in listening are similar,*[25] students will have the same problem in reading. A common test of reading has been to ask students to read a passage aloud with careful attention to diction, phrasing, and intonation. A student performing well on this task will not necessarily be able to answer questions on the content of what he has just read, without first being given the opportunity to reread the passage silently. With his attention concentrated on identifying meaningful segments, interrelating these in sentences distinguished by certain intonational patterns, and pronouncing individual words and groups of words comprehensibly, the student may have engaged his cognitive system in too much activity to be able also to recirculate segments and recode them for long-term storage.

6. When students have selected segments for the construction of the message they are extracting, they will no longer have access to the rejected segments (unless these were recirculated as alternatives and retained because the student was in doubt). If students have misunderstood the tenor of the message, the solution is not to question them further in an attempt to extract the correct message. They should be given some indication of where they misinterpreted the message and the opportunity to hear it again so that they can construct a new version of it.

7. It is a mistake to make all listening comprehension exercises tests with strict limitations. Students should be *allowed to listen to material as often as they need to* until they are able to "hear" and retain the content. Relaxed conditions, with no feelings of apprehension, are essential, since emotional tension greatly affects our ability to "hear" a message. Students should have frequent opportunities to listen to material purely for the pleasure of comprehension without the threat of grading.

8. *The recirculation of material in the memory takes place during the pauses in speech,* so the pauses are vital. In normal speech, pauses are lengthened by hesitation expressions (*mm . . . ah . . .* etc.), whereas in edited speech, or careful speech, these extensions of the pauses are missing. This allows less processing time for the listener. Speech which appears "too fast" to the inexperienced listener should be "slowed down" by lengthening slightly the pauses between segments, rather than by slowing down the delivery within the segments. The latter procedure distorts the natural sounds of the language by creating diphthongs, eliminating customary linking, and so on.

Recoding of material for storage in long-term memory

We store what we hear in long-term memory in a simplified form. In common parlance, *we retain the gist of what was said,* that is, the basic semantic information, rather than the actual statements with all their complications of structure.

C52 We may hear the following discussion of private schools in Germany:

A   Gibt es überhaupt Privatschulen in Deutschland?
B   Ja, es gibt auch in Deutschland Privatschulen, aber die Privatschulen stehen allgemein nicht in einem guten Ruf, was ihre Leistung anbetrifft. Das liegt vielleicht zum großen Teil daran, daß man doch hin und wieder die Erfahrung gemacht hat, daß derjenige auf den Privatschulen . . auf einer Privatschule gut versetzt wird, dessen Vater gut bezahlt. Also es kommt da nicht so sehr auf Leistung an, sondern auf die Zahlungsfähigkeit des Vaters.

Und weil da eben keine staatliche Kontrolle unmittelbar vorgeschaltet ist, mißt man den Zeugnissen von Privatschulen nicht so viel Wert bei, wie den Zeugnissen von staatlichen Schulen.[26]

C53 If asked what this passage was about, a student might come up with a series of statements like these:

Man spricht über die Privatschulen in Deutschland.
Die Privatschulen stehen nicht in einem guten Ruf.
Auf einer Privatschule ist das Geld des Vaters wichtig.
Ein Schüler von einer reichen Familie kommt da weiter.
Nicht so wichtig ist die Leistung des Schülers.
Es gibt keine staatliche Kontrolle für die Privatschulen.
Ein Zeugnis von einer Privatschule hat nicht so viel Wert.
Ein Zeugnis von einer staatlichen Schule hat mehr Wert als das Zeugnis von einer Privatschule.

Commentary

1. In reducing what he heard to a set of factual statements, the student has produced *a series of simple active affirmative declarative sentences* (SAAD's to the psychologist). This is the basic type of sentence in most grammars. Facts in this form are the easiest to recall because all relationships are reduced to subject-verb-object, with some adverbial modifications.

2. A set of basic utterances like these is quite *redundant* in that much information is repeated from sentence to sentence, thus providing associational tags which make it easier to retrieve all the information about any one aspect, as in the following questions:

C54 In welchem Ruf stehen die Privatschulen in Deutschland?

Die Privatschulen stehen nicht in einem guten Ruf. Das Geld des Vaters ist wichtig. Die Leistung des Schülers ist nicht so wichtig. Wichtiger ist die Zahlungsfähigkeit des Vaters.

Or: Hat ein Zeugnis von einer Privatschule so viel Wert wie eins von einer staatlichen Schule?

Nein, das Zeugnis von einer staatlichen Schule hat mehr Wert. Es gibt keine staatliche Kontrolle für die Privatschulen. Übrigens, Geld ist auf einer Privatschule wichtiger als Leistung.

3. Note that *a certain amount of the information in the original has been dropped*. Without looking back to check the details, our reader, like the student listener, will probably not recall, for instance, that the speaker qualifies his statements (*Das liegt vielleicht zum großen Teil daran*) and that he is speaking from general experience. In preparing questions which require retrieval of information from long-term memory, teachers should keep in mind how this information is stored and *focus on the central line of thought and the basic facts,* rather than on peripheral detail.

Where there is ambiguity, the listener, by reducing the message to its basic elements, clarifies interpretatively relationships between what he has assimilated and what he is hearing.

C55 The listener hears:

Der Verlust der Freunde ist bitter.

He recodes this information for long-term storage as
   A. X verliert die Freunde, und das ist bitter.
or B. Die Freunde verlieren Y, und das ist bitter.[27]

If he has selected interpretation A for recoding for storage, this is what he will recall and he may even argue forcefully that this is exactly what was said, as listeners often do in native-language communication situations. After he has constructed interpretation A from what he has heard, interpretation B will be accessible to him only if a contiguous segment forces him to readjust interpretation A while he is still recirculating what he heard through his short-term memory.

Since psychological experiments and empirical intuition seem to indicate that recoding is basic to long-term memory storage, *we can help our students develop efficiency in listening comprehension,* and in retention and recall, by:
   1. presenting them with an outline of the main ideas in basic SAAD sentences before they listen to a structurally complicated version;

2. by asking them to state in basic SAAD sentences what they have
retained of a listening comprehension exercise;

3. by asking questions on the text which require SAAD sentences as
answers.

The teacher's expectations

We cannot expect students to extract and retain from foreign-language
listening material more than they do in the native language. Experiments
have shown that average-ability adults recall a very low percentage of the
possible information from broadcast talks (about 20 percent when they
were not aware that they were to be tested, 28 percent when they knew
they were to be tested). Other studies suggest that college students comprehend about half of the basic matter of lectures. The degree of listening
efficiency on any particular occasion depends, of course, on the type of
material and its organization, the interest the material holds for the listener,
the way it is presented (speed, audibility, variations in tone of voice, situational relevance), and even such factors as the acoustics of the room and
the emotional state or physical fatigue of the listener. Nevertheless, "evidence on the ability of people to be trained in listening makes it clear that
many people listen below capacity"[28] in the native language. We may
expect a higher degree of concentrated attention to a foreign-language
listening exercise because students are aware of its difficulty for them, but
we must not look for total or near-total recall of detail. In order to correct
any unrealistic expectations, it is often useful to try out a listening comprehension exercise on a native speaker before giving it to foreign-language
learners.

✱ Reduce the basic facts in the following text to SAAD sentences and write
some questions which would extract from the listener this series of related
facts, rather than a few isolated details.

C56 *Diskussion über die Ehe*[29]

A   Ja, denn das ist nämlich für uns ein wirkliches Problem, die Ehe ist,
wie man so sagen kann, doch, meinem Wissen nach, eine christliche
Einrichtung. Oder nicht?

B   Nein, die Ehe ist eine gesellschaftliche Einrichtung,

A   Ja,

B   nicht christlich.

A   Hat sie nicht 'ne tiefe Wurzel auch im Christentum?

B   Das Christentum oder vor allen Dingen die Bibel nimmt Stellung zu
der Ehe, und sie nimmt Stellung zu den Problemen der Ehe.

A   —Ja—

B   Aber die Ehe selbst ist meiner Ansicht nach also das Natürlichste und das Ursprünglichste einer Gesellschaft.

A   Oh nein, das möchte ich . . . würdest du das wirklich sagen, das Ursprünglichste, das Natürlichste? 's kann doch genau so gut sein—man spricht davon—, daß die Männer polygam veranlagt sind, genauso die Frauen. Man müßte jetzt wirklich Untersuchungen anstellen über die verschiedenen Rassen in verschiedenen Erdteilen, ob da überhaupt die Ehe als das Ursprünglichste und Natürlichste der Welt (die Ehe) geführt wird. Das möcht' ich unheimlich bezweifeln, denn denk doch an die Mohammedaner, die hatten alle mehrere Frauen.

B   Sicher, aber sie haben schließlich auch eine Ehe gehabt, ja? Sie hatten bestimmt unter den vielen Frauen eine, die ihnen besonders zugetan ist, ja? Also, ich meine . . .

A   Ja, aber das ist doch noch nicht Ehe. Ich meine, unter Ehe verstehen wir doch nicht nur eine Liebe, 'ne besondere Liebe zu einer Frau, sondern Ehe ist eine ganze Institution mit sagenhaft vielen Verpflichtungen, die beide Partner gegenüber haben . . .

Strategies of perceptual segmentation

For the psychologist Bever, "the internal logical relations are a major determiner of perceptual segmentation in speech processing."[30] This view aligns well with that of the linguist G. Lakoff of the generative semantics group, that logical categories and logical classes provide the natural basis for grammar and, therefore, ultimately of language use.[31] In other words, since our experience of the real world has taught us to expect such functions as agents, actions, objects, and place, time, and manner modifications,[32] we identify these in what we hear.

Bever has identified four strategies[33] we seem to employ in the perception of speech.

1. First of all, we tend to segment what we hear into sequences which could form *actor-action-object . . . modifier* relations. This segmentation strategy Bever calls Strategy A. Clearly, for this elementary segmentation, we need to be able to identify, at least approximately, syntactic groups. Fortunately, languages generally supply a certain number of surface indicators of function, or syntactic cues, which we use to separate out different clauses within the sentence.[34] This aspect of perceptual segmentation has already been discussed as stage two of the active process of constructing a message, and exercises have been proposed for developing this ability in a foreign language.

2. In English at least, we learn to expect *the first N . . . V . . . (N)* (that is, noun . . . verb . . . optional noun) *to be the main clause* (that is, to set out the overriding idea of the sentence) unless morphemes like *if, when,* or *before* warn us that we are dealing with a subordinate clause. The latitude for variation is greater in German. Although Segmentation Strategy B is frequently true for the principal clause, the student must be trained to expect the inflected verb as the second element in statements even when the first element is something other than the subject. The student must also learn to expect the inflected verb at the end of subordinate clauses introduced by subordinating conjunctions, and he must interpret readily such cues as *wenn, als, bevor, da,* which indicate subordination. At the advanced level the student must be able to recognize such deviations from the usual pattern as the not uncommon sentence opening segment *adverb + past participle,* which he might encounter in more formal listening materials, e.g., *davon abgesehen, können wir feststellen, daß all seine Werke diese Markmale besitzen.*

3. In applying Strategy C, we seek the meaning by *combining the lexical items in the most plausible way.* Thus, *the dog bit the man* is easily comprehended, whereas *the man bit the dog,* not being consistent with our normal experiences of the real world, gives us pause. We may "hear" it as *the man was bitten by the dog,* but be forced to reprocess it as subject-verb-object when later segments make it clear that something unusual has happened. Alternatively, we may ask the speaker to repeat his statement.

4. Sometimes there is no specific semantic information to guide us in assigning relationships. We then fall back on a primary functional labeling strategy, based on the apparent order of lexical items in a sentence— Strategy D. We assume that any *noun-verb-(noun), NV(N), sequence* represents the relations *actor-action-object.* It is for this reason that we understand the active construction *the dog chased the cat* more quickly than the passive form *the cat was chased by the dog.* Since the latter allows semantically for reversal of roles, it will often be heard as *the cat chased the dog,* especially by children. In a continuing message, later information which does not support this interpretation will cause us to pause and reprocess the utterance syntactically. We then search for cues (passive form of the verb, agent *by*-phrase) which indicate to us the order *logical object–verb–logical subject.* Although somewhat different, the German passive may also be misinterpreted by the student until he can recognize readily the syntactic cues of verb position and case indicators.

SEMANTIC-SYNTACTIC DECODING

Schlesinger has called the process of relying at first on semantic expectations and resorting to syntactic processing only in doubtful cases *semantic-*

syntactic decoding.[35] In summary, we perceive the semantic cues and rapidly assign these such roles as actor (or experiencer or instrument), action, object, or modifier according to our knowledge of the real world. It is when our initial interpretation does not fit into the developing message that we pause to analyse syntactic cues to function.

Because of this initial tendency in listening to take the easier road of semantic decoding, students with an *extensive vocabulary* can often interpret a great deal of what they hear by sheer word recognition and logical reasoning. A person listening to a news broadcast might identify the following lexical items:

C57 . . . Flughafen . . . Baranquilla . . . Nordkolumbien . . . Luftpiraten . . . Passagierflugzeug . . . zwanzig . . . Landung . . . Reifen . . . Maschine geplatzt . . . Sprecher . . . erklärte . . . Entführer . . . Zwischenlandung in Cali . . . dreißig Reisende freigelassen . . . nach Kuba fliegen.

With this basic information, his knowledge of similar situations, and his powers of inference, the student would probably have little difficulty deducing the following facts:

C58 Auf dem Flughafen von Baranquilla in Nordkolumbien halten Luftpiraten in einem von ihnen entführten Passagierflugzeug weiter etwa zwanzig Geiseln fest. Bei der Landung waren mehrere Reifen der viermotorigen Maschine geplatzt. Ein Sprecher der Fluggesellschaft erklärte, die Entführer, die bei einer Zwischenlandung in Cali dreißig Reisende freigelassen hatten, wollten offenbar nach Cuba fliegen.[36]

✱ As an exercise in introspection, try to remember which of Strategies A-D you employed in your perception of the meaning of C57.

AURAL RECOGNITION VOCABULARY

Since combining lexical items in a plausible way plays such an important role in listening comprehension, attention should be given to building an extensive aural recognition vocabulary.

For many students, particularly above the elementary level, the greater part of their vocabulary is acquired in association with reading and writing. It is not surprising, therefore, that many of them have problems in recognizing by ear the words they already know in graphic form. They also have difficulty recognizing words derived from these, and even the cognates and the rapidly disseminated vocabulary of contemporary technology, science, politics, and social diversions (*der Smog, das Schöpchen, der*

Nylon, der Jumbo Jet, der Föderalismus, die Dynamik, die Blue Jeans). Many of these terms are pronounced in a sufficiently different fashion in German to appear novel to the inexperienced ear. In C58, for instance, even [ɛtvɑ tsvɑntsIç] when spoken at normal speed may not be obvious to a visually trained person, while words like [landUŋ] and [fiʁmotɔRIç] may elude recognition, and [lUftpiRɑt] may not be recognized as a compound of [piRɑt].

To develop confidence in aural recognition of words originally encountered in graphic form, students need to understand and apply constantly the rules of sound-symbol correspondence in German. Knowledge of such rules often helps a student to visualize the probable spelling of a seemingly new word and so to relate it to what he knows. This is an ability which is important to a person who has been accustomed to learning the language graphically or who by modality preference is visually oriented.

All kinds of practice techniques and competitions can foster transfer from visual to aural recognition and from aural to visual.

1. Clearly *comprehensible pronunciation of all new words* should be expected as they are encountered, so that the students' ears are kept tuned to a high pitch. This is particularly important beyond the elementary level, where students and teacher often relax their efforts in this regard. It is no wonder that such students fail to recognize words pronounced so differently from the classroom norm.

2. Flashcards should be made of *groups of words which follow certain rules* of sound-symbol correspondence and competitions organized with points allotted to the first person who gives the correct pronunciation for the series, e.g.:

Stahl, Stein, Stuhl;

Wand, Stand, Band;

Öde, blöde, schnöde.

Later, more rigorous competitions can be conducted with the words isolated from the series and presented in short sentences.

3. Conversely, students should hear words in short sentences and be asked to *identify* which of the *spellings* on three cards represents the word they heard, e.g.:

[bInən] Biene, Beine, binnen;

[vɛtə] Wette, Wetter, Vetter.

4. Students should be shown cards of words in *special problem groups* and drilled in their pronunciation, e.g.:

[tsĭon] Kaution, Nation, Demonstration;

[pf] Pferd, Pflicht, Pfund.

5. Spelling bees may be conducted to arouse enthusiasm for a high level

of performance. Words are given in sentences, then repeated in isolation, or in short word-groups, for the student to write down, e.g.:

Es ist ziemlich *kühl* heute—*kühl;*

Er hat *kein Verständnis* für unsere Probleme—*kein Verständnis.*

Those making mistakes are progressively eliminated until a champion is found.

6. These may be paralleled by pronunciation bees. Sentences are flashed on the screen or wall by overhead projector, or are shown on flashcards, and elimination contests are conducted for acceptable pronunciation, e.g., Wo ist *die Schweiz?*

Note: Items for both 5 and 6 should be kept to words students may be expected to meet. Common words which follow foreign models of pronunciation will be introduced, e.g., *Er ist Journalist.* Any unfamiliar word which follows regular sound-symbol correspondence rules is admissible, e.g., *Genie, Gehölz, jammern, Schnurrbart.* Teams may work out elimination lists to try on each other.

7. *Spot dictation* is useful at the elementary level (see R26), and continuous dictation passages at higher levels.

8. Students should be trained to recognize aurally a *root word in derivatives and compounds* in which there is a sound change, e.g.:

Buch, Bücher, Bücherei, Büchlein;

[bux] [bYçəʁ] [bYçəʁaI] [bYçlaIn]

Bad, baden, Bäder.

[bɑt] [bɑdən] [bedəʁ]

Students may work out series of this type by dictionary search and then dictate them to each other.

9. Students should be given regular practice in finding and interpreting *pronunciations in dictionaries.* Teaching phonetic symbols for recognition purposes can arouse interest in this exercise.

10. If students are to understand radio newscasts and documentary films, they should be given regular training in the aural identification of the *contemporary vocabulary for matters of international-preoccupation,* e.g., [ølkʁizə] *Ölkrise,* [tɛmpo lImIt] *Tempo-Limit.*

Some people will object that the above recommendations relate the aural too closely to the graphic and that aural vocabulary should be learned only by ear. This may be advisable for specialized aural courses, although, even in this case, student modality preferences must be allowed some play. Most intermediate and advanced foreign-language classes have multiple aims. Students who have been trained to depend on visual information need the liberating realization that there are predictable relationships between the pronunciation of a word and its written form. In this way, what they have learned in one modality can become available to them in the other, and the students' limited processing capacity will be used more economically and efficiently.

Macro or micro?

With listening, as with all other aspects of language learning, we must keep in view the final goal of *macro-language use* (the ability to use language holistically for normal life-purposes). *Micro-language learning* (the learning of elements of language and their potential combinations) is only a means leading to this end.

In the macro context, listening can be evaluated only by response: How does the listener react emotionally? How does he respond—verbally or by action? Does he do what he has been asked or told? Does he use the information offered? Does he fill the supportive role of the listener? (In other words, does he utter, at appropriate intervals, agreeing or consoling interpolations, exclamations of surprise, or tut-tutting noises—such expressions in German as *Ja! Ah so! So? Wie? Und ob! Na! Aber nein!*) Does he laugh or smile at the right moments? Is he absorbed by what he is hearing?

Because micro-language learning is more easily assessed than macro-language use, there is a tendency to think of the evaluation of listening comprehension in terms of multiple-choice and true/false items. Certainly, these can play a useful part in directing the students' efforts in listening and helping them assess the accuracy of their comprehension. The importance of understanding fine detail at crucial points in some aural tasks cannot be ignored, since puzzlement can cause an emotional or cognitive block, which overloads channel capacity so that the student loses the thread. On the other hand, there are students who tackle aural comprehension almost heuristically with considerable success. Students who can cope with macro-language use practically from the start may be wasting their time on micro-tests of detail. Other students need the developmental, step-by-step approach, and their needs should not be neglected. Even for the latter, however, functional comprehension in real situations must be the ultimate criterion.

For these reasons, listening comprehension is particularly suited to individualized arrangements, with students working at their own level and their own pace. Teachers should assemble all the materials they can find into *developmental listening kits,* each containing micro-training exercises for particular purposes, but culminating in a macro-activity. Students should be encouraged to work their way through a series of these kits in their own manner and at their own pace. Taking one's own time is important in listening, where individuals require differing lengths of time for processing. Students who are capable of doing so should be encouraged to jump from macro-activity to macro-activity, until listening to the foreign language becomes for them natural and effortless. Eventually most students will reach the stage where their listening is completely integrated with communication activities of the kind outlined in Chapter 2.

ASSESSMENT OF MACRO-LANGUAGE USE

We must place the student in a situation where listening comprehension plays an essential role, then see how he copes. Macro-language evaluation should be related to the normal uses of listening in life-situations:

1. as part of a purposeful communicative interchange;
2. for receiving directions or instructions;
3. for obtaining information;
4. for the pleasure of an activity like watching a play, a film, a TV show, or a fashion parade, or listening to a sports commentary, a newscast, or group discussion on the radio;
5. for participating in social gatherings (listening to small talk, listening to others conversing, and so on).

Any items in the B and D sections of the *Chart of Listening Comprehension Activities,* C67, are appropriate for macro-language assessment.

ASSESSMENT OF MICRO-LANGUAGE LEARNING

Many aspects of micro-language learning have already been discussed in this chapter (discrimination of sounds which change meaning; recognition of intonation patterns, syntactic segments, and word groups with high frequency of occurrence; aural vocabulary recognition). Any activities in the A and C sections of the *Chart of Listening Comprehension Activities,* C67, can be adapted to micro-language testing.

One of the commonest forms of assessment of this developmental phase of listening comprehension is the use of *multiple-choice questions,* yet the preparation of this type of test holds many pitfalls for the inexperienced.

The test items often consist of *short questions or comments in isolation,* like those in C59, for which students choose appropriate rejoinders (sometimes completions) from multiple-choice options.

C59 1. Wohin gehen Sie heute?
2. Wie spät ist es, bitte?
3. Was ist das drüben?

In natural interaction, there is a context for such short utterances which helps in the interpretation of the fleeting sounds, e.g., place, time, relationship of the person speaking to the person addressed, previous utterance, gesture of pointing or eyes turned in a certain direction, facial expression of exasperation, surprise, or expectancy. If the person addressed is taken off-guard, the interlocutor frequently makes a circumstantial comment before repeating the question, thus bringing it into focus, e.g.:

C60 A Wohin gehen Sie heute?
B Wie bitte?
A Es ist sehr früh. Wohin gehen Sie?

Materials writers often seem not to realize that isolated short utterances are more difficult to "hear" correctly than longer, contexualized segments.

In real life, the responses which would actually occur to such short, non-contexualized utterances may well be some of the options considered "incorrect" by the writer of the multiple-choice exercise. Choosing the "appropriate" response then becomes a question of reading the mind of the item-writer or the corrector of the exercise.

C61 Circle the letter corresponding to the most appropriate response to the question you hear.

> *Recorded voice: Wohin gehen Sie heute morgen?*
> A. Ich komme eben vom Bahnhof.
> B. In die Kirche. Kommen Sie mit?
> C. Ich? Ich werde einen Brief schreiben.
> D. Ich warte auf einen Freund.

Any of the above is an "appropriate response" in a certain context.

A. *Ich komme eben vom Bahnhof.* (I may be walking along the street, but I'm not *going* anywhere. I'm *coming back*.)

B. *In die Kirche. Kommen Sie mit?* (The "appropriate response" anticipated.)

C. *Ich? Ich werde einen Brief schreiben.* (I'm not going anywhere this morning. I've got far too much to do here at home.)

D. *Ich warte auf einen Freund.* (I may look as if I'm waiting for the lights to change so that I can cross the road, but I'm not.)

As any experienced teacher knows, students who dispute the grading of such short multiple-choice items can often justify their choices quite logically. Some kind of context should be built into every listening item.

C62 (Cf. C59.)
1. Sie ziehen Ihren Mantel an! Wohin gehen Sie jetzt?
2. Ich habe Hunger! Wie spät ist es, bitte?
3. Was ist das drüben? Auf der anderen Seite der Straße?

Students should also be given opportunities from time to time to select more than one "appropriate response," adding a brief note indicating a possible context. This encourages projection of expectations of the kind provided also in *Situation Tapes* (C33).

The following fully contextualized passage for listening would actually be easier than a short, non-contextualized utterance (if we exclude clichés and sentences students have heard over and over again in class):

C63 (1) *Recorded voice:*

Es war sehr heiß, und das Wasser war erfrischend. Überall sah man Leute, die badeten. Peter lag auf seinem Rücken im Schatten eines Felsens. Er ließ den Sand durch seine Finger fließen. In der Ferne fuhr ein Schiff nach Helgoland. Was machte Peter?

Choices supplied:

A. Er fuhr mit einem Schiff ab.
B. Er badete im Meer.
C. Er ruhte sich auf dem Strand aus.
D. Er baute ein Sandschloß.

The recorded passage contains a number of associated concepts which provide clues to the correct answer. The student who has understood some parts clearly, but not all, has more opportunity in a longer passage like this to reconstruct by conjecture those sections he did not comprehend fully.

DESIGNING MULTIPLE-CHOICE ITEMS FOR LISTENING COMPREHENSION

Many of the problems of multiple-choice items discussed in Chapter 7, in the section *Assisting and Assessing Reading Comprehension* (p. 214) apply also to multiple-choice items for assessing listening comprehension. There must be no ambiguity in the choices. The correct choice should not repeat word for word some sentence in the listening text. The correct choice should not depend on comprehension or non-comprehension of one unusual vocabulary item. Where there is a series of questions on one passage, the correct choices should not form an obvious sequence which students can detect without understanding the passage (a later item can sometimes supply the answer sought in an earlier question). Care must be taken to see that the items do not test powers of logical deduction, or ability to recognize exact paraphrases, rather than actual comprehension of the passage.

Apart from the general problems of preparing multiple-choice questions, items for listening comprehension present problems peculiar to this modality. The items have to be prepared in such a way that they give a clear indication of what the student "heard," that is, constructed personally from the sound signal. The item-writer must be able to imagine himself in the place of the neophyte and reconstruct what the latter may be "hearing." For these reasons, it is difficult for a native speaker to construct suitable choices for foreign-language listeners, unless he has had long experience with their particular problems.

It is useful to analyze the types of confusions one is anticipating on the part of the listeners by the choices one proposes. If there is no predictable rationale for a certain choice, it can be considered a "donkey item" which will be chosen only by a student who interpreted almost nothing of the sound signal. There should never be more than one "donkey item" in each set and this particular item must be very plausible, if it is to be selected at all. Unless it has some obvious relationship to the rest of the set, or re-echoes closely what was heard, even the donkeys will shy away from it.

C64   (E) *Recorded voice:* Sind Sie gestern früh schlafen gegangen?

    A. Ja, wir wollten gestern morgen viel schaffen.

    B. Ja, ich gehe heute gern vor neun ins Bett.

    C. Ja, ich habe mich um acht Uhr ins Bett gelegt.

    D. Ja, Sie sind früh ins Geschäft gegangen.

Commentary

A. The student who chooses A identifies

1. the question form with the pronoun *Sie,* requiring the answer *ich* or *wir;*

2. the lexical items *gestern* and *früh,* but misinterprets the intonation and therefore the meaning;

3. the sentence frame *sind . . . gegangen* as an indicator of a past action;

4. the presence of a dependent infinitive, but hears only the [fən] of [ʃlafən] which he recognizes in *schaffen* without distinguishing between [ɑ] and [a].

B. The student who chooses B identifies

1. the question form with the pronoun *Sie,* requiring the answer *ich* or *wir;*

2. the lexical item *früh* which he finds restated as *vor neun;*

3. the grammatical structure of *schlafen gehen* as a verb with a dependent infinitive, but misinterprets the tense structure. A student who is still unaccustomed to the use of *sein* as the auxiliary for forming the perfect tense of certain verbs may decode what he hears according to his

knowledge of English, thus deciding that the German sentence has a structure similar to the English present progressive. A student who is weak enough to choose this item may rationalize that *gern,* which has some acoustic resemblance to *gestern,* was what he heard.

C is the correct response.

It expresses the main concept in nearly synonymous terms (*schlafen gehen—sich ins Bett legen*), thus testing the apprehension of meaning, and contains a response element which is consistent with the question element (*gestern früh—um acht Uhr*). This avoids the possibility that the student is not comprehending but selecting the choice with the most items in identical form.

D. The student has not understood the question but the D response matches his audial image of parts he perceived (*Sie sind früh . . . gegangen*) and seems plausible, so he chooses D, which is a "donkey item" in that it makes no pretense at answering the question.

C65 (I) Viele kennen München als die Bierhauptstadt der Welt. Sie glauben, die Münchner trinken den ganzen Tag Bier und essen Wurst. Aber die Brauereien sind nur eine unter vielen Industrien in einer Großstadt Deutschlands. München ist eine Großstadt mit einer Tradition von Kunst, Theater und Musik—eine Industriestadt, die zugleich ein kulturelles Zentrum ist. Viele Touristen besuchen das Hofbräuhaus und glauben, sie haben alles gesehen, was es in München zu sehen gibt. Das ist ein großer Fehler!

Was haben Sie von München gehört?

A. Neben den Unterhaltungsmöglichkeiten findet der Fremde in München viele Industrien.
B. Wenn man München gut kennen möchte, dann braucht man nur ins Hofbräuhaus zu gehen.
C. Die Brauereien sind die wichtigste Industrie in München.
D. Im Hofbräuhaus findet man viel Theater und Musik.

Commentary

An additional source of error in this example may be the student's lack of knowledge of the German way of life.

A. The correct choice draws elements from several sentences and requires comprehension of a sequence of ideas.

B. This choice echoes a complete sentence the student has heard and reflects a common misconception about the subject. If the student has not related what he is hearing at this point with what he has heard previously, he may select this item.

C. The student who chooses C has heard clearly a statement like this but has not noted the structural interrelationships (in this case, the influence of *eine unter vielen Industrien* on the meaning of the sentence).

D. The student choosing D has not followed the line of thought, but has recognized the name *Hofbräuhaus* with its connection to *Bier* and the lexical items *Theater* and *Musik,* which are cognates. Since this type of student has a rather elementary knowledge of German, this choice is deliberately constructed by using only words commonly found in elementary courses.

✱ *Analyze* in similar fashion the anticipated reactions of the students who will choose the various alternatives in the following listening comprehension exercise.

C66 Wie? Sie ist schon weg? um sechs Uhr in der Frühe?

A. Ja, sie verläßt uns bald.
B. Ja, der Wecker klingelt jeden Tag früh.
C. Ja, du weißt, Inge arbeitet sehr weit von hier.
D. Nein, ich fahre nie vor sechs Uhr morgens ab.

C67 *Chart of Listening Comprehension Activities*[37]

In the following chart, the activities are divided into four learning stages:

A. *Identification:* perception of sounds and phrases; identifying these directly and holistically with meaning.

B. *Identification and selection without retention:* listening for the pleasure of comprehension, extracting sequential meanings, without being expected to demonstrate comprehension through active use of language.

C. *Identification and guided selection with short-term retention:*[38] students are given some prior indication of what they are to listen for; they demonstrate their comprehension immediately in some active fashion.

D. *Identification and selection with long-term retention:* students demonstrate their comprehension, or use the material they have comprehended, after the listening experience has been completed; or they engage in an activity which requires recall of material learned some time previously.

Elementary Level (E)

A. IDENTIFICATION (E)
Macro

1. Listening to tapes of various languages to detect the language one is learning.

2. Listening to songs and poems for the pleasure of the sounds (in classroom, listening room, or listening corner).

3. Amplifying songs and poems in language laboratory for atmosphere.

4. Hearing original sound tracks of documentary films before being able to understand them.

Micro

5. Aural discrimination with pictures.

6. Short-phrase discrimination with pictures.

7. Listening to segments of dialogue to be learned.

8. Responding with miming actions to segments from dialogue learned or from classroom conversation.

9. Responding with flashcards to names of letters of the alphabet.

10. Backward buildup in imitation of a model (C48).

B. IDENTIFICATION AND SELECTION WITHOUT RETENTION (E)

11. Games involving miming of words and phrases learned.

12. Listening to conversation-facilitation dialogues, songs, or poems already learned.

13. Listening to retelling of stories already read, reacting in some way to variations from the original.

14. Listening to a conversation which is a variant of a dialogue studied.

15. Listening to an anecdote based on reading material studied.

16. Teacher gives some background information on a topic, then tells an anecdote, or describes an experience.

With visual

17. Listening to description of pictures or slides.

18. Listening to an anecdote, story, or dialogue illustrated with a flannelboard.

19. Listening to a *Show and Tell* oral report.

With action

20. Total physical response activity or *Jakob sagt* (C45–C46).

21. Obeying classroom instructions.

22. Listening to simple narration, raising hands whenever a color (or occupation, or kind of food, etc.) is mentioned.

23. *Letter Bingo:* letters of alphabet called randomly; each student checks against word in front of him; first student with complete word wins.

24. *Number Bingo:* numbers called randomly; students check numbers on their cards; first student with all numbers correctly checked wins.

C. IDENTIFICATION AND GUIDED SELECTION
WITH SHORT-TERM RETENTION (E)
With visual

25. Discrimination of numbers, dates, and times of day by pairing with multiple-choice items, clockfaces, lists of famous events, or flight schedules.

26. Learning a dialogue with vanishing techniques (see *Dialogue Exploitation* in Chapter 1, p. 30).

27. True/false questions supplied beforehand; student listens to variation of dialogue or story read and checks answers.

28. Multiple-choice answers supplied beforehand; student listens to dialogue or story using recombinations of vocabulary and structures learned and checks appropriate answers.

With action

29. Miming the actions in story being narrated.

30. Obeying complex classroom instructions for class exercises and tests.

31. Completing a diagram according to instructions.

32. *Subjekt oder Anderes?* (C50): miming when subject stands first, but not when some other element begins statement.

With speaking

33. Directed dialogue (C24).

34. Group piecing together of a new dialogue from initial hearings.

35. Participating in Cummings device (C29).

36. Participating in Gouin series (C11–13).

37. Participating in verbal-active series (C15).

38. *Wer ist es? Was ist es? Wo ist es?* (guessing who, what, or which place is being described by teacher or student).

39. Intensive practice exercises varying syntactic segments (see Chapter 4).

40. Running commentary: listening to a story and giving the gist at the end of each sentence in SAAD's (see C52–53).

With writing

41. Writing down words which are dictated letter by letter.

42. Writing from dictation series of numbers in increasing length and complexity.

43. *Information Search* (*Nur das Treffende,* C49): writing down segments which answer particular questions.

44. Dictation: students repeat to themselves what they think they heard before they write it.

45. Spot dictation (R26).

D. IDENTIFICATION, SELECTION, AND LONG-RANGE RETENTION (E)

46. Listening to a continuation of a story (with same vocabulary area, same setting, and same characters).

47. Listening to a story different from, but with similar vocabulary to, one already read.

48. Listening to a conversation similar to one studied.

49. Listening to skits prepared by other students.

50. Listening to dramatizations of stories read.

51. Listening without the text to the expressive reading (on tape, by the teacher, or by a student) of a poem already studied.

52. Listening to other students reciting poems in a poetry competition.

53. Checking answers to aural questions given before or after a passage for listening.

54. Checking appropriate choices for multi-choice continuations (or rejoinders) given orally after a listening passage.

With speaking

55. Listening to a story, then giving the gist at the end in SAAD's (see C52–53).

56. Answering questions orally on a passage just heard.

57. Responding to others in spontaneous role-playing.

58. Listening to and discussing oral reports of other students.

59. Chain dialogue (C25).

60. Rubbishing the dialogue (C26).

61. Acting out learned dialogues with others (paraphrasing the sense rather than repeating by rote).

62. Learning and acting a part with others in a skit or original dialogue.

63. *Erraten Sie meinen Beruf:* student mimes a series of actions, others ask yes-no questions until they have guessed what the student does for a living.

With writing

64. Student answers questions in writing after listening to a story or conversation.

65. Students write down what they have learned from other students' oral reports.

66. Cloze test on content of what has been heard (W28).

Intermediate Level (I)

A. IDENTIFICATION (I)

1. Aural discrimination of small sound distinctions which change meaning of sentences.

2. Recognition of characteristics of familiar level of speech with assimilation and reduction of syllables (e.g., *danken* [daŋkn̩] and *haben* [hɑbm̩]) through listening to authentic informal speech on tapes, disks, or film sound tracks.

With visual

3. Aural recognition of German pronunciation of names of foreign personalities and places (supplied on scrambled lists).

4. Aural recognition of German/English cognates from scrambled lists.

With action

5. Recognition of aural indicators of tense: *Ich oder von mir?* (C51) — tapping for passive voice, miming future tenses.

With writing

6. Demonstrating recognition of German equivalents of contemporary international scientific, technical, political, and social vocabularies by writing these down.

B. IDENTIFICATION AND SELECTION WITHOUT RETENTION (I)

7. Listening to complete reading of story studied in sections.

8. Listening to dramatization of story read.

9. Listening to the acting out of scenes from play read.

10. Listening to disk or tape of reading by German professional of short story, poem, or extracts from novel.

11. Listening to a version in SAAD's before listening to a more complicated version (see C52–53). No questions asked.

12. Listening to teacher or another student telling amusing incident which happened on the way to school or at school.

13. Listening to a news item told by teacher or another student.

14. Listening to teacher or another student give background information for news item.

15. Listening to teacher or another student give background information for reading or for a class or group project.

16. Following the line of discussion in a group conversation.

17. Listening to German songs.

With visual

18. Listening to a presentation of slides of some aspect of Germany, Switzerland or Austria, German, Swiss or Austrian history, or the arts.

19. Watching and listening to a documentary film on some aspect of Germany, Switzerland or Austria or German, Swiss or Austrian life.

20. Watching and listening to a final showing of a scholastic film, with background of contemporary German culture which has already been studied in class.

21. Listening to a story as one is reading it silently, to improve fluent reading techniques.

With action

22. Following directions for classroom organization.

C. IDENTIFICATION AND GUIDED SELECTION
WITH SHORT-TERM RETENTION (I)

23. Selecting from aural choices completions for sentences heard.

24. Listening to oral compositions of other students.

25. Listening to skits and spontaneous role-playing of other students.

26. Students discuss news beforehand; then listen to newscasts to find answers to certain questions raised.

27. Students listen to exchange tapes and correspondence tapes.

28. *Was beschreibe ich?* (guessing object described by fellow student). Alternatives: *Wo bin ich? Wer ist es?*

With visual

29. Student is provided with multiple-choice or true/false questions beforehand, then checks answers as he listens, or immediately afterwards.

30. Student chooses among written completions for sentences given orally.

31. Student practices reading aloud with tape model: student reads segment, listens to model reading, then rereads segment.

32. Students watch films of which they have previously studied sound track or synopsis.

33. Students watch films in which they are looking for specific cultural details, certain interactions of characters, or particular developments of the story.

With action

34. Following instructions for making something.

With speaking

35. Providing oral sentence completions at end of longer and longer sequences.

36. Student is asked questions aurally beforehand, hears passage, hears aural questions again, and gives oral answers.

37. Student gives spontaneous responses on Situation Tapes (C33).

38. *Verbessern Sie mich* (C47): noting inappropriate words in story given orally and suggesting appropriate replacements.

39. *Einundzwanzig Fragen:* group asking of eliminative yes-no questions to discover name of famous person selected for the game. Alternatives: *Identität, Tierreich-Pflanzenreich-Steinreich.*

40. *Weder ja, noch nein:* group elimination game where students are asked all kinds of questions which they may answer in any way they can, so long as they never use *ja* or *nein.*

41. Oral spelling bees.

42. Taking part in Lipson-type puzzle exercises.

43. Fulfilling the supportive role of the listener (*So?... Ach, ja...*).

With writing

44. Written spelling bees.

45. Spot comprehension: students are given incomplete statements about the content of what they will hear; after listening, they fill in the blanks with the missing details, expressed in short phrases.

46. Dictation: gradually increasing length of segment to be retained.

47. Taking dictations containing information on cultural matters discussed: e.g., famous sayings of leading historical figures, famous anecdotes every German child knows (e.g., Wilhelm Tell shooting the apple off his son's head).

48. Taking from dictation notes on the lives and achievements of historical figures, painters, musicians.

D. IDENTIFICATION, SELECTION, AND LONG-TERM RETENTION (I)

49. Listening without a script to readings of plays studied.

50. Listening to a part of a play for which students will develop impromptu continuations later.

51. Listening to episodes of a mystery serial.[39]

With speaking

52. Answering aural questions asked after a long listening passage.

53. Group conversations and discussions on an assigned topic.

54. Preliminary discussion for preparation of oral compositions.

55. Questions and discussion after listening to other students' oral compositions.

56. Participating in spontaneous skits and role-playing.

57. After listening, answering questions asked in SAAD's (see C52–53).

58. Listening to a passage, then giving the gist in SAAD's.

59. Listening to a mystery without hearing the conclusion; then discussing possible explanations.

60. Taking map journeys (C14).

61. *Der Angeklagte* (discovering crime of which one is accused and defending oneself).

62. Participating in simulated telephone conversations or authentic telephone conversations with monolingual, or presumed monolingual, German speakers.

63. Interviewing visiting German native speaker to find out who he is, what he does, what he thinks, and so on.

64. *Was ist mein Geheimnis?:* discovering the secret a fellow student is concealing (can be pet peeves, career plans, weekend plans, etc.).

65. *Wer sagte die Wahrheit?* Three students pretend to be the person whose unusual experiences are recounted at the beginning; other students try to find out, by questioning, who is the real Herr Sowieso (Frau Sowieso).

66. *Scharaden:* see *Categories of language use* 10 in Chapter 2, p. 50.

67. *General Knowledge Quizzes:* students can choose such categories as German history, institutions, contemporary life, current events, language, literature, art, music, sport, exploration, famous German men and women.

68. *Verbessern Sie den Erzähler* (C43–44) as a test of cultural information.

69. Listening to and discussing exchange and correspondence tapes.

70. Taking part in general conversation at German clubs, German tables, German camps, German festivals, during summer abroad programs.

With writing

71. Listening to a passage and then writing the gist in SAAD's (see C52–53).

72. Listening to a mystery which stops before the conclusion, then writing an explanation.

73. Listening to a segment of dialogue, then writing a composition which gives it a context and conclusion.

Advanced Level (A)

A. IDENTIFICATION (A)

1. Aural discrimination of features of rapid spoken style, regional accents, levels of language, through listening to authentic tapes, films, radio broadcasts, plays.

With writing

2. Transcribing and retranscribing tapes of unedited authentic speech until student has absorbed the material (to learn, through personal observation, characteristics of unedited speech and tune ear to understand it).[40] Student plays back any sections of the tape as often as he wishes.

B. IDENTIFICATION AND SELECTION WITHOUT RETENTION (A)

3. Listening to a sequel to a passage read.
4. Listening to recordings of plays and poems already studied.
5. Listening to scenes from other plays by the same playwright.
6. Listening to other poems by the same poet.
7. Listening to debates and panel discussions by fellow-students.
8. Listening to German newscasts for personal information and pleasure.
9. Listening to commercials recorded from German radio broadcasts or mock commercials prepared by fellow-students.
10. Listening to recordings of German *Schlager* or *Lieder.*
11. Continuing tape correspondence with German friend.

C. IDENTIFICATION AND GUIDED SELECTION
WITH SHORT-TERM RETENTION (A)

12. Listening to student presentation of mock radio program, call-in program, or TV talk show.

With visual

13. Watching German films.
14. Listening to student presentation of fashion parade.

With speaking

15. Listening to lecturettes by other students on aspects of German civilization, culture, or literature and asking questions.
16. Listening to an aural text and recording answers to questions on the text.
17. Group conversations with visiting native speakers.
18. Micro-texts: see *Categories of language use* 9 in Chapter 2, p. 49.

With writing

19. Students practice taking notes on classroom lecturettes, first with an outline of points to be covered, then without guidance.

20. Dictation: students are expected to listen to and retain whole sentences before writing.

D. IDENTIFICATION, SELECTION, AND LONG-TERM RETENTION (A)

21. Listening to lectures by visiting German speakers on aspects of contemporary German life.

22. Watching performances of German plays by visiting actors.

23. Watching performances of German plays by school German club or on the invitation of other schools.

24. Listening to recordings of group conversations of German speakers discussing subjects of interest.

25. Listening to readings of plays not studied previously.

With visual

26. Extracting different lines of thought from a listening passage: listening with one set of printed questions, then listening again with a different set of questions.

27. Visiting German art show and listening to commentary in German.

With action

28. Seeking information from documentaries, tapes, and records for group projects or class discussions.

29. Listening to lengthy instructions for a task one has to perform.

30. Learning German cooking from oral instructions.

31. Visiting a German restaurant, discussing menu with German-speaking waiter, and eating a German meal in company with other German-speaking students.

32. Making preparations for a German festival with a German exchange student, or teacher, who explains what to do in German.

33. Activities at German club, German camp, or during study abroad tour.

With speaking

34. As much of the lesson as possible is conducted in German.

35. Listening to a passage and recording oral answers to questions about it.

36. Listening to recordings of plays, poems, and speeches and discussing them afterwards.

37. Learning German songs from recordings.

38. Learning a part for a play from a professional recording.

39. Group conversations and discussions on cultural subjects which students have researched, films they have seen, or books and journals they have read.

40. Discussion of newscasts from Germany.

41. Asking questions at lectures by visiting German speakers or exchange students.

42. Talking on telephone with German native speakers, seeking information for projects or for reporting back to class.

43. Interviewing visiting, or local, German speakers or exchange students to find out information on German life, institutions, and attitudes, for group project on contemporary German culture.

44. Watching German film and being able to discuss afterwards questions which require aural comprehension, rather than kinesic or visual interpretation.

45. Engaging in debates and discussions on controversial subjects.

46. Showing German-speaking visitors around school or town.

47. Listening to a story which members of the class will dramatize spontaneously later.

48. Listening to tapes of radio discussions with German authors and civic leaders, or speeches by political figures, and discussing these in the context of contemporary German life.

49. Listening to newscasts in order to act as daily or weekly reporter for the class.

50. Taking part in such competitions as Intermediate activities 61, 64, 65, and 67.

51. *Nacherzählung.* As a preliminary study of the differences between spoken and literary language, leading later to *explication de texte* or *Kommentar zu einem literarischen Text,* students listen to a poem or short literary extract and, with the help of systematic questioning from the teacher, reconstruct it orally.

With writing

52. Taking dictations containing information related to cultural subjects being researched.

53. While listening to a speech, lecture, or taped discussion, students take notes for use with a group project.

54. Listening to a speech, lecture, or taped discussion and writing afterwards a summary of main points for use with a group project.

55. *Nacherzählung.* After having done 51, students reconstruct the text in writing, individually or as a group, and then compare their version with the original as an exercise in stylistics.

56. As an ambitious project for a class in which listening comprehension is a major objective, or as an independent study project: students

listen to German broadcasts to draw out information on cultural differences. They write up the results of their research in German. (Much can be learned from the types of news reported and what this conveys about German interests and preoccupations; the types of goods advertised on German-speaking commercial stations and the way they are advertised; the kinds of interviews conducted, and with whom; the types of music played on different stations; the subject matter of comedy hours, situation comedies and *Kabarett,* and the types of questions asked by listeners.)

4

Oral practice for the learning of grammar

Deductive or inductive?

At some stage students must learn the grammar of the language. This learning may be approached *deductively* (in which case the student is given a grammatical rule with examples before he practices the use of a particular structure) or *inductively* (the student sees a number of examples of the rule in operation in discourse, practices its use, and then evolves a rule with the help of the teacher; or he sees a number of examples, evolves a rule from these examples with the help of his teacher, and then practices using the structure). In either of these approaches, there is a phase when the student practices the use of grammatical structures and applies the various facets of grammatical rules in possible sentences. This subject is discussed in greater depth in Chapter 8.

Oral exercises

In many classrooms, the greater part of grammatical practice has always been in writing. Here, we are concerned with the contribution that can be made by oral practice exercises of many kinds. In this chapter, we shall:

1. examine types of exercises traditionally found in textbooks and see which ones are suitable for or can be adapted to oral practice;

2. study examples of more recently developed drills and exercises and discuss their features;

104

3. categorize, exemplify, and discuss six types of oral practice exercises (repetition, substitution, conversion, sentence modification, response, and translation exercises).

Traditional types of exercises

To make the discussion of different exercises comparable we will select those suitable for practicing the forms of the dative with the definite and indefinite articles (the *der*-words and *ein*-words). There are *various structural uses* of the dative.
1. It is used to indicate the indirect object. (*Ich kann meinem Bruder das Geld nicht geben.*)
2. It is used with some verbs that require the dative. (*Er konnte dem Lehrer sofort antworten.*)
3. It is used with certain prepositions that govern the dative. (*Er bleibt bei seiner Familie.*)
4. It is used with certain prepositions that can take either the dative or the accusative. (*Das Buch ist in meinem Zimmer.*)
5. It is used with certain adjectives. (*Das kann dem Kind schädlich sein*).[1]
In addition to the uses of the dative the student is also confronted with the *various forms* of the dative:
a. the dative singular and plural of the articles and of the *der*-words and *ein*-words;
b. the dative plural of nouns;
c. the dative forms of the personal pronouns.

The first decision to be made is: with which use and forms will the student begin his practice or will all be learned at once? (This decision is usually made for the teacher by the textbook writer, but the type of approach adopted by the author will influence the teacher in his selection of a textbook.)

1. GRAMMAR-TRANSLATION TYPE EXERCISES

If we examine older textbooks we find that many of them introduce the students to the dative through paradigms illustrating the grammatical forms. To practice the forms learned from the paradigm, the students are asked to analyze phrases and are given sentences to translate.

G1 *Paradigm*

	Masc.	Fem.	Neuter	Plural (all genders)
Nom.	der	die	das	die
Dat.	dem	der	dem	den
Acc.	den	die	das	die

Nom.	(k)ein	(k)eine	(k)ein	keine
Dat.	(k)einem	(k)einer	(k)einem	keinen
Acc.	(k)einen	(k)eine	(k)ein	keine

This schematic presentation is occasionally supplemented with an explanatory paradigm:

G2 Nom.   mein Bruder   meine Schwester   mein Kind *my brother,*
sister, child

Dat.   meinem Bruder   meiner Schwester   meinem Kind *to (for)*
my brother, etc.

To practice the forms learned from the paradigm, the students are given exercises like the following.

G3 1. Give the dative forms of the following:
der Freund, ein König, meine Mutter, das Gebäude, ihr Geheimnis, die Frau.
2. Translate, and then explain the grammatical forms of the italicized words:
a. Hans gibt *seinem Vater eine Zeitschrift.*
b. Was antwortet *der Student dem Professor?*
c. Ich kaufe *meinen Eltern Blumen.*

Commentary

1. The students learn to *analyze* grammar. They are expected to observe the grammatical form in the paradigm and to distinguish the forms of the dative from the other forms of the articles. The exercises are designed to instill a recognition of grammatical forms. As a result the students acquire an abstract comprehension of the grammar without the ability to produce the language actively.

2. The table is useful as a summary of what the student has learned, but it can easily become *an end in itself* if the students are called upon to reproduce such paradigms on tests and quizzes. Time is thus spent in the memorization of grammatical rules at the expense of practice in using the language.

3. *There is no systematic teaching practice* of one form of the dative and then of the next, e.g., practice of *dem (Vater)* as distinct from *der (Frau)* and these as contrasted with *den (Gebäuden)* for which the students must also know that all nouns except those that form the plural with -*s* must end in -*n* in the dative plural.

4. Exercises like these are clearly designed to *develop skill in reading by translating* and provide no opportunity for the student to develop his ability to use German for normal communication.

5. The first exercise, in which the student is asked to supply the dative article, becomes a mechanical, mindless chore. The student supplies the forms of the dative without producing a meaningful utterance in the language he is learning.

6. The entire presentation is *teacher, or textbook, directed.* There is no place for student creativeness, for enjoyment or even mild interest.

Such paradigms are frequently accompanied by translation exercises which provide the student with his only opportunity for active production of German.

G4 Translate the following into German:

a. To whom does the teacher give a book?
b. You send the brother a pen.
c. I hand the girl a pencil.
d. Do you give the book to the child?

Commentary

1. All of these sentences sound stilted because it is difficult to imagine immediately a context in which any one of them would be used. The first sentence, for example, makes sense only if one imagines that the student is being asked about the content of a story in which the teacher's gift of a book to a particular child is important.

2. The sentences are modeled on the expected response in German with the result that they do not sound like authentic English. The student faces a curious sort of English that is then converted into something stranger still. He is trained from the beginning to *think from German to English and English to German* and to seek a one-to-one equivalence even if it is necessary to distort the English expression in doing so. The second sentence would make more sense if it read: So! You are giving your brother a pen!

3. *Translation of short sentences* has its uses (see G45–53), but only when the sentences are ones the student might conceivably use. The disregard for probability and authenticity still found even in carefully constructed pattern drills leads quickly to the attitude that German is an artificial classroom game which is irrelevant to real life and best forgotten as fast as possible with other school nonsense.

2. FILL-IN-THE-BLANK EXERCISES

These exercises are found in textbooks which profess to teach aural-oral skills as well as in texts oriented to written practice in grammar. They are discussed here because they are often used for oral practice in the classroom. (As written exercises they are examined in detail in Chapter 8.)

G5 Supply the suggested forms of *der, unser,* or *ein.*

a. Sagen Sie es (to the) Chef!
b. Wir zeigen es (to our) Mutter.
c. Er gibt es (to a) Freund.

Commentary

1. This exercise provides a context for the use of the dative by presenting complete sentences, thus alleviating a problem encountered in similar exercises which only present the student with phrases [*zu (this) Stadt; bei (his) Mutter*]. It also supplies the student with a controlled range of choices (*der, unser, ein*). Nevertheless the student is likely to jot down the German *replacement in isolation* in his exercise book without reading, let alone hearing or saying, a complete German sentence. The mixture of German and English encourages the student to think of German as disguised English and of language learning as essentially translation.

2. When the exercise is completed orally by having the students read aloud either the correct response alone or the entire sentence, the student may still not understand the sentence. He needs to recognize only the gender and number of the word following the blank. Then the exercise can be completed rather like a crossword puzzle. Since the student is "learning the rules" in isolation, it is unlikely that there will be any high degree of transfer to a spontaneous utterance without further practice of a different nature.

G6 Supply the correct ending of the dative case:

a. Erika gibt d_____ Vater ein Buch.
b. Karl kauft d_____ Mutter Blumen.
c. Sein_____ Schwester schickt er eine Karte.
d. Schicken Sie Ihr_____ Sohn ein Paket?

Commentary

1. This exercise avoids the use of English but, even more than the preceding exercise, encourages students to find "answers" for segments. In

this case, the student needs only to check to see if the word following the blank is feminine or masculine/neuter.

2. Students are encouraged to *think of the nominative forms first* and then to transform them to the dative instead of learning the dative articles and endings directly as a German form of expression and practicing them frequently in context.

3. If items c and d were to be read aloud by either student or teacher before being answered, *incorrect German* forms would be used which might then be impressed on the minds of the students.

4. The vocabulary in this exercise is connected with the everyday world of the student. With the aid of carefully selected pictures or with a list of nouns on the chalkboard the same task could be accomplished in a *rapid oral exercise* in which students are asked questions like: *Wem geben Sie das Buch?* or *Wem schicken Sie das Paket?* for which the teacher indicates the appropriate response by holding a picture or pointing to a word: *Ich gebe es meiner Mutter, Ich schicke es meinem Bruder.* (See also G12.)

G7 Fill in the blanks in the following sentences with the dative article:

a. Wir helfen _____ Lehrer.
b. Kurt hilft _____ Freundin.
c. Der Bleistift gehört _____ Kind.
d. Ich folge _____ Tante.

Commentary

1. The student *does not see incorrect forms* in print.

2. He may still *not see complete sentences* in German since all the information he needs to complete the sentence correctly is supplied by the final segment.

3. This exercise, even more than G5 and G6, is first of all a *visual* task (blanks cannot be spoken by the teacher). If the answers are read aloud in their full context, students at least articulate a complete German sentence. Otherwise, they rush through, rapidly "filling in the blanks."

3. REPLACEMENT EXERCISES

G8 Replace the italicized word by the noun indicated, making any necessary changes.

a. Ilse antwortet der *Freundin.* (Vater)
b. Franz gibt dem *Kind* Milch. (Tochter)
c. Gehört dieses Bild einer *Studentin?* (Student)

Commentary

1. The student sees or hears a *complete German sentence* and responds in a complete German sentence.

2. The exercise can be given orally. This is actually close to the substitution drill technique of G9. However, because of the continual changes in structural formation and lexical content in successive sentences, it would be difficult to hold the sentences in the memory while making substitutions orally. For this reason, it is *essentially an exercise for written practice.* In the next section we shall see how by observing certain restrictions it could be transformed into an oral exercise.

More recently developed oral practice exercises
1. PATTERN OR STRUCTURE DRILL EXERCISES

These types of exercises are found in most contemporary textbooks and on language laboratory tapes. They are designed for rapid oral practice in which more items are completed per minute than in written practice. Some teachers mistakenly use them for written practice, thus giving students a boring, tedious chore.

Pattern drill exercises are useful for demonstrating structural variations and familiarizing students with their use. They serve an *introductory function* and are useful only as a preliminary to practice in using the new structural variations in some natural interchange, or for consolidation of the use of certain structures when students seem in doubt.

When pattern drills are used, it is important that students understand the rationale of the variations they are performing. Sometimes a grammatical feature has been encountered in listening or reading material or in a dialogue. Its functioning has been experienced, or explained, and a rapid drill is conducted to familiarize the students with the feature in use in various contexts. Sometimes a demonstration pattern drill introduces the grammatical feature, which is then explained, before being practiced again in a drill sequence which requires thought.

Intensive practice exercises or drills are useful for learning such formal characteristics of German as verb endings, word order in statements and questions, negation, the use of pronouns and so on. They can be of many types, as we shall see in this chapter.

Teaching series

G9 Repeat the model sentence you hear. In successive sentences replace the last word by the cue words given, making any necessary changes. You will then hear the correct sentence. Repeat it if you have made a mistake. (The modeled correction and the repetition of the correct response will be given here only for the first item, as a demonstration of the technique.)

a.	MODEL SENTENCE	Ich helfe dem Chef.
	CUE	Kaufmann.
	RESPONSE BY STUDENT	Ich helfe dem Kaufmann.
	CORRECT RESPONSE CONFIRMED	Ich helfe dem Kaufmann.
	REPETITION BY STUDENT OF	
	CORRECT RESPONSE (IF DESIRED)	Ich helfe dem Kaufmann.
	FURTHER CUES	Lehrer, Mädchen, Briefträger, Bäcker

b. Ich helfe der Nachbarin.
(Lehrerin, Polizei, Studentin, Firma...)

c. Ich helfe einem Arbeiter.
(Amerikaner, Kind, Ausländer, Freund...)

d. Ich helfe einer Schülerin.
(Dame, Freundin, Engländerin, Kusine...)

e. Ich helfe meinem Großvater.
(Onkel, Bruder, Vetter, Neffe...)

f. Ich helfe meiner Schwester.
(Tante, Mutter, Familie, Frau...)

g. Ich helfe den Ärzten.
(Freunde, Tiere, Eltern, Kellner...)

h. Ich helfe dem Opa.
(Großmutter, Vater, Schwestern, Kinder, Italienerin, Nichte...)

Commentary

1. This is called a *four-phase drill*. When the student does not repeat the correct answer after the model, it is referred to as a *three-phase drill*. The fourth phase is useful for the student who has made a mistake. The third phase (confirmation of correct response) is usually included on a laboratory tape, but it can become irritating in class when students are giving correct responses smartly. It should be used only when needed.

2. In this exercise there is a *fixed increment*, that is, a segment which is repeated in each utterance in a series. Here it is *ich helfe,* which makes the use of many different nouns in the dative possible. The fixed increment reduces the memory load for the student and allows him to concentrate

on the minimal change he is asked to make. It is usually retained during *six to eight items* especially when a new structure is being learned.

3. The sentences are *short,* thus lightening the memory load.

4. The *lexical content is restricted* to vocabulary with which the student is familiar so that he can concentrate on the structural rule he is applying.

5. Each sentence the student utters is one which could possibly appear in conversation.

6. There is *no ambiguity in the exercise.* The instructions are clear and each item is so composed that only one response will be correct. This makes it possible for the acceptability of the response to be confirmed by a correct response modeled by the teacher or the voice on the tape.

7. Although the endings of the possessive adjectives are the same as those of the indefinite article, the students need to practice these endings since their usage in German contrasts with English usage.

8. Series h is *the testing phase* of the drill. It ranges over various possibilities in eight (or more) items. Through it the teacher can tell whether the students need further practice of specific variations of the feature they have been learning.

9. Note the peculiar problems of h: words like *Fahrer, Kellner, Bäcker* are ambiguous as cues since the singular and plural forms are alike except in the dative case. (In g the problem is not the same since the pattern is plural and the students expect the cues to follow the pattern.)

10. It will depend on the age and maturity of the students and the intensiveness of the course whether this series is taught gradually over a period of days, or weeks, or taught in one lesson.

11. Since words are grouped according to gender and number, the operation of the drill can become mechanical and cease to be useful, because students are no longer concentrating on the grammatical point at issue. It should not be continued beyond the point where students have acquired familiarity with the forms.

Patterned response

The drill in G9 would be *less monotonous* and the students would be participating in a more realistic way if the response were not a simple repetition but required an answer form.

G10 a. Practice with the model (students repeat sentences demonstrating the structural model) :

Ihre Schwester macht die Arbeit allein?
Nein, ich helfe *meiner Schwester.*

b. The drill continues, following the same pattern:
CUE   Ihre Mutter macht die Arbeit allein?
RESPONSE   Nein, ich helfe *meiner Mutter.*
(Confirmation)

CUE   Ihre Nachbarin macht die Arbeit allein?
RESPONSE   Nein, ich helfe *meiner Nachbarin.*
(Confirmation)

CUE   Ihr Bruder macht die Arbeit allein?
RESPONSE   Nein, ich helfe *meinem Bruder.*
(Confirmation)

Chain drill

A *final practice* at the end of this series can be a chain drill on the following pattern: each student in turn invents his own contribution and produces a cue for his neighbor. Students should be encouraged at this stage to be as original as they can within the limitations of the pattern.

G11 STUDENT A TO STUDENT B   Dein Freund macht die Arbeit allein?
STUDENT B   Ja, ich helfe meinem Freund nicht.
(TO STUDENT C)   Ihre Oma macht die Arbeit allein?
STUDENT C   Nein, ich helfe meiner Oma jeden Freitag.
(TO STUDENT D)   Glaubst du deinem Lehrer?
STUDENT D   Ja, ich glaube dem Lehrer immer.

This chain drill can be a *team game,* each team gaining a point for each correct link in the chain (with a limit on the time for reflection to keep the game moving). The chain passes to the other team each time an error is made or a student fails to respond within the time allowed.

Patterned response in a situational context

A drill of this type is more interesting and has more reality if it is given a *situational* context.

G12 Context can be provided by the use of objects, pictures, or actions and by introducing a simple phrase exemplifying the use of the dative after prepositions (*Das ist ein Bild von . . .*). The students are shown pictures or advertisements cut from magazines of items within the range of their vocabulary (*das Kind, die Schule, das Haus, der Mann . . .*). The drill is conducted first in choral fashion with the students describing the picture held up by the teacher (*Das ist ein Bild von einer Stadt*). Then the drill moves to individual response, with students pointing out things to each other (*Das ist ein Bild von einer Schule; Das ist ein Bild von einem Amerikaner*).

Finally a *game* develops.

1. Team points are awarded for correct answers to the question *Was ist das?* Students understand that the answer must contain a phrase with *von;* they respond with such expressions as *Das ist ein Bild von einem Pferd* or *Das ist ein Bild von zwei Frauen.*

2. Alternatively, students are given a list of pictures they must collect, and the pictures are distributed to the class. The student asks *Wer hat das Bild von . . . ?* until he has the complete list. He proceeds to ask for pictures as long as he makes no grammatical mistakes.

With a little practice and some choral responses at the beginning, a game of this type can proceed as smartly as an oral drill. Swift response can be elicited by pausing a short time for one student to reply, then moving to another if the student is still hesitating.

Successful completion of an oral drill does not guarantee that the student will use the correct form in *autonomous production*. The student must try to express himself outside of a framework which forces him to produce certain answers.

G13 The lesson may conclude with the students asking each other questions: *Was gibst du deinem Freund? Zeigst du der Mutter das Bild?* Alternatively, they may play a game such as *Wem gehört dieses Foto?* Students guess: *Gehört es dem Lehrer? Gehört es deiner Schwester? . . .* until they find the right answer.

Suggestions for encouraging autonomous production are given in Chapter 2.

* Try to write a series of drills to teach and test the *prepositions governing the accusative* or the formation of the *perfect tense* (which is more complicated). Think of *situational contexts* in which these could be practiced and *games* which would produce the same types of responses as a drill. Then see if the types of games you have invented work smoothly by trying them out on other students.

2. SUBSTITUTION OR VARIATION TABLES

Oral drilling can also be performed with the use of variation or substitution tables[2] such as the following:

G14 Was macht Peter?

Peter	dankt	dem	Onkel	
	antwortet	der	Lehrerin	
	hilft	dem	Kind	
	gibt	den	Freunden	die Bilder
	schenkt	den	Schwestern	eine Uhr

Commentary

1. This is a *mixed drill* and presumes some prior learning of the specific structural items either in dialogues, reading material, oral work in the classroom, or earlier more restricted drills on the different forms of the dative. It serves a useful purpose in drawing together in a systematic way what has already been learned. (See also W1–3.)

2. The drill may be conducted with the complete table in front of the students in an initial *learning phase*. The teacher points to various items on a chart to elicit different combinations from the students, or the students respond to oral cues while looking at their books. In the second or *testing phase,* the students close their books and work from a chart where items have been jumbled and column 3 omitted:

G15

Peter	hilft		Freunden	
	gibt		Kind	die Bilder
	antwortet		Schwestern	
	schenkt		Onkel	eine Uhr
	dankt		Lehrerin	

The exercise can be varied by asking the students to insert the proper form of the possessive adjective (*sein*). Finally, students move on to practice with items not on the original chart, and here suggestions from G12 for *applications in situational contexts* will apply.

3. If the items, as is usually the case, are related to dialogue or reading material already studied, the variations may be taught without books or chart by using *flashcards or pictures* of characters familiar to the students. After considerable practice in this purely aural-oral fashion, students will then look at the chart in their books.

4. As with G9, this practice with variation tables is preliminary learning of grammatical structures. It must be accompanied by more extensive, and more spontaneous, applications of the variations in some form of *personal interchange* between students and teachers. (See G13.)

Six groups of oral exercises

For each type of exercise in this section a brief description with an example will be given, some comments will be made on common faults to be avoided in constructing such exercises, and some German structural features for which this type of oral exercise would be useful will be listed.

Oral exercises fall into six groups: repetition, substitution, conversion, sentence modification, response, and translation drills.

1. REPETITION OR PRESENTATION DRILLS

In simple repetition drills, the instructor gives a model sentence containing a particular structure or form to be manipulated and the students repeat the sentence with correct intonation and stress. Repetition drills are not, in one sense, a special category of exercises which will be used for practicing certain types of structure; they represent, rather, a commonly used technique for familiarizing the student with the *specific structure,* with the *paradigm,* or with the *procedure for the practice.* For this reason they are sometimes called *presentation drills.* They are useful as *introductory material,* but it must be remembered that from mere repetition, no matter how prolonged, the student will learn little except the requirements of the drill.

G16

MODEL	Wo ist das Kino?	So, jetzt sehe ich es.
STUDENT	Wo ist das Kino?	So, jetzt sehe ich es.
MODEL	Wo ist der Bahnhof?	So, jetzt sehe ich ihn.
STUDENT	Wo ist der Bahnhof?	So, jetzt sehe ich ihn.
MODEL	Wo ist die Post?	So, jetzt sehe ich sie.
STUDENT	Wo ist die Post?	So, jetzt sehe ich sie.

Commentary

1. This example highlights one of the defects of many repetition drills: their unreality and lack of application to the students' situation. Unless the students are looking at a picture showing the buildings in a town, G16 could become completely mechanical,[3] with students attending only to the cue words *der, die, das.* In this case, the structure could just as easily be presented with nonsense words: *Wo ist das Bimbolein? So, jetzt sehe ich es,* a procedure which the students might actually find more amusing and which might focus their attention on the cues in the drill.

2. If students are to use in other situations the object pronouns being demonstrated, they should be concentrating on the meaning of what they

are saying. Some reality can be introduced by referring to objects the students can see and having them point to them as they respond: *Wo ist die Landkarte? So, jetzt sehe ich sie.*

2. SUBSTITUTION DRILLS

Commonly used types are simple substitution, double substitution, correlative substitution, and multiple substitution drills.

a. *Simple substitution drills* have been demonstrated in G9.

b. *Double substitution drills* are similar to simple substitutions in that the student has no other operation to perform apart from substitution of a new segment in the place of an existing segment, but they require the student to be more alert because they continually change the wording (and, therefore, the meaning) without changing the structure. They are *still mechanical,* however, because each segment is usually signaled in such a way that it can be substituted in the correct slot without the student necessarily understanding its meaning.

G17	MODEL	Wenn ich es finde/ gebe ich es dir.
	CUE	*Wenn du willst*
	RESPONSE	*Wenn du willst/* gebe ich es dir.
	CUE	*schickt er dir das Buch*
	RESPONSE	Wenn du willst/ *schickt er dir das Buch.*
	CUE	*Wenn er es finden kann*
	RESPONSE	*Wenn er es finden kann/* schickt er dir das Buch.
	CUE	*bekommen wir es morgen*
	RESPONSE	Wenn er es finden kann/ *bekommen wir es morgen.*

Commentary

1. The pattern of activity the student learns is "substitute in alternate slots, retaining the new segment for two responses (as in the sequence: A*B*, C*B*, C*D*, E*D*, E*F* . . .)."

2. If the instructor makes clear what elements are being manipulated (in this case "verb in final position in the *wenn* clause: verb in the principal clause immediately follows *wenn* clause"), the student will find this type of substitution useful for familiarizing himself with the correct slot in the utterance. He will, however, need a more demanding type of activity later, such as an innovative *chain drill* (G11), a *game,* or a *structured interchange* (where he invents conditional statements himself) if the teacher is to be sure that he can really use the pattern in communication.

c. In *correlative substitution drills* each substitution requires a correlative change to be made elsewhere in the model sentence. (See G9h.)

G18   MODEL   Das *verstehe ich auch* nicht.
        CUE   *du . . .*
        RESPONSE Das *verstehst du* auch nicht.
        CUE   *Peter und Ilse . . .*
        RESPONSE Das *verstehen Peter und Ilse* auch nicht.

This type of drill is useful for learning such things as tense inflections, possessive forms, reflexive pronouns, irregular verbs, and certain sequences of tenses in related clauses.

Correlative substitution drills can also be used to practice adjective endings.

G19 Replace the last word of the sentence with the word you hear and make all necessary changes:

        MODEL   Er kauft *ein neues Auto.*
        CUE   *Hut*
        RESPONSE Er kauft *einen neuen Hut.*

Correlative substitution can be made *more realistic* by designing the cue with a natural-sounding tag which elicits a response that completes a conversational interchange.

G20   CUE   Ich trinke morgens Kaffee zum Frühstück.
                  Und Hans?
        RESPONSE *Hans trinkt* morgens auch Kaffee.
        CUE   Ich nehme Zucker in meinem Kaffee. *Und ihr zwei?*
        RESPONSE *Wir nehmen* auch Zucker in unserem Kaffee.

This type of tag can also be used to practice the possessive adjectives:

G21   CUE   Ich habe mein Heft. *Und du?*
        RESPONSE Ich habe *mein* Heft auch.
        CUE   Also, du hast dein Heft. *Aber Paul?*
        RESPONSE Er hat *sein* Heft auch.
        CUE   Ja, Paul, du hast dein Heft mit. *Und Inge?*
        RESPONSE Inge hat *ihr* Heft auch mit.

d. *Multiple substitution drills* are a *testing device* to see whether the student can continue to make a grammatical adjustment he has learned while he is distracted by other preoccupations—in this case, thinking of the changing meaning of successive sentences so as to make substitutions in different slots. In order to make the substitutions in the appropriate slots, students have to think of the meaning of the whole sentence, which changes in focus with each substitution. For this reason, students need to be very alert to perform this exercise successfully.

After study and practice of the dative the following multiple substitution drill could be used:

G22   MODEL   Ich kaufe meiner Mutter Blumen.

         CUE   *seine Mutter*

   RESPONSE   Ich kaufe *seiner Mutter* Blumen.

         CUE   *Jürgen*

   RESPONSE   *Jürgen kauft* seiner Mutter Blumen.

         CUE   *ein Buch*

   RESPONSE   Jürgen kauft seiner Mutter *ein Buch.*

         CUE   *sein Onkel*

   RESPONSE   Jürgen kauft *seinem Onkel* ein Buch.

         CUE   *geben*

   RESPONSE   Jürgen *gibt* seinem Onkel ein Buch.

         CUE   *seine Brüder*

   RESPONSE   Jürgen gibt *seinen Brüdern* ein Buch.

The last two responses, requiring changes in the verb stem in one sentence and the additional ending on the noun for the dative plural in the last sentence, provide a challenge for an enthusiastic class which enjoys showing how much it has learned.

3. CONVERSION DRILLS

The term *transformation* has long been applied to the types of exercises in which affirmative sentences are changed into negative sentences, statements are changed into questions, simple declarations are converted into emphatic declarations, active voice is converted into passive voice, or a present tense statement is changed into a past tense statement. Such exercises have been the staple of foreign-language classes for many years. Some of these processes happen to parallel what are known as "transformations" in transformational-generative grammar (e.g., negativization, passivization, and the interrogative transformation), and others do not, but when they do, this is more a coincidence than a derivative relationship. The term "transformation" is, therefore, misleading to some people because of a presumed connection with transformational-generative grammar. For this reason, the term "conversion drill" will be used for exercises in changing sentence type, combining two sentences into one, moving from one mood or tense to another, changing word class (e.g., replacing nouns by pronouns), substituting phrases for clauses or clauses for phrases (e.g., adverbial phrases for adverbial clauses, infinitive phrases for clauses), and substituting single words for phrases or phrases for single words (e.g., adverbs for adverbial phrases, adjectives for adjectival phrases).

These are conversions rather than substitutions in that they require the use of a different form (frequently with a correlative change), a change in word order, the introduction of new elements, or even considerable restructuring of the utterance. They are useful for developing flexibility in the selection of formal structures for the expression of personal meaning.

a. *General conversion drills*

In our discussion of the construction of common types of conversion drills and the weaknesses to be avoided, we will use examples based on *negation*. Negatives are among the most frequently used forms in the language and practice with them can easily be given a *situational context* and a *personal application*.

G23 Negate the following statements:

CUES   a. Im Mai beginnt die Touristensaison.
        b. Maria ist gesund.
        c. Inge kommt gut an.
        d. Die Sonne scheint schön.
        e. Schmidts haben Geld.
        f. Ich habe eine Krankheit.

Commentary

1. When c and d are converted to negative sentences, they produce utterances that are grammatically correct, but have zero probability of occurrence. Yet such sentences can still be found in books in use at the present time. It is obvious that these examples were chosen to demonstrate the position of *nicht* with regard to separable prefixes and adverbs. A better example for c would have been *Abends machen wir die Fenster zu* and for d *Er fährt schnell*.

2. Statement f illustrates the type of exercise that disregards normal

usage. While it is entirely appropriate to say *Er hat eine Krankheit,* it is extremely unlikely that a speaker of German (or of English) would say of himself that he has a disease. One expects: *Ich bin krank.* This may not be a grave fault, but it deepens the impression many students acquire that language study is mere manipulation of words and has no reality or relevance.

3. In these six sentences the student is *tested* first for his ability to choose between negation with *nicht* or *kein* and then to decide on the position of *nicht.* This exercise should come after a *series of learning exercises* in which the student encounters the various aspects of negation, including the position of *nicht,* and practices them step by step. Each exercise in the series will consist of six or more sentences, with familiar vocabulary, which will produce after the conversion utterances semantically related, as in the following.

G24 Negate the following statements according to the model:

REPEAT   Dieses Motorrad gehört mir.
           Dieses Motorrad gehört mir nicht.
CUES   a. Ich kenne deinen Freund Max.
       b. Er braucht mich.
       c. Ich verkaufe das Motorrad.
       d. Er bekommt es morgen.

A *complete series on negation with nicht* should include a set with separable prefixes, a set with predicate adjectives and nouns, a set with directives, a set with modal auxiliaries and other verbs governing dependent infinitives, a set with modal auxiliaries including directives or predicate adjectives, a set with the perfect and other compound tenses, a set with adverbs of manner. Some review drills would be interpolated. Some study of many of these aspects, although not necessarily all at once, would normally precede a mixed exercise of the G23 type. At some stage also, students will learn to differentiate between negation with *nicht* or *kein* and to practice the position of *nicht* in subordinate clauses. At some later period students will also learn that the position of *nicht* can vary to negate specific parts of the sentence.

The great *advantage of oral exercises* is that so much more practice can be accomplished in the time available and this allows for step-by-step progression through a series of rules. The practice sets will normally be spread over several lessons. The amount of subdivision within these sets and the number of sets presented at any one time will depend on the level of instruction, the maturity of the students, and the intensiveness of the course. For elementary classes, the forms necessary for simple communication will suffice. For more mature students, discussion of the various possibilities can reduce the necessity of proceeding by one-feature-at-a-time drills.

The *problem of appropriateness of items after conversion* must be constantly kept in mind. This applies especially when sentences are changed from singular to plural (*Meine Mutter besucht meine Tante*), when statements are converted to questions (*Ich habe einen Bruder*), and when practicing tenses by changing verbs from present to simple past (*Du kaufst dir ein Auto*).

Before selecting a textbook the teacher should look through it carefully to see that the German it elicits from the students is probable, useful, and contemporary.

Situational and personal application

Another set of grammatical rules commonly practiced through conversion drills is the series determining the form, position, and order of pronouns which occur as direct and indirect objects of the verb. Most textbooks resort here to the replacement in sentences of nouns by pronouns.

G25 In the following sentences replace the italicized nouns by pronouns and make any other appropriate changes:

    a. Paul gibt *seinem Vater die Zeitung*.
    b. Inge erzählt uns *eine Geschichte*.
    c. Wann kaufst du das *deinem Vater?*
    d. Schicken Sie Ihrem Vater *eine Uhr?*

The question of the form and position in the sentence of pronoun objects appears complicated to the student. In addition to the problems occasioned by the replacement of direct and indirect nouns by pronouns, students are frequently puzzled by the forms used in German for replacing non-personal nouns after prepositions. (Ich habe *von Pauls Reise* gesprochen: Ich habe *davon* gesprochen; *Wovon* haben Sie gesprochen? and Wir haben *über Paul* gesprochen: Wir haben *über ihn* gesprochen; *Über wen* haben Sie gesprochen?) The conversion exercises necessary for assimilating these rules can be made more vivid by associating structure with action. Students may be asked to respond to instructions by making statements of their own invention, as in a normal conversational interchange, along the following lines:

G26 (I) Maria, erzählen Sie uns von Ihrer Reise nach Österreich!
      Ich habe schon gestern davon erzählt.

      Haben Sie etwas von Ihrem Vetter in Berlin gehört?
      Ja, ich habe einen Brief von ihm bekommen.

Denken Sie an Ihre Aufgaben für heute abend!
Woran soll ich denn sonst denken?

Commentary

1. If students prepare ahead of time they can come to class with instructions to give each other which will require quick-wittedness in responding and cause quite a lot of amusement for the class.

2. A *mixed practice* of this type presumes preliminary sequential learning, but it is very effective in providing for *review of a complicated set of rules.* Conducted orally, without hesitation, it enables the student to absorb the rhythm of the sequences. This is an aid to memory which is quite lost if the student constantly writes out his responses—editing and re-editing his first attempts as he "puts the objects in the right place" in a conscious, artificial way.

b. *Combinations*

Combinations are a form of conversion drill which has also been used for many years. It involves a process which reflects certain features of transformational grammatical analysis and can be very illuminating in differentiating some aspects of the rules. For instance, students often have difficulty in understanding the different uses of *der/die/das* and *wer/was* as relative pronouns. If we examine the sentence

Wo ist die Zeitschrift, die wir gestern gekauft haben?

we find it combines two underlying sentences:

Wo ist die Zeitschrift?
Wir haben die Zeitschrift gestern gekauft.

Asking students to combine these two underlying sentences by using a relative pronoun involves moving from a deeper level of structure to surface structure. The relative pronoun *die,* in the example above, replaces one occurrence of the element found in both sentences (*die Zeitschrift*), the final choice of form depending on the gender of the antecedent and on the function the relative pronoun performs in the expanded sentence (object of *gekauft haben*).

On the other hand, the combining of two underlying sentences such as

A schreibt eine gute Arbeit
A fällt nicht durch,

(where *A* refers to something not explicitly stated in either sentence) requires the appropriate form of *wer* to form the sentence

Wer eine gute Arbeit schreibt, fällt nicht durch.

(Contrast with these the pair

Meier fällt nicht durch,
Meier hat eine gute Arbeit geschrieben,

which combine as

Meier, der eine gute Arbeit geschrieben hat, fällt nicht durch.)

The following oral exercises, G27-28, require more active construction of sentences with relative pronouns than the traditional fill-in-the-blank exercise of the type:

Hier ist der Amerikaner, _____ ich in Berlin getroffen habe.

G27 Combine the following pairs of sentences using *der* or *den* as required. In each case make the first sentence the main clause.

    a. Hier ist der Amerikaner. Ich habe den Amerikaner in Berlin getroffen.
    b. Hier ist der Hund. Der Hund stand gestern vor unserer Tür.
    c. Hier ist der Bericht. Wir müssen den Bericht für heute fertig haben.

Exercises for practicing the relative pronoun should include a series in which the students have to choose from the nominative form, a series for the dative singular and plural forms of the relative pronoun, especially after prepositions, and a series for the genitive forms.

G28 Combine the following pairs of sentences using *wer, wen* or *wem* as required:

    a. A unternimmt nichts.
       A lernt auch nichts.
       RESPONSE   Wer nichts unternimmt, lernt auch nichts.

    b. Er vergißt A nie.
       Er trifft A bei einer Party.
       RESPONSE   Er vergißt nie, wen er bei einer Party trifft.

These sets of exercises would be expanded with sets using sentences with different subjects (*A fragt Else nach Hilfe/Sie hilft A—Wer Else nach Hilfe fragt, dem hilft sie*) and with sets using *was* as a relative pronoun. Mixed drills reviewing the various uses of the relative pronoun would be interspersed throughout these exercises.

The procedure of combining sentences to form one utterance can also be used for creating other types of subordinate clauses (*Heinrich ist heute nicht mitgefahren/Er hatte eine andere Verabredung—Heinrich ist heute nicht mitgefahren, weil er eine andere Verabredung hatte*), or for practicing coordinating conjunctions as well as the use of *sondern*. It is also useful for situations that require a special sequence of tenses in successive clauses, e.g., sentences with *nachdem* and *bevor*. (Where one clause will be subordinate to another, it must be clear to the student which of the two sentences to be combined will be the main clause and which the dependent clause.)

c. *Restatement*

Restatement is another useful kind of conversion drill.

G29 One frequently used type of *directed dialogue* is a restatement exercise. (See also C24c.)

CUE	Sagen Sie Paul, daß Sie Hans heißen.
RESPONSE	Paul, ich heiße Hans.
CUE	Fragen Sie Georg, was er heute macht.
RESPONSE	Georg, was machst du heute?
CUE	Sagen Sie ihm, Sie möchten mitkommen.
RESPONSE	Ich möchte mitkommen.

A series of this type is usually based on a dialogue which has been learned, but all kinds of restatements can be invented to practice different grammatical features. A realistic note is added if one student pretends to be giving directions to a third party by telephone, while a second student tells him what to say.

G30 A *running commentary* by one student on what another student or the teacher is saying softly gives practice in restatement of direct speech in indirect speech form.

(I)	STUDENT A	Ich bin eben angekommen, aber ich muß gleich fort.
	STUDENT B	Er sagt, daß er eben angekommen ist. Er muß aber gleich fort.
	STUDENT A	Warum schaust du mich so an?
	STUDENT B	Sie fragt mich, warum ich sie so anschaue.

Another type of restatement (sometimes called a *contraction*) consists of the replacing of a clause with a phrase, or a phrase with a single word, while retaining the basic meaning.

G31 Restate each of the following sentences, replacing the adverbial clause with an adverbial phrase of similar meaning:

a. *Nachdem wir angekommen waren,* haben wir ihn gesucht.

RESPONSE *Nach unserer Ankunft* haben wir ihn gesucht.

b. *Bevor wir wegfahren,* müssen wir zur Bank.

RESPONSE   *Vor der Abfahrt* müssen wir zur Bank.

G32   In each of the following sentences replace the descriptive clause with an adjective of equivalent meaning.

a. Die Erlebnisse, *die ich damals gehabt habe,* sind jetzt vergessen.

RESPONSE   Die *damaligen* Erlebnisse sind jetzt vergessen.

b. Das Kleid, *das aus Seide ist,* hat sie nur einmal getragen.

RESPONSE   Das *seidene* Kleid hat sie nur einmal getragen.

c. Der Mensch, *der fünfundachtzig Jahre alt ist,* kann noch viel unternehmen.

RESPONSE   Der *fünfundachtzigjährige* Mensch kann noch viel unternehmen.

d. Ihr Aufenthalt, *der sechs Monate gedauert hat,* war sehr angenehm.

RESPONSE   Ihr *sechsmonatiger* Aufenthalt war sehr angenehm.

✱ List for yourself other areas of German grammar for which some form of restatement would be a suitable exercise and try to think of ways in which this restatement can be incorporated into a natural communication activity.

4. SENTENCE MODIFICATIONS

Sentence modification exercises are of three kinds: expansions, deletions, and completions.

a. *Expansions*

Expansions serve two purposes. Type A requires strictly grammatical manipulation and is useful for learning such things as the position of adverbs. It can be teacher or student directed. Type B is more spontaneous; it gives students the opportunity to create new and original sentences from a basic sentence, often in an atmosphere of competition.[4] Students should be encouraged to spice the exercise with humorous items.

Type A expansions. The question of word order in the middle (or inner) sentence field is a complicated one to which the student will have to devote attention throughout his study of German. The position of adverbs and adverbial phrases of time and place is a recurrent problem in the student's acquisition of German. The following observations can be made about these groups of adverbs:

Observation 1: Adverbs and adverbial phrases like *gestern, nächstes Jahr, dort, im Kino* precede a. directives like *nach Hause, in die Stadt,* b. pred-

icate nouns and adjectives, and c. direct objects preceded by indefinite articles (*ein Bild,* plural: *Bilder*).
Compare: Ich möchte *morgen früh* nach Berlin fahren.
Er war *gestern* sehr fleißig.
Sie hat *in der Schule* ein Bild gezeichnet.

Observation 2: Adverbs of time and place generally follow all pronouns, nouns in the nominative serving as the subject, indirect objects, and direct objects preceded by definite articles (including *der*-words and possessive adjectives).[5]
Compare: Gestern habe ich ihm *in diesem Geschäft* ein Buch gekauft.
Er kauft seinen Eltern *heute* Blumen.

Observation 3: If adverbs of time and place are used in the same sentence, adverbs of time generally precede adverbs of place.
Compare: Ich habe seinen Vater *letzte Woche im Restaurant Krone* gesehen.

Observation 4: When more than one adverb of time is used, the more specific adverb of time follows the more general.
This complex set of rules can be practiced very effectively in an oral expansion of Type A.

G33 (E or I)

MODEL SENTENCE Er kauft ein Buch.
CUE morgen
RESPONSE Er kauft morgen ein Buch.
CUE in der Stadt
RESPONSE Er kauft morgen in der Stadt ein Buch.
CUE nachmittag
RESPONSE Er kauft morgen nachmittag in der Stadt ein Buch.

Students would also be given a set of exercises in which the direct object is preceded by the definite article. Later they will have to learn that the position of certain elements in the inner field can vary, depending on the news value of a particular item.[6]
Many other grammatical features can be practiced in a Type A expansion.

G34 a. Insert in the sentences you hear the expressions supplied in the cues, making any necessary changes:

BASIC SENTENCE Sie hat einen Mantel.
CUE Neu?
RESPONSE Sie hat einen neuen Mantel.

CUE	Aus Leder?
RESPONSE	Sie hat einen neuen Mantel aus Leder.
CUE	Weich?
RESPONSE	Sie hat einen neuen Mantel aus weichem Leder.

b. Insert at the beginning of the sentences you hear the expression supplied in the cues, making all necessary changes:

BASIC SENTENCE	Er besucht uns.
CUE	Morgen?
RESPONSE	Morgen besucht er uns.
CUE	Trotz des Schnees?
RESPONSE	Trotz des Schnees besucht er uns morgen.

Type B expansions provide students with the opportunity to create new sentences from a basic frame by expanding the frame as they wish, as often as they wish. In this type of practice no two students would produce exactly the same answer.

G35

CUE	Der Mann geht über die Straße.
STUDENT A	Der alte Mann, der ein Bier trinkt, geht langsam über die Straße.
STUDENT B	Der Mann, der sehr besorgt ist, geht über die Straße, ohne auf den Verkehr achtzugeben.

A Type B expansion may be conducted as a *chaining activity,* with each student in succession adding a new element to the sentence until a limit seems to have been reached. At that stage, a new chain begins with another simple sentence.

b. *Deletions.*

Flexibility in manipulating structures can be developed by reversing the processes discussed above.

Type A deletions, which are the reverse of Type A expansions, provide further variety in practice.

G36 Delete the modals in the following sentences:

CUE	Ich muß morgen nach Chicago fahren.
RESPONSE	Ich fahre morgen nach Chicago.
CUE	Er möchte das ganze Buch lesen.
RESPONSE	Er liest das ganze Buch.
CUE	Seine Eltern wollten zu Hause bleiben.
RESPONSE	Seine Eltern blieben zu Hause.

Type B deletions serve a less useful purpose than Type B expansions. Expansions require the student to decide at which point in the sentence to insert additional information of his own choosing. Deletions of extra information usually require only formal changes, as practiced in Type A deletions. For this reason deletions are not creative.

c. *Completions*

In completions, part of the sentence is given as a cue and the student finishes the sentence either with a semantically constant segment in which some syntactic or morphological change must be made according to the cue (Type A_1), with a suitable segment which is to some extent semantically governed by the cue (Type A_2), or with a segment of his own invention (Type B).

Type A_1 completions.

G37 (I) In the following exercise you will hear the model sentence: *Wenn wir Geld hätten, würden wir nach Berlin fahren.* Throughout the exercise, you will retain the same concluding notion, varying the segment from subjunctive to indicative as the introductory segment changes.

MODEL SENTENCE Wenn wir Geld hätten, würden wir nach Berlin fahren.

CUE Wenn das Wetter schön wäre . . .

RESPONSE Wenn das Wetter schön wäre, würden wir nach Berlin fahren.

CUE Wenn wir Zeit haben . . .

RESPONSE Wenn wir Zeit haben, fahren wir nach Berlin.

CUE Wenn du mitfahren könntest . . .

RESPONSE Wenn du mitfahren könntest, würden wir nach Berlin fahren.

Type A_2 completions.

G38 (I) In the following exercise you will hear the model sentence: *Er gibt mir meinen Bleistift zurück, wenn er seinen findet.* Throughout the exercise you will retain a concluding segment of similar meaning to *wenn er seinen findet,* but as the introductory segment varies you will vary the person referred to in the concluding segment.

MODEL SENTENCE Er gibt mir meinen Bleistift zurück, *wenn er seinen findet.*

CUE Ich gebe dir deinen Bleistift zurück . . .

RESPONSE   Ich gebe dir deinen Bleistift zurück, *wenn ich meinen finde.*

CUE   Wir geben ihm sein Buch zurück.

RESPONSE   Wir geben ihm sein Buch zurück, *wenn wir unseres finden.*

Commentary

With an exercise involving a correlative change of this type, it is usually advisable for the student to repeat two, or even three, items with the instructor at the beginning in order to be sure of the kind of manipulation required.

A Type A_2 completion is very useful for *vocabulary learning.*

G39 Complete the following statements with the appropriate occupational term, according to the model:

MODEL   Wer die Post bringt, *ist Briefträger.*

CUE   Wer Fleisch verkauft . . .

RESPONSE   Wer Fleisch verkauft, *ist Metzger.*

CUE   Wer Kranke behandelt . . .

RESPONSE   Wer Kranke behandelt, *ist Arzt.*

Type B completions. A Type B completion allows the student to make his personal semantic contribution within a syntactically fixed framework. It is useful for practicing such things as the governance of infinitives with *zu* and without *zu,* the use of the subjunctive, and word order in subordinate clauses.

G40 (I) Invent a completion containing an infinitive construction for each sentence you hear, according to the following model: Ich rate dir . . . / Ich rate dir, *Anna nach der Stunde zu sprechen.*

CUE   Ich höre . . .

RESPONSE   Ich höre *meinen Bruder laut schreien.*

CUE   Ich finde es langweilig . . .

RESPONSE   Ich finde es langweilig, *nur Englisch zu sprechen.*

Commentary

In a Type A_1 completion on governance of infinitives the concluding segment would remain the same throughout the exercise, except for the change of link: Ich empfehle dir / *mit ihm zu sprechen;* Ich möchte / *mit ihm sprechen;* Er sieht mich / *mit ihm sprechen.* An exercise of Type A₁ may precede the Type B exercise above in order to familiarize the student with the required structures, or to refresh his memory. All practice should, however, move toward Type B exercises where the student supplies something of his own invention, and then beyond Type B to creative practice, like that described in Chapter 2 under *Autonomous Interaction,* p. 44.

✳ Look for other areas of grammar for which sentence modifications would be useful and try to think of original ways of presenting them which draw close to the real purposes of communication.

5. RESPONSE DRILLS

All oral exercises may, in one sense, be called response drills. In the particular type to which we are referring here, *question-answer* or *answer-question* procedures are used, or students learn to make appropriate conventional responses (*rejoinders*) to other people's utterances.

a. *Question-answer practice*

Ability to ask questions with ease and to recognize question forms effortlessly, so that one can reply appropriately, is of the essence in communication. It has always been a basic classroom activity. Unfortunately, much question-answer material is very stilted, questions being asked for the sake of the form, without attention to their real interest to the student. The structure of the question form itself can be practiced through conversion exercises; question-answer practice is useful for such things as forms and uses of tenses, various kinds of pronouns, and forms of emphasis. It is most frequently associated with a picture, slide, or film, reading material, some project or activity, or a game. It can, however, be carefully structured for language-learning purposes. Since the form of an appropriate answer is nearly always a reflection of the question, the teacher can elicit the forms and uses he wants by skillful construction of his questions. In the following series, for instance, successive questions elicit the use of different tenses from the student, yet the communicative interaction develops naturally.

G41 (The students have been reading about or viewing a film of the adventures of a group of young people in Munich.)

Q. Warum sind sie so spät zurückgekommen?

A. Sie sind so spät zurückgekommen, weil die Nacht schön war und der Mond hell schien.

Q. Kommen Sie abends auch oft spät nach Hause?
A. Nein, ich komme lieber früh nach Hause, weil ich gerne warm esse.

Q. Aber wenn Sie im Juli Ferien haben, dann werden Sie sicher öfters spät zurückkommen, oder?
A. Ja, das stimmt. Im Sommer gehe ich immer schwimmen.

Q. Was würden Sie tun, wenn Ihre Mutter sich wegen der Verspätung ärgerte und kein Abendessen vorbereiten wollte?
A. Ich würde sie um Geld bitten, um mir einige Hot Dogs zu kaufen.

Commentary

The development of this type of interchange is not predictable, but the alert questioner can keep on switching the conversation to a different time perspective. The same type of approach can be developed at the elementary level through discussion of an action picture.

Many *situations* can be created in the classroom for the asking of questions and the obtaining of answers.

G42 With a simulated telephone link, all kinds of situations can be invented which elicit questions and answers from students.

1. Student A calls student B on the phone. Student B asks questions until he is able to identify the person calling and his purpose.
2. Student C calls student D to get some information from him. Student D has a German brochure, menu, or a collection of advertisements from which he gives the information requested.

b. *Answer-question practice*

Frequently the teacher asks all the questions, yet in a foreign-language situation it is more commonly the language learner, or foreign visitor, who needs to be able to ask questions with ease. Certainly, in a natural conversation, each participant passes freely from the role of interlocutor to respondent. Answer-question practice takes place when the teacher, or some student, has the answer and the others must find out what it is. This type of exercise takes place naturally and interestingly in such games as *Einundzwanzig Fragen, Tierreich-Steinreich-Pflanzenreich* and *Identität.*

G43 In *Einundzwanzig Fragen* one person (A) thinks of someone or something. By asking eliminating questions to which A may reply only *Ja* or *Nein,* the players narrow the field of possibilities until they are able to guess the person or object in question. Only twenty-one questions may be asked before the game is lost.

Tierreich–Steinreich–Pflanzenreich is similar except that the first eliminations are in these three categories and the number of questions is not limited.

In *Identität,* A thinks of a person and an object typically associated with this person. Forms of questions will be more varied than in the first two games because A may give information, although he tries to do this as ambiguously as possible. When the students have guessed the person, they must guess the object associated with this person (e.g., the school janitor and his keys; Luther and his ink well).

c. *Rejoinders*

In every language there are conventional ways of responding to the utterances of others which ease social relations and make continued communication less effortful: ways of agreeing, disagreeing, expressing pleasure, astonishment, surprise, displeasure, or disgust, ways of responding to another person's monologue so that one appears to be participating, and ways of acknowledging replies to one's questions. These common responses are frequently not taught in any systematic way to foreigners, with the result that the latter often offend, either by not contributing as they should to an interchange or by contributing too forcefully or pedantically. Some rejoinders will be learned incidentally because the teacher will use them frequently; others can be practiced in an oral exercise from time to time.

G44 (I) Listen to the following sentences and respond to each with an appropriate exclamation or rejoinder:

CUE	Also, wir treffen uns heute abend um acht.
RESPONSE	*Abgemacht!*
CUE	Wir wollen heute einen Ausflug machen. Kommst du mit?
RESPONSE	*Gerne!*
CUE	Mir hat sie gesagt, sie wollte mich nie wiedersehen!
RESPONSE	*Na, so was!*

Commentary

This mixed exercise is, of course, a review and presumes preliminary learning of appropriate rejoinders, either through a series of exercises on particular rejoinders or through the teacher's continual use of them in class. Rejoinders learned artificially, out of context, are easily forgotten. Students should be encouraged to intersperse them liberally through their communication activities.

* Begin keeping a list of frequently used German rejoinders so that you can employ them yourself in class and teach them to your students. Your list will certainly include such expressions as *Das tut mir leid! Abgemacht! Na, so was! Wie bitte? Schmeckt's? Gleichfalls! Gewiß! Verzeihung! Eben! Mir geht's genau so! Großartig! Leider! Schade! Sicher! Unbedingt! Na, klar! Gern! Kaum! Und? Und ob! Macht nichts.*

6. TRANSLATION DRILLS

Translation exercises have slipped into disfavor in recent years. This is not because translation itself is reprehensible. In fact, it is a natural process with many practical uses. Unfortunately, for many teachers it became an end, rather than a means of improving the student's control of the structure of the language. As a result, many translation exercises became tortuous puzzles. (Try translating a sentence like: Didn't you wish the old woman had died before she knew about it?) The question of translation, and how it can be used most effectively, is discussed in depth in Chapter 9.

The habit of translating everything one hears or says (or reads or writes) can become a hindrance to fluency. Many students do not realize that it is possible to learn to comprehend and think in the foreign language directly; hence the need for procedures which encourage and develop this ability. For these reasons translation drills, if used at all, should be used sparingly, and then only for linguistic features which are difficult to practice entirely in German.

Oral translation drills differ from the older types of translation exercises in several ways:

1. Since the native language serves solely as a stimulus for the production of authentic German utterances, only natural idiomatic utterances that the student could conceivably use in communication are introduced.

G45 *He went home early.* Er ist früh nach Hause gegangen.

2. Stimulus sentences are *short,* centering exclusively on the grammatical feature being practiced.

G46 *I saw him.* Ich habe ihn gesehen.
I didn't see him. Ich habe ihn nicht gesehen.

3. Stimulus sentences remain within a *familiar vocabulary range* so that the student's attention is not distracted from the grammatical feature being practiced.

4. Translation drills do not encourage students to look for one-to-one equivalences between English and German by distorting the English, as in the following example from a grammar-translation type textbook.

G47 *What did you let fall?*
Was haben Sie fallen lassen?

Instead they require students to produce a German utterance which is *semantically equivalent* to the English stimulus.

G48 *Do you like it?*
Gefällt es dir?

In this way, they encourage students to think in German. They are particularly useful for practicing distinctively German idioms.

G49 *It turned out that he was right.*
Es hat sich herausgestellt, daß er recht hatte.
Don't be mad at me.
Sei mir nicht böse.

5. Although stimulus sentences are short, they are not fragments, but *complete utterances* providing a context which indicates usage. Instead of being asked to translate: *he came, she went, they left,* students are presented with more likely utterances such as:

G50 *He left yesterday.* Er ist gestern weggefahren.
I went to the post office. Ich bin zur Post gegangen.

6. As with other oral drills, translation drills provide practice of one grammatical feature consistently through six or seven items before the drill moves on to a related feature, or to a further complication of the same feature.

G51 Set of stimulus sentences for practicing the present perfect with *haben* or *sein* as auxiliary:

Sagen Sie auf deutsch!
a. He came last night.
b. She stayed home.
c. She visited us.
d. He bought a book.
e. He ate quickly.

f. She drove to Frankfurt.

g. He became ill.

h. She slept late.

Commentary

This is a mixed practice exercise, to be conducted after other practices which have been limited to one aspect of this complex feature. Here, the student is expected to decide rapidly to which category the different verbs belong, as he would have to do in communication. See also W62.

7. After several drills developing familiarity with a certain feature, a mixed drill may be given (as in G9).

8. Translation drills provide a stimulus for quick production of verb forms as in G52 and for contrasting tense usage in German and English as in G53.

G52 *He can find it.* Er kann es finden.
We can find it. Wir können es finden.

G53 *He's coming today.*   Er kommt heute.
Are they coming tomorrow?   Kommen sie morgen?
Do they always come on Mondays?   Kommen sie immer am Montag?
He always comes alone.   Er kommt immer allein.

9. Translation drills are *useful for quick review*—for refreshing students' memories and pinpointing persistent inaccuracies. Conducted orally, at a brisk pace, they do not give the students time to pore over the German equivalents and edit them, as they do with written exercises.

Simultaneous interpretation

When some grammatical features are well learned, oral translation drills for review may be placed in a more realistic setting by giving individual students the opportunity to act as German simultaneous interpreters for the poor monolingual English-speaking teacher, or a fellow-student. With classroom-laboratory facilities, an authentic simultaneous interpreting situation can be staged. The passage for interpretation will be carefully prepared by the teacher so that it is possible for the student to interpret successfully. (It can also be designed to elicit certain features, for instance, specific tenses.) Other students will be asked to comment on the success of the interpreting and have the opportunity to improve on it. This type of activity is also suitable for recording in the language laboratory.

* Form small groups of students interested in different types of oral exercises.

1. Find examples of the selected type of oral exercise in textbooks, workbooks, or laboratory manuals, and discuss whether or not they are well constructed.

2. Try writing an exercise of this type for a structural feature for which it is appropriate.

3. Try your exercise out on the class to see if it is effective.

4. Take some poorly constructed oral exercises of this type, rewrite them in a more effective form, and then try them out on other students.

5
Teaching the sound system

Understanding descriptions of phonological systems: a little terminology[1]

In order to follow the discussion in this section, the reader needs to be familiar with certain commonly used terms. The sounds we make are *phones*. Although the number of phones that can be produced by any individual speaker is practically unlimited, only certain sounds are recognized by the speakers and hearers of a particular language as conveying meaning. The smallest unit of significant or meaningful sound has been called a *phoneme*. A phoneme is actually an abstraction rather than a concrete description of a specific sound. Any particular phoneme comprises a group or *class* of sounds that are phonetically similar but whose articulations vary according to their position relative to the other sounds which precede or follow them. The environmentally conditioned variants of any particular sound occurring in complementary distribution are *allophones*. "In complementary distribution" means that these sound variants are regularly found in certain environments where they do not contrast with each other, e.g., variant A may occur perhaps only in medial position between vowels, whereas variant B always occurs in initial or final position.

In *articulatory phonetics,* we study the positions of the organs of speech, e.g., the tongue, lips, or vocal cords, in the production of different sounds. These articulatory descriptions are intended to help us to form unfamiliar sounds. In speech, however, the organs are in continual motion, so that

138

sounds may vary slightly as they are produced in association with other sounds or are given differing degrees of stress. This variation must remain within a certain band of tolerance if it is not to hinder comprehension (that is, if the phonetic variants are still to be recognizable to a listener familiar with that language as manifestations of the same phoneme).

The concepts mentioned above are useful for the teacher in understanding and defining problem areas which speakers of one language encounter when attempting to learn another. For example, the German /l/ is phonemic, as shown by the fact that *wild* and *wird* have different meanings which are signalled only by the change of the element /l/ to /r/; in English, /l/ is also phonemic, as witness *it's a lot* and *it's a pot*. The phonemes of the two languages, however, have a different range. Whereas the German phoneme /l/ occurs as the so-called *clear l* [l], the English phoneme /l/ has two allophones, the *clear l* [l] and the *dark (velarized) l* [ɫ], which occur in different environments ([l] before vowels and /j/, and [ɫ] after vowels) and are therefore in complementary distribution. Since these varying sounds always appear in certain environments they may be termed allophones of the phoneme /l/. (They are not merely accidental or dialectal variants, because they do not alternate with each other in the same position but each has a clearly defined distribution.)

The recognition of the phoneme is basically a psychological process which results from experience with a particular language. Many English speakers do not notice the difference between [l] and [ɫ] in their own language, because these sounds are non-distinctive in English, that is, they do not clearly differentiate one word from another. Students need to be made aware of differences to which they are not accustomed but which may be phonemic in a new language; otherwise, they may unwittingly transfer their English speech habits to the new language. Naturally teachers of German need to be very familiar with the significant differences between the German and the English sound systems if they are to help their students acquire a pronunciation acceptable and comprehensible to a native speaker.

In *generative phonology,*[2] sound systems are not described in terms of phonemes, but of *distinctive features*. These features are *binary,* that is, either present (+) or absent (−), which enables the phonologist to represent the phonological system of a language by a feature matrix. Features are described in terms which may be *articulatory* (taking into account such things as place and manner of articulation), *acoustic* (referring to information detectable by technical instruments), or *perceptual* (e.g., syllables or stress). Generative phonologists are attempting to establish a set of *universal* distinctive features which may be used to characterize the sounds of all languages. To the generative phonologist the pronunciation of a word is a surface representation resulting from the application of transformational rules to an abstract underlying form. This approach has brought to light some interesting relationships between surface sound realizations and traditional spelling systems.

Variation and change in German sounds: speech levels and dialects

In German, as in English, there is a wide range of variation for each single sound. While the native speaker, either consciously or unconsciously, adjusts to differences in pronunciation, the student of a foreign language at any stage may be baffled by a sound he simply does not recognize. Such variations may be influenced by a number of factors, but the situational level of speech (see Chapter 1) and dialect peculiarities are of particular significance to the student of German.

For half a century the pronunciation established in 1898 by Siebs' *Deutsche Bühnensprache* remained the guide to standard High German. Although Siebs is still considered by many the absolute standard for *Hochlautung,* a more relaxed modified standard (*gemäßigte Hochlautung*) has gained considerable acceptance in recent years, and even the variations produced in everyday casual speech have drawn increasing attention.[3]

Even in the classroom the student of German will be confronted with variations of the same sound, for the language teacher adjusts his enunciation and speaking tempo to the mood of the situation and the reaction of the class and may fall into everyday habits of speech. Under such circumstances endings tend to be reduced, e.g., the [ən] of *guten Tag* becomes [ŋ]. Tense vowels in monosyllabic words or before *r* tend to become lax, e.g., *Bad* from [bɑːt] to [bat] or *mir* from [miːʁ] to [mɪʁ]. Assimilation is more frequent, so that the student is more likely to hear [habm̩] than [habən] or even [habn̩] for *haben.*[4]

A second major cause of confusion to the language-learner is the many variations of sound and of intonation (*Sprachmelodie*) resulting from differences in dialect. In the last twenty-five years the redistribution of population in Germany and the growing importance of radio and television have favored the acceptance of a unified language norm, but more recently there has been a counter-movement to promote the use of dialects in German schools so that the regional character of language will not be entirely lost.

The sounds prevalent in dialects affect the non-dialect standard of speech in certain geographical areas.[5] For the language-learner, this means that he will encounter many sounds which contradict what he has learned. He may even hear teachers produce sounds which do not conform to the "rules" for the standard. Students may struggle to master the correct pronunciation of the [pf] in *Pfanne* only to notice that their teacher from northern Germany consistently uses [f] when he is not teaching pronunciation.

Two sounds in particular require an explanation from the very beginning.

The German *r* occurs in two forms (as well as several allophones not to be discussed here), the uvular [R] which is articulated by raising the back of the tongue toward the uvula, and the apical or trilled [r] (*Zungen-r*) which is produced by bringing the tip of the tongue against the alveolar ridge. The older [r] is still regarded to be preferable by Siebs, but in practice the uvular [R] is in use today in most urban areas of Germany while the [r] is prevalent in the speech of rural and southern German speakers as well as of Swiss and Austrian speakers. Likewise, the [ɛ:] sound of *Käse* is still known to most Germans who use it to clarify which of two similar words is meant (*Segen/sägen*). In northern Germany, however, no distinction is generally made between [ɛ:] and [e], while in southern areas they are frequently distinguished from one another.

Which variants of sounds a teacher chooses to teach in addition to the modified standard will depend on his own habits of speech and dialect influences. But it can in any case be both helpful and entertaining to students to learn what major forms of sound variation they may encounter in their experience with the German language.

Languages contrast: major differences between the German and English phonological systems

A number of sounds in English and German are remarkably similar, but the differences, both small and large, invariably cause students difficulties in understanding and speaking. The most evident contrasts exist between the two vowel systems.

Speaking of the English vowel system Delattre states:

Comparatively, English vowels are predominantly low, back, unrounded, with a strong tendency to center the short and unstressed (except when very low). Duration contributes to vowel distinctions. All English vowels are more or less diphthongized. Most characteristic series: the somewhat back-unrounded /u, ʊ, ə, ʌ/.

. . . Comparatively, German vowels are predominantly high, fronted, rounded, more extreme than English . . . Differences of duration play an important role in vowel distinction (more than in English). For every long vowel except /ɑ/ there is a corresponding one which is more open. There is no diphthongization, not even in long, close /e/ and long, close /o/. Most characteristic series: the front rounded /y, Y, ø, œ/.[6]

Although Delattre does not note the tense/lax distinction which is an important characteristic of the German vowel system (to be treated later in this chapter), his observations point to areas of difficulty in learning German sounds. For English speakers, cultivating a forward position of the tongue and a strong rounding of the lips to which they are not accustomed and producing vowels which are not diphthongized but which vary significantly in duration and articulation will pose particular problems.

It is lack of realization of basic contrastive differences such as these which result in a marked "foreign accent" as the student tries to make a few new sounds and fit them into his native-language phonological system. The teacher will not explain these differences to his students in scientific terms, except to an interested adult group, but he will need to understand them himself if he is to help his students form correct German sounds. Slight distinctions in sound which can hinder comprehension of a message are made by movements of the tongue and other organs in the teacher's mouth and throat which the students cannot normally see. Consequently, merely making German sounds which are different from English sounds and urging students to imitate these, without giving some indication as to how they can be produced, may not be sufficient to ensure accurate production by the students. This is the case particularly when a specific sound does not exist in English, as with [y] and the German [R], or when the German sound varies in some significant way from a familiar English sound, as does the German [l].

Articulatory descriptions and empirical recommendations

Articulatory descriptions for the production of a particular sound, using terms like those in the previous section, are useful for the preparation of the teacher. They make clear to young teachers what they themselves have been doing, perhaps intuitively rather than consciously, in the pronunciation of German. They highlight the types of articulatory difficulties English speakers may be expected to encounter. The teacher does not usually give such descriptions to the students at the introductory stage (although they may be helpful for remedial work and of interest to older students or to students learning a third language). Instead, from their knowledge of the articulatory data,[7] teachers develop empirical recommendations to help their students produce sounds they do not seem to acquire easily by imitation.[8] (This subject is discussed in more detail below under *Remedial Training,* p. 155.)

TEACHING A GERMAN [R]

We may take as an example a sound which often proves difficult for speakers of English, the German uvular [R]. (The apical [r], which presents fewer learning problems, has been gradually replaced in many regions of Germany by [R] and is thus taught more and more rarely in the classroom.) In teaching students to produce the [R], we must first consider the student's native language *r.*

Prator's advice for the production of an American r is as follows:

S1 "Pronounce the vowel /a/. As you do so, curve the tip of your tongue up and slide the sides of the tongue backward along the tooth ridge, and you should have no difficulty in producing a perfect American /r/."[9]

Armstrong describes the production of the British English fricative r, usually transcribed [ɹ], as follows:

"1. The tip of the tongue is raised to the back part of the teeth-ridge.
2. The passage is narrowed at that point, but not sufficiently to cause much friction.
3. The sound is voiced."[10]

The production of the German [R] on the other hand, is described in the following manner by Hans-Heinrich Wängler:

S2 "Der Mund is geöffnet. . . . Die Zungenspitze berührt die Unterzahnreihe, der hintere Teil des Zungenrückens wölbt sich gegen das Velum auf, das seinerseits dem stimmhaften Phonationsstrom den Weg zur Nase versperrt. Der Phonationsstrom passiert die orale postdorsal-velare Enge und bringt die Uvula dazu, gegen den hinteren Teil des Zungenrückens zu flattern."[11]

From these three descriptions it seems clear that the first step for an English speaker learning to pronounce a German [R] is to keep the tip of the tongue down behind the lower teeth. This prevents him from making either kind of English r described above and forces him to use other organs in the production of the German r. This simple, essential fact is rarely explained to the student. With the tip of the tongue accounted for, the student may then proceed as recommended by Moulton:

S3 ". . . say to the student: 'Tip your head back and enjoy a good dry gargle.' This may seem to be a peculiar way of putting things, but it is sound phonetic advice. In gargling, the back of the tongue is raised close to the uvula and the back of the velum. . . ."[12]

Other ways of teaching a German [R] have been suggested, but in all cases the tongue must be kept behind the lower teeth, with tip lowered to give the tongue the convex fronted shape required for the German [R].

S4 The student may begin, for instance, with [x] as in *Bach* (the [x] rarely poses great difficulties even though it may be a new sound to beginning students). In forming the [x] the student is forced to raise the back of his tongue and also to bring his vocal cords into a position for voicing. He should then be told to produce the same sound as far back in his mouth as possible and to add voicing. Once he has found the sound he will no longer need to start with [x].

In neither S3 nor S4 is any articulatory description given to the students but the correct articulatory positions are induced through the production of familiar movements which lead to the unfamiliar movement desired. These are, then, empirical recommendations.

* From your knowledge of English and German articulatory movements, work out in similar fashion empirical recommendations for inducing students to make correct [y] and [ç] sounds.

Teaching German sounds as a system

Teachers often concentrate on correct articulatory production of those distinctive German sounds which do not exist in English (the so-called "difficult" sounds), while allowing students to produce English near-equivalents for the rest. Unfortunately, incorrectly articulated consonants affect the production of vowels just as incorrect vowel production affects the contiguous consonants.

EFFECT OF INCORRECT PRODUCTION OF FINAL *l*

Many students do not realize that in English they are using two *l*'s: the so-called *clear l,* as in *leaf* and *lack,* which is different from the so-called *dark l* of *bull, fell,* or *table.* The *l* used in initial positions in English is not very different from the German *l.* In English the initial *l* is produced by the tip of the tongue touching the tooth ridge, whereas in German the *l* used in all positions is produced with the tip of the tongue down against the upper (sometimes lower) teeth. This new position should be practiced. When, however, the student unwittingly uses an English *dark l* in final position in German he distorts and tends to diphthongize and to lower vowels like [ɛ] in *hell* and [I] in *still* because the general tongue position for the English *final l* is close to the position of [U] as in *pull.* The efforts the teacher has made to teach students to pronounce correctly [ɛ] and [I] are thus negated by failure to teach the correct pronunciation of [l].

THE TENSE AND LAX VOWELS

The German vowel system tends to cause students persistent problems throughout the process of learning the language. The difficulty arises in

part because fourteen of the nineteen vowel sounds of German are introduced to students as seven pairs of long and short vowels. The terms
"long" and "short" mislead English-speaking students to think of the
differences between the members of the pairs in terms of duration only, or
to equate the German vowels too closely to those of English and to think
of length as diphthongization.

Much confusion can be avoided by making it clear from the very beginning that the most important considerations regarding the seven pairs
of vowels are the positions where they are formed in the mouth (high-mid-
low and front-central-back) and the amount of muscular activity involved
in forming the sounds (tense versus lax). The German vowels formed
in a relatively central position in the mouth require less muscular effort
and are therefore designated "lax" (instead of "short"), whereas the relatively decentralized vowels requiring more muscular effort are "tense"
(instead of "long"):

> lax   [a, ɛ, I, ɔ, U, Y, œ];
> tense [ɑ, e, i, o, u, y, ø].

It is true, of course, that tense vowels are longer than lax vowels when
both are in stressed position, but when unstressed the tense vowels are
short in duration while still retaining their distinctive qualities. Compare
Typ [ty:p] to *Typographie* [typogʀafˈiː] and *Los* [loːs] to *zeitlos*
[ˈtsaItlos]. The exception is the pair [a, ɑ] which cannot be distinguished
in unstressed position, e.g., *achtsam* [ˈaxtzɑm], although in relaxed speech
the distinction may disappear in other cases as well.[13]

✱ The above discussion of the differences between the English and German
  sound systems is illustrative only and by no means exhaustive. Be sure you
  are aware of and able to help students with other problems, such as the
  aspiration of the final consonants *p, t, k;* the difference in pronunciation
  between English and German consonant clusters as in stool and *Stuhl,*
  spring and *springen,* knee and *Knee;* the maintenance in German of vowel
  contrasts before *r* as in senator/*Senator;* juncture and glottal stops; differences in stress and in patterns of intonation.[14]

Aural discrimination

Students confronted with strange sounds will at first tend to perceive them
as variants of the categories of sounds with which they are familiar in their
native language. If this continues, it will, of course, affect comprehension,
and it will also hinder the development of a near-native pronunciation. The
student who is not aware of the existence of certain distinctions of sounds
is unlikely to produce these correctly, except by chance on random occasions. When he is able to "hear" the differences, that is, discriminate

between sounds aurally, he can work toward perfecting these distinctions in his own production.

German sounds which have no counterparts in English will at first be difficult for English speakers to distinguish. They will not perceive the difference between *würden* [vYʁdən] and *wurden* [vUʁdən] of between *lügen* [ly:gən] and *lugen* [lu:gən]. In fact, inexperienced English-speaking students tend to identify German [Y] and [y] with English [U] as in *soot* or more likely with English [u] as in *too,* a sound similar but not exactly equivalent to German [u]. If they do hear a difference, they may associate German [Y] and [y] with the English phoneme [i] as in *feet*. They will also fail to hear the difference between [x] as in *Loch* and [ç] as in *ich,* since neither occurs in English; to the naive speaker both sounds may resemble the [k] in *lock.*

German sounds for which there are *apparently similar sounds in English* may pose problems as great, or even greater, than those for which there are no corresponding sounds in English. Students will tend to hear the German [ɑ] of *Staat* and the German [a] of *Stadt* as the English [a] in *father*. Although they may be aware that similar vowel oppositions exist in English (except in the case of Eng. [a]), they will be confused by the tense and lax vowels in German simply because the latter are never exactly equivalent to their English counterparts. Even sounds existing in both languages may not be recognized by the English speaker when they occur in unfamiliar positions or combinations in German. Thus the untrained English ear will be likely to mistake German [ts] as in *zu* [tsu:] for [z] and [pf] as in *Pfeil* [pfaIl] for [f].

AURAL DISCRIMINATION PROBLEMS

Exercises may be designed to help students discriminate sounds which are causing them difficulty, once the kind of problem involved has been identified. Particular German sounds should be differentiated both from closely related German sounds and from English sounds that may be interfering with the student's perception.

Just how much difficulty a particular English-speaking student may have in distinguishing one sound of German from others depends on a number of factors, such as his individual sensitivity to distinctions of sound, the pronunciation of the teacher, and how carefully the student happens to be listening on that day. As a rule, the students are first taught to discriminate a problem sound from a similar sound in German, or from an interfering sound in English. If the students' inability to distinguish the sound persists because of confusions with other sounds, then the number of discrimination exercises is increased to cope with this complexity. Problem areas in German which involve one or more discriminations are illustrated in examples S5–9. In the diagrams accompanying these examples, the sounds to be discriminated are connected by arrows. The various discriminations involved in each example are numbered.

1. A simple German-English discrimination.

S5 Ger. [ɔ]   Eng. [ɔ]
(1)

Problem: The student must learn to discriminate the German lax mid back [ɔ] of *Tonne* from the English lax low back [ɔ] of *tawny*.

2. Distinguishing a German sound from two English interfering sounds.

S6

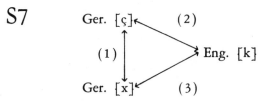

Problem: The student must learn to discriminate the German [e] of *geht* from the English [ei] of *say* and the English [e] of *gate*.

3. Distinguishing two German sounds which do not exist in English from an English sound to which the student tends to assimilate them.

S7

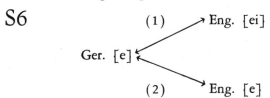

Problem: The student must learn to discriminate the German [ç] of *ich* from the [x] of *ach* and not to confuse either German sound with the English [k] of *ache*.

4. Distinguishing two German sounds from each other and from two interfering English sounds.

S8

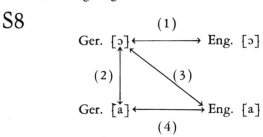

Problem: The student who continues to have difficulty recognizing the German [ɔ] must learn not only to discriminate between the German [ɔ] of *Tonne* and the English [ɔ] of *tawny* but also to distinguish the German [ɔ] from the German [a] of *Tanne* and both these German sounds from the English [a] of *tot*.

5. Distinguishing three German sounds from each other and from an interfering English sound.

S9

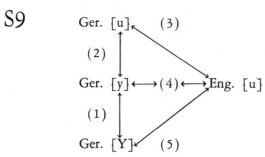

Problem: The student must learn to discriminate the German [Y] of *Flüsse* from the German [y] of *Füße* and the latter from the [u] of *Fuß;* he must also learn that none of these is identical with the English [u] of *food*.

✱ Show diagrammatically the discrimination problems an English speaker can encounter in understanding *Finger* or in learning to distinguish *bitte* and *bitter; Zehen* and *sehen; Betten, beten* and *bäten*.

TYPES OF AURAL DISCRIMINATION EXERCISES

These exercises are necessary only when discrimination problems become evident. Often they serve remedial purposes. Which types of exercises and how many are used at one time and how these are interspersed with production exercises will vary according to the needs of a particular group of students at a particular time. Usually, after some aural discrimination exercises, students will be encouraged to produce the sounds themselves to demonstrate what they have observed. If confusions are still evident, more aural discrimination exercises may be tried.

The sounds [ø] and [œ], which are easily confused by English speakers, will be used for demonstration purposes in the following examples. These sounds may be identified and practiced separately, discriminated from each other and from interfering English sounds (e.g., Ger. *Öl* and Eng. *earl*), and finally produced in close proximity (*schöne Töchter, größere Dörfer*).

Type 1: Identification of the sound, e.g., [ø]
The sound will have been encountered in dialogue or conversational narrative, or in oral work in the classroom, in an utterance like: *Danke schön, Hans,* or *Das ist nicht nötig.*

1. The sound in a familiar context.

S10 Listen carefully to these sentences:

a. Danke schön, Hans.
b. Danke schön, Hans.
c. Danke schön, Herr Fischer.

2. The sound in single words.

S11 Listen again to the sound [ø] in the following words:

d. schön, böse, hören

3. The sound in a larger context.

S12 How many times do you hear the sound [ø] in the following sentences?

e. Danke schön, Herbert.
f. Hans ist größer als seine Brüder.
g. Mögen Sie dieses Möbelstück?

Type 2: Minimal pair technique
1. Discrimination between similar sounds in German and English.

S13 Listen to the difference between the German [ø] and the English [ɜ].

a. Öl / earl
b. hör' / her
c. böser / bursar

2. Discrimination between similar sounds within the German phonological system.

S14 The sound [ø] is not the same as [œ]. Listen carefully to the difference between the following pairs:

d. Höhle / Hölle
e. Schöße / schösse
f. Öfen / öffnen

   g. Goethe / Götter
   h. Es ist eine Höhle / Es ist eine Hölle

Type 3: Same-different exercises

   Listen carefully to the vowel sounds in these pairs of words and tell me
   (or: mark on your answer sheet) if the two vowel sounds are the same or
   different.

       1. German/English

S15 (For ø/ɜ):   a. *Höhle, Höhle*   (same)
                  b. *blöd,* blurt   (different)
                  c. earl, earl   (same)

S16 (For œ/ɜ):   d. *dörrt,* dirt   (different)
                  e. *Hölle, Hölle*   (same)
                  f. Burl, *Böll*   (different)

       2. German/German

S17 (For ø/œ):   g. schön, schön   (same)
                  h. Höhle, Hölle   (different)
                  i. dörrt, dörrt   (same)
                  j. schösse, Schöße (different)

S18 k. In der Höhle, in der Hölle   (different)
     l. Er hört die Töne, er hört die Töne (same)

   With German/German discriminations it is possible to use larger contexts than single words as long as the only difference in sound is the change
   of vowel.

Type 4: Differentiation exercises

   You will hear three sounds numbered 1, 2, and 3. Write down (or: tell me)
   the number of the one which is different from the others.

       1. German/English

S19 (For ø/ɜ):   a. 1. earl   2. *Öl*   3. earl   (2)
                  b. 1. *blöd*   2. *blöd*   3. blurt   (3)

S20 (For œ/ɜ):   c. 1. *Götter* 2. *Götter* 3. girder (3)
                  d. 1. dirt   2. *dörrt*   3. dirt   (2)

2. German/German

S21 (For œ/ø): e. 1. Götter   2. Goethe   3. Goethe   (1)
f. 1. In der Höhle 2. In der Höhle 3. In der Hölle (3)

S22 *Variation.*

In the following groups of words, one does not have the same vowel sound as the others. Make a check mark for each word as you hear it, crossing the one which has a different vowel sound from the others:

g. Töne, Möbel, Ströme, Söhne, *Stöcke*
h. er gönnte, er könnte, *er hörte,* er öffnete, er röstete

Type 5: Rhyming exercise (combining aural discrimination and production)

S23 Listen to the following word and give me as many words as you can think of which rhyme with it:

TEACHER   Flöße
STUDENTS Blöße, Größe, Stöße, ~~schösse, genösse,~~ Schöße, Klöße

✳ Construct items similar to those in Types 2, 3, and 4 of this section to help students discriminate:

1. German [y] from German [Y], and both of these from English [u];
2. German [o] from German [ɔ], and both of these from English [o].

Production
INTRODUCTION OF THE GERMAN SOUND SYSTEM

Should the learning of a language begin with a series of lessons on the sound system? This is the approach of some textbooks. Sometimes, when this is done, little attention is paid to the usefulness of the words in which the sounds are produced or whether they will be used in classwork in the early lessons. In a quick check of several older textbooks the following words were found for practice: *Aas, Baal, Bö, Dachs, glitzern, Laich, Löß, Knolle, Kutte, Reeder,* none of which appear in Pfeffer's *Basic (Spoken) German Dictionary for Everyday Usage*[15] and one of which does not even occur in Wahrig's *Deutsches Wörterbuch.* In presenting minimal pairs (which are admittedly difficult to find in some cases), textbooks frequently resort to far too many words which are even more specialized than those listed above. This approach may be acceptable for highly motivated adult learners to whom the rationale of the teaching has been explained, but it is unwise for elementary, junior high school, or senior high school classes. It can become boring and its relevance is not understood by the students, who are anxious to be able to say something practical in German.

In the early lessons, the students can be introduced to the whole array of German sounds which they try to repeat after the teacher, before being drilled carefully in particular problems of pronunciation. Sentences like the following are frequently the first the student learns: *Guten Tag, Inge. Wie geht's?* [guːtən tɑk Iŋə viː geːts]. These five words contain thirteen different sounds, of which only three, [g, t, ə], are repeated and less than half pose no problem at all for English speakers. A normal reply: *Sehr gut, danke. Und dir?* [zeːʁ guːt dankə Unt diːʁ] introduces four more, making a total of seventeen distinct sounds. This shows the impracticality of trying to keep early material within the limits of certain sounds, if natural, usable utterances are to be learned. Sentences such as *Oh, oh, ich sehe dich doch noch nicht auf dem Podium stehen* which are artificially constructed to introduce only one or two sounds at a time may have some place in laboratory drill, particularly of a remedial nature, but their utility is limited in developing conversational interchange. Tongue-twisters like *Ob er über Oberammergau oder aber über Unterammergau kommt, ist ungewiß,* for practicing initial vowels, may be used for relaxation in the classroom and to focus attention on a particular problem. Repetition of such concentrated conglomerations of one sound gives some practice in the correct articulation of the sound. This, of itself, does not ensure equally successful transfer to utterances where the sound is more sparsely distributed. The sound will need to be practiced in many contexts if it is to reappear correctly articulated in spontaneous utterances.

EARLY TEACHING OF THE SOUND SYSTEM

Language learning usually begins either with the simple dialogue, useful expressions for classroom interchange, or a conversational narrative in the textbook. As the student listens to the teacher or model, his ear becomes attuned to the overall system of sounds of the language and its characteristic rhythm (*Rhythmus*), stress (*Akzent*), and intonation or melodic patterns (*Satzintonation, Satzmelodie*). *Approximations to correct pronunciation* are sought in everything the student reproduces, without insistence on perfection at every point since this is too discouraging for the students at this early stage.

Problem sounds are singled out at intervals in the first few weeks and practiced, with attention to acceptable and comprehensible production.

1. The teacher begins with *short phrases* from current work, then, if necessary, isolates *specific words,* gives practice in *a specific sound,* returns to the practice of *words* and then to *the complete phrase,* moving, e.g.,

from *sehr gut, danke* to *sehr gut,* to *sehr* (and if absolutely necessary to [e], then rebuilding to *sehr, sehr gut,* and finally *sehr gut, danke.*

Students may be asked to produce the sound in isolation a few times if they are having trouble with it, but not for long. Most sounds are rarely heard in isolation, and students must become accustomed to the slight variations which occur when sounds are made in association with other sounds.

2. Where possible, the sound is practiced in *stressed* position (*betont*) then in *unstressed* position (*unbetont*). Students should thus learn that tense vowels in unstressed position retain full quality, even when shorter in length (except for [ɑ]).

S24 a. *Stressed*   *Unstressed*
Stoff   Bischof
in dem Staat   auf dem Sofa

Vowels other than [ə] in unstressed position occur most frequently in foreign words; in such cases contrasting German to English can often clarify significant differences.

b. zwei min*u*s eins   two min*u*s one   (unstressed)
er ist phil*o*s*o*phisch   he is phil*o*s*o*phical   (unstressed/stressed)

3. When the teacher senses that students would profit from intensive practice in specific pronunciation problems, the training should move from *identification* of the sound (associated with aural discrimination of similar sounds, when necessary, as in S6–19), to *imitative production.* When imitative production is well advanced, the practice moves to *guided non-imitative production* (where the exercise is so structured that the student is induced to produce the sound without first hearing the model). The goal must be *autonomous production* of the correct sound in non-structured contexts.

During intensive training in the production of a certain sound, it is helpful for the student to hear a correct model after he has produced the sound himself. He needs to be sensitized to the differences between his own production and the desired pronunciation if he is to improve in unsupervised practice. Where his own production has been faulty he should correct it immediately, while he still retains the auditory image of the model. (The four-phase format of G9 is often employed for this reason.)

STAGES OF INTENSIVE PRACTICE

1. Identification: Student listens.

S25 MODEL   In die Schule . . . die Schule . . . in die Schule . . . die Schule . . . die Schule . . . in die Schule.

2. Imitative production.

S26   MODEL   In die Schule.
       STUDENT   In die Schule.
       MODEL   In die Schule.
       Student repeats after the model to correct his production or confirm it.

A similar four-phase format continues while the student imitates *die Schule, Schule, die Schule, in die Schule,* thus practicing the sound in reduced contexts and then producing it once more in the larger context.

The practice moves on to such expressions as:

S27   Das ist meine Schule; Ist das Ihre Schule?
      Ich gehe zur Planck-Schule; Zu welcher Schule gehen Sie?
      Meine Schule ist nicht weit von hier; Wo ist deine Schule?

3. Guided non-imitative production.

S28   TEACHER   Zu welcher Schule gehen Sie?
      STUDENT   Ich gehe zur Planck-Schule.

      TEACHER   Die Planck-Schule? Ist das deine Schule?
      STUDENT   Nein, das ist nicht meine Schule.

      TEACHER   Fragen Sie Hanno, zu welcher Schule er geht.
      STUDENT   Hanno, zu welcher Schule gehst du?

4. Autonomous production.

S29   An interchange takes place between students, with the students themselves selecting the way they will ask the questions or answer them.

Wo ist deine Schule?
      Meine Schule ist in der Theaterstraße.

Zu welcher Schule gehst du?
      Zu der Planck-Schule hier in der Nähe.

Welche Schule ist auf deinem Heimweg?
      Eine Volksschule ist nicht weit von unserer Wohnung.

Die Planck-Schule? Ist das deine Schule?
      Nein, das ist nicht meine Schule.

Wo ist deine Wohnung?
>Nicht weit von der Volksschule.

In welcher Straße ist die Schule von Hans?
>Er besucht die gleiche Schule wie ich.
>*or:* Das weiß ich nicht.

If the interchange is truly autonomous, students will occasionally produce sentences which do not contain the sound being practiced.

In the early lessons it is not only particular sounds which are practiced, but also juncture and glottal stops. (Make sure you are familiar with contemporary usage in these areas.[16])

What degree of perfection should be expected in the early stages?

Practice should concentrate on errors of pronunciation which would hinder comprehension, e.g., [Iç fY:lə mIç vo:l] for *ich fühle mich wohl,* and errors which force students into other errors (like those discussed above under *Teaching German Sounds as a System*). The teacher will need to return again and again, in an unobtrusive fashion, to certain persistent faults which are crucial to comprehension or acceptability, while continuing to improve the overall standard of pronunciation.

Remedial training

A distinction must be drawn between the types of exercises suitable in the very early stages, when the student knows only a little of the foreign language and appropriate exercises for remedial training at a later stage. At first, emphasis is laid on phonemic distinctions which hinder comprehension. Later, advanced students often need intensive practice in the production of certain problem sounds or sequences of sounds to correct a "foreign accent."

Remedial work at an advanced level usually takes the form of a *systematic review of the German sound system.* At this stage, students have a wide-ranging vocabulary and considerable knowledge of grammatical structure. After a certain number of retraining drills (see S35–38), exercises can be used which exploit the students' knowledge of the language, eliciting from them the sounds being reviewed while they are concentrating on grammatical conversions and manipulations (see S39).

REMEDIAL PRODUCTION EXERCISES

Exercises of this type are usually constructed on a contrastive basis, highlighting problems of interference from English sounds which are close to the German sounds being practiced, and from other German sounds which to an English ear appear similar to the particular sound to be produced (see S5–9). The remedial exercises in production may be preceded by *aural identification exercises* in which the sound is used in short utterances which are meaningful.

1. Remedial production exercises are frequently preceded by *articulatory instructions* for the correct production of the sound, with warnings about English habits which interfere with correct articulation. These are sometimes accompanied by photographs or diagrams showing the recommended position of the speech organs. (Articulatory information, can, of course, be supplied without the use of technical terms. In the instructions below, *alveolar* and *aspirated* can be omitted and the explanations of these terms used instead.)

In general, German consonants (other than [ç, R, l]) cause less serious difficulties to students than the German vowel system. Nevertheless certain aspects of consonant production will require some attention.

S30 *Articulatory instructions for the production of a German final* [t]

German [t] is an *alveolar stop,* i.e., the breath stream is stopped briefly as the tip of the tongue touches the alveolar ridge. The English [t] is formed similarly, and in both languages the [t] is strongly *aspirated* (that is, a puff of air is emitted when the air flow is released) initially and medially before a stressed syllable. In German, however, the [t] is also sometimes aspirated in medial position and almost always in final position, whereas in English the [t] is usually *unaspirated* and may even be unreleased in both positions.

These articulatory instructions are often accompanied by *empirical recommendations* for achieving the correct articulation or for testing whether the sound is being correctly produced.

S31 *Empirical recommendations: German* [t]—*English* [t]

Hold a piece of paper (or a lighted match) in front of your mouth as you say English *top* and notice how the paper (or flame) is blown by the puff of air emitted with the [t]. Now say *colt* and notice that the paper moves very little. Finally, practice saying *Tag* and *kalt,* making sure that the paper moves appreciably after [t] in both cases.

S32 *Articulatory instructions for the production of German* [y]

German [y] is a high front, rounded tense vowel. The tongue is arched high in the front of the mouth, not quite so far forward as for [i], but higher and farther forward than for [Y]. The lips are rounded. The vowel is tense and not diphthongized, that is, it does not have the glide of English [u] or [iu].

S33 *Empirical recommendations: German* [y]

1. Some books recommend that the student put his mouth into a correct position for whistling and then try to say [i] without unrounding his lips. (The whistling position moves the tongue into the high front position with tongue firmly against the lower teeth which is essential for the production of [y]. It also requires tense muscular control.) If students do not know how to whistle they may be told to round their lips firmly and thrust them forward while pressing the tongue tip against the lower teeth.

2. Other books recommend taking the mouth position for German [i] with lips stretched as for a wide smile and then, without moving the tongue, rounding the lips and saying [y]. Rapidly moving from [i] to [y] to [i] to [y] makes the student conscious of the tenseness of these two vowels and the similar tongue position. If the tongue or lips are relaxed in the switch from [i] to [y] the student will tend to produce English [u] which has an element of glide in it.

Note: Students may be able to produce an acceptable [y] in isolation but fail to do so when it follows a consonant. This is because they are not aware of the characteristic *vowel anticipation* in German, which means that the mouth must have already taken the rounded or unrounded position of the vowel when articulating the preceding consonant. Contrast *riechen* with unrounded lips for [R], and *rühren* with rounded lips for [R]. For this reason it is essential to practice German vowels with preceding consonants. (This contrasts with the characteristic consonant anticipation of English which, if transferred to German, tends to diphthongization of vowels as the mouth position changes in mid-vowel.)

2. Production exercises *should not begin with the sound in isolation.* This is useful only when articulatory movements are being practiced. No German phoneme occurs normally in isolation, except in a few exclamations and tags, e.g., *ah! oh! eh!* The various relationships into which a sound enters modify it slightly and it is these natural sequences which must be learned. Production exercises begin, then, with the *sound in single words or short phrases* which demonstrate the various environments in which it can occur. For instance a consonant may be practiced in initial, medial, and final positions and in association with certain other consonants; a vowel

may be practiced in stressed and unstressed position, and after or preceding certain consonants. This is the stage of *imitative production.* The words in which the sounds are practiced should be words which students can use, rather than nonsense words.

S34 *Relationships in which the consonant* [t] *may occur*

a. Tal, teuer, Tier, Thema, Töpfe (*initial* followed by various vowels)
b. trotz, Tscheche, Zug; Stil, Straße, Szene (in *initial consonant clusters*)
c. Atom, Auto, etwa, natürlich; bitte, sollte, wartet, Winter (*medial* in various relationships)
d. Bad, Boot, nett, Tod, Zeit (*final* preceded by various vowels)
e. deutsch, echt, hart, oft, Pfund, Welt; Blitz; Arzt (in *final consonant clusters*)

S35 *The vowel* [y] *in various positions*

a. Bühne, Duisburg, üben, typisch, Menü (stressed)
b. Mythologie, dynamisch, demütig (unstressed)

The above examples also provide practice in pronouncing [y] in various environments.

3. The sound is then practiced in short sentences, also in various environments and intonation patterns. This is still imitative production.

S36 *The consonant* [t] *in short sentences in various environments*

a. Eine Tasse Tee? Bitte.
b. Er fährt mit dem Zug.
c. Sie ist Deutsche.
d. Sprichst du Tschechisch?
e. Es tut mir leid.

4. Remedial exercises often *practice two similar sounds at the same time* in order to highlight auditory and kinesthetic differences, since it is oppositions and contrasts within the sound system which make a language meaningful.

S37 *Vowel contrasts* are demonstrated in such pairs as:

a. sie tritt auf die Bühne: sie tritt auf die Biene;
b. die Spülmaschine läuft: die Spulmaschine läuft;
c. sie besitzt Güte: sie besitzt Goethe.

S38 *Difference in voicing* distinguishes the meaning of the following pairs:

   a. die Gasse: die Kasse;
   b. er leidet gern: er leitet gern.

   5. Exercises are next introduced which, through some form of grammatical manipulation, force the student to *produce the sound unmodeled.* This is guided non-imitative production.

S39 *Vowel production*

   1. A change of *die Kuh* from the singular to the plural forces the student to produce the sound [y] in *die Kühe,* while concentrating on the grammatical manipulation he is asked to perform.
   2. A change from the present tense *ich mag* to the subjunctive form *ich möchte* forces the student to produce [œ] and [ç] in combination.

   6. The sound is then practiced in *longer utterances,* in mixed environments, or in sections of discourse. In this way the effects of proximity to other sounds in characteristic sequences, and the influence of intonation, stress, and juncture are more fully experienced. This practice need not be purely repetitive and imitative. It can take the form of a question-answer series, so designed as to induce the student to produce certain sounds.

S40 *The vowel* [y]

   a. Sind Sie m*ü*de nach dem langen Schultag?
      Nein, m*ü*de bin ich nicht, nur schläfrig.

   b. War das Wetter k*ü*hl *ü*ber das Wochenende?
      Ja, es war k*ü*hl über das Wochenende.

   c. Was haben Sie heute zu Fr*ü*hstück gegessen?
      Ich habe gar nicht gefr*ü*hstückt.

   In application practice of this type, there is no need to concoct sentences loaded with a particular sound like: Es gr*ü*nt so gr*ü*n, wenn Spaniens Bl*ü*ten bl*ü*hen. Such artificiality makes the student over-conscious of what the exercise demands of him and the resulting production is no real indication of what he will produce autonomously.

   7. Sounds may finally be practiced *in a formal context* such as the reading of *poetry or literary prose,* since much of the language in earlier exercises will have been informal. It is important that students learn the differences between the formal and informal styles of spoken German.

If a passage is read after a model, this is merely imitative production. If it is later read by the student alone, this is guided non-imitative production.

8. There is a place for some *anticipation practice*. The student reads each section first before hearing it read by a model. He then has the opportunity to reread this section and continue reading the next section before again hearing the model. This can be done as spaced reading on tape, provided that the natural pauses between word groupings are as obvious as in the following passage of simple conversation.

S41 [o – ɔ] *contrasts*

STUDENT	Vor einem Monat bin ich von Ostfriesen weggefahren.
MODEL	Vor einem Monat bin ich von Ostfriesen weggefahren.
STUDENT	Vor einem Monat bin ich von Ostfriesen weggefahren, sagte Herr Hofe.
MODEL	. . . sagte Herr Hofe.
STUDENT	. . . sagte Herr Hofe. Jetzt habe ich nur noch eine Woche Sommerferien.
MODEL	Jetzt habe ich nur noch eine Woche Sommerferien.
STUDENT	Jetzt habe ich nur noch eine Woche Sommerferien. Doch wollte ich meine Oma in Oberwalden besuchen.

9. The goal of this type of remedial practice is for the student to demonstrate control of the sound he has been practicing when he is engaged in autonomous production in conversation.

✱ *Questions to discuss* in class or with other teachers.

1. Should remedial production exercises be conducted with book open or with book closed? (What has been your own experience?)

2. Why do you think proverbs and short verses, like the ones in S42, are often used for pronunciation practice?

S42 a. Leben ohne denken
ist Dürsten ohne Schenken.

b. Einer acht's,
der andre veracht's,
der dritte verlacht's,
was macht's? [17]

3. How would you help a student correct the following faults: pronouncing initial [ts] like [z]; pronouncing *Staat* the same as *Stadt;* pronouncing *schlüpfen* as though it rhymed with *schöpfen;* failing to put

strong stress on the separable prefix of a verb (e.g., *eingéhen* instead of *éingehen*)?

* *Find some short poems* which would be useful for practicing certain types of sounds. They must be attractive and simple in content, with vocabulary and structures appropriate for the level at which you propose to use them. A certain amount of repetition of lines, or segments of lines, will make them more useful, particularly if this involves alliteration of a feature to be practiced or assonance involving vowels requiring special attention. Short lines are an advantage if you wish the poem to be memorized.

STIMULATING INTEREST IN REMEDIAL PRONUNCIATION PRACTICE

If students need corrective training but have become bored with the usual sound production exercises, this remedial work can be associated with the study of the *International Phonetic Alphabet* (IPA) as applied to German. As students concentrate on learning which sounds are represented by which symbols and as they endeavor to write down dictated passages in phonetic symbols, they become more sensitive to fine distinctions of sound. The reading aloud of passages in phonetic symbols can be a useful remedial production exercise. The transcribing of passages in IPA into normal written German draws the students' attention to the relationships between the German sound and spelling systems (a study for which the term *Orthoepie* is used). These new intellectual interests often stimulate motivation to improve pronunciation where "more pronunciation exercises" would fail.

Similarly the organization of a poetry recitation competition, the production of some short one-act plays by different groups for a festival or an inter-school social gathering, or the exchange of letter-tapes with German, Swiss, or Austrian correspondents will make students conscious of the need to improve their pronunciation and intonation.

MONITORING ONE'S OWN PRODUCTION

When working with tapes on their own, students have difficulty in detecting their errors of pronunciation. Aural discrimination exercises help the students to refine their ability to perceive distinctions.

To make them more conscious of these distinctions in their own production, students may be asked to read on to tape a series of aural discrimination exercises of Types 3 and 4 (S15–21) and then, later, to use this recording as an exercise, comparing their final discrimination decisions with the original script from which they recorded the exercise.

Students can be encouraged to evaluate their progress in perfecting their pronunciation by marking their weaknesses and their successes on a *pronunciation checklist* (S43).

1. When *working with tapes,* students should keep the checklist beside them as a guide to the features of the German sound system to which they should be attentive.

2. If the practice session is monitored, students should mark on the checklist the weaknesses in pronunciation which the monitor has drawn to their attention, so that they may concentrate on improving their production of these features.

3. The monitor should keep a cumulative record on a pronunciation checklist for each student, so that at each session he may refresh his memory of the weaknesses he has already drawn to the attention of the particular student to whom he is listening. In this way he will be able to emphasize some faults at one session and others at another, thus making maximum use of the short time at his disposal.

4. If pronunciation tapes are checked from time to time by the teacher, comments may be entered on a duplicate pronunciation checklist for the student's consideration when recording.

S43 *Sample Pronunciation Checklist*

Features for Attention	Estimate of Quality (E, A, or U)*	Monitor's Comments or Personal Notes on Progress
General Features		
1. Tense muscular control		
2. Vigorous lip and facial movement (rounding, unrounding, opening)		
Vowels		
3. Purity of vowels (no diphthongization)		
4. [ɑ/a]† distinction		
5. [e/ɛ] distinction		
6. [i/I] distinction		
7. [o/ɔ] distinction		
8. [u/U] distinction		
9. [ø/œ] distinction		
10. [y/Y] distinction		
11. [ə/əʀ] distinction		

Features for Attention	Estimate of Quality (E, A, or U)*	Monitor's Comments or Personal Notes on Progress
Consonants		
12. [l]		
13. [R]		
14. [ç/x] distinction		
15. nasal [ŋ]		
16. clusters such as [ʃp, ʃt, pf, kn]; initial [ts]		
17. medial [t]		
18. final aspirated [p, t, k]		
Intonation		
19. Short statement		
20. Long statement		
21. Yes-no question		
22. Information question		
23. Exclamations and interjections		
General Fluency		
24. Word stress, especially in compounds and verbs with prefixes		
25. Open and close juncture (and glottal stops)		
26. Grouping of words		
Orthographic Recognition		
27. [ɔI] (spelled *äu*)		
28. [aI/i] distinction (spelled *ei* and *ie*)		
29. Unvoicing of final *b, d, g* (as in *Feld, lieb, klug*)		
30. [z] (spelled *s*)		
31. [v] (spelled *w*)		
32. [j] (spelled *j*)		

* E = Excellent (near-native); A = Acceptable (but not yet perfect); U = Unacceptable (needs attention).

† / indicates that sounds must not be confused in pronunciation, e.g., [ç/x].

* Use this checklist to evaluate a recording of your own speech in German. You will have to ask another student, a fellow teacher, or your instructor to evaluate points 1 and 2 for you by watching you. Later, discuss in class how the list can be improved. Is it too long for practical use? Could certain categories be evaluated together?

* Sometimes teachers (and students) use, for initial or final evaluation of pronunciation, a recording of a passage such as the following which was specially written to include most of the features in the sample checklist. Try to evaluate a recording of this passage by one of your fellow students.

S44 Evaluation passage

Study the following passage carefully for three minutes to see that you understand the development of the dialogue, but do not make any marks on the paper. Read the passage clearly and expressively into the microphone with your tape recorder set at Record. Do not read the names Ursula and Peter.

Zum Postamt

URSULA   So gehts nicht weiter, Peter! Fragst du jetzt endlich? Vielleicht stört es dich nicht, den ganzen Tag herumzuirren, aber meine Zeit wird knapp.

PETER   Na, gut! Ich frage den Polizisten, der drüben steht. Entschuldigung, Herr Polizist, wie kommt man zum nächsten Postamt?

POLIZIST   Geradeaus, dann die erste Straße links. Es liegt nur zehn Schritte von hier.

PETER   Vielen Dank. Siehst du, Ursula, es ist gar nicht weit. Wir können zu Fuß gehen. Möchtest du noch mit?

URSULA   Sicher. Aber dann müssen wir nachher zu Mittag essen. Es ist schon halb eins. Heute früh habe ich um sechs Uhr gefrühstückt, und jetzt habe ich einen Riesenhunger.

PETER   Von mir aus. Wunderschönes Wetter, nicht wahr? Und die grünenden Bäume! Die ganze Stadt geht bei dieser Frühlingsluft spazieren.

URSULA   Ja, im Mai fängt München an, richtig zu blühen. Aber sag mal, wieviele Marken brauchst du? Wir stehen schon vor der Post.

PETER   Zwölf zu siebzig Pfennig. Was ich an Briefschulden habe!

II
THE WRITTEN WORD

6
Reading I:
purposes and procedures

Most students learning German expect to be able to read the language sooner or later. Their desires and expectations vary from wanting to be able to read a novel by Kafka, or a scientific journal, to being able to read a menu, a tourist brochure, or advertisements in the Munich *U-Bahn*. Fortunately, reading is a completely individual activity and students in the same course may be reading at very different levels of difficulty in German just as they do in English.

To be able to read in German in the sense of extracting meaning from a graphic script is not an aim in itself: the student's aim is to be able to extract something specific—something personal of interest to him—and this must be kept in mind from the beginning. Many a German textbook started the student reading with such inanities as:

R1 Es regnete draußen. Die Familie war im Hause. Herr Schmidt las eine Zeitung. Karl hat die Zeitung gekauft. Nur er war draußen gewesen. Die Frau nähte. Die Frau war Karls Mutter. Karls Schwester Ilse war auch da. Sie las ein Buch.

Reading activities should, from the beginning, be directed toward *normal uses of reading*. We read normally:

1. because we want information for some purpose or because we are curious;

2. because we need instructions in order to perform some task for our work or for our daily life (we want to know how an appliance works, we are interested in a new recipe, we have forms to fill in);

3. because we want to act a play, play a new game, do a puzzle, or carry out some other activity which is pleasant and amusing;

4. because we want to keep in touch with friends by correspondence or understand business letters;

5. because we want to know when or where something will take place or what is available (we consult timetables, programs, announcements, menus, or we read advertisements);

6. because we want to know what is happening or has happened (we read newspapers, magazines, reports);

7. because we seek enjoyment or excitement (we read novels of all kinds, short stories, poems, words of songs).

Activities for developing reading skill should exploit these natural desires and impulses, preferably by supplying something which cannot be readily obtained in the native language: something which is interesting, amusing, exciting, useful, or leads to pleasurable activity.

R2 A quick check reveals reading material in some recent textbooks which is not likely to encourage the development of reading skill in German:

Long *dialogues,* which tend to be stilted and too obviously contrived to illustrate particular points of grammar which are to be taught in that unit (adjective endings, use of cases, the passive).

Lengthy *prose passages* about Germany, packed with geographical and historical detail which cannot be absorbed in such density and are therefore tedious.

Long, detailed *descriptions* of people, the small actions they perform from day to day, and the places where they live, work, and play, with no unusual happenings to relieve the monotony. Because such texts are frequently constructed to introduce an unrealistic number of vocabulary items, they become dull and rambling.

Almost all of the readings lack the flashes of humor and whimsy that could make the learning experience more enjoyable for both student and teacher, and from the student's point of view the most expressive sentences he encounters in reading may well be:

Und was macht er? Er langweilt sich.

∗ Look at the reading material in several elementary and intermediate textbooks and class this material according to the normal uses of reading. Mark in each case whether it is interesting in content, amusing, exciting, useful, or promotes some activity.

There are various ways of approaching the teaching of reading. The approach will be selected according to the objectives of the students. Teachers now realize that students must be attracted to the learning of a foreign language by the assurance that they will be able to attain the kind of competence they themselves are interested in, rather than being "put through the mill" according to some one else's preconceptions of the ideal foreign language course.

There are five possible objectives for a reading course: reading for information; reading of informal material; fluent, direct reading of all kinds of material; literary analysis; and translation of texts.

A. *Reading for information*

Some students may wish to learn merely *to extract certain kinds of information from German texts* (scientific, historical, political, philosophic, economic, sociological). They wish only to learn to *decipher,* to break the code sufficiently for their purposes. Courses of this type appeal particularly to students in the senior years of high school (especially those who are anxious to acquire some knowledge of a third language), and they fulfill the needs of certain undergraduate and graduate students.

Courses (and materials) can be designed to teach them to extract information with only a recognition knowledge of basic grammatical relations[1] and of the commonly used function words (determiners, prepositions, conjunctions, common adverbs, interrogative and negation words), words which commonly emerge among the first two hundred words in frequency lists. The students can then achieve their purpose with the help of specialized dictionaries of terms used in their particular fields of interest. Students can be taught to guess audaciously at the content. They then discuss the reasons for their guesses and reasons for the inaccuracy of some of these guesses.[2] From the beginning students read texts of interest to them, carefully selected to provide a gradation of difficulty. In a course of this type the students do not want, nor expect, to learn fine points of pronunciation or aural-oral or writing skills, nor do they want to learn to read directly and fluently in the foreign language for pleasure. They gain their pleasure from their ability to draw the information they want from the text rapidly, without attention to style.

These students need the following skills:

1. *Complete control in recognition of points of grammar which impede comprehension of written German.*

R3 One such problem area is the *der/den* distinction.

The unwary student equates in meaning the two sentences:

Die Dame hat *den* Schaffner nicht gesehen.

Die Dame hat *der* Schaffner nicht gesehen.

* List five other points of *recognition grammar* which could cause problems for the English-speaking reader.

2. *Knowledge of word formation* which will help them to recognize the functions and nuances of meaning of words derived from the same radical.

R4 They should be able to separate *prefixes and suffixes* from the radical and recognize the part of speech indicated by the suffix:

kaufen, einkaufen
sehen, wiedersehen, versehen, besehen, einsehen, ersehen
Kind, Kindlein
Haus, Häuschen
Freund, Freundin; Student, Studentin
Bild, Bildung, Einbildung, Bildner, bildnerisch, bilden, ausbilden, bild-
    lich, bildsam, Bildlichkeit
reich, bereichern, Reichtum, reichlich
alt, Alter, altern, veraltern, ältlich, Altertum, altertümlich
vier, vierfach, viertens, viermal, Viertel, der Vierte
schön, Schönheit; krank, Krankheit; gesund, Gesundheit
breit, Breite; groß, Größe; tief, Tiefe
rot, Röte, röten, rötlich, Röteln

R5 They should be able to extract meaning from compound forms, which are especially prevalent in German:[3]

Tankstelle; Speisewagen; Hausfrau
Todesangst, Liebesbrief; Herzenspein; Sonnenschein, Kirchenlied (The
    use of the genitive case in forming compounds can be demonstrated
    with such examples as: Vaterland-Landesvater.)
Kleinbahn, Altvater, Scharfsinn
taubstumm, rotbraun, altklug
schamrot, weltfremd; wirklichkeitstreu, leistungsfähig, liebeskrank; blau-
    äugig

* Make up some word games which would develop sensitivity to word families and compound words, e.g., competitions in listing derivatives and compounds, in constructing as many words as possible from letters supplied, in extending radicals with affixes to make new words.

3. *Practice in recognizing German-English cognate radicals.* Although many of the cognates are basic words in English which are derived from Germanic roots, the students may often fail to recognize them. The area

of meaning the cognates cover and the way they are used in the two languages, that is, their distribution, often do not coincide, which creates a further difficulty.

R6 *Es wundert mich, daß er uns besucht.* The English verb "to wonder" is not used in an impersonal construction and means "to ask oneself a mental question" rather than "to be surprised."

R7 *Die Güter sollte man weitertransportieren.* With the radical "transport" sandwiched between the suffix *-ieren* on one side and the separable prefix *weiter-,* which is not expressed in the same manner in English, the inexperienced student is likely to seek the help of his dictionary.

R8 *Der Pfadfinder*
The student who has no knowledge of the relationship between English *p* and German *pf,* as well as between English *th* and German *d* will look on *Pfad-* as a new word, even though he recognizes *-finder.* In the dictionary he will discover that the word is not only the title for Cooper's popular book *The Pathfinder* but also the German term for "Boy Scout."

Many German/English cognates are disguised by historical change, and often these disguises are systematic enough to be useful to the reader.[4]

R9 a. Ger. *f* or *ff* or *pf* often equals Eng. *p* or *v,* as in:
Pfeife,   *pipe*
Pfennig,   *penny*
hoffen,   *hope*
Schaufel, *shovel*

b. Ger. *z* or *ß* (*ss*) often equals Eng. *t:*
weiß,   *white*
beißen,   *bite*
zehn,   *ten*
zu,   *to*

c. Ger. *ch* often equals Eng. *k* or *gh:*
Woche,   *week*
wachen,   *wake*
Sicht,   *sight*

d. Ger. *b* often equals Eng. *v* or *f:*
lieben,   *love*
selber,   *self*

e. Ger. *t* often equals Eng. *d:*

Tag,   *day*

hart,   *hard*

f. Ger. *d* often equals Eng. *th:*

denken,   *think*

baden,   *bathe*

g. Ger. *g* often equals Eng. *y:*

Auge,   *eye*

Garten,   *yard*

* Share notes within the class on other regular features of German/English cognates and disguised cognates that you have observed or can discover.

4. *Recognition knowledge of the most frequent "falsche Freunde"* (that is, cognates whose meanings have diverged in the two languages). Students should begin a self-constructed cumulative list of *falsche Freunde* which should contain for each item a short sentence illustrating its use.

R10 *Falsche Freunde:*

Ger. *Gift* = Eng. *poison*

In den Großstädten versucht man, die Ratten mit Gift zu töten.

Ger. *Geschenk* = Eng. *gift*

Die Uhr ist ein Geschenk von ihrem Bruder.

Ger. *bekommen* = Eng. *receive*

Ger. *werden* = Eng. *become*

Wenn ich ständig Werbung durch die Post bekomme, werde ich wütend.

* Add to this list by sharing with others in your class the *falsche Freunde* which have caused you trouble.

WHAT DO WE DO ON THE FIRST DAY?

As with all teaching, the way the students are oriented toward the course at the beginning can be crucial to their progress. In a course where students are reading for information they should be *given confidence* from the first lesson that they will be able to read German without difficulty in a very short time. Because of the cognates in German and English this is possible very early with carefully selected texts. The teacher should *explain to the students the techniques* that will be employed to extract meaning from the text and impress on them that they must acquire rapidly a *recognition knowledge of basic grammar* and an automatic recognition knowledge of *common relational words,* like prepositions, conjunctions, adverbs, and pronouns, so that these no longer impede their extraction of meaning. They must also learn thoroughly the *most frequently used nouns and verbs* so that these can provide a framework for guessing the meaning of new words from the context. Very early, they must begin a *personal list of words* which often cause them to pause as well as of specialized vocabulary of interest to them (their *utility vocabulary* which will be discussed later in this chapter).

A PLAN FOR THE FIRST LESSON

1. Begin with all the German words you and your students can think of which are commonly used in English:

R11 kindergarten, zwieback, gestalt theory, blitzkrieg, hinterland, zeitgeist, sauerkraut, sauerbraten, hausfrau, lederhosen, strudel . . .

As you write each word on the chalkboard, pronounce it in German and ask students to repeat it after you. The length of the list will impress the students with the number of German words they already know.

2. Have a short discussion on the history of the English language with its intertwined Anglo-Saxon (Germanic) and Norman-French (Latin) origins (and many subsequent borrowings). Show how we tend to use the two strands in parallel:

R12 *Informal* Germanic strand: start; leave; end.
Formal Latin-derived strand: commence; depart; terminate.

3. Ask the students to think of as many English parallels of this type as they can. Write these on the chalkboard with their German equivalents and use them as a further incidental introduction to German pronunciation.

R13

Orient	East	*Ost*
award	prize	*Preis*
nation	land	*Land*
phantom	ghost	*Geist*
timid	shy	*scheu*
nourish	feed	*füttern*
odor	stink	*Gestank* (from *stinken*)
novel	new	*neu*

By this time students should begin to see that differences in spelling are a thin disguise for cognates.

4. Give them sentences to read based on cognates, like:

R14 Er stillt den Durst mit Milch.
Der Präsident beendet das Gespräch.

Design these sentences so that you can point out incidentally simple German function words like: *der, das, die; ein, eine; kein; zu; um; an, für* (*das Für und Wider* is a useful expression here to highlight the meaning of the definite article).

5. Give some further sentences which show that determiners and verbs vary more in form in German than in English, and that this helps to make the meaning clear:

R15 The fish in the ocean: how many are there?
Der Fisch im Ozean: D*ie* Fisch*e* im Ozean.
The German expression tells you twice it is plural, so you cannot miss it.

Das kleine Mädchen sieht *den* Fisch.
Here the German determiner clearly indicates that *Fisch* is not the subject, but rather the object of the sentence.

6. At this point, the effect of case on German word order may be discussed, using as examples simple sentences with cognates:

R16 Das kleine Mädchen sieht *den* Fisch. *Den* Fisch sieht das kleine Mädchen. *Der* Fisch sieht das kleine Mädchen.

Die Frau grüßt *der* Mann. Die Frau grüßt *den* Mann. *Den* Mann grüßt die Frau.

The students may be asked to identify the word that makes clear the subject/object relationship in each case. The flexibility of word order in German sentences will become most evident to the students as they attempt to supply English equivalents using the same word order as that in the German sentences.

7. The first lesson should end with a group deciphering of a short passage with a great number of cognates, so that the students can leave the class "knowing how to read German already."

A passage like the following could be used to illustrate the pervasive influence of English on German in recent years:

R17 Im Drugstore von Schwabing
Petra: (in Blue Jeans und einem zu großen Lumberjacket) Schade, daß du nicht bei dem Happening warst, das dieser Pop-Art-Sammler gegeben

hat! Es war eine tolle Show mit Underground-Filmen und Lichtballett! Die
Tänzer traten mit Walkie-Talkies auf und die Tänzerinnen mit freien
Midriffs. Supersexy, sag ich Dir!
Evelyn: (... Sie trägt Shorts und einen Sweater in French Blue) So ein
richtiger Kultur-Smog. . . .
Petra: Wo warst du denn am Weekend?
Evelyn: Ich war gar nicht in der City. Du weißt doch, mein Hobby ist
Camping. Am Abend gingen wir noch zu Karls Beach-Party.
Petra: Karl ist ein großer Hi-Fi-Fan. Wie war es denn?
Evelyn: Ach, es war Okay! ... Hot Jazz, Blues, Rock, Pop, Beat und
Protest Songs . . . wir hatten eine richtige Jam-session! Um Mitternacht gab
es Snacks. Inge hatte Crackers, Sandwiches und Coca-Cola mitgebracht . . .
und Klaus und Bernd mixten ganz verrückte Milch-Shakes![5]

8. As preparation for the next lesson, ask the students to make a list
of expressions, slogans, trade names, hotel names, quotations, inscriptions,
and proper names in common use which are borrowed from German. (Use
these in the second lesson for pronunciation practice and further incidental
teaching.)

ACTIVITIES IN THE READING FOR INFORMATION CLASS

As soon as students have acquired some skill in extracting information from
a German text they may begin to work in small interest groups, in pairs,
or individually, according to temperament, as a supplement to large group
guidance on aspects of written German. Gradually, large group activity is
reduced to those occasions when students feel the need for further help in
specific areas. Students begin seeking out the types of reading materials in
which they are most interested. The task of the teacher is then to be available to help with language problems, to draw the attention of the students
to interesting chapters in books or articles in contemporary foreign-language magazines, and to discuss with them what they have been reading.

Every possibility for encouraging autonomous activity should be explored. One such avenue is the preparation of group projects centered
around special interests. Students in the project group may fan out in
exploratory reading for a certain period in order to report back and
establish a list of what is worthwhile reading for all members of the group.
Alternatively, students may assign each other specific articles or sections of
books on which the readers will report back to the group for a sharing of
the information gathered.

Eventually, students should become interested in seeking out information
in the foreign language to enhance research projects in other subjects and
thus develop the habit of using their newly developed skill purposefully.

B. Reading of informal material

Some students, more interested in German for interpersonal communication, may want only to be able to *read correspondence, notices, newspaper headings, and advertisements.* For these a course emphasizing listening and speaking will be complemented with practice in reading informal German materials and in writing informally, with some study of the clichés of officialese and popular journalism. These students will be most familiar, for instance, with the present tense (*ich spreche*) and the present perfect (*ich habe gesprochen*), although they will also know the simple past (*ich sprach*). Forms such as the past perfect (*ich hatte gesprochen*) are of no great importance to them, and their knowledge of subjunctive forms will be limited to passive recognition. The implied future (*ich spreche*) will be more frequently used by them than the explicit future (*ich werde sprechen*). They will not often employ complicated structures such as the extended adjectival phrase (*das schon vor Jahren angefangene Buch*). In other words they will write very much as they speak, and read German written in the same informal style rather than in a formal literary style. Their reading (and writing) will thus reinforce their speech patterns.

The earlier stages of reading training described later in this chapter will prepare this group for their objectives.

C. Fluent, direct reading of all kinds of material

Students who want to learn to use German flexibly in all modalities, who hope to be able to pick up a novel, a biography, a newspaper, or a magazine (light or serious) and read the contents fluently for pleasure as well as being able to communicate orally and in writing, will require a course which provides balanced development of all language skills. It is to this group that the six stages of reading development described in this chapter and the next apply. This is the group which aims at attaining the stage of reading directly in German without mental translation and without constant recourse to a dictionary.

D. Literary analysis

Some of Group C will wish to develop also the skill of in-depth analysis of literary material, which requires considerable refinement in perception of nuances and choices in language. For this they require special training.

Teachers interested particularly in the preparation of this group are referred to:

Die Unterrichtspraxis IV, 2 (1971), spec. ed. K. Schaum, on the theme: "Focus on Literature";

"The Times and Places for Literature," F. André Paquette et al., in

Foreign Languages: Reading, Literature, Requirements, ed. T. E. Bird (Northeast Conference on the Teaching of Foreign Languages, 1967), pp. 51-102;

Modern Language Journal 56, 5(1972), spec. ed. W. Lohnes, on the theme: "The Teaching of Foreign Literatures"; and

W. Ruttkowski and E. Reichmann, *Das Studium der deutschen Literatur* (Philadelphia: National Carl Schurz Association, 1974).

E. Translation

Other students may want to *translate German texts* accurately into English. This is an art which requires an increasingly sophisticated knowledge of English as well as German. A course with finesse of translation as its objective will concentrate on fine distinctions of syntax and vocabulary, and contrastive aspects of sentence and paragraph formation. The perfecting of pronunciation, fluency in oral communication, and composition in German will. not be emphasized. Translation for scientific and industrial purposes requires a more than superficial acquaintance with many fields and much experience with the many dictionaries available for the specialized vocabularies of medicine, physics, engineering, chemistry, electronics, business, and so on. Translation of literary works requires a sensitivity to nuances and subtleties of meaning, speech registers, and levels of style in German and a perceptive awareness of the flexibility and potentialities of the English language. Such a course can be engrossing for those with a special fascination for language but tedious and frustrating for any who are not in the course of their own volition. Translation is discussed more fully in Chapter 9.

Each of these five objectives is, of course, legitimate. In designing or selecting reading materials and learning activities, the teacher needs to keep clearly in mind the specific purpose toward which the course, or a particular student's interests, are directed.

The remainder of this chapter will concentrate on the needs of Group C (which covers in its earlier stages the needs of Group B, and from which Group D and some of Group E will later emerge). Some of what is said about this program for progressive development of reading skill can be adapted also to certain aspects of courses for Group A. The teacher of the latter course will extrapolate what seems to him to be appropriate.

Lexical, structural (or grammatical), and social-cultural meaning

The reader must learn to extract from the graphic script three levels of meaning: lexical meaning (the semantic implications of the words and expressions), structural or grammatical meaning (which is expressed at times by semantically empty function words, but also by interrelationships among words, or parts of words), and social-cultural meaning (the evaluative dimension which German people give to words and groups of words because of their common experiences with language in their culture). When we consult a dictionary we find an *approximation of lexical meaning,* usually in the form of a synonym (which has a non-matching distribution of meaning) or a paraphrase. A study of grammar rules and experience with language in action help us to apprehend *structural meaning.* It is *social-cultural meaning* which is most difficult for a foreigner to penetrate. This is meaning which springs from shared experiences, values, and attitudes. When this type of meaning is not taken into account, or when the student interprets a German text according to his own cultural experiences, distortions and misapprehensions result. Living among German people for a long period will give a teacher or student an insight into this aspect of meaning, but the average student will need at first to depend on footnotes and his teacher's explanations. As his vicarious experience of German life and attitudes increases through much reading, he will come to a deeper understanding of the full meaning of a text.[6]

R18 In the following passage a German writer tries to explain his attachment to Cologne, the German city in which he lives. His impressions of seemingly unimportant events that create a certain atmosphere will be comprehensible to anyone who has grown fond of a particular city or town.

Ich lebe in Köln. Seit mehr als fünfundzwanzig Jahren. Als Imi, als imitierter Kölscher, als Zugereister also. Warum?

Das habe ich mich schon oft gefragt. Broterwerb? Ja, aber nicht allein. Meinen Beruf könnte ich auch anderswo ausüben. Geographische Lage, Umgebung? Ja. Die eine hat praktischen, die andere sogenannten Freizeitwert. Aber beides genügt nicht. Um mich irgendwo festzuhalten, bedarf es anderer Gründe. Einer: Köln ist meine Heimat geworden.

Aber mit dieser Feststellung ist nichts beantwortet. Man muß weiter "warum" fragen. Also?

Vielleicht erklären ein paar Erlebnisse das Problem. Lassen Sie mich erzählen . . .

Zum Beispiel neulich. Ein Sommerabend; ein bißchen warm, vielleicht zu warm für unsere Breitengrade, eine Luft, die an den Süden erinnert. Ich liebe es, an solchen Tagen nicht etwa im Grünen, sondern mitten in der Stadt zu spazieren. Im Geschäftsviertel. Das ist an solchen Abenden anderswo totenstill. In Köln nicht. Gestern hockten auf den Steinen eines Brunnens vorn größten Kaufhaus der Stadt zehn oder fünfzehn Jungen und Mädchen, um einem französischen Chansonsänger, einem Mann in ihrem Alter, zuzuhören. Durchreisender? Hängengebliebener? . . .[7]

Commentary

The expression *Heimat* can be comprehended fully only when a person is familiar with German life styles and attitudes.

Heimat has a *lexical meaning. Der Sprach-Brockhaus* gives the meaning as "der Ort, wo man zu Hause ist, der Wohnort und seine Umgebung oder der Geburtsort." This has been translated in the widely used *Cassell's German Dictionary* as "home, native place or country, homeland." To the native of a country other than Germany, neither Brockhaus nor Cassell's conveys a satisfactory connotational meaning of *Heimat.* As the author of the passage states, Cologne is not his birthplace, and his reasons for staying are not strictly practical. *Heimat* does not simply designate the place where one lives; it also suggests fondness for a particular location coupled with a sense of belonging. Even with increasing mobility, many Germans choose to spend a good part of their lives in one place. They come to know well the people and atmosphere of their immediate surroundings through many experiences both great and small which leave a lasting impression on thought and feeling (i.e., through *Erlebnisse*). The specific attachment may be to a small town with *Fachwerkhäuser* surrounded by a *Stadtwall*, to a modern postwar metropolis of *Hochhäuser*, or most commonly to a city which combines old with new. The *Rathaus* may be located on the *Marktplatz* next to a *Kaufhaus*; a *Tiefgarage* is built almost under the foundations of a medieval *Dom.* The many types of people on a *Stadtbummel* provide movement and *Stimmung.* But the feelings for *Heimat* extend beyond the city limits to the neat *Schrebergärten* on the outskirts and to the *Landschaft* that lies beyond. The term *Heimat* in its broadest usage designates the country to which one is bound by a strong sense of national loyalty (*Heimatliebe*). The *social-cultural* meaning of *Heimat* can be understood only by a student who has come to know German life styles and surroundings.

Understanding structural meaning is, of course, a prerequisite to penetrating any text.

R19 . . . eine Luft, die *an* den Süden erinnert. Ich liebe es, an solchen Tagen nicht etwa im Grünen, sondern mitten in der Stadt *zu* spazieren.

Commentary

In this sentence, neither *an* nor *zu* can be assigned a precise lexical meaning, yet they are essential if the sentence is to be understood; they show structural relationships between parts of the sentence and may therefore be said to have *structural* or *grammatical meaning*.

Word counts and frequency lists

Several lists of the most frequently used words in the German language have been published. The two word counts most often used in the editing of texts for students are B. Q. Morgan, *German Frequency Word Book,* Publications of the American and Canadian Committees on Modern Languages, IX (New York: Macmillan, 1929); and J. Alan Pfeffer, *Grunddeutsch. Basic (Spoken) German Word List. Grundstufe* (Englewood Cliffs, New Jersey: Prentice-Hall, 1964) and *Mittelstufe,* Preliminary Edition (Pittsburgh, Pennsylvania: The University of Pittsburgh Institute for Basic German, 1970).[8]

Morgan's work is based on F. W. Kaeding's *Häufigkeitswörterbuch der deutschen Sprache* (1898), which was established from a count of almost eleven million running words derived from German newspapers, magazines, legal documents, belles lettres, and other sources.[9] The 2402 basic words in Morgan's list are arranged by descending frequency, although the exact rates of occurrence are not noted because they could not be determined from Kaeding's data. A second list of 6000 words arranged alphabetically includes these basic words and their most common derivatives.[10] A handy dictionary of approximately 2150 words, the *Minimum Standard German Vocabulary* (New York: F.S. Crofts & Co., 1934), was prepared from Morgan's work by Walter Wadepuhl and has been reprinted frequently since then. The basic vocabulary in Morgan's list (and in the Morgan-Wadepuhl dictionary) is useful as an aid for students learning to read traditional materials, but as Morgan himself pointed out in 1929, the list is limited because the original word count was undertaken before the advent of words like *Auto.*

Pfeffer's *Grunddeutsch. Grundstufe* (GD-G) was established from a corpus of 595,000 spoken words (recorded topical discussions of 401 persons from various parts of Germany, Switzerland and Austria whose speech represents differences in sex, education, vocation, and location). From 25,000 lexical units 737 were selected for inclusion in the *Grundstufe.* For the sake of syntactical balance the oral list is supplemented by a topical list of 347 words. These utility words were gathered from 5,400 students in 82 intermediate schools. These two lists are augmented by a third carefully selected empirical list of 185 items which correct disparities in the previous two lists. The resulting first volume of *Grunddeutsch* contains 1,269 words arranged first in alphabetical order, then by parts of speech, and finally in the order of frequency. A second volume, *Mittelstufe* (GD-M) lists 1,536 words deriving in equal proportion from three sources: 1) spoken and topical counts, 2) a collation of earlier word lists, and 3) a statistical analysis of 500,000 words appearing in 500 books, periodicals, and newspapers from 23 fields or areas. The lists for the two levels are combined and expanded in *Grunddeutsch: Basic (Spoken) German Dictionary For Everyday Usage* (Englewood Cliffs, New Jersey: Prentice-Hall, 1970). This dictionary contains over 3,000 words and numerous idioms with sentences to illustrate each meaning, and Pfeffer maintains (p. ix) that the "contents represent over 90 per cent of the lexical and semantic fields of all the free and restricted forms of any ordinary conversation or printed page in German today."

Despite the usefulness of frequency lists in the acquisition of basic vocabulary, 3,000 words are obviously insufficient for fluent reading of all kinds of texts. Pfeffer distinguishes *frequency vocabulary* from *utility vocabulary* and even supplements the oral list of GD-G with a limited number of basic topical words, for at any level the interest of the student will often be drawn by vocabulary too specialized to be found among the words of a frequency list.

R20 As an example of this distinction, on reading the sentence: *Mein kleiner Bruder, der hinter einen Baum verschwunden war, sagte plötzlich, "Ich habe eine Spinne gefunden,"* a student is more likely to be interested in the word *Spinne* (which does not occur in either the Wadepuhl/Morgan vocabulary or in the Pfeffer dictionary) than in words such as *mein* (GD-G 48), *eine* (GD-G 4), or *sagen* (GD-G 40). *Mein, eine,* and *sagen* belong to the frequency vocabulary; *Spinne* would be added to the student's personal utility vocabulary, that is, available to him in a situation where spiders are relevant.

Knowledge of a basic vocabulary will ensure that a student knows the most widely used words which provide the framework of any sentence, revealing to him a set of relationships that will serve as a basis for "intelligent guessing" or "inferencing" when he encounters unfamiliar content words. (R24 demonstrates this process.) Each student will need, then, to build his own *personal vocabulary* (his *utility vocabulary*) from his reading, and for this he should be encouraged to keep an individual notebook in which he copies words he wishes to remember, setting them out in short sentences demonstrating their use in context.

How an unfamiliar text appears to a student

> In the following discussion, a slightly adapted version of the beginning paragraphs from the first pages of "Ein Tisch ist ein Tisch" by Peter Bichsel[11] will be used for demonstration. The full text is given at the end of this section (R25). Our readers should refrain from referring to it until they have worked through this section in order to get the feeling their students may have on being confronted with this text for the first time.

R21   Text from "Ein Tisch ist ein Tisch" as it would appear to a student knowing only the first 200 words of Pfeffer's *Grunddeutsch. Basic (Spoken) German Word List. Grundstufe* (GD-G). Only the words in the Oral Frequency List have been considered. On the right are shown additions and deletions to be made to the text if the student has learned the first 200 words of Morgan's *German Frequency Word Book* (Morgan). Numbers refer to the order of blanks in the line.

Ich will von einem alten Mann erzählen, von	omit *erzählen*
einem Mann, der kein ____ ____ sagt, . . . Er	(1, 2) add *Wort* & *mehr*
____ in einer kleinen Stadt, am ____ der ____	omit *Stadt;* (2) add *Ende*
oder nahe der ____. Es ____ sich ____ nicht,	
ihn zu ____, ____ etwas ____ ihn von andern.	omit *etwas*
Er ____ einen ____ ____, ____ ____, einen	(1) add *tragen*
____ ____ und im ____ den langen ____ ____,	
. . . die ____ ____ sind ihm viel zu weit.	
Im ____ ____ des Hauses hat er sein ____,	
vielleicht war er ____ und hatte Kinder, viel-	omit *vielleicht, Kinder*
leicht ____ er früher in einer anderen Stadt.	omit *früher, Stadt*
Bestimmt war er einmal ein Kind, aber das war	omit *bestimmt, Kind*
zu einer Zeit, wo die Kinder wie ____ ____	omit *Kinder*
waren. Man sieht sie so im ____ der ____. . . .	
Auf einem kleinen ____ in seinem ____ steht	
ein ____, ____ liegen alte ____ und das ____,	
an der ____ ____ ein ____ und ein ____.	
Der alte Mann machte ____ einen ____ und	
____ einen ____, sprach ein ____ ____ mit	(4) add *Worte*
seinem ____ und ____ ____ er an seinem ____.	(3) add *saß*
Das ____ sich ____ . . . . Und wenn der Mann	(1) add *änderte*
am ____ ____, ____ er den ____ ____.	(2) add *saß*

R22   Text from "Ein Tisch ist ein Tisch" as it would appear to a student knowing only the first 200 words of GD-G and Morgan and recognizing certain cognates. Notes on cognates appear in correspondingly numbered sections of the commentary immediately following the passage.

Ich will von einem alten Mann erzählen, von einem Mann, der kein Wort mehr sagt, . . . Er _____ in einer kleinen Stadt, am Ende der _____ oder nahe der _____. Es _____ sich _____ nicht, ihn zu _____, _____ etwas _____ ihn von andern. Er trägt einen grauen Hut[1], graue _____, einen grauen _____ und im Winter den langen grauen Mantel[2], . . . die _____ _____ sind ihm viel zu weit.

Im _____ _____ des Hauses hat er sein _____, vielleicht war er _____ und hatte Kinder, vielleicht _____ er früher in einer anderen Stadt. Bestimmt war er einmal ein Kind, aber das war zu einer Zeit, wo die Kinder wie _____ _____ waren. Man sieht sie so im Fotoalbum der Großmutter[3]. . . . Auf einem kleinen _____ in seinem _____ steht ein _____, _____ liegen alte _____ und das Fotoalbum, an der _____ hängen[4] ein _____ und ein _____.

Der alte Mann machte _____ einen _____ und _____ einen _____, sprach ein paar[5] Worte mit seinem _____ und _____ saß er an seinem _____.

Das änderte sich _____ . . . . Und wenn der Mann am _____ saß, _____ er den _____ ticken.

Commentary

1. *Hut:* the possible meanings are limited to clothing by "tragen," and students will easily recognize "hat." (*Hut* is also in the first 50 words of the topical list of GD-G.)

2. *Mantel:* it is unlikely that all students would be familiar with the cognate "mantle" and discern the correct meaning, "coat," instead of "cloak." The words "winter" and "long" are of some assistance. (*Mantel* is present among the first 50 words of the topical list of GD-G.)

3. *Großmutter:* the student would know the two separate elements of this compound word, which are included among the first 200 words of *Grunddeutsch,* but he may hesitate before connecting the more common meaning "great" with "grand."

4. *Hängen:* some inexperienced students will be disconcerted by the umlaut and hesitate to identify the word with "hang." The preposition *an* will facilitate the identification of *hängen.*

5. *Paar:* although students would probably associate this word with "pair," they may have trouble arriving at the meaning "a few." The context (*sprach* and *Worte*) may help to suggest the correct meaning.

R23 This passage shows how the text from "Ein Tisch ist ein Tisch" would look if the 200 most frequent words from GD-G and Morgan were omitted.

____ ____ ____ ____ ____ ____ ____, ____ ____ ____, ____
____ ____ ____ ____, ... ____ wohnt ____ ____ ̤____ ____, ____
____ ____ Straße ____ ____ ____ Kreuzung. ____ lohnt ____ fast
____, ____ ____ beschreiben, kaum ____ unterscheidet ____ ____
____. ____ ____ ____ grauen Hut, graue Hosen, ____ grauen Rock
____ ____ Winter ____ ____ grauen Mantel, ... ____ weißen Hemd-
kragen ____ ____ ____ ____.
____ obersten Stock ____ ____ ____ ____ ____ Zimmer, ____
____ ____ verheiratet ____ ____ ____, ____ wohnte ____ ____
____ ____ ____ ____. ____ ____ ____ ____ ____ ____, ____
____ ____ ____ ____ ____, ____ ____ ____ ____ Erwachsene ange-
zogen ____. ____ ____ ____ ____ ____ Fotoalbum ____ Großmutter.
... ____ ____ ____ Tisch ____ ____ Zimmer ____ ____ Wecker,
daneben ____ ____ Zeitungen ____ ____ Fotoalbum. ____ ____ Wand
hängen ____ Spiegel ____ ____ Bild.
____ ____ ____ ____ morgens ____ Spaziergang ____ nachmittags
____ Spaziergang, ____ ____ paar ____ ____ ____ Nachbarn ____
abends ____ ____ ____ ____ Tisch.
____ ____ ____ nie .... ____ ____ ____ ____ ____ Tisch ____,
hörte ____ ____ Wecker ticken.

Commentary

Here we have a clear demonstration of the indispensability to meaning of function words (like *zu, wenn, der, kein*); common verbs (*sein, haben, sagen*); adverbs (*so, einmal*); prepositions and conjunctions (*an, oder, und*), and pronouns (*er, ihn, das*).

R24 This passage shows how the text from "Ein Tisch ist ein Tisch" would look to a student knowing the 650 most frequent words of GD-G and Morgan. The obvious cognates not in the first 650 words are given in parentheses and obvious derivatives of the first 650 words are italicized.

Ich will von einem alten Mann erzählen, von
einem Mann, der kein Wort mehr sagt, ... Er
wohnt in einer kleinen Stadt, am Ende der Straße

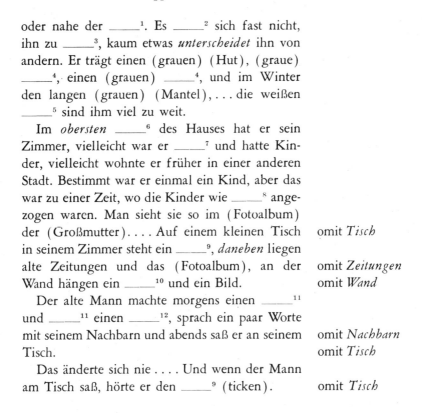

oder nahe der _____¹. Es _____² sich fast nicht,
ihn zu _____³, kaum etwas *unterscheidet* ihn von
andern. Er trägt einen (grauen) (Hut), (graue)
_____⁴, einen (grauen) _____⁴, und im Winter
den langen (grauen) (Mantel), . . . die weißen
_____⁵ sind ihm viel zu weit.

Im *obersten* _____⁶ des Hauses hat er sein
Zimmer, vielleicht war er _____⁷ und hatte Kinder, vielleicht wohnte er früher in einer anderen
Stadt. Bestimmt war er einmal ein Kind, aber das
war zu einer Zeit, wo die Kinder wie _____⁸ angezogen waren. Man sieht sie so im (Fotoalbum)
der (Großmutter). . . . Auf einem kleinen Tisch   omit *Tisch*
in seinem Zimmer steht ein _____⁹, *daneben* liegen
alte Zeitungen und das (Fotoalbum), an der   omit *Zeitungen*
Wand hängen ein _____¹⁰ und ein Bild.   omit *Wand*

Der alte Mann machte morgens einen _____¹¹
und _____¹¹ einen _____¹², sprach ein paar Worte
mit seinem Nachbarn und abends saß er an seinem   omit *Nachbarn*
Tisch.   omit *Tisch*

Das änderte sich nie . . . . Und wenn der Mann
am Tisch saß, hörte er den _____⁹ (ticken).   omit *Tisch*

Commentary

Once the reader is familiar with the function words and common verbs,
adverbs, pronouns, prepositions, and conjunctions and has a recognition
knowledge of some basic vocabulary, he can usually work out the meaning
of most of the remaining words in a passage by intelligent guesswork or
inferencing. Inferences will be indicated with an asterisk.

1. This is obviously a location, and it would seem likely that the location is as general as *"am Ende der Straße."* Although the exact meaning
of the word cannot be determined unless the students perceive that it is a
cognate (*Kreuzung:* crossing), the significance of the phrase is clear:
*somewhere in the town, it does not really matter where.

2. and 3. These words are best considered together. The student will
recognize in 3 a word he knows, *schreiben,* and probably assume the
meaning: *write about (*beschreiben:* describe). The impersonal statement
beginning *"Es lohnt sich nicht, . . ."* initiates a generalization concerning

the old man: if he scarcely differs from anyone else, writing about him *is not really worthwhile.

4. Both words clearly represent articles of outer clothing which do not differentiate the old man from other people. The articles in question are grey, which suggests a man's suit. *Hosen* may at first be interpreted as hose or stockings, but the student will then move to *trousers. Only one major item of external attire remains, a *jacket (*Rock*). (Both *Hose* and *Rock* are included among the first 150 topical words of GD-G.)

5. The item is part of the sequence describing the old man's clothing. In contrast to the previously mentioned articles this one is white, and the students will probably surmise quickly that it is part of a shirt (especially as *Hemd* is among the first 150 topical words of GD-G). That the garment is too large would be most immediately evident from the *shirt collar. (The students who recognize that the compound word *Hemdkragen* represents more than just a shirt will be most likely to make this final inference.)

6. The old man's room is located in a house on the uppermost *floor (*Stock*).

7. If the old man had children, he would also have been *married (*verheiratet*).

8. The students know *wachsen* ("to grow") from the first 650 words of Morgan and the sentence implies that although the old man was once technically a child, he never really had the appearance of one. In his childhood he was dressed in an unchildlike manner, i.e., like *grown-ups (*Erwachsene:* adults).

9. The object, as we learn the second time it is mentioned, ticks and must therefore be a clock. The students may identify the clock as an *alarm clock because it is standing on the table, especially if they recognize the cognate "wake" in *Wecker*.

10. We know that the object hangs on the wall and is not a picture. While it is unlikely that the exact meaning of the word (*Spiegel:* mirror) will be inferred from this information, the word itself is not essential to the story.

11. The old man would have to leave his room to talk to his neighbors. The students who associate *Gang* with the past participle of *gehen* will be able to infer that the old man took a *walk of some sort (*Spaziergang:* walk).

12. The student already knows the analogous forms of *morgens* and *abends,* and the three adverbs are used in a logical sequence (morning-

afternoon-evening). An analysis of *nachmittags* will reveal the cognate "midday" (*Mittag*) and the meaning will be quickly discerned: *afternoons, in the afternoon.

R25 Complete adapted text from "Ein Tisch ist ein Tisch" (P. Bichsel). Parentheses indicate additions and suspension points indicate deletions from the original text.

Ich will von einem alten Mann erzählen, von einem Mann, der kein Wort mehr sagt, ... Er wohnt in einer kleinen Stadt, am Ende der Straße oder nahe der Kreuzung. Es lohnt sich fast nicht, ihn zu beschreiben, kaum etwas unterscheidet ihn von andern. Er trägt einen grauen Hut, graue Hosen, einen grauen Rock und im Winter den langen grauen Mantel, ... die weißen Hemdkragen sind ihm viel zu weit.

Im obersten Stock des Hauses hat er sein Zimmer, vielleicht war er verheiratet und hatte Kinder, vielleicht wohnte er früher in einer anderen Stadt. Bestimmt war er einmal ein Kind, aber das war zu einer Zeit, wo die Kinder wie Erwachsene angezogen waren. Man sieht sie so im Fotoalbum der Großmutter.... Auf einem kleinen Tisch (in seinem Zimmer) steht ein Wecker, daneben liegen alte Zeitungen und das Fotoalbum, an der Wand hängen ein Spiegel und ein Bild.

Der alte Mann machte morgens einen Spaziergang und nachmittags einen Spaziergang, sprach ein paar Worte mit seinem Nachbarn und abends saß er an seinem Tisch.

Das änderte sich nie .... Und wenn der Mann am Tisch saß, hörte er den Wecker ticken ....

Six stages of reading development

To help the student to develop progressively his ability to read more and more fluently and independently materials of increasing difficulty and complexity, six stages of reading development are recommended. Materials in German of an appropriate level of difficulty for each stage are presented and discussed, and suitable activities are suggested for reinforcing the developing reading skill and for ensuring a clear grasp of the meaning of what is read. More detailed discussion will be found in *Teaching Foreign-Language Skills* (Rivers, 1968), pp. 221–37.

The six stages do not represent six levels of study (in the sense in which Brooks used this term).[12] Stage One may begin after the first oral presentation of a short dialogue, or after some active learning of simple actions and statements in the classroom context, or in simulated situations. Should teacher and class prefer it, Stage One may be postponed to allow for two or three weeks of entirely oral work. This is often the case with younger students. As soon as students acquire some familiarity with sound-symbol correspondences in German and the word order of simple sentences, they pass from Stage One to Stage Two (reading of recombinations of familiar material). For a while Stage Two may alternate with Stage One. A more mature group of students, already adept at native-language reading, may pass rapidly through Stages One and Two and move on to Stage Three (reading of simple narrative and conversational material which is not based on work being practiced orally). Some textbooks plunge the student directly into Stage Three at the beginning, particularly if development of reading skill is the primary objective. Progress through Stages Three, Four and Five becomes a largely individual matter as students outpace one another in ability to read increasingly complicated material.

Stage One: Introduction to reading

The introduction to reading will be very short or longer depending on the age of the students and the intensive or non-intensive nature of the course.

Students learn to read what they have already learned to say either in short dialogues, in informal classroom conversation, or through the oral presentation of the initial conversational narrative. Questions require only recognition of material in the text.

The major emphasis is on the identification of *sound-symbol correspondences* so that the student perceives in graphic form the meaning with which he has become familiar in oral form.

Reading is an integrated part of language study, not a specialized activity. At this stage:

Reading is linked with listening.

Students learn to segment an oral message[13] (that is, to identify its phrase structure groupings) and then try to recognize these groupings in graphic form.

Reading is linked with speaking.

Students learn to say a few simple things in German and then to recognize the graphic symbols for the oral utterances they have been practicing. The script helps them to remember what they were saying, to see more clearly how it was structured, and to learn it more thoroughly. It also provides further variations of these utterances for them to use orally.

Reading is linked with improvement in pronunciation and intonation.

Students practice correct production of sounds and appropriate phrasing as they learn to associate symbols with sounds.

Reading is linked with writing.

Students consolidate sound-symbol associations through dictation or spot dictation exercises. They confirm this learning by copying out, with correct spelling, sentences they have been learning. They write out sentences associated with pictures and use, as practice in reading, what their fellow students have written. Teacher or students write out instructions which others read and then put into action.

R26 *Spot dictation*

Spot dictation enables the teacher to focus the attention of the students on the correct spelling of certain words and on slight differences in the spelling of near-homographs. It is a testing device to encourage the mastery of the spelling system, as contrasted with word recognition. Sometimes students write the words separately, sometimes in blanks on a partial script.

The teacher reads a complete sentence to the class so that the students hear the word in context.

TEACHER   Peter hat einen Freund, der Wolfgang heißt.

The teacher then repeats a particular word or group of words which the students write down.

TEACHER   *heißt* . . . (Students write *heißt*.)
TEACHER   Peter hat einen Freund, der Wolfgang heißt.
             Wolfgang hört gerne Musik.
             hört gerne . . . (Students write.)
             Er hört gerne Musik.
             Musik . . .
             Er hört gerne Musik, aber er hat wenig Zeit dazu.
             wenig Zeit . . .
             Er hat wenig Zeit, weil er viele Aufgaben für die Schule
               machen muß.
             für die Schule . . .

Reading is linked with the learning of grammar.
Students see in written form what they have been learning orally and consolidate their grasp of grammatical structure.
Reading is linked with learning about language.
Students become conscious of differences in the surface structure of German and English. Students take language universals for granted because they are universals, e.g., the fact that sentences consist of noun phrases and verb phrases. They tend to expect other features to be universals too. Many surface differences are more clearly observable in written language, e.g., the manifestations of gender and number agreements in German.

Reading is linked with learning about the culture of the speakers of the language.

The written script in textbooks should be accompanied by illustrations and photographs which elucidate many aspects of the life and customs of the people and add new meaning to even the simplest of exchanges in the foreign language. Even culturally neutral material (see Rivers, 1968, p. 275) becomes more alive when the student sees how everyday situations vary in other cultures and have a different import. Some time should be spent from the earliest lessons in arousing the students' interest in German life and attitudes. (As reading skill develops and students read more widely, this particular link becomes more and more important.)

RECOGNITION OF SOUND PATTERNS REPRESENTED BY THE GRAPHIC SYMBOLS

Although the student beginning to read German probably will not encounter serious difficulties in comprehending sound-symbol correspondences, spelling variants and combinations may at first prove confusing, e.g.,

R27   1. [i]   *lie*ben [liːbən]
             Fam*i*lie [famiːliə]
             *ih*n [iːn]
             *zieh*en [tsiːən]
             Z*y*linder [tsilIndəʁ]
      2. [f]   *f*ühlen [fyːlən]
             *v*on [fɔn]
      3. [p]   *P*ost [pɔst]
             a*b* [ap]

R28   A speaker of English will also find that some words spelled like English words (and even in some cases having a similar meaning to their English counterparts) which he has hitherto pronounced in English with an [i] sound now have a distinctly different pronunciation in German: e.g., *leer* will now be pronounced [leːʁ]; *Sphere* will now be pronounced [sfeːRə].

R29   On the other hand *-i-*, which the English speaker has just learned to pronounce [i] in German, will be pronounced [I] in such words as *in* [In] and *Sinn* [zIn]; *-v-* can be pronounced [f], but also occurs as [v] in cases such as *V*ase [vɑzə] and *v*ital [vitɑl].

The student will become more conscious of variations of the types described if, instead of merely repeating after the teacher as he reads or is corrected, he also constructs lists from his reading of different combinations of letters which are pronounced the same, and combinations of letters which have several possible pronunciations.

* Compare notes in class on sound-symbol areas which you yourself have found particularly confusing.

MATERIALS FOR STAGE ONE

If a dialogue-learning approach is being used, an early dialogue the student will read, after having practiced it orally, may resemble the following:

R30 *Unit One: Basic Dialogue Three*[14]

GÜNTHER Willst du ins Kino gehen?

KLAUS Nein, ich möchte gerne nach Hause gehen.

GÜNTHER Wirklich? Was ist denn los? Bist du müde? Du siehst so aus.

KLAUS Ich? Müde? Durchaus nicht! Ich bin nur so hungrig. Ich möchte etwas essen und trinken.

(Construction of suitable dialogues is discussed in detail in Chapter 1.)

Commentary

1. The subject matter is of interest to high school students.

2. The utterances are authentic.

3. The speech patterns are typical of informal German (e.g., idiomatic use of *möchte gern(e)*; familiar form *du;* particles *denn* and *so;* contraction *ins*).

4. The sentences are short or break into short semantically and structurally replaceable segments (e.g., *was ist los, ins Kino gehen*), thus providing opportunities for variation and recombination practice.

5. Useful exclamations and tag phrases are provided (e.g., *Wirklich? Durchaus nicht!*).

6. Provision is made for the study of basic grammar (*bin-bist;* vowel change in *siehst;* formation of questions; use of modal auxiliary and infinitive: *Willst du . . . gehen;* separable prefixes: *Du siehst . . . aus*).

7. With additional vocabulary supplied, this dialogue provides a natural stepping stone to the recombinations for reading practice of Stage Two. The forms provided permit interesting recombinations.

8. Sound-symbol correspondences: about two-thirds of all vowels and consonants in German are represented in this passage. There is ample material for practice in contrasting German syllabification and in glottal stops. Contrasting German sounds which do not exist in English are demon-

strated, e.g., i*ch* – na*ch, G*ü*nther* – m*ü*de, as are contrasts with English phonic values, e.g., hu*n*gri*g*, s*ieh*st, wi*ll*st.

When dialogues are not used, the first reading material consists of a graphic representation on the chalkboard, in the textbook, on the overhead projector, or on flashcards of the German sentences being learned orally in the classroom context or in simulated situations.

R31 In one variation of this approach, illustrations accompany sentences containing new vocabulary words which are drilled through questions and answers.

1. Das ist Hans.
   Hans ist ein Junge.
   Hans ist ein Freund von Helga.
   Der Junge ist freundlich.
   . . .
1. Ist Hans ein Junge?
2. Wer ist ein Junge?
3. Was ist Hans?
4. Ist Hans freundlich?[15]

Stage Two: Familiarization

Students read rearrangements and recombinations of material they have been learning orally. These recombinations may be situational dialogues, conversations that can be acted out in class, or take the form of interesting narratives.

The recombinations may be written by the students themselves, thus linking writing practice with reading. All materials will be written in informal style. Students may write out such things as directions from the school to their home; these may be passed out to the class and other students asked to identify the address. Students may write down things they are presumed to be doing while other students try to identify the time of day or place associated with these actions. Many other realistic activities can be invented which use the vocabulary and structures the students have learned at this particular stage.

MATERIALS FOR STAGE TWO

R32 When dialogues like R30 have been used in Stage One, a *recombination conversation* like the one below[16] may be used for Stage Two. (The previous occurrence of a similar item in the book from which this passage has been taken is indicated by the following symbols: P—preliminary unit; BD—basic dialogue; R—a previous recombination.)

UWE   Bist du müde (BD 3)? Du siehst so aus (BD 3).

HELGA   Nein, ich bin nur so hungrig (BD 3). Ich möchte etwas essen und trinken (BD 3).

ILSE   Ist dein Freund krank (BD 1 and R)?

PETER   Nein, er sieht nur so aus (BD 3). Er sagt, er möchte ins Kino gehen (P and BD 3).

HEINZ   Was ist denn los (BD 3)? Bist du krank (P and R)? Du siehst wirklich so aus (BD 3).

R33   When classroom conversations like R31 are used *recombination readings* like the following[17] are appropriate. (Vocabulary which has not been practiced in previous lessons is glossed in the margin.)

                  Es ist ein Nachmittag im August. Wir sind in Hannover. Im

kühl   August ist es schon kühl hier in Niedersachsen. Heute nach-

cool   mittag gehen Gertrud und ich einkaufen. Wir gehen zu *Bren-ninkmeyer*. Das ist ein Kaufhaus in Hannover. *Brenninkmeyer* hat Sommerschlußverkauf, und die Preise sind herabgesetzt.

meisten   Alles ist sehr billig. Die meisten Geschäfte in Deutschland

most   haben jetzt zwei Wochen Sommerschlußverkauf.

                  Gertrud braucht viele Sachen. Ich brauche nichts, aber ich gehe doch mit Gertrud, denn ich gehe gerne einkaufen. Gertrud findet einen Rock. Er ist schön, und sie kauft ihn.

R34   Sometimes a little whimsy helps. The following passage modified slightly from the Bichsel story "Ein Tisch ist ein Tisch"[18] presents the results of an elderly gentleman's efforts to transfer the meanings of words to other words. (The students should have been introduced to the vocabulary in previous work.)

Am Morgen bleibt der alte Mann lange im Bild liegen, um neun läutet das Fotoalbum, der Mann steht auf und stellt sich auf den Schrank, damit er nicht an die Füße friert, dann nimmt er seine Kleider aus der Zeitung, zieht sich an, schaut in den Stuhl an der Wand, setzt sich dann auf den Wecker an den Teppich und blättert den Spiegel durch, bis er den Tisch seiner Mutter findet.

It is certain that the student who could read and understand such a passage would not be depending solely on recollection of memorized sentences, and juggling the nouns to arrive at more usual sentences proves an amusing exercise.

R35 *Recombinations in narrative form*

As a further step away from dependence on what has been learned in conversational form, the following recombination narrative reintroduces words, phrases, and structures previously learned and practiced, but extends the vocabulary range by the use of cognates (indicated by an asterisk), and creates a completely new and entertaining narrative which is nevertheless conversational in tone.

Ein Geschenk für Irmgard[19] (Unit 6)

Werner ist traurig. Seine Schwester Irmgard hat am Freitag Geburtstag, und er hat noch kein Geburtstagsgeschenk. Was Irmgard nur möchte? Einen Schal? Eine Bluse oder einen Pullover? . . . Einen Pulli! Ja, bestimmt! Pullis sind jetzt so modern*, und Irmgard findet sie sehr schick. Ach, aber sie kosten so viel, und Werner hat nur fünf Mark für ein Geschenk.

Und für fünf Mark bekommt er keinen Pulli . . . keine Handtasche . . . kein Buch. Kein Buch? Aber Paperbacks* sind billig! Was für eine Idee*! Für fünf Mark bekommt er drei Paperbacks! Werner kauft aber nur zwei. Für zwei Mark kauft er Briefpapier. Irmgard hat nie Papier, wenn* sie einen Brief schreibt. Und sie schreibt so viel! Sie hat viele Freunde.

At Stage Two students are trained to recognize meaningful segments of thought and read in coherent word groupings. The familiarity of the structure and of most of the lexical items enables students to relate segments of meaning in what they are reading to what has preceded and to keep all of this in their immediate memory while processing what follows. Students are acquiring reading habits basic to fluent direct reading. For this reason reading practice at this stage is best done in class where the teacher can guide the student in techniques rather than being set as homework. Questions require answers which force students to recombine known elements in new combinations.

Stage Three: Acquiring reading techniques

Students read simple narrative and conversational material with an uncomplicated and entertaining theme. They are introduced to written style and more complicated structure. Vocabulary remains largely in the area of the known, with some unfamiliar words whose meaning can be deduced from illustrations, from cognates, or from the context. (See examples of inferencing in comments on R24.) Reading materials are a step behind what is currently being learned in order to encourage direct reading in German, a process which becomes exceedingly difficult when too many novelties of vocabulary and structure are encountered at the same time.

A recombination narrative like R35 bridges the gap between Stages Two and Three.

MATERIALS FOR STAGE THREE

R36 Finding suitable materials for this level frequently proves difficult, but letters or descriptions written by children, children's books, or simple selections from contemporary literature can be successfully employed. The following example is taken from Werner Schmidli's "Geschichten vielleicht." [20]

Ich muss jeden Tag um sieben Uhr aufstehen. Um acht muss ich an der Arbeit sein. Über Mittag bleibe ich in der Fabrik. Ich esse in der Kantine. Du kannst essen, was du willst, es schmeckt alles gleich. Den ganzen Tag hast du die gleichen Leute um dich, von früh bis spät. Um sechs komme ich nach Hause; dann können wir meistens gleich essen. Ich muss mich mit den Kindern abgeben, schau mir das Fernsehprogramm an, wenn die Kinder im Bett sind. Ich unterhalte mich mit meiner Frau. Die Zeitung habe ich aber noch nicht gelesen. Gegen elf gehe ich zu Bett. Ausschlafen kann ich jeden Samstag, am Sonntag fahren wir aus, gehen spazieren. Am Montag fängt es wieder von vorne an. Das geht schon achtzehn Jahre so. Da soll man ein fröhliches Gesicht machen. Ich bin keine Maschine.

Commentary

1. The passage was written by a native speaker in authentic contemporary style.

2. The sentences in the passage are short; the structure of the sentences is uncomplicated and can be easily recognized. The vocabulary is appropriate for the elementary level. Those words not to be found in Pfeffer's *Grundstufe* can be understood in the context (e.g., *anschauen*) or derived from known roots (e.g., *ausschlafen, ausfahren, fröhlich*); only *abgeben* requires some explanation.

3. The extract shows a blend of activities from the foreign culture and of familiar situations from the native culture of the learner. The description of the course of the regular daily routine is easy for the students to follow. At the same time the social problem portrayed through the description is one common to all modern industrial societies.

When fluent reading is considered the primary objective,[21] Stages One and Two are frequently omitted and simple, entertaining narrative and conversational material with much repetition of vocabulary and structures, often profusely illustrated, is used from the beginning. These passages are usually written in such a way that they can be used for dramatic readings or role-playing; in this they resemble the dialogues of Stage One. An example of such material is given below. The meaning of the italicized expressions is made clear in the book by illustrations; the new words marked here with °, unfamiliar punctuation, and so forth are explained at some length in the margin (not included here).

R37 *Spielen Sehen Lesen 2*[22]

Es war einmal°
ein Riese°; der° hatte großen Hunger.
Da setzte°
er sich° an seinen riesengroßen *Tisch*.
vor seinen riesengroßen *Teller*.
Seine Frau nahm den riesengroßen *Topf*
vom riesengroßen *Herd* und füllte
ihm die Suppe auf; die° aß er mit seinem
riesengroßen *Löffel*.
Dann gab sie ihm ein Stück Fleisch
aus einer riesengroßen *Schüssel*.
das aß er mit seinem riesengroßen *Messer*
und mit seiner riesengroßen *Gabel*.
Danach° aß er noch° Pudding
aus einer riesengroßen *Schüssel*.
Dann war er satt°.
Nun hatte er großen Durst.
Da nahm seine Frau die riesengroße
Kanne und tat° ihm Milch
in seine riesengroße *Tasse*.
Weil° er aber keine Milch mochte°,
wurde er böse. Da setzte die Frau den
riesengroßen *Kessel* auf und wollte
Kaffee kochen, aber° den mochte der Riese
auch nicht. Da nahm er den riesengroßen
Krug und stampfte aus dem Haus.
Ich weiß nicht, wohin° er ging.

Commentary

The cultural background in this passage is neutral. The text includes a number of structures in various contexts: prepositions followed by the accusative case (*vor seinen riesengroßen Teller, in seine riesengroße Tasse*); the simple past tense; verbs with separable prefixes (*füllte . . . auf, setzte . . . auf*); many examples of variation in German word order.

For students who have passed through Stages One and Two materials for reading at Stage Three will be more demanding than the extract just quoted. In the following passage, specially written by a native speaker, new words beyond the usual vocabulary of classroom texts are introduced at the rate of about one or two words in every hundred running words. Each new word (marked with °) is glossed in the margin on its first appearance.

Details of German life are introduced in a narrative about several young Germans and their activities (thus providing an opportunity for the American student of German to identify himself in his reading with people of his own age and interests).

R38 Günther und Jochen sind schon lange gute Freunde. Sie gehen in dieselbe° Klasse, und sind auch sonst viel zusammen. Jochen ist gern bei Bergers, denn in einer kinderreichen° Familie ist immer etwas los. Günther besucht Jochen gern zu Hause, denn wo es nur zwei Kinder gibt, ist es stiller und niemand ärgert einen — das ist auch mal schön! Schmidts Uschi, Jochens "kleine" Schwester, ist ja auch schon sechzehn.

Zweimal° in der Woche geht Günther zu Schmidts rüber, um Uschi mit der Mathematik zu helfen, für die sie, wie auch Jochen, wenig Talent hat. Nach ihren zwei Fünfen[1] im Oktober hat Günther angefangen, ihr Nachhilfe zu geben, und dann ist es nach ein paar Wochen besser geworden. Jetzt bekommt sie gewöhnlich eine Drei, und einmal war es sogar eine Zwei. Günther ist sehr gut in Mathe. Wenn Englisch für ihn nur so leicht wäre!

Eigentlich wollte Günther kein Geld für die Nachhilfe nehmen. Aber Uschi will sich von einem Jungen nichts schenken lassen und ihr Vater hält es für seine Pflicht, Günther wenigstens eine kleine Summe zu geben . . .

---

[1] The grading system in German schools is 1, 2, 3, 4, 5, 6, that is, *sehr gut, gut, befriedigend* (satisfactory), *ausreichend* (fair, just passing), *mangelhaft* (unsatisfactory), and *ungenügend* (failing)—corresponding to A, B, C, D, and F in American schools.[23]

RECOGNITION OF STRUCTURAL CLUES

For fluent reading, the student must be able to detect rapidly meaningful groups of words, even when their lexical content is not clear to him.

Through Stages Three and Four, students will be learning to detect effortlessly the indicators of word classes (parts of speech), of persons and tenses of the verb, and of cases of the noun; the words which introduce phrases (*bei, aus, vor, während, nach* . . .) and clauses (*wenn, seitdem, bevor, während, weil* . . .) and the particular modifications of structure and meaning they indicate; the adverbs and adverbial expressions which limit the action in time, place and manner (*jetzt, oft, morgen; da, hier, irgendwo; ganz, sehr, zu, überhaupt* . . .); the indicators of interrogation (*Was? Wann? Wie? Wo? Warum?* . . .) and negation (*nicht, nichts, nie* . . .). Questions will be designed to attract the students' attention to these structural clues.

R39 For rapid comprehension, students should be trained to recognize such features as the *-t-* which in regular verbs is always present as an indicator of past time or of some type of unverified, hypothetical or unrealized action:

Ich lern*t*e Deutsch (contrast: ich lerne Deutsch);
Sie sagt, sie lern*t*e Deutsch;
Wenn ich Deutsch lern*t*e, könnte ich deutsche Zeitungen lesen;
Lern*t*e sie nur Deutsch! (presumption—she has not yet learned German).

R40 Students should be conscious of the relationship between two people indicated by the function words *dem, der,* and *den* (articles in the dative case) so that they will understand the sense of the sentence no matter what the word order:

Dem Gepäckträger, der ihr jetzt ins Gesicht schreit, sagt sie kein Wort mehr.
Maria stellt ihn der Schwester vor.
Das neue Haus zeigen sie den Freunden.

R41 Students should be made aware of the usefulness of *wohin* as a directional indicator. They might be asked to explain the reasons for the different answers to the following versions of the question "Where are you going?"

Wo gehen Sie? Auf der Straße gehe ich!
Wohin gehen Sie? Ich gehe nach Hause.

∗ Discuss other structural clues on which you depend to clarify the meaning of what you are reading.

7
Reading II:
from dependence to independence

Stage Four: Practice

Students now practice their reading skill with a wider range of language. Reading is of two kinds: *intensive* where reading is linked with further study of grammar and vocabulary, and *extensive* where the student is on his own, reading for his own purposes or for pleasure. In both cases texts are authentic writings by German authors, but they are carefully selected to be accessible to the student at this stage of his development, that is, difficult or complex style or esoteric vocabulary is avoided. As the student progresses through this practice stage he reads material of increasing complexity with a wider and wider range of vocabulary. The 3,000 words of the Pfeffer dictionary as a recognition vocabulary seem a reasonable limitation. This will, of course, be augmented by cognates and some specialized vocabulary associated with a specific topic.

INTENSIVE READING

This provides material for close study of problem areas.

1. The systems and subsystems of the language[1]

English-speaking students frequently have difficulty understanding the German system for expressing point of view or unverified opinion through the use of the subjunctive.

R42 In the course of reading the student becomes conscious that in German the subjunctive may be employed to report objectively what someone has said or to emphasize that a statement represents one particular perspective.[2]

Sein eigentliches Bestreben, so erzählen sie, sei es, theoretisch zu arbeiten; . . . Nun aber ist ihm die Politik in die Quere gekommen. Er verfolge seine Ziele, die verschiedenen Besucher und Anrufer die ihrigen; er durchschaue sie nicht.

Commentary

Erzählen and *ist gekommen* form the factual framework of the passage; *sei, verfolge, durchschaue* are all actions and reactions attributed to a person by an unnamed source, i.e., they represent hearsay reported objectively by the writer of the passage.

Compare the viewpoints presented by the use of the subjunctive in the following passages.

R43 So saß er eines Tages wieder etwas mißmutig und bedrückt zu Hause und las über einen sehr berühmten holländischen Maler. Er las, daß dieser Maler von einer wahren Leidenschaft, ja Raserei besessen gewesen sei, ganz und gar beherrscht von dem einen Drang, ein guter Maler zu werden. Der junge Mann fand, daß er mit diesem holländischen Maler manche Ähnlichkeit habe. Im Weiterlesen entdeckte er alsdann mancherlei, was auf ihn selbst weniger paßte. Unter anderem las er, wie jener Holländer bei schlechtem Wetter, wenn man draußen nicht malen konnte, unentwegt und voll Leidenschaft alles, auch das geringste, abgemalt habe, was ihm unter die Augen gekommen sei.

HERMANN HESSE, "Märchen vom Korbstuhl."[3]

R44 Die Landschaft gefalle ihm nicht besonders, aber es gebe dort gute Arbeitsplätze, sagte er. Ja, Geld lasse sich viel verdienen, wenn man nur ein bißchen tüchtig sei . . . Ob ich auch in Syndlingen aussteige oder noch weiter fahre? So, das wisse ich noch nicht, das wolle ich erst einmal sehen?

Ich stand auf, nahm meinen Koffer und setzte mich nach hinten auf einen anderen Platz. Ich hauchte die überfrorene Scheibe an und bekam einen Fleck frei. Ich hätte mir denken können, daß es nichts zu sehen gab.

WOLFGANG HERMANN KÖRNER, *Krautgärten.*[4]

Commentary

To make students more aware of the difference in perspective achieved through the use of the subjunctive, they may be asked questions like the following:

1. Discuss the reasons for the use of the subjunctive in R43. How does *habe* (1.6) differ from the other subjunctives in the passage and what nuance of meaning is conveyed?

2. Why is the whole first paragraph of R44 presented in the subjunctive? Attempt to reconstruct the dialogue which took place, and explain what effect results from the use of the subjunctive instead of the indicative.

Focusing the students' attention on the use of the subjunctive by German writers who wish to convey certain effects will make the German manner of expressing opinions and perspectives appear more rational and meaningful. Many other problems of contrastive German-English usage are also more efficiently studied through the thoughtful analysis of a text than through the study of a rule, illustrated by examples detached from the wider context of interacting rules. Nor is translation of sentences from English to German particularly effective in such areas of contrast just because at these points English does not make a particular distinction in parallel fashion.

* Look for passages of German which show clearly the use of passives which express an action (actional passives) as opposed to passives which describe the state resulting from the action (statal passives), for example: *Das neue Hotel wird gebaut* (construction is underway at the moment) and *Das neue Hotel ist gebaut* (construction is completed and the building stands finished). Work out questions which would bring a student to an understanding of this distinction.

2. *Contrastive problems of meaning*

It is in functioning language that students will begin to assimilate the differences in coverage of semantic space of German words which seem to be equivalent in meaning to certain English words.

R45 The concept of the German verb *lassen* does not coincide in all cases with English "to leave."

> *Laß* mich in Ruhe! *Leave* me alone!
> *Laß* uns gehen! *Let's* go!
> Er hat es bauen *lassen.* He *had* it built.

Das *läßt* sich nicht ändern. Nothing *can* be done about it.
Sie kann das Rauchen nicht *lassen*. She cannot *give up* smoking.

The basic meanings of the German verb *lassen* are expanded even further through the use of separable and inseparable prefixes.

Die Nachfrage *läßt nach*. The demand *slackens*.
Er wurde *entlassen*. He was *dismissed* (or *released* or *discharged*).

R46 On the other hand, a familiar concept with an extensive range like "to put" becomes a problem to the English speaker because there is no single equivalent in German.

Sie *stellt* die Weinflasche auf den Tisch. She *puts* the wine bottle on the table.
Wie er es *ausdruckt*, . . . As he *puts* it, . . .
Unterschreiben Sie unten! *Put your signature* at the bottom!
Er *steckt* das Geld in die Tasche. He *puts* the money in his pocket.
Versetzen Sie sich in meine Lage! *Put* yourself in my place!
Er *zieht* den Mantel *an*. He *puts on* his coat.
Sie *schiebt* es immer *auf*. She always *puts* it *off*.

Such uses as these must be encountered in context on many occasions if they are to be used spontaneously.

Students come to appreciate the resources of the German language when they *listen* to the plays, poems, and prose they have studied intensively being acted, recited, or read by German actors and sometimes by the writers themselves.

This is the stage for intellectually challenging ideas and the cultivation of aesthetic values. Material for Stage Four should be selected for the literary, informational, or provocative value of its content, not merely as a language vehicle. Questions should go beyond Who? What? When? Where? How (manner)? and yes-no questions, to considerations of implications, that is, Why? If . . . then what? and How (explanation)? questions.[5]

EXTENSIVE READING

This gives the student the opportunity to use his knowledge of the language for his own purposes. It is an individualized or shared activity as the student prefers. With some help from the teacher in selection as he needs it, the student reads for his own pleasure short stories, plays, short novels, newspapers, or magazines specially written for schools, or selected articles and advertisements (particularly those profusely illustrated) from West German, East German, Austrian, or Swiss sources. He may read for information about a topic which interests him or prepare a project, a report, or a debate with a friend or a group of friends. He attempts to increase his reading speed; setting timed goals may help him in this. He learns to tolerate a certain vagueness, reading whole sections at a time in order to establish the general meaning, so that he can develop his ability to deduce from semantic and syntactic clues the meaning of unfamiliar words and phrases.

MATERIALS FOR STAGE FOUR

Passages like R38 may be read and discussed in class at Stage Three to supplement the steady diet of the intermediate level textbook or may be used for the *extensive reading* of Stage Four which should always be at a lower level of difficulty than material for intensive reading.

R47 One of the traditionally favored sources for easy reading material with general appeal has been *Märchen* and *Erzählungen,* which abound in German. But such materials are not always as simple as they may at first seem to be. The version of the story from which the following passage was taken appeared in an elementary reader at the end of the nineteenth century in a section recommended "for rapid reading." In this passage we have italicized all words, except cognates, not contained in the 3,000 words of the Pfeffer dictionary.

Der Mensch hat wohl täglich Gelegenheit, Betrachtungen über den *Unbestand* aller *irdischen* Dinge anzustellen, wenn er will, und zufrieden zu werden mit seinem *Schicksal,* wenn auch nicht gebratene *Tauben* für ihn in der Luft herumfliegen. Aber auf dem seltsamsten *Umweg* kam ein deutscher Handwerks*bursche* in Amsterdam durch den Irrtum zur Wahrheit, und zu ihrer Erkenntnis. Denn als er in diese grosse und reiche Handelsstadt, voll *prächtiger* Häuser, *wogender* Schiffe und *geschäftiger* Menschen, gekommen war, fiel ihm sogleich ein grosses und schönes Haus in die Augen, wie er auf seiner ganzen *Wanderschaft* von Duttlingen bis nach Amsterdam noch keines erlebt hatte. Lange betrachtete er mit *Verwunderung* dies *kostbare* Gebäude, die sechs *Kamine* auf dem Dach, die schönen *Gesimse* und die hohen Fenster. Endlich konnte er sich nicht *entbrechen,* einen Vorübergehenden *anzureden:* "Guter Freund," *redete* er ihn *an,* "könnt ihr mir nicht sagen, wie der Herr heisst, dem dieses

wunderschöne Haus gehört, mit den Fenstern voll Tulipanen, Sternen-
blumen und *Levkoien?*" Der Mann aber, der *vermutlich* etwas wichtigeres
zu thun hatte, und zum Unglück gerade so viel von der deutschen Sprache
verstand als der Fragende von der holländischen, nämlich nichts, sagte
kurz und *schnauzig: "Kannitverstan!"* und *schnurrte* vorüber.

J. P. HEBEL, "Kannitverstan."[6]

Commentary .

The same story, which really is genuinely amusing, has since appeared with
various slight modifications in several intermediate readers and has still
been used during the last decade.

1. Quite a number of the words will probably be recognized rapidly
as derivatives (*Unbestand, Umweg, prächtig, geschäftiger, Wanderschaft,
Verwunderung, kostbare, anreden, vermutlich*). Presuming that students
know all the words in the Pfeffer dictionary (which is not at all certain
at this stage), the passage still contains 11 unknown words in 195 running
words (excluding *Kannitverstan,* which must be explained), a rate of one
new word in 18. Scherer recommends a rate of one new word in 35.[7]
Scherer also recommends that the new words be spaced evenly, that the
new vocabulary be useful, that cognates be signalled in some way, and
that new words be surrounded by "contextual clues so that it is possible
to infer the meaning."[8] The reader should look again at the italicized
words in the preceding passage with these recommendations in mind.

2. The sentences in the passage are also long and rather complicated,
placing a strain on the memory of the student who is making an attempt
at direct reading of the extract.[9]

We may say that this passage was intended for intensive reading and
therefore for extension of vocabulary and knowledge of structure. But a
number of the words italicized are not likely to be encountered frequently
in further reading or communication (*Levkoien, schnauzig, schnurren,
entbrechen,* and so on); the cognate *Tulipanen* is now archaic. On the other
hand, in the following passage, which is taken from a book of Heinrich
Böll's short stories,[10] four words of 117 running words are not in Pfeffer,
and one of these is a readily comprehensible derivative (*durchsuchen*). All
three (*Karteikarte, Zettel,* and *Bedürfnisanstalt*) are useful and can be
understood fairly well within the context (particularly as both *Karte* and
Bedürfnis are in Pfeffer). The passage is more suitable for Stage Four students than R47.

R 48 Sie haben mir jetzt eine Chance gegeben. Sie haben mir eine Karte ge-
schrieben, ich soll zum Amt kommen, und ich bin zum Amt gegangen.
Auf dem Amt waren sie sehr nett. Sie nahmen meine Karteikarte und
sagten: "Hm." Ich sagte auch: "Hm." "Welches Bein?" fragte der Beamte.
"Rechts."
"Ganz?"
"Ganz."
"Hm." machte er wieder. Dann durchsuchte er verschiedene Zettel. Ich
durfte mich setzen.
Endlich fand der Mann einen Zettel, der ihm der richtige zu sein schien.
Er sagte: "Ich denke, hier ist etwas für Sie. Eine nette Sache. Sie können
dabei sitzen. Schuhputzer in einer Bedürfnisanstalt auf dem Platz der
Republik. Wie wäre das?"
"Ich kann nicht Schuhe putzen; ich bin immer schon aufgefallen wegen
schlechten Schuhputzens."

It may be objected that this passage is too simple with regard to verb
tenses and structure, but with little trouble we can find in the same book
a passage which demonstrates various verb tenses, passives, and complex
sentences.[11]

R 49 Wir waren in jener gräßlichen Stimmung, wo man schon lange Abschied
genommen hat, sich aber noch nicht zu trennen vermag, weil der Zug noch
nicht abgefahren ist. Die Bahnhofshalle war wie alle Bahnhofshallen,
schmutzig und zugig, erfüllt von dem Dunst der Abdämpfe und von
Lärm, Lärm von Stimmen und Wagen.
Charlotte stand am Fenster des langen Flurs, und sie wurde dauernd
von hinten gestoßen und beiseite gedrängt, und es wurde viel über sie
geflucht, aber wir konnten uns doch diese letzten Minuten, diese kost-
barsten letzten gemeinsamen unseres Lebens nicht durch Winkzeichen aus
einem überfüllten Abteil heraus verständigen . . .
"Nett", sagte ich schon zum drittenmal, "wirklich nett, daß du bei mir
vorbeigekommen bist."
"Ich bitte dich, wo wir uns schon so lange kennen. Fünfzehn Jahre."
"Ja, ja, wir sind jetzt dreißig, immerhin . . . kein Grund . . ."
"Hör auf, ich bitte dich. Ja, wir sind jetzt dreißig. So alt wie die russische
Revolution . . ."
"So alt wie der Dreck und der Hunger . . ."
"Ein bißchen jünger . . ."
"Du hast recht, wir sind furchtbar jung." Sie lachte.

Commentary

Here in 168 words there are 11 words which are not in the Pfeffer dictionary, but 6 of these are regularly constructed derivatives (*zugig, Abdämpfe, beiseite, kostbar, überfüllt,* and *Abteil*) and therefore comprehensible. This leaves five new words, or a little more than three per 100 running words. One cannot maintain that suitable texts are easy to find, but it is evident that the works of modern writers like Böll generally prove to be more fruitful sources for completely unadapted material at this level than do nineteenth-century *Erzählungen* of the type shown in R47.

✱ Examine some reading passages in textbooks in common use for Stage Four to see how they measure up to the criteria discussed. Then find some suitable passages in novels and short stories in the library and share them with your fellow students, before adding them to your personal file.

Stage Five: Expansion

At Stage Five, students can read without becoming discouraged a wide variety of materials in their original form. At most there will have been some judicious editing to eliminate occasional paragraphs of excessively complicated structure and rare vocabulary. Once again the material that the student is encouraged to read entirely on his own, his extensive reading, will be more readily accessible in language and content than that which is being studied intensively. Reading is now a technique, not an end, and language is a vehicle and a model. Students are expected to be able to discuss not only the content but the implications of what they have been reading.

Material for intensive reading is chosen with a view to developing the student's aesthetic appreciation, imagination, and powers of judgment and discriminative reasoning. Students learn to scan for information, to read with careful attention, and to extract the major ideas and arguments. Attention is paid to matters of style in writing, and students are given some experience in exact translation from German to English to make them more conscious of the choices involved in literary writing and the potentialities of their own language, as well as the German language. Reading is still linked with *listening* (to plays, poems, readings, speeches), with *writing* (of reports, summaries, commentaries, and, for self-selected students, even poetry), and with *speaking* (discussion of ideas, themes, and values). Students seek to penetrate the mind and heart of the German people and compare and contrast their attitudes and aspirations with their own. They continue to read widely on subjects which interest them personally (political, social, scientific, artistic, practical) and prepare presentations in which they share what they have enjoyed with their fellow students.

Teachers need not feel at a loss in providing widely diversified reading for their Stage Five students, since material now being made available by publishers is much more varied than in previous decades.

✱ Examine advertisements in recent journals and publishers' catalogues to see how many areas of interest you can identify in recently published books of readings.

Students at Stage Five still need help with more difficult aspects of German written style. Many students, for instance, never grasp the essential differences between the common logical connectives such as *also, dagegen, danach, dann, dennoch, deshalb, doch, endlich* and *zuerst,* yet words such as these are indispensable for understanding the development of thought and drawing implications. A situational technique may be used to familiarize students at this level with their meaning.

R50 A key sentence is selected, such as:

Er hat seine Schulden nicht bezahlt.

A situation is described in German and the student is asked to link this key sentence with the idea: du hast ihm schon wieder Geld geliehen, in some way such as: Er hat seine Schulden nicht bezahlt, *dennoch* hast du ihm schon wieder Geld geliehen.

Other possibilities are:

Er hat seine Schulden nicht bezahlt.	Er hat keine Absicht sie zu bezahlen.
Er hat seine Schulden nicht bezahlt.	Er hat *auch* keine Absicht sie zu bezahlen.
Er hat seine Schulden nicht bezahlt.	Er geniert sich, wenn er mich sieht.
Er hat seine Schulden nicht bezahlt.	*Deshalb* geniert er sich, wenn er mich sieht.
Er hat seine Schulden nicht bezahlt.	Ich nehme seine Einladungen nicht mehr an.
Er hat seine Schulden nicht bezahlt.	*Also* nehme ich seine Einladungen nicht mehr an.

Important clue words like these are frequently omitted entirely from the German course, with the result that students continue for years to express themselves in simple sentences, or link sentences only with *und* and *aber,* and are incapable of recognizing the significance of these logical connectives in modifying the meaning of what they are reading. A careful study should be made of the way an argument is developed in German through a succession of such connectives.

READING WITH WRITING

A class which is reading for information would find practicing these connectives orally very difficult. A written exercise which requires analysis of the logical development and choice among possible connectives may be used instead.

R51 Write out the following passage as a paragraph, selecting from the logical connectives supplied those which will provide the most natural development of thought.

Ich gebe dir das Buch zurück. Ich habe versucht, es zu lesen, (doch, daher, danach) verstand ich kein Wort. (Endlich, daher, schließlich) kann man nicht erwarten, daß ich etwas ganz Unverständliches lese. Ich werde ein leichteres Buch kaufen, (denn, dann, aber) das Thema "Redekunst" interessiert mich noch. Ich möchte die Theorie der Redekunst nicht nur verstehen, (aber, sondern) sie auch anwenden können. Ich habe dich ja (dagegen, deshalb, dennoch) gefragt, was auf diesem Gebiet zu empfehlen ist.

MATERIALS FOR STAGE FIVE

Some textbooks propose for intensive reading in a general course at this level material like the following:

R52 *Hoffnung*

Es reden und träumen die Menschen viel
Von bessern künftigen Tagen,
Nach einem glücklichen Ziel
Sieht man sie rennen und jagen;
Die Welt wird alt und wird wieder jung,
Doch der Mensch hofft immer Verbesserung.

Die Hoffnung führt ihn ins Leben ein,
Sie umflattert den fröhlichen Knaben,
Den Jüngling locket ihr Zauberschein,
Sie wird mit dem Greis nicht begraben;

Denn beschließt er im Grabe den müden Lauf,
Noch am Grabe pflanzt er — die Hoffnung auf.

Es ist kein leerer schmeichelnder Wahn,
Erzeugt im Gehirne des Toren,
Im Herzen kündet es laut sich an:
Zu was Besserem sind wir geboren.
Und was die innere Stimme spricht,
Das täuscht die hoffende Seele nicht.

F. SCHILLER[12]

The vocabulary and syntax of the poem, especially after the first stanza, require a good deal of explanation. Important, and moving, as the poem is, it is not clear how the average intermediate-level student could do more than decipher it, whereas he would be able to read easily and with enjoyment simpler poems of Goethe, Brentano, or Brecht. For a general textbook, then, this poem is unsuitable, whereas it would fascinate Group D, which has chosen to specialize in literary analysis.

A poem which has delighted many non-specialized students and made German poetry accessible to them is this brief poem by Goethe, *Wanderers Nachtlied*. It has been reprinted in numerous textbooks and anthologies for students of German for well over a hundred years, but poetry is timeless in its appeal to new generations.

R53 *Wanderers Nachtlied*

Über allen Gipfeln
Ist Ruh,
In allen Wipfeln
Spürest du
Kaum einen Hauch;
Die Vögelein schweigen im Walde.
Warte nur, balde
Ruhest du auch.

This poem, in contrast to R52, is easily understood by all students. Its theme is universal, yet immediate, calling forth an emotional response with little need for explanation.

Many twentieth-century poems are equally accessible to the general student. The concrete poetry of such poets as Ernst Jandl can be used even at very elementary stages of language learning to involve students in basic sound and word relationships of German.[13] As an example for a

slightly more advanced level we may take the following poems by Bertolt
Brecht:[14]

R54 *Der Radwechsel*

Ich sitze am Straßenhang.
Der Fahrer wechselt das Rad.
Ich bin nicht gern, wo ich herkomme.
Ich bin nicht gern, wo ich hinfahre.
Warum sehe ich den Radwechsel
Mit Ungeduld?

Der Rauch

Das kleine Haus unter Bäumen am See.
Vom Dach steigt Rauch.
Fehlte er
Wie trostlos dann wären
Haus, Bäume und See.

Again the themes are universal and appealing to modern students, and when
compared, the poems could lead to a discussion of change and permanence.
At the same time, any of the three poems above could be easily committed
to memory by the students and added to their store of treasured literary
memories. In this way poetry becomes a personal experience, not another
arduous classroom assignment.

With prose readings similarly, care must be exercised in the selection of
materials for Group C. (Group D, as we have noted, is a self-selected
group of specialized interests with a declared desire to explore literature.)
Some books offer selections like the following where the language is not
inaccessible and there are some cognates, but the content is very difficult
for the average student of German.

R55 Aber in dem Maße, wie seine Gesundheit geschwächt ward, verschärfte
sich seine Künstlerschaft, ward wählerisch, erlesen, kostbar, fein, reizbar
gegen das Banale und aufs höchste empfindlich in Fragen des Taktes und
Geschmacks. Als er zum ersten Male hervortrat, wurde unter denen, die es
anging, viel Beifall und Freude laut, denn es war ein wertvoll gearbeitetes
Ding, was er geliefert hatte, voll Humor und Kenntnis des Leidens. Und
schnell ward sein Name, derselbe, mit dem er seine ersten Reime an den
Walnußbaum, den Springbrunnen und das Meer unterzeichnet hatte, dieser
aus Süd und Nord zusammengesetzte Klang, dieser exotisch angehauchte
Bürgersname zu einer Formel, die Vortreffliches bezeichnete; denn der

schmerzlichen Gründlichkeit seiner Erfahrungen gesellte sich ein seltener, zäh ausharrender und ehrsüchtiger Fleiß, der im Kampf mit der wählerischen Reizbarkeit seines Geschmacks unter heftigen Qualen ungewöhnliche Werke entstehen ließ.   THOMAS MANN, *Tonio Kröger*.[15]

A passion for the chronological presentation of literary masterpieces must be curbed at this stage if students are to become fluent in reading and using contemporary language. If the oral skills are to be kept at a high level, reading material must be such that the students can discuss its content and implications with ease and confidence. This does not mean that the content must be of little literary or philosophical value, as the following extract from Wolfgang Borchert's story "Die Hundeblume" demonstrates.[16]

R56 Was ist so komisch: Ein blasierter, reuiger Jüngling aus dem Zeitalter der Grammophonplatten und Raumforschung steht in der Gefängniszelle 432 unter dem hochgemauerten Fenster und hält mit seinen vereinsamten Händen eine kleine gelbe Blume in den schmalen Lichtstrahl—eine ganz gewöhnliche Hundeblume. Und dann hebt dieser Mensch, der gewohnt war, Pulver, Parfüm und Benzin, Gin und Lippenstift zu riechen, die Hundeblume an seine hungrige Nase, die schon monatelang nur das Holz der Pritsche, Staub und Angstschweiß gerochen hat—und er saugt so gierig aus der kleinen gelben Scheibe ihr Wesen in sich hinein, daß er nur noch aus Nase besteht.

Da öffnet sich in ihm etwas und ergießt sich wie Licht in den engen Raum, etwas, von dem er bisher nie gewußt hat: Eine Zärtlichkeit, eine Anlehnung und Wärme ohnegleichen erfüllt ihn zu der Blume und füllt ihn ganz aus.

Er ertrug den Raum nicht mehr und schloß die Augen und staunte: Aber du riechst ja nach Erde. Nach Sonne, Meer und Honig, liebes Lebendiges! Er empfand ihre keusche Kühle wie die Stimme des Vaters, die er nie sonderlich beachtet hatte und der nun soviel Trost war mit seiner Stille—er empfand sie wie die helle Schulter einer dunklen Frau.

Commentary

This story is relevant to the relationship of the individual to modern society as well as to nature and would lead to a discussion of interest to the students, yet in language it is within the reading scope of Stage Five. Scherer suggests a vocabulary of at least 5,000 words for the last stage before liberated reading.[17] All but nine words in R56 either occur within the 3,000 word limit of Pfeffer's *Grunddeutsch. Basic (Spoken) German*

Dictionary for Everyday Usage or can be readily derived from the stems of words contained in Pfeffer. Although it is impossible to calculate exactly how many words would be unfamiliar, all but two words (*blasiert* and *Pritsche*) are common and useful enough that students might be expected to recognize them in context. (Some students may even find *blasé* in the stem of *blasiert*.)

* Look for suitable poems, stories, essays, scenes from plays, and short novels which you think would appeal to Stage Five and which are accessible in vocabulary range and complexity of structure to students. (Keep careful notes of bibliographic details and page references!) Share your discoveries with others in your class and add to your file for future reference.

Stage Six: Autonomy

Students who have reached this stage should be encouraged to undertake an independent reading program tailored to their special interests. They should be able to come to the teacher on a personal basis at regular intervals to discuss what they have been reading and share the exhilaration of their discoveries.

Their reading may be in some special area of literature which interests them, or they may be reading widely with the aim of finding out as much as they can about the cultural attitudes or the civilization of the German people. On the other hand, they may have some specialized interest they wish to pursue: a contrastive study of German and American advertising, or of the content of popular magazines; the theories behind modern German architecture; urban problems; or folklore. An independent reading unit becomes more purposeful if it leads to some form of display: a one-man show at a German club festival, an illustrated presentation to interested German classes, an article for the school magazine, or the elaboration of a plan for study abroad in the area of the student's interest. Independent study of this type for advanced students stimulates self-disciplined motivation and is an excellent preparation for autonomous intellectual exploration in later life.

Ordering the reading lesson

The reading lesson is not a quiescent interlude as some teachers seem to think. Because students have learned to associate sound and symbol in their native language, it does not follow that they know how to extract the full meaning from what they see in print. For the teacher the reading lesson or reading assignment has six parts.

1. *Selection* of suitable material at an appropriate level of reading difficulty for this particular group of students; selection of the right amount

of material for the time available and for arousing and maintaining interest in the content of the text.

2. *Preparation* by the teacher, who checks on: the necessary background information; words that need explaining (and how best to explain them—by visual, action, German definition or synonym, or translation); structural complications; obscurity of meaning or allusion; and the most effective way to arouse interest in this particular text.

The teacher who has prepared the material ahead of time can often slip some of the unfamiliar vocabulary into class discussions and exercises in a preceding lesson, or can center an oral lesson on a semantic area germane to the reading text, thus not only introducing useful vocabulary but also preparing students unobtrusively for intelligent guessing when they are face to face with the text. A review of certain grammatical features may refresh the students' memory so that comprehension is not impeded by structural complexity.

3. *Introduction* of the material to the students. This introduction may take the form of the provision of background information or some explanation of cultural differences, either directly—visually or orally—or indirectly, during some other activity when the students may have been given the opportunity to find out information which will be useful for a later reading lesson. Sometimes the introduction will take the form of a provocative discussion on a question which is raised in the reading text, with the students then reading more alertly as they find out how the author has viewed the problem or whether the outcome is as they had anticipated. This approach is particularly valuable at Stage Five when a writer is developing difficult concepts or setting out a complicated discussion of ideas. Stimulating the student's own thinking about the central issue or problem helps him to anticipate the probable meaning of unfamiliar vocabulary and to perceive disguised cognates in the matrix of the development of ideas.

4. *Reading.* Throughout this section, and particularly in the discussion of the different stages, many practical suggestions have been given as to ways to approach the actual reading of the passage. These should be exploited on different occasions to ensure that the reading lesson does not fall into a set pattern. Individualized reading assignments also should be designed with a variety of activities in mind. The cardinal principle for each approach (except for Group E: *Translation*) is that it should encourage students to keep looking ahead for meaning, rather than stopping at each word to seek an exact English equivalent.

5. *Discussion.* It is at this point that the teacher is able to gauge and increase the student's overall comprehension of the passage, not by explaining and restating, but by encouraging the student to go back to the passage and look into it more carefully. Suggestions for improving this part of the lesson are developed in the next section.

6. *Application.* Reading is not an isolated activity. In a language class

it should lead to something, and thus be integrated with the improvement of all skills. This idea is developed below in the section *Integrating the Language Skills,* p. 229.

✱ From all the indications scattered throughout this section draw up three different lesson plans for the reading of R57 below.

Assisting and assessing reading comprehension

The following passage will be used as a basis for demonstration and evaluation of various methods for assisting and assessing the student's comprehension of reading material. In each example, items given are for illustration only and in no case represent a complete set.

R57   War die Sonne mal weg, oder es regnete, gingen wir in den Zoo. Wir   1
kamen umsonst rein; Vater war mit dem Mann an der Kasse befreundet.   2
Am häufigsten gingen wir zu den Affen; wir nahmen ihnen meist, wenn   3
niemand hinsah, die Erdnüsse weg; die Affen hatten genug zu essen, sie   4
hatten bestimmt viel mehr als wir.   5
Manche Affen kannten uns schon; ein Gibbon war da, der reichte uns   6
jedesmal alles, was er an Eßbarem hatte, durchs Gitter. Nahmen wir es   7
ihm ab, klatschte er über dem Kopf in seine langen Hände, fletschte die   8
Zähne und torkelte wie betrunken im Käfig umher. Wir dachten zuerst, er   9
machte sich über uns lustig; aber allmählich kamen wir dahinter, er ver-   10
stellte sich nur, er wollte uns der Peinlichkeit des Almosenempfangens   11
entheben.   12
Er sparte richtig für uns. Er hatte eine alte Konservenbüchse, in die tat er   13
alles, was man ihm am Tag zu essen gegeben hatte, hinein. Wenn wir   14
kamen, sah er sich jedesmal erst besorgt um, ob uns auch niemand beob-   15
achten könnte; dann griff er in seine Büchse und reichte uns die erste   16
Erdnuß, nachdem er sie sorgfältig am Brustfell saubergerieben hatte,   17
durchs Gitter. Er wartete, bis wir eine Nuß aufgegessen hatten, darauf   18
reichte er uns die nächste hinaus. Es war mühsam, sich dann nach ihm zu   19
richten; aber er hatte wohl seine Gründe für diese umständliche Art, uns   20
die Nüsse zu geben; und wir mochten ihn auch nicht beleidigen, denn er   21
hatte Augen, so alt wie die Welt . . .   22

W. SCHNURRE, "Der Verrat."[18]

Commentary

Most of the words in this passage are either in the Pfeffer dictionary or are cognates. The meanings of words not in the dictionary (*Gitter, Käfig, klatschen, fletschen, torkeln*) can be inferred with little effort from the context and from the situation, although *Konservenbüchse* will require an explanation. (*Freund, Mühe, Umstand, stellen, heben, Brust* are in Pfeffer, so *be-freund-et, müh-sam, umständ-lich, ver-stellen, ent-heben,* and even *Brust-fell* should pose no problems.)

1. *Content questions,* that is, Who? What? When? Where? How (manner)? and yes-no questions, are most appropriate at Stage Three.

R58 a. Wohin gingen der Vater und Sohn, wenn es regnete?
        Sie gingen in den Zoo.
     b. Worin sparte der Affe die Erdnüße?
        Er sparte sie in einer alten Konservenbüchse.
     c. Was für Augen hatte der Affe?
        Er hatte Augen, so alt wie die Welt.

Commentary

Questions of this type are too simple for Stages Four and Five. Answers to the questions can be copied directly from the text with a little infusion of words from the question itself. They do not necessarily require comprehension of the text; once the student has identified the place in the text where the answer can be found he responds to structural clues—*Wohin? in . . . in den Zoo; Worin? in . . . in einer alten Konservenbüchse; was für Augen? Augen, so alt . . .*

2. *Implication questions,* that is, Why? If . . . then what? and How (explanation)? questions, should be asked at Stages Four and Five.

R59 a. Warum gingen der Vater und Sohn in den Zoo?
        Weil das Wetter schlecht war (oder auch: weil sie Hunger hatten und Erdnüße von den Affen bekamen).
     b. Wie hat der Gibbon seine Freundlichkeit gezeigt?
        Er sparte Erdnüße für den Vater und Sohn (oder: Er hat sich verstellt, weil er sie nicht beleidigen wollte; oder: Er hat jede Erdnuß saubergerieben, bevor er sie überreichte).

Commentary

Question (a) requires the student to answer a question from line 1 from information contained in lines 1–5. Question (b) is based primarily on lines 10–12, but requires an answer from various sections (lines 6–12, 13, 16–18). Some teachers insist that students copy out, or repeat, the relevant part of the question and thus always answer with a complete sentence. If the aim is to evaluate degree of reading comprehension, this is really busy work at this point and can become laborious for the student, with no particular gain in skill. The student who has not done so should not be penalized. Note that with questions of this type there will be a number of possible answers depending on the way the student chooses to express the idea.

The problem arises: If one is evaluating reading comprehension, should one require skill in composition, written or oral, at the same time? If the student has demonstrated quite clearly that he has understood the passage by giving the right facts in answer to the questions, should he be penalized for writing or phrasing his answers in incorrect German, since this has nothing to do with reading comprehension? At Stage Five one should expect students to be able to express themselves in simple correct German. For some students at Stage Four, and certainly at Stage Three, it may be better to try other methods of eliciting information gained from reading. If the method outlined is used because students are seeking to attain a high level in all skills, a form of dual credit will be adopted: allowing some credit for comprehension and some for the way the answer is formulated.

    3. *Multiple-choice questions* are frequently used.
    a. At Stage Three, *sentence completions* requiring only discrimination among several short alternative phrases may be used. The choices are usually set out in written form; if they are given orally, they also test listening comprehension and auditory memory.

R60   Choose a completion for each of the following sentences according to the information given in the text you have just read:

Der Gibbon hatte die Gewohnheit, die Erdnüße
A. dem Sohn abzunehmen;
B. sauberzureiben, bevor er sie in den Mund steckte;
C. aus dem Käfig zu reichen;
D. für sich zu sparen.

Commentary

The choices are designed so that the correct answer (C) is quite clear to the student who understood the text. (A), (B), and (D) pick up expressions in the text which may attract students who do not understand completely. (A) points to lines 7–8: *nahmen wir es ihm ab.* (B) could attract a student who did not understand the passage very well but who sees in line 17: *nachdem er sie sorgfältig am Brustfell saubergerieben hatte.* (D) could attract the student who is unsure about the difference between *uns* and *sich.* Multiple choice selections must always be designed so that they reflect some element in the text which may have been misunderstood, but the correct version should never reproduce word for word some sentence in the text. The choices should also be plausible completions—in this case (A), (B), (C), and (D) all describe the kinds of things monkeys do. There must be no ambiguity in the choices which would cause an intelligent student to hesitate between possibilities. If students are warned in advance, there can occasionally be more than one correct choice in a set.

Variation: Sometimes single word completions are used.

R61 Der Gibbon hat die Erdnüße, die er zu essen bekam, gleich _____ .

    A. aufgefressen
    B. aufgespart
    C. angesehen
    D. weggegeben

Commentary

With single word completions, once again, it is important that the correct completion does not parallel a sentence the student can identify in the text without understanding its meaning. Since the purpose of this exercise is to assess comprehension of the passage, it is important that the choices contain words whose meanings the students may be expected to know.

    b. At Stages Four and Five, multiple choice sets will consist of *longer statements* which the student must be able to comprehend as well as the original text.

R62 Nachdem der Sohn eine Erdnuß empfangen hatte,

    A. rieb er sie gleich sauber;
    B. wartete er, bis er die nächste bekam;
    C. wurde es ihm zu mühsam, sich nach dem Gibbon zu richten;
    D. sah er sie erst besorgt an.

Commentary

Once again, each of the choices is plausible in the context. (A) draws attention to line 17 where *nachdem* and *saubergerieben* occur; (B) is correct; (C) points to lines 19–20 (*es war mühsam, sich da nach ihm zu richten*) where part of the correct answer lies, but puts a wrong interpretation on this sentence; and (D) is for students who did not understand the passage but who see *sehen* in line 15 (*sah er sich jedesmal erst besorgt um*).

Variation: In an expository text, one sentence important in the comprehension of the development of ideas may be drawn out and students asked to select a correct paraphrase for the idea in the sentence from several alternatives.

DIGRESSION

In "How to Pass Multiple-Choice Tests when you Don't Know the Answers" Hoffman[19] sets out for ambitious but indolent students a few rules based on common faults of multiple-choice tests. Below are seven which are applicable to reading comprehension tests.

1. With five alternatives the correct answer tends to be the third, with four alternatives the second or third.

2. An alternative which is much longer or shorter than the others tends to be the correct answer.

3. With a sentence to complete: if the alternative when added to the stem does not make a grammatical sequence, that alternative is not the correct item.

4. Look for clues in other questions.

5. If two alternatives are exactly the same except for one word, one of them is usually the correct answer.

6. "None of the above" is usually wrong.

7. Find out before the test if there is a penalty for guessing the wrong answer.

* Apply these rules to some tests you have constructed to see if wily students could have "guessed" their way to an A.

4. *True-false-don't know checks.* True-false checks are useful as a quick assessment of reading comprehension, particularly for extensive-reading assignments. If students are given two points for a correct answer, lose a point for an incorrect answer, but do not lose a point for answering Don't Know, they will be less likely to make wild guesses and the score will more truly reflect their comprehension of the passage.

R63   Read the following statements and check whether each is T (True) or F (False) according to the information in the passage you have just read. If you are not sure circle D (Don't Know). (If the instructions are written in German the terms *Richtig, Falsch,* and *Unentschieden* will be used.)

1.   T   F   D   Da der Sohn den Mann an der Kasse kannte, brauchte er nicht zu bezahlen, um in den Zoo zu kommen.
2.   T   F   D   Der Gibbon steckte immer die erste Nuß in den Mund und reichte die zweite hinaus.
3.   T   F   D   Der Gibbon war besorgt, daß man sehen würde, wie er dem Vater und Sohn Nüße gab.
4.   T   F   D   Der Affe tat wie ein Betrunkener, um den Vater und Sohn zu beleidigen.

Commentary

As with multiple-choice items, all statements must be plausible in the context and must be based on possible misunderstanding of specific phrases in the text. Care must be taken not to develop a pattern of correct responses, e.g., TFTFTF or TFFTTFFTT. There is no need for an equal number of T's and F's: students are quick to discover that this is usually the case and will adjust their answers accordingly. Correct statements should not be so phrased that they repeat exactly the words of the text. True-false questions provide a good opportunity to test the student's attention to structural clues, e.g., "Der Vater und Sohn gingen in den Zoo, *um* die Affen *zu* besuchen."

   5. *Questions in German requiring answers in English.* We have discussed the particular problem of reading comprehension questions requiring written or spoken answers in German. Some teachers avoid this problem by asking questions in German to which the students respond in English. This makes it impossible for a student to frame a response using words from the question or the text without knowing their meaning. It also requires comprehension of the questions, which are in German.

R64   Hat der Sohn immer verstanden, was der Gibbon tat? Erklären Sie Ihre Antwort!

   No, the son did not always understand what the monkey intended with his behavior. He realized at one point that the gibbon was trying to spare both father and son the embarrassment of accepting food, but the boy could not understand why the monkey insisted on passing out the nuts one by one.

Commentary

Many students who have understood the text perfectly would have trouble saying all this in correct German. This method enables the teacher to dig more deeply into the student's comprehension of what he has read. If this approach is used, questions should not move methodically through the text so that the student can pinpoint the particular sentences in which the answers can probably be found, but should require the student to think about and interpret the content of large sections of the text.

6. *Questions in English to be answered in English* are not advisable. The questions in English often solve problems of vocabulary and structure for some of the students, and the very sequence of the English questions sometimes supplies a kind of résumé of the meaning. *Questions in English to be answered in German* would be pointless. Students capable of answering the questions in German would also be capable of understanding the questions in German, and once again the questions would supply the students with clues to the meaning of many sections of the text.

7. *Anticipatory questions.* With a difficult text, the student may be supplied with questions before he begins to read. These questions are designed to lead the reader to search for certain information which will make the passage clearer to him. Anticipatory questions are more appropriate for expository and informational passages than for a narrative like R57. However, questions like the following would make the student look carefully at the text.

R65 1. Was taten der Vater und Sohn gewöhnlich, wenn sie in den Zoo gingen?
2. Waren die Affen freundlich zu ihnen?

8. *Zusammenfassung with key words omitted.* After the student has read the text and put it away, he may be supplied with a *Zusammenfassung* in German of the content with certain words omitted. He then shows by the way he completes the *Zusammenfassung* how well he understood the text and how much attention he paid to the vocabulary.

R66 _____ es, gingen der Erzähler mit seinem _____ in den Zoo. Wenn _____ hinsah, nahmen sie den Affen _____ weg, weil die Affen mehr zu _____ hatten _____ sie. Ein Gibbon sparte für sie in einer _____ und _____ ihnen alles durchs Gitter.

9. *Assessing overall comprehension.* Depending on the content of the passage students may be asked to do such things as:

a. supply in German a suitable title for a film of the story and subtitles for the main sections into which it could be divided;

b. make a chart of the relationships of the persons in the story;

c. sketch (or describe) a suitable stage setting for a dramatization of the scene;

d. draw a map showing the various areas in which the action took place;

e. write a brief day-to-day diary of the hero's adventures;

f. outline the plot under the headings: presentation of characters, development, climax, dénouement (or unraveling of the complications).

10. *Assessing comprehension of expository reading.* (Exercises of the types below would be suitable for R67: *Land ohne Hauptstadt.*)

a. Give the passage a suitable title. (In this case no title would be supplied with the text.)

b. For each paragraph, give the main gist in one sentence, then set down the important details related to the central idea, showing clearly their relationships in the development of this idea. (Exercises (a) and (b) would be given and completed in English for Group A who are reading for information, but in German for Groups C and D.)

c. Below are four sentences for each paragraph in the text. Select from the four choices in each case the one which best sums up the central idea of the paragraph. (Choices are given in German.)

d. Rearrange the following statements to form a simplified but consecutive account of the development of ideas in the passage you have just read. (The student is presented with a jumbled set of paraphrases of statements made in the text. The statements are in German, but are so worded as not to be identifiable by simple matching with the text.)

e. For Group A: In which paragraphs are the following ideas discussed? (Paraphrased summaries of the ideas in the passage are given in German, care being taken to see that they are so expressed that they cannot be matched from the text without being fully understood. To give the student practice in reading rapidly to extract the main ideas, a time limit is set within which to complete the exercise.)

✳ Below is a reading passage suitable for Stage Four or Stage Five. Develop some questions of the different types which have just been described and discuss in class their effectiveness.

R67 *Land ohne Hauptstadt* [20]

Es ist aus verschiedenen Gründen nicht leicht, über die Bundesrepublik zu schreiben—sogar dann, wenn man in diesem Land seit mehr als fünf Jahren diplomatischer Korrespondent ist.

Selbst wenn man lange in Westdeutschland ist, kann man nur die Eindrücke summieren, aber es ist nicht möglich, die in jeder Hinsicht komplizierte Situation zu bewältigen.

Will man ein Land kennenlernen, dann beginnt man die Beobachtung in der Regel in seiner Hauptstadt. Westdeutschland jedoch hat im Grunde genommen keine Hauptstadt und hat bisher kein Zentrum geschaffen, das als Ort für eine solche Beobachtung geeignet wäre. Eine Hauptstadt in des Wortes eigentlicher Bedeutung ist Bonn nicht—genausowenig wie Washington oder Ankara oder Brasilia. Die Entstehung einer Hauptstadt kann man nicht anordnen. Daher ist Bonn bestenfalls Sitz der staatlichen Verwaltung und des Bundestages.

Die Beobachtung des Besuchers ist also vom Startort abhängig—davon, ob er eine Reise durch Deutschland in Hamburg oder in München beginnt, im Ruhrgebiet oder in Frankfurt am Main. Fast ein Jahrhundert nach dem ersten Versuch, Deutschland von oben zu vereinen, hat der traditionelle Partikularismus keineswegs aufgehört, die charakteristische Eigenschaft der deutschen Landschaft auch in politischer Hinsicht zu sein.

Aus der ZEIT

Building and maintaining an adequate vocabulary (Stages Four and Five)

Moulton gives foreign-language students three practical recommendations for acquiring vocabulary: "First, never 'look a word up' until you have read the whole context in which it occurs—at least an entire sentence. . . . Second, don't be afraid of making 'intelligent guesses.' . . . Third, make a special list of your 'nuisance words'—the ones you find yourself looking up over and over again. Put them down on paper and memorize them."[21] These recommendations may well be passed on to students as an essential form of personal discipline. Going beyond this, however, the teacher may develop exercises to help the student "increase his word power" in German through focusing on form, focusing on meaning, expanding by association, and recirculating the vocabulary he has acquired.

FOCUSING ON FORM

Often students are not given guidelines for multiplying the vocabulary they already know through recognition of related forms.

Many are not familiar with simple facts about the German language such as those exemplified in R4 and R5.

They have never been taught to recognize the many *nouns derived from the various forms of verbs:*

R68

schlafen	der Schlaf
suchen	die Suche
helfen	die Hilfe
tun	die Tat
geben	die Gabe
versenden	der Versand
verstehen	der Verstand
	das Verständnis
	das Verstehen

They do not know how to discover the meaning of *words prefixed by common prepositions or adjectives* with which they are familiar:

R69

mit	mitbringen
gegen	die Gegenerklärung
	der Gegenangriff
nach	die Nachhilfe
	nachholen
durch	durchschauen (with separable prefix: see through)
	(with inseparable prefix: penetrate, understand)
voll	volljährig, vollbeschäftigt
	die Vollmacht
gut	gutgelaunt
	gutwillig

Recognition of the common *meanings of inseparable prefixes* will help them discern the meaning of unfamiliar verbs:

R70

zergehen
zerfallen
zerfließen

verspielen
sich versprechen
verkennen

✱ Think of words that can be deciphered through recognition of *ent-* as meaning "away from."

Common suffixes give clues to the meaning of seemingly "new" words.

R71 *-eln* and *-ern* are used to form verbs from verbs or other parts of speech, diminishing the action of the verb and frequently expressing repetition:

lachen (to laugh)	lächeln (to smile)
tropfen (to drop or drip)	tröpfeln (to fall in drops or to pour drop by drop)
steigen (to climb)	steigern (to raise, to increase)
krank (sick)	kränkeln (to be sickly)

Teachers who are not familiar themselves with these formal indications of variation in meaning will find much of interest in Herbert Lederer et al., *Reference Grammar of the German Language* (New York: Scribner, 1969), pp. 20-43.

Exercises

1. Students may be asked to give nouns corresponding to adjectives (*hart, die Härte*), adjectives corresponding to nouns (*das Glück, glücklich*), verbs corresponding to nouns (*der Trost, trösten*), verbs corresponding to adjectives (*frei, befreien*), and so on.

2. Students may be asked to change the meaning of sentences by the addition of a prefix to a word italicized (Seine Ankunft hat mich *glücklich* gemacht; Seine Ankunft hat mich *unglücklich* gemacht) or to complete sentences with a word with a different suffix (Es ist nicht ganz *rot;* Es ist eher *rötlich*).

FOCUSING ON MEANING

Valuable practice in vocabulary building is provided when students are asked to do exercises like the following:

1. To supply paraphrases or definitions for words in the text (*Er entkleidete sich, Er zog sich aus*).

2. To identify from multiple-choice items the correct paraphrases or definitions for certain words in the text (in R57: *torkeln* = A. *springen*, B. *rennen*, C. *unsicher gehen*, D. *auf der Erde herumrollen*).

3. To find words in the text to match paraphrases of definitions supplied (in R57: Find the words in the text which mean a. *unsicher gehen*, b. *komplizierte Weise*).

4. To complete sentences, based on the text, with certain words on which they will need to focus their attention. These sentences should not reproduce the original text exactly and should usually require the student

to reuse the vocabulary in a different form, e.g., in a different person, number, or tense.

R72 Complete the following sentences with words from the text you have just read (R57).

    a. Der Gibbon hat dem Vater und Sohn das eigene Essen durchs Gitter

_____.

    b. Der Affe verstellte sich, weil die Situation für den Vater und Sohn sonst zu _____ wäre.

    c. Es machte dem Vater und Sohn große _____, sich nach der umständlichen Art des Gibbons zu richten.

    5. *Exercises may be unrelated to a known text,* e.g., students discover for themselves, through dictionary search, synonyms and antonyms (*klug, intelligent; gut, schlecht*). They may compete to see who can find the largest number of synonyms and antonyms in a given period of time. Learning to enjoy a purposeful search for information in dictionaries and grammars is an important preparation for autonomous student progress. (See also W68-75.)

    6. Students complete an unfamiliar text in a plausible way by supplying for each blank a word carefully selected from multiple-choice alternatives. This type of exercise can be developed with simple texts or more complex texts, serving as an amusing and challenging exercise right through to the advanced level.

R73 Es gibt (Aufsätze, Tage, Theaterabende), die wie alle (anderen, Schriften, Unternehmungen) beginnen und die plötzlich eine (normale, unerwartete, glückliche) Wendung nehmen. An diesem (Morgen, Abend, Nachmittag) bin ich wie (manchmal, sonst nie, immer) früh (eingeschlafen, heimgefahren, aufgewacht).

Commentary

A passage such as this teaches the student to pay attention to distinctions of meaning, but it is also an exercise in reading comprehension. The student should write out his completed version as a coherent paragraph, rather than merely circling choices. In this way he can read his version through to see that it makes sense and then read it aloud to his fellow students. With a little ingenuity, passages can be designed to have several possible final versions, and students can be encouraged to reconstitute the several possibilities. Advanced students may like to prepare such passages for the other students to complete. (A teacher or student who does not feel confident in constructing a passage in German himself can easily adapt paragraphs from books or magazines.)

* Find in various composition and reading texts other types of exercises which focus on meaning distinctions and discuss their effectiveness.

EXPANDING BY ASSOCIATION

We tend to recall words through meaningful associational bonds, and words tend to appear in texts in collocations, that is, in relation to centers of interest of semantic areas (*Brot* is likely to appear in a text in which *Bäcker* appears; *Reifen, Panne,* and *Wagen* are very likely to occur together). It is for this reason that learning vocabulary in context is much more valuable than learning isolated words.

Exercises

Many possibilities suggest themselves, and each teacher can think of his own once he understands the necessity for developing chains of associations and for expanding nuclei. Many of these exercises can take the form of games or team competitions which can be directed by the students themselves. Three come immediately to mind.

R74 What action do you associate with the following objects? Follow the pattern:

Das Brot? Man ißt es.

In each case give as many alternatives as you can find. The team gains points for every alternative its team members can discover.

Die Blumen?   Man kann sie anschauen.
              Man kann sie sammeln.
              Man kann sie pflanzen.

Das Buch?   Man macht es auf.
              Man liest es.
              Man macht es zu.

R75 As each object is named, give the German word for a person you associate with it. You must answer in three seconds.

das Papier?   der Schüler
die Kreide?   der Lehrer

der Zug? der Schaffner
das Restaurant? der Kellner/der Ober

Alternatively: When a person, animal, or object is named, give the German word for a place you associate with it. You must answer in three seconds.

das Brot? die Bäckerei
der Kuchen? die Konditorei/das Café
das Rindfleisch? die Metzgerei

R76 Intelligence test series can be adapted as follows. This exercise can be used from elementary to advanced levels and, again, students may be encouraged to make up further exercises themselves.

In the following lists, underline the word which does not seem to belong with the others in the series.

blau, rot, kalt, grün
der Garten, die Blume, der Rasen, der Schrank
die Kälte, heiß, die Kühle, die Ehre (This item can be answered in two ways: by form or by semantic area.)

RECIRCULATING VOCABULARY ACQUIRED

Students learn new words with every passage they read. Often they forget them rapidly because they do not encounter them again for a long while. All kinds of games and exercises can be introduced to enliven the class while giving students the opportunity to retrieve words they have learned in the past and recirculate them through their conscious minds. In this way the ease with which these words can be retrieved, when required, is increased. The following suggestions will bring to mind other possibilities. They are arranged in approximate order of difficulty.

R77 From the parallel lists of words given select pairs which have a natural association.

das Meer das Brot
der Bäcker die Seite
das Buch die Wellen

Students working in teams may make their own parallel lists to try out on members of the other teams.

R78 Begin with the word *der Baum* (or . . .) and write down rapidly any ten German words which come to your mind. Write whichever word you think of. Do not try to develop a logical series. (With each noun, include the correct definite article.)

The lists, when completed, may be read aloud for amusement. Series may come out like the following:

der Baum, die Blume, der Duft, die Frau, die Kleidung, der Schneider, das Geschäft, die Straße, die Polizei, das Gefängnis.

der Baum, der Vogel, das Nest, das Ei, das Frühstück, der Morgen, die Schule, das Klassenzimmer, die Bücher, die Bibliothek.

R79 *Semantic areas.* Write down as many words as you can think of which have a natural association with *der Baum* (or . . .). Points will be given to the team having the largest number of different words. (Include the correct definite or indefinite article with each noun.)

der Baum, das Blatt, der Zweig, der Wald, das Obst, die Blumen, der Stamm, die Nadel . . .

Or: Write down all the words you know which have a similar meaning to *das Haus*. (Include the correct definite or indefinite article with each.)

das Haus, die Wohnung, das Schloß, die Burg, die Hütte . . .

R80 Make as many words as you can from the letters in "Das ist ein Baum." No letter can be used more times than it appears in the sentence.

das, ist, ein, Baum, dein, mein, nein, sein, Saat, Daumen, Mund, Taube . . .

R81 Write down all the idiomatic expressions you can think of which contain the word *Kopf* (or . . .) and make up a sentence to show the use of each:

den Kopf voll haben
einen harten Kopf haben
aus dem Kopf aufsagen
beim Kopf nehmen
etwas im Kopf behalten

R82 List any five words on the chalkboard and ask students to make up a brief story incorporating all five, e.g.: das Gold, der Rotkohl, das Zollamt, die Grippe, der Berg.

R83   *Kreuzworträtsel.* Simple crossword puzzles may be constructed by the students as exercises, then tried out on their fellow students. These provide practice in recalling words from their definitions or by association. Students may use definitions they find in monolingual dictionaries, thus giving them a purposeful familiarity with such dictionaries. One source of German crosswords in published form is: Susanne Ehrlich, *Das Kreuzworträtsel-buch* (National Textbook Company).

Scrabble sets geared to the letter frequencies of particular languages are also available.

Vocabulary enrichment and retrieval should be woven into the lesson fabric or the learning packet as an important and purposeful activity, not dredged up to fill in time on the day when the teacher and the class are suffering from end-of-the-week fatigue. By encouraging the students to play with words, the teacher can help to increase their interest in words in relation to concepts and in association with other words, and to refine their appreciation for nuances of meaning.

* Think of further ideas for vocabulary expansion and retrieval, and develop these into possible classroom or individual activities.

Integrating the language skills at Stages Three to Five
READING AND WRITING

Students may be asked a series of questions which, when answered in sequence, develop a summary or *Zusammenfassung* of the material read. They may write an ending to a story or play of which they have read part or develop a different ending from the one in the book. They may write letters which one character in the story might have written to others. Completed compositions may be passed around, with the writer's consent, to be read by other students. Students may create their own stories on similar themes to those they have been reading. They may write skits based on some parts of the narrative which will be acted in class or at the German club. Comprehension of extensive reading undertaken on an individualized basis will often be demonstrated in activities of this kind.

After reading a play, students may write the story as it might appear in a theater program, adding short descriptions of the characters. Should opportunity arise to act parts of the play before other classes, the best synopsis will be printed in a program for distribution.

Further suggestions for integrating reading and writing will be found in Chapter 9.

READING AND LISTENING COMPREHENSION

Students may listen to a story, play, poem, or speech by a famous person and then read it, or they may read first and then listen to a worthwhile reading or dramatic presentation of what they have read. The aural element adds vividness and life to the reading unit. Students may take turns listening to tapes of news broadcasts from a German-speaking source (the Federal Republic, the German Democratic Republic, Switzerland, Austria), and then write summaries of the news which will be posted for other students to read, thus integrating listening, writing, and reading in a purposeful activity. Before listening to a German play, students may read a synopsis of the action. In this way they are better prepared to comprehend because they have some expectations to help them project meaning.

In some ways the processes of fluent, direct reading for meaning appear to parallel the processes of listening. comprehension. We recognize in a quick, impressionistic way meaningful syntactic units, interrelating those we have selected and are holding in our memory with what follows, then rapidly revising expectations when these are not supported by the later segments we identify. Practice in direct reading of a text which is readily accessible to the student at his level of knowledge, while listening to a taped model reading it in meaningful and expressive segments, can help the student develop useful habits of anticipation and syntactic identification in both of these skills. Later he can practice rapid reading of a text to which he has already listened without a script.[22] (For further suggestions, see Chapter 3.)

READING AND SPEAKING

Students should be provided with frequent opportunities to give in German the gist of what they have been reading. They may be encouraged to prepare their own questions to ask of others in the class. When small groups are engaged in similar extensive reading projects they should discuss together what they have discovered. Students reading individually may share what they have been reading with others. Some of the material read will serve as a basis for oral presentations of projects; some will be dramatized in the original form or through extempore role-playing; and some will provide ammunition for discussions and debates. Many other ideas can be gleaned from Chapter 2.

READING AND PURPOSEFUL ACTIVITY

At all levels students should be encouraged to do research reading in an area which interests them in order to find the information necessary to carry out some activity. A few indications are outlined below, but at Stages Three through Five students should be expected to propose their own.

1. Students read advertisements for a particular type of product in magazines in order to prepare a commercial for a class television or radio show.

2. Students find out information about a popular German singer in order to introduce a session of records of his songs.

3. Students read a play carefully in order to design a stage setting for a class performance or play-reading.

4. Students seek out information on events, people, costumes, or social customs at a particular period in German history in order to produce a pageant for some historical anniversary.

5. Students study tourist brochures, guide books, geography, history, and art books in order to give an illustrated lecture or slide commentary on some part of Germany.

6. Students read through German cookbooks in order to prepare some German dishes for a German club festivity.

7. Students undertake tasks set out by the teacher or another student in the form of detailed instructions which lead to the collecting or making of something which can later be brought back as proof of the completion of the task.

At Stage Three, the well-known *Scavenger Hunt* (*Suchfahrt*) game can be adapted to the German class. Students work in pairs to find and bring to the class next day a series of strange objects which are described in German on instruction cards. They win points for their team for each object they find.

R84   One list might be: eine Taschenlampe ohne Batterien, zwei hartgekochte Eier, ein Stück Seidenpapier, eine chinesische Briefmarke, ein weißes Haar, ein kanadisches Geldstück, ein Büchsenöffner, eine Anzeige für eine möblierte Wohnung mit 2 1/2 Zimmern, ein Bierdeckel, ein Schnecken-haus.

While students are looking for these things they read and reread the list so that the words become impressed on their minds. Then, when showing the objects in class, they must state what each one is and how they came to acquire it.

Improving reading speed

The reading speed of different students varies considerably in their native language. The teacher must therefore expect considerable variation in the reading of the foreign language. To become fluent readers, however, the students must acquire the skill of reading whole word groups and whole sentences in German and of holding material in their memory over larger and larger sections as they move on with the developing thought.

1. At Stages Two and Three an overhead projector can be used to encourage continuity of reading. The text is moved slowly upward on the roll, so that the slower reader is encouraged to keep his eyes moving forward while the faster reader is not impeded, as would be the case if only one line were shown at a time. This is the process frequently used in films or on television where there is a long introduction to, or explanation of, the story. This procedure will be associated with silent reading for information, rather than reading aloud, since the aim is to help each student to improve his own reading rate.

2. At Stages Three and Four, students may be timed as they read a certain number of pages to a pre-established comprehension criterion level. Mere pace without adequate comprehension is pointless. Since this is an individual endeavor, students should be encouraged to improve their own rate rather than compete with others in number of pages read.

3. As an encouragement to practice *scanning,* which is a very useful reading skill, students may be given questions to which they are to find as many answers as possible in a given time.

4. Students will increase their reading speed in a natural way if they have set themselves the clearly defined goal of reading in a stated period of time a certain amount of material selected by themselves because of the interest of the subject matter.

8
Writing and written exercises I: the nuts and bolts

What is writing?

The Soviet psychologist Vygotsky draws our attention to the fact that all the higher functions of human consciousness, that is, those which involve more than mere physical skill, are characterized by *awareness, abstraction, and control*.[1] Learning to say [ø] by a process of successive approximations in imitation of a model may be relatively easy. Learning to say [ø] in response to various graphic combinations in a script and in a variety of graphic contexts is already more complicated. It demands the recognition of abstract representations and their conversion from a visual to a phonic form, before the skill acquired in the simpler act can come into operation in the new situation. In short, it requires awareness of the relevance of the graphic symbol, recognition of what it stands for in the phonic medium, as well as control of the production of the sound. Similar abstract processes are in operation when one writes *ö* in response to the sound [ø].

That a graphic representation of sound combinations is an abstraction with an arbitrary relationship to that which it represents is frequently overlooked. Convention alone makes the relationship between sound and written symbol predictable. The abstract quality of a written communication is intensified by:

    1. its *complete detachment from expressive features,* such as facial or

body movement, pitch and tone of voice, hesitations or speed of delivery, and emotional indicators such as heightened facial color or variations in breathing;

2. its *lack of material context:* surroundings, feedback from inter-locutors, relevant movement (hence the attraction of the comic book for modern readers);

3. its *displacement in time:* a written communication may be read as soon as it is written (like a note slipped to a companion) or months, years, or centuries later. It is interesting that we often do not understand a note we ourselves wrote when we find it years later.

The operation of writing, unlike speaking, must be performed as it were in a void, in response to a personal internal stimulus. Consequently, the writer must compensate for the absence of external contextual elements by the deliberate inclusion and elaboration of explanatory details which the speaker would omit.

For reasons such as these, Vygotsky suggests that the comparative difficulty for the child in acquiring facility in speech and in writing approximates that of learning arithmetic and algebra. All children learn to speak and express themselves effectively in speech at about the same age, even though some by personality and temperament may be more articulate than others. On the other hand, many people never learn to express themselves freely in writing. Even with careful instruction, there is a considerable lag between the achievement of an expressive level in speech in one's native language and a similar level of expressiveness in writing—a gap which, for many, widens as their education or life experience progresses. Certainly, many learn quite quickly to "write things down," if these are not too complicated, but this is the least demanding aspect of writing. Many who know how to "write things down" in their native language avoid expressing themselves in writing almost completely, even in personal letters. To write so that one is really communicating a message, isolated in place and time, is an art which requires consciously directed effort and deliberate choice in language. The old saying, "If you can say it, you can write it," is simplistic in its concept of the communicative aspect of writing. On the other hand, "He talks like a book" emphasizes the elaborations and comprehensive explanations of written messages which are quite unnecessary in face-to-face communication.

WRITING AND OTHER LANGUAGE ACTIVITIES

We must not be surprised, then, that a high level of written expression is so difficult to attain in a foreign language. It cannot be achieved by chance, as a kind of by-product of other language activities, although it draws on what has been learned in these areas. Good writing implies a knowledge of the conventions of the written code (the "good manners" of the medium); to be effective, it néeds the precision and nuances which derive from a thorough understanding of the syntactic and lexical choices the language offers; to be interesting, it requires the ability to vary structures and patterns for rhetorical effect. So good writing will not develop merely from practice exercises in grammar and vocabulary choice. Experience in speaking freely seems to facilitate early writing, which often parallels what one would say. For the development of a writing style, however, much acquaintance with the practical output of native writers in all kinds of expressive styles is essential. Familiarity with the great variety of expression to which the language lends itself gives the neophyte writer an intuitive feel for an authentic turn of phrase which he can acquire in no other way.

Included in this chapter are activities which associate writing with experiences in listening, speaking, and reading. (Further suggestions are to be found in Chapters 3 and 7.)

WHAT ARE WE TEACHING WHEN WE TEACH "WRITING"?

As with oral communication, we can classify writing activities as either *skill-getting* or *skill-using* (see model C1), with the same need for bridging activities which resemble the desired communicative activity to facilitate transfer from one to the other. *Interaction through the written message* is the goal: what is written should be a purposeful communication, on the practical or imaginative level, expressed in such a way that it is comprehensible to another person. Otherwise, we are dealing with hermetic or esoteric writing of purely personal value which can be set down in any idiosyncratic code.

Skill-getting, for oral or written communication, is based on knowledge of the way the language operates (*cognition*). Many grammatical rules are the same for speech and writing (e.g., the agreement of subject and verb in certain conventional ways: *Wir gehen* [viːʁ geːən]; the position and form of the relative pronoun: *der, die, das* for the subject of the relative clause, *den, die, das* for the direct object, both appearing invariably at the beginning of the clause, in close proximity to the expression for which they are acting as a substitute). Other rules vary according to the degree of formality of the spoken or written communication (e.g., formal writing: "Der Mann ist klug"; informal speech: "Der ist klug, der Mann!"[2] Note that a personal letter may retain many of the features of an informal chat, whereas a scholarly lecture given on a formal occasion adheres in the main to the same rules as a written paper or scientific report. In an orally oriented course, early writing will consist of the writing down of what one would say, moving further away from oral forms as knowledge of the rules of written language advances.

Learning the rules and conventions of written language is reinforced by writing out examples and applying the rules in new contexts, thus developing *awareness of the abstraction and control of its graphic manifestation*. For written language, this activity parallels the oral-practice exercises which help students develop flexibility in structuring their oral expression. Writing things out helps with the organization of material to be held in memory and clarifies rules at points of uncertainty. It gives concrete expression to abstract notions. All of this is, however, merely preliminary activity which is pointless unless it is serving some clearly understood purpose of meaningful communication.

Considerable disappointment and frustration will be avoided if the nature and purpose of any particular writing task are clearly understood by student and teacher alike. In this chapter and the next, we will discuss writing under four headings. These do not represent sequential stages but, rather, constantly interwoven activities. They are:

I. *Writing down:* learning the conventions of the code.

II. *Writing in the language:* learning the potential of the code (we shall include here grammatical exercises and the study of samples of written language to develop awareness of its characteristics).

III. *Production:* practicing the construction of fluent, expressive sentences and paragraphs.

IV. *Expressive writing or composition:* using the code for purposeful communication.

Finally, *translation* will be discussed at some length as a separate activity.

I. Writing down

Activities of this type, although apparently simple, contribute to awareness. The student either copies or reproduces without the copy in front of him. To do this accurately, he must focus his attention on the conventions of writing: spelling, capitalization, punctuation, diacritical marks (umlauts, apostrophes), number conventions (W6), abbreviations (*bzw., d.h., u.s.w.*), indicators of direct discourse and quotation (*Anführungszeichen, Gedankenstrich*), and so on.

This activity prepares for eventual expressive writing. It is, however, useful in itself. Language users need to be able to interpret and copy down printed schedules, timetables, records, details of projects, charts, formulas, prices, recipes, new words and phrases they wish to remember. They should be capable of writing down accurately and comprehensibly oral arrangements and instructions for themselves and others. As students studying in the language they may need to copy accurately diagrams, details of experiments, quotations from literary works.

COPYING

1. (E) Students are given dittoed sheets with simple *outline illustrations,* or stick figures, suggesting the lines of a dialogue or parts of a narrative they have been studying. They transcribe from the text sentences which are appropriate to each sketch.

2. (E) Each student copies a line of dialogue and passes it to his neighbor who copies out an appropriate response. This operates like a *chain dialogue* (C25), with students selecting utterances and appropriate responses from any material they have studied.

3. (E) Students copy the initial part of an utterance and pass it on to their neighbors for a *completion,* or students choose and copy completions for parts of utterances supplied on a dittoed sheet, trying to make as many different sentences as they can with each opening phrase.

4. (E) Students make new sentences by copying segments from *substitution tables.* This activity familiarizes the students with the logical segmentation of sentences into subject, verb, object, and adverbial extensions.

W 1 (E) Make six different sentences by selecting one segment from each column in the following table:

Heinz	sieht	Ursula	vor dem Restaurant
Die Wirtin	findet	die Katze	auf der Straße
Das Mädchen	sucht	den Polizisten	hinter dem Haus
Der Lehrer	trifft	das Kind	gegenüber von der Schule

If pronoun subjects of different persons and numbers are used, it is advisable to keep subject and verb in one column to accustom elementary-level students to the correct combination of pronoun subject and verb ending:

W 2 (E)

Wir treffen	die Mutter von Paul	vor dem Kino
Sie finden	den Polizisten	gegenüber von der Schule
Ich sehe	das Kind	auf der Straße

Developing sentences from a substitution table becomes a more thoughtful process when only some subject items can be appropriately used with some of the verb items, some of the objects, and so on. The following exercise illustrates such a table: [3]

W 3 (E)

	Flugzeug	ist	abgeflogen			das Kind				
	Katze		angekommen			Fritz				
der	Wagen				aber	sie	hat	es		gemerkt
die	Vogel		gebellt			die Kinder	haben	sie	nicht	gesehen
das	Hund	hat	gesungen			du	hast	ihn		gehört
	Tante					Inge				

New tables of this type can be developed as a writing exercise by groups of students for use by other students, thus moving into the second activity, writing in the language.

5. (E) Students copy from the chalkboard a simple poem they have been learning orally. A familiar poem like Uhland's "Der gute Kamerad," with its segments of interpolated speech, can be a useful copying exercise. The use of the present tense to actualize the past can be explained to the students as a feature of literary language, as well as of effective dramatic speech. Other poems, for example, Goethe's "Maifest," serve to illustrate how essentially "spoken" structures such as exclamations produce particular effects in formal written language.

✻ Find for your personal file some suitable short poems for elementary classes. Share these with other members of the class and discuss their appropriateness.

REPRODUCTION

Copying activities 1, 2, and 3 may also be reproduction exercises, with students writing the utterances, or completing them, from memory.

6. (E) *Scrambled sentences* are sometimes used as a stimulus to the reproduction of a dialogue or narrative. This technique forces students to think of the meaning of what they are reproducing. Credit should be given for ingenuity in working out novel but possible recombinations.

7. (E) Students write down from *dictation* utterances they have learned, or recombinations of familiar segments, or they may concentrate on the spelling of more difficult words in *spot dictation* (see R26).

(E and I) The spot dictation may focus on subjects and verbs (tense endings, irregularities), or on article, noun, and adjective agreements.

8. (I and A) *Dictation of unfamiliar material* as an exercise in auditory recognition and accurate reproduction has been a standard classroom technique for centuries. The passage to be dictated should normally have some thematic relationship to something already read or discussed. It can often provide supplementary material worth keeping on a subject of cultural interest. The standard procedure is described below. There are also several possible variations which are useful language-learning aids.

a. *Standard procedure.* The material is read in its entirety at a normal, but unhurried, pace. It is then dictated in meaningful, undistorted segments, each segment being read twice. After students have looked over what they have written, corrected obvious mistakes, and tentatively filled in gaps according to semantic or grammatical expectations, the passage is read again at a normal pace to enable students to check on doubtful segments. After opportunity for a final check, students correct their own versions from a model. If one student has written his dictation at one side of the chalkboard or for projection on the overhead projector, the correction process is facilitated: students suggest corrections and the teacher is able to comment on errors probably committed by other students as well or answer questions about problem segments. Each dictation should be regarded as an opportunity for learning, not as a test. For this reason, immediate correction is desirable, before students have forgotten which segments they found difficult and why they solved the problems as they did. Since it is difficult for students to detect all the errors in their own work, they should exchange papers for a final check by a classmate.

b. *Variations.*

i. (E) *Students are encouraged to repeat the segment* to themselves before writing it. This forces them to make identification decisions before they begin writing and strengthens their memory of what they have heard.

ii. (E and I) If interpreting the aural signal and writing the message down accurately is a valuable exercise, there is no reason why students should be limited to an arbitrary number of repetitions of the segments. The dictation may be taped and *students encouraged to keep playing the passage over* until they have been able to take down the complete message.

iii. (E and I) Students are asked to *hold longer and longer segments in their immediate memory* before beginning to write. In this way they are not working with echoic memory, but are forced to process the segments, that is, interpret them and situate them syntactically in the structure of the sentence, before reproducing them. Dictation then becomes more challenging and more meaningful.

iv. (I) *The speed of the dictation is gradually increased* as students become more adept at making the various morphological adjustments, particularly those which are not apparent in the spoken signal.

v. (I and A) *The repetition of segments is eliminated* and students are expected to listen carefully, retain the segment they have heard only once, and write it down without expecting further help. This forces students to concentrate on the message and the semantic and syntactic expectations it arouses.

vi. (A) Finally, students should be able to *take down a dictated letter or report,* with their own set of abbreviations, and write it out, or type it up correctly, as they might be expected to do in a business situation. This activity can be practiced individually with tapes.

FOCUSING ON SPELLING, CAPITALIZATION, AND COMMAS

1. (E and I) This goes beyond the initial stages. The teacher can focus students' attention on spelling conventions by asking them to work out for themselves, from reading passages or dialogues they have studied, *probable rules of spelling* like the following:

W 4 [s] is spelled *ss* medially after a lax vowel (*Flüsse, gegossen*). It is spelled *ß* instead of *ss*
a. medially after a tense vowel (*Straße, Füße*);
b. medially before another consonant (*mußte, läßt*); and
c. finally after either a tense or lax vowel (*Fuß, Fluß*).
(In modern practice *ss* may be substituted for *ß*, but never *ß* for *ss*.)
It may also be spelled *s* in all positions except medially between two vowels (although [s] initially is rare: *Satin*).

This is a suitable small group activity. It can be undertaken whenever particular spelling problems emerge in dictation or writing practice.[4]

2. (E and I) Although beginning students are sometimes uncertain where to put the umlaut (diaresis), they seldom have serious problems once they know that only *a, o,* and *u* are umlauted and have learned to distinguish sounds. On the other hand, capitalization and commas may pose persistent difficulties which students do not anticipate. To become acquainted with common practice they may be given the research project of finding out from printed texts when and where capitals and commas are used. Through personal observation they will easily discover facts like the following:

W 5 1. *Groß oder klein?*

a. All nouns are capitalized in German, including those which have been formed from verbs (*das Singen*), adjectives (*die Alte*), prepositions (*das Für und Wider*), pronouns, or any other part of speech. There is a decided difference between "Das liebe ich" and "Das liebe Ich."

b. The pronoun *Sie* ("you" in formal usage) and its corresponding adjective *Ihr* are capitalized. *Du, dein, ihr,* and *euer* are only capitalized when used for direct address in letters.

c. Proper adjectives are not capitalized unless part of a name or title: *der deutsche Mensch,* but: *die Deutsche Bank.*

d. Times of the day are not capitalized when they consist of combinations with *heute, morgen* and *gestern* or with the names of weekdays: *heute abend, Sonntag nacht.*

2. How are commas used?

a. All dependent clauses are set off by commas: *Gina, die heute ankommt, bleibt bei uns; Ich weiß, daß er ungern liest.*

b. Extended infinitive clauses are preceded by commas (although simple infinitives are not): *Sie hat keine Lust, so früh aufzustehen* (but: *Er hatte keine Zeit zu gehen*); *Sie ist um zehn Uhr hingefahren, um ihn abzuholen; Er ist weggezogen, ohne sich abzumelden.*[5]

When students have discovered regular patterns of usage for capitals and commas, they find them easier to remember. (I and A) This project may be continued to cover more intricate rules of capitalization and comma use.

Note: Although correct use of capitals and commas can affect meaning, the subject should not be so heavily emphasized that it becomes an important element in the grading or evaluation of writing in the beginning stages. A discussion of plans to reform spelling by abandoning traditional practices of capitalization may help students understand both the problems and advantages of the German system.

LEARNING NUMBER CONVENTIONS

Misunderstandings can result from the use of English numerical conventions in German writing.

W 6 (E) Students should be familiar with such differences as the indicators for decimals and for thousands, e.g., English 21.5 = German 21,5; English 3,365,820 = German 3.365.820; with abbreviations like 3,65 m and 11.000 km; Nr. 2; 1., 2.; 4 PS; and with ways of writing times: 15.45 Uhr and dates: 31.V.75 or den 31. Mai 1975. It is also useful for students to learn the handwritten forms for German numbers, particularly $\mathcal{1}$ and $\mathcal{7}$.

These special features can be practiced in projects such as *describing a trip from München to West Berlin,* in which the student studies timetables, route maps, and area maps, and gives full details of times of departure and arrival, distances traveled, and heights of surrounding mountains. Prices of rooms and meals can be found in guides or information sheets obtained by writing to the Städtisches Verkehrsamt in towns on the way and in West Berlin itself.

PROOFREADING

It is a commonly held opinion that students should not be shown incorrect German because they will learn the errors in the text and these misapprehensions will be difficult to eradicate. This assumption does not seem to have been scientifically tested. It is clear that young teachers improve in their control of the syntax and spelling of the language as they teach it, yet they see a great deal of incorrect German in the process. The difference, in the latter case, is that these young teachers are looking for errors and check facts in grammars or dictionaries whenever they are uncertain about correctness of usage or form in the exercises they are grading. This attitude of alertness to erroneous forms, and pleasure in finding the facts when in doubt, needs to be developed in students so that they will take an interest in proofreading their own work before submitting it for checking or grading by the teacher. It can be cultivated by an occasional problem-solving competition along the following lines:

W7 (E and I) *Die Vorbereitung eines fertigen Textes*

1. The teacher takes a text of a level comprehensible to the students and types it out, double- or triple-spaced, with a certain number of spelling errors (*orthographische Fehler*) of the type students themselves tend to make (e.g., *wen ich ihn kenne, Flüße*), some errors in capitalization (e.g., *das fahren ist gefährlich*), a few typing slips (*Tippfehler*) which do not change pronunciation (e.g., *er boot* or *Leerbuch*) and some other typing slips which constitute morphological or syntactic inaccuracies in written language (e.g., *der jungen Mann; das Buch, was ich gekauft habe*).

2. The students work in pairs or small groups to prepare a perfect text for the final typing. Each group has a different text, a pencil of a distinctive color, and a group symbol which they put beside each correction they make. Students may check in dictionaries, grammars, or their textbooks.

3. Points will be awarded for every correction made and deducted not only for errors not detected but also for miscorrections.

4. After a time, corrected texts are passed on to the next group for

rechecking. Groups gain further points for discovering miscorrections and undetected errors in the texts from other groups, but they lose points for wrongly challenging another group's corrections. (In this second round, it is essential that groups remember to put their group symbol beside their corrections and recorrections.)

5. Final results in points for each group will usually have to be deferred till the next day, to allow the teacher time to sort out the different corrections and challenges. The perfected texts, with corrections still visible, are then retyped on dittoes by those students who are learning business skills. The final text is then used for some class or individualized activity.

6. When the next composition is due, students are given some class time to proofread each other's work and write suggested improvements in colored pencil.

✻ The regular *relationships between many noun endings and the gender* of the noun is frequently not made clear to students, yet it can provide a considerable shortcut to the mastery of this troublesome feature. It is also reassuring to students to know that the gender of a new noun is not completely unpredictable.

Make notes for your teaching file on these regularities, with lists of words of high frequency in each of the categories and the common exceptions.[6] Work out an interesting activity students could undertake to discover many of these regularities for themselves, e.g.,-*er* m. nationalities and agents: *Spanier, Amerikaner, Italiener, tanzen—Tänzer, anfangen— Anfänger, verkaufen—Verkäufer, sprechen—Sprecher, backen—Bäcker* (the few feminine and neuter nouns ending in -*er* [*Mutter, Tochter, Ader; Alter*] do not fit into this category); -*ung* f. action or result thereof: *Erfindung, Teilung, Warnung, Endung, Landung,* etc.

II. Writing in the language

Writing down words from a German dictionary inserted into native-language patterns in native-language word order is not "writing in the language."

W 8   Diese Gedichte sind gleich in Thema, aber es sieht zu mir als, sie waren nicht in demselben Jahr geschrieben.

Commentary

This extract from a student's composition comparing two poems is clearly *gemischte pickles* (English structure dressed in German lexicon)—a form of fractured German which may, or may not, be comprehensible to a German, depending on his patience and imagination, or his knowledge of English. Our students will want to go beyond this stage. Unless they can eventually write so that their meaning is immediately comprehensible to a German reader, they are wasting a great deal of precious time on this demanding activity.

To acquire an adequate foundation for autonomous writing the student studies the potential for diversity of meaning of the German syntactic system. He seeks to understand how it works (*cognition* in model C1) and essays the expression of a variety of meanings in written exercises (thus learning *production* through the *construction* of fluent, idiomatic sentences). This controlled micro-practice, like limbering up exercises, is useful for developing the linguistic flexibility needed to communicate specific meanings.

PRESENTING THE GRAMMAR: COGNITION AND ABSTRACTION

Students must not only understand the grammatical concepts they encounter, but also appreciate how each, like a link in a coat of chain mail, interrelates with all the others in one fabric—the German language system. They may practice a concept in isolation, the present tense to express the past: *Ich wohne seit zehn Jahren hier,* becoming familiar with its form and primary function. No concept, however, is fully assimilated until it can be used, or its specific meaning recognized, in a matrix of other grammatical concepts (e.g., *Er wohnt seit zehn Jahren in Berlin und will noch zehn Jahre bleiben* as contrasted with *Er hat zehn Jahre in Berlin gewohnt, bevor er nach Amerika versetzt wurde*). The student must be able to select, with conscious differentiation of meaning, what he needs from this matrix (e.g., whether *er wohnt, er hat gewohnt,* or *er wohnte* is most appropriate).

It is this need for our students to comprehend grammatical concepts in relation to, or in contrast with, other grammatical concepts which guides us in selecting among the *various ways of presenting the grammar.*

1. The teacher, or more usually the textbook writer, decides, for example, that the students should now learn a past tense (or negation or the relative pronoun). This decision is an arbitrary one, and the next lesson is designed accordingly. The forms of the past tense are set out in a paradigm, and the way it is used is explained and demonstrated in some example sentences. Students are then asked to write out the past tense forms of some verbs and to use them in written (or oral) exercises or translation sentences.

This is the standard *deductive approach.*[7] It highlights aspects of the grammar extracted from the matrix. The new forms being learned then need to be incorporated into reading or oral activities, where their relationships with other aspects of the grammar may be observed; otherwise, the students will tend to think of them as separate "rules" rather than elements in an interacting system. This deductive approach is incorporated, in a non-arbitrary fashion, as part of 3 below.

2. The student may encounter a new aspect of the grammar in a matrix of language and become curious about its function. This is the initial stage of *inductive learning.*

a. The student may hear a form which is unfamiliar to him as he is listening to oral German. He may look puzzled or ask about it. In response, the teacher explains that this is a way of expressing past action and discusses its use. Opportunity is then provided for the student to hear other examples of the use of this past form in further oral work.

b. The past form may be encountered in reading material. Its function may be inferred from the context and then discussed in relation to other expressions of time relations. The forms and use of the past tense are then practiced orally in other contexts or in written exercises.

3. The student may need an expression of past time for something he wishes to say or write. He asks for the form he needs. The teacher tells him briefly how to create past tenses from known verbs and explains the difference between expressions for past action continued to the present, a repeated action in the past, or a single past action. The teacher then encourages the student to use other past forms in what he is trying to say or write. This is a *deductive approach in response to a felt need.*

Each of these approaches has its use for specific age-groups or for particular aspects of the language. The deductive approach is most useful for mature, well-motivated students with some knowledge of the language who are anxious to understand the more complicated aspects of the grammatical system; students who have already learned one foreign language and are interested in the way this language deals with certain grammatical relationships; and adult students in intensive courses who have reasons for wishing to understand how the language works as fast as possible. The inductive approach is very appropriate for young language learners who have not yet developed fully their ability to think in abstractions' and who enjoy learning through active application; students who can take time to assimilate the language through use; and those studying the language in an environment where they hear it all around them. Most classroom teachers use a mixture of inductive and deductive approaches according to the type of student with whom they are dealing and the degree of complication of the problem being presented.

What about grammatical terminology?

Grammatical terminology has long been the bugbear of foreign-language teachers. Even switching from traditional terms to those used by any of the several competing systems of contemporary grammatical study does not seem to solve the problem. Students learn new terms and a schematic apparatus readily enough without coming to grips with the concepts they represent.

Ultimately, foreign-language teachers must take the responsibility themselves for teaching the student as much, or as little, abstract grammar as seems to be needed by each particular group for the specific language they are learning. Teachers must feel free to adapt or invent terminology which they find helps their students grasp the concepts and use the language effectively. In German, for instance, it is often more useful in the early stages to talk about *der, die,* and *das* nouns and ramifications of their behaviour, rather than about masculine, feminine and neuter nouns. The latter concept, in its German form, seems extraordinary to the average English-speaking student and causes him to hesitate about such usages as *Er hat sein neues Dienstmädchen gelobt* and *Er hat seine Putzfrau gelobt.* The concept of *der, die,* and *das* nouns is of great assistance in moving to indefinite articles (*ein, eine,* and *ein*). The forms of the definite articles (augmented by the plural) and of the indefinite articles carry the student to relative pronouns (also *der, die,* and *das*) and to a large group of various kinds of limiting adjectives commonly called "*der*-words" (*dieser, jener, mancher, welcher,* etc.), as well as to the possessive adjectives (*mein, dein, ihr,* etc.), which are frequently referred to as "*ein*-words." Thus what might otherwise seem to the student an endless number of new endings to be learned can be simplified considerably when presented as a system. Each teacher should experiment with his own ways of talking about grammar and continue with those that work.

How do written exercises for learning grammatical concepts differ from oral practice?

1. Oral exercises provide the opportunity for many more examples of the rule to be practiced, immediately corrected, and repracticed in a given time.

2. When exercises are practiced orally, the observant teacher can judge more accurately when to skip some exercises which performance indicates are not needed, and when to add further exercises to ensure assimilation of the rule.

3. Oral exercises can be used to prepare students for written exercises by allowing opportunity for questions and comment on obvious areas of misunderstanding and a rapid repracticing of the point at issue.

4. Written exercises provide useful reinforcement of what has been practiced orally; they help to build in concepts through the abstract process of thinking out the written forms.

5. Written exercises have an individual diagnostic function, revealing

what sections of the work have not been thoroughly assimilated by a particular student and where their application in wider contexts is not fully understood. It is in written exercises that one focuses the student's attention on specific problems, rather than in expressive writing where the student is attempting to do a number of things at the same time.

6. Because they allow time for editing and re-editing, written exercises are less likely than oral exercises to reflect slips due to inattention or momentary distraction, and are often better indicators of genuine misunderstanding of the functioning of the system.

7. A few aspects of the language cannot be practiced except in writing, e.g., capitalization, punctuation and common abbreviations.

8. It is easier for the student to submit in writing several possible versions, in which he can show how one rule parallels, interacts with, or contrasts with other rules.

9. Written exercises allow time for consulting references (dictionaries, grammars, or the textbook) and can, therefore, take on problem-solving characteristics.

10. Written exercises allow students with physical or emotional aural difficulties, or with slow response reactions, to demonstrate what they know through a medium in which they feel more relaxed.

COGNITIVE EXERCISES

Whether the grammar has been presented deductively or inductively, a time comes when the students need to try for themselves whether they can use the various parts of it in novel contexts to express specific meanings. Through cognitive exercises they explore its possibilities and become more conscious of the constraints it imposes. They also clarify for themselves their individual areas of vagueness and miscomprehension.

Several very commonly used types of exercises may be termed cognitive, in the sense that they require of the student an abstract comprehension of the workings of a grammatical system. It is not surprising, therefore, that in form some of them resemble various well-known tests for estimating intelligence and ability to undertake abstract learning tasks. Success in these types of exercises does not necessarily mean that the student will be able to think of the appropriate rule at the appropriate moment when he is composing sentences himself. Nevertheless, it is a step on the way, since this basic knowledge is indispensable for effective language use. Students must, however, clearly understand that such exercises mark only a beginning—a foundation on which to build the all-important structure of personal meaning.

Under this heading, we will consider multiple-choice exercises, fill-in-the-blank and completion exercises, the cloze procedure, and exercises in living language for the inductive exploration of particular problems of grammar. Conversions, restatements, expansions, and combinations will be considered under *Production*.

Some of these types of exercises are also dealt with in Chapter 4 and occasional reference will be made to the discussion in that section. Most of these exercises are also commonly used as *tests*.

Multiple-choice exercises

A *typical multiple-choice grammar exercise* will look like the following:

W 9 (E or I) Circle in the margin the letter corresponding to the correct form to complete the following sentences when

A = den
B = dem
C = die

1. Wenn es zu regnen anfing, lief er unter ____ Baum.   A   B   C
2. Sie setzte sich neben ____ Brüder.   A   B   C
3. Er fährt seinen Wagen hinter ____ Ratskeller, um da zu parken.   A   B   C
4. Mein alter Mantel hängt an ____ Nagel im Schrank.   A   B   C
5. Das kleine Mädchen hat sich auf ____ Boden gelegt.   A   B   C
6. Oft muß man stundenlang über ____ Flughafen kreisen, bevor man landen kann.   A   B   C
7. Während eines Ausverkaufs laufen die Leute wie Verrückte in ____ Läden der Stadt herum.   A   B   C
8. Gestern ist Petra hingefallen, als sie vor ____ Bus stand.   A   B   C

Commentary

1. This exercise forces the student to think over carefully the various aspects of the rules for the use of either the dative or accusative case after certain prepositions. He must understand the whole sentence and the implications of each part to be able to select successfully.

2. There are enough choices that the student is not likely to succeed through guessing, except by a fluke. The fluke probability is also reduced by the fact that the student thinks he knows at least some of the items and so is not depending on pure guesswork for the complete exercise.

3. If a separate computer answer-sheet is used, the exercise may be machine-scored as a test. The answer format of W9 can be rapidly checked

with an easily constructed punched-stencil key (with holes punched to mark the positions of the correct answers).

4. The W9 format provides a useful mechanism for students in individualized programs to check their mastery of certain concepts and their readiness to move on.

5. It is easy to construct from a basic model several equivalent versions of an exercise of this type by changing the lexical items, and thus the semantic context, while retaining the grammatical context. The following three items are equivalent in grammatical difficulty and test the same rule:

W10 a. Das kleine Mädchen hat sich auf _____ Boden gelegt.
   b. Die Vase stellt sie auf _____ Tisch.
   c. Am liebsten sitzt er auf _____ harten Stuhl am Fenster.

From the point of view of knowledge of the rule, the following items are also equivalent:

   d. Die Kellnerin bleibt keine halbe Minute an _____ Tisch stehen.
   e. Meine Tante stieg keuchend in _____ Eilzug ein, ohne zu merken, daß er in die verkehrte Richtung fuhr.

Note, however, that (e) contains expressions and vocabulary of a level of difficulty above the level of the grammatical item sought. *Verkehrt* is advanced level, or at least intermediate; *Eilzug* may disconcert elementary-level students if they have not yet learned about German trains.

6. It is essential in this type of exercise or test that each of the items be unambiguous. Students should not have to hesitate over possible interpretations while they try to decide what the instructor had in mind.

W11 a. Die Kinder laufen in _____ Garten.
   b. Die Kinder laufen in den Garten.
   c. Die Kinder laufen in dem Garten.

Both (b) and (c) are possible German sentences in the appropriate context. Clearly the constructor of item (a) had in mind the use of the accusative case when the verb of the sentence denotes motion and therefore expected (b). With more context, as in W12, the correct choice is clear:

W12 a. Die Kinder spielen nicht auf der Straße. Sie laufen lieber in _____ Garten herum.
   b. Die Kinder laufen aus dem Haus in _____ Garten.

This multiple-choice format can be used for a number of aspects of grammar, even the *use of tenses:*

W13 (I) Read the following sentences carefully. Circle in the margin the letter corresponding to the tense and mood of the verb that you would use to complete the sentence when

A = present indicative
B = simple past (imperfect) indicative
C = subjunctive I
D = subjunctive II [9]

1. Wenn es schön wäre, _____ ich spazieren gehen. A   B   C   D
   (können)
2. Früher _____ er jeden Tag eine Zeitung.   A   B   C   D
   (kaufen)
3. Ich _____ schon zehn Jahre in New York.   A   B   C   D
   (wohnen)
4. Obgleich sie kein Geld hat, kleidet sie sich, als ob sie A   B   C   D
   reich _____.
   (sein)
5. Ich weiß, was du morgen _____.   A   B   C   D
   (machen)
6. _____ er nur einen Wintermantel!   A   B   C   D
   (Haben)
7. Sie haben uns versprochen, daß sie gleich _____, A   B   C   D
   (kommen)
   doch sind sie immer noch nicht da.

8. Erika _____ schon eine Stunde, als ich sie anrief. A   B   C   D
   (warten)

Commentary

1. This is clearly a review exercise since it requires comparative knowledge of the use of two tenses in two different moods.

2. The exercise tests knowledge of the functioning of the language system, not ability to produce the forms required. As it is constructed, it is useful as an objectively corrected test of cognitive assimilation of the rules. When using W13 as an exercise, students would, of course, also fill in the appropriate forms of the verbs in the blanks.

3. In constructing items to test ability to select correct tenses, sufficient

indicators of time relationships must be given to make the appropriate choice clear. In most of the above examples, tenses and moods required in the blanks are either syntactically constrained by other tenses in associated clauses (as in 1: *Wenn es schön wäre, könnte ich spazieren gehen*), semantically and temporally constrained by a superordinate verb (as in 7: *Sie haben uns versprochen, daß sie gleich kämen, doch sind sie immer noch nicht da*), or clearly indicated by an adverbial phrase of time (as in 3: *Ich wohne schon zehn Jahre in New York*).

4. Other factors which have been kept in mind in constructing the items are:

a. that the sentences should be of a type that the students might encounter or wish to use;

b. that the vocabulary and general construction of the sentence should be of a level that the students can easily comprehend, so that they are not distracted from the real task of deciding on tense and mood.

The same format can be used for practice in *distinguishing among expressions* whose precise usage is often confusing.

W 14

(I) Circle in the margin the letter corresponding to the most appropriate completion for the following sentences when

A = kennt   D = weiß
B = erkennt   E = erlebt
C = kann

1. Mein Vater _____ Herrn Schmidt aus seiner Schulzeit.   A B C D E

2. Er _____ ein Mittel, wie man schnell Deutsch lernt.   A B C D E

3. Er lernt alles sehr schnell und _____ schon sieben Sprachen.   A B C D E

4. Er hat mich seit zehn Jahren nicht gesehen und ist unsicher, ob er mich wieder _____.   A B C D E

Commentary

In this example, the number of items is not equal to the number of choices. This is one way to avoid selection by pure elimination procedures. Another way is to write the items so that some of the choices are appropriate for more than one item.

The novice multiple-choice item constructor should not be misled by the final product into underestimating the difficulty of constructing unambiguous, useful test items in this format. The first step is to make a careful list of exactly which items it is desirable to include. After the test has been constructed and carefully scanned for ambiguities, inappropriate vocabulary, unintentional comprehension difficulty or obscurity, stilted expressions, unlikely meanings and a regular pattern order of correct choices (e.g., A B C A B C),[10] it should be passed on to another person to be read and checked for these weaknesses. Even an experienced test constructor is sometimes temporarily blinded by the knowledge of his intentions.

A similar format may be used for testing the student's understanding of the *meanings of words*.

W15 (E or I) Circle in the margin the letter corresponding to the phrase which correctly completes the sentence:

1. In einer Konditorei kauft man   A   B   C   D
   A. Obst.
   B. Schweinefleisch.
   C. Kuchen.
   D. Marmelade.

2. Ein Berliner ist   A   B   C   D
   A. eine Gebäckart.
   B. eine Biersorte.
   C. ein Nordseefisch.
   D. ein Käsegericht.

3. In einer Apotheke verkauft man   A   B   C   D
   A. Parfüm.
   B. einen Rasierapparat.
   C. Zigaretten.
   D. Aspirintabletten.

Commentary

1. Items 1 and 3 are based on traditional, but still existing, German shopping patterns. (Teachers will keep up, through reading and visits, with the changes taking place in Germany as elsewhere, e.g., the rapid spread of *Kaufhäuser* and *Supermärkte*.)

2. These items would not be given to students out of the blue. The exercise is obviously based on material in the students' textbook.

3. This type of exercise can be fun to make up and groups of students may be asked to construct exercises for other groups of students. Another format, which is not suitable for a test because of the fifty-fifty chances it provides, but which is very entertaining for students to construct while broadening their vocabulary, is as follows:

W 16 (I) Some of the following statements are sensible and some are ridiculous. Circle in the margin

A: if the sentence is sensible,
B: if the sentence is ridiculous.

1. Bei einer Bäckerei kauft man Backen.	A	B
2. Ein Klempner beschäftigt sich mit Wasserleitungen.	A	B
3. Einen Schluß kann man mit einem Schlüssel öffnen.	A	B
4. Ein Stammtisch ist ein Möbelstück aus festem Holz.	A	B
5. Ein Fehler ist ein Schüler, der immer fehlt.	A	B
6. Ein Tageblatt ist eine Zeitung, die täglich erscheint.	A	B

The multiple-choice format can be used also to test appreciation of *appropriate rejoinders, responses, or comments* as in the following:

W 17 (E) Circle in the margin the letter corresponding to the most appropriate response to the following questions:

1. Können Sie einen Dollar wechseln?   A   B   C   D
   A. Ein Dollar hat einen Wert von ungefähr 2,50 DM.
   B. Nichts zu danken.
   C. Schön!
   D. Ich glaube ja . . .

Alternatively, the student may be asked to select the appropriate response in a particular situation.

W 18 (E) Circle in the margin the letter corresponding to the appropriate response in the situation described.

1. Auf der Straße treffen Sie den Rektor der Schule, in
   der Sie unterrichten. Sie sagen zu ihm: A   B   C   D
   A. Guten Tag, Herr Rektor. Wie geht es Ihnen?
   B. Servus, Herr Rektor.
   C. Tag, Herr Rektor. Wie steht's?
   D. So, du machst auch einen Spaziergang?

✳ Construct a multiple-choice test for the forms of the relative pronoun or the uses of *es ist* and *es gibt*. Try the test out on other members of the class. Discuss the strengths and weaknesses of the various tests constructed by the class members.

Fill-in-the-blank exercises

Some weaknesses of this format have already been discussed in Chapter 4, particularly the type of construction which makes these exercises mechanical busywork. To earn a place as a cognitive exercise, the fill-in-the-blank activity must demand of the student *understanding of the complete sentence and careful thought*. W13 can be altered to meet this criterion as a fill-in-the-blank exercise by requiring the student to write in the correct form of the verb for the tense and mood selected. The same type of exercise may also be used successfully without guides to the blanks.

W19 (E or I) Read the following sentences carefully and write in the blank the most appropriate form of the definite article.

1. Sie hat den Scheck in _____ Handtasche gesteckt.
2. _____ Professor hat er gestern vor der Universitätsbuchhandlung getroffen.
3. Das Markstück, das der Junge auf der Straße fand, gehörte _____ alten Herrn Fink.
4. Es ist am Donnerstag, _____ 7. Mai, passiert.
5. Er hat _____ ganzen Tag an seiner Aufgabe gearbeitet, und er ist immer noch nicht fertig.
6. Gestern abend hat Ulrich _____ drei Mädchen eine Gespenstergeschichte erzählt.

Commentary

1. In this exercise, the students must consider the various relationships within the sentence: Is the article required by the noun *der, die* or *das?* What case is required in the context, e.g., if the article and noun follow a preposition, what case is called for? What kind of object does the verb take?

2. If items are written in, the exercise cannot be scored mechanically.

3. Students may be asked to write out the whole sentence. This depends on whether W19 is used as a practice exercise in writing or as part of a test with a large number of items to be covered in a restricted amount of time. If students do write out the whole item, points should not be de-

ducted for slips in copying other parts of the sentence when the fill-in item is correct. If the copying is careless throughout, a penalty of two or three points may be deducted from the total for this specific fault.

4. Note that in sentence (6), *Mädchen* was used rather than a noun which does not end in *n* throughout the plural (e.g., *Gäste*) so that it is not necessary to add an *n* for the dative plural, thus giving away the case. The number *drei* clarifies that the noun is plural rather than singular. Careful attention must also be given to other such indications of which case is sought, e.g., adjective endings. The substitution in (3) of *alten Frau* for *alten Herrn Fink* would eliminate the accusative case as an alternative and make the answer clear.

At the intermediate and advanced levels fill-in-the-blank exercises can become very demanding as in a *mixed, overall structure test* with no guides to the blanks:

W20 (I and A) Complete the following sentences appropriately as indicated by the clues in the sentences.

1. Es ist erst Februar, und mein Bruder freut sich schon _____ die warmen Sommertage, weil er gern ins Freibad geht.
2. Der Schriftsteller, _____ Buch ich vor zwei Monaten gelesen habe, hält morgen einen Vortrag.
3. Sie glaubt alles, _____ man ihr sagt.
4. Er interessiert sich sehr _____ die Naturwissenschaften, nicht wahr?
5. Sag mir, _____ Schuhe du schöner findest.
6. Sie hat getan, _____ sie reich wäre. Das war aber nicht der Fall.
7. Sie kann _____ kein neues Kleid leisten, weil sie ihr ganzes Geld schon ausgegeben hat.
8. Guten Tag. Ich bin Amerikaner und komme aus New York. _____ kommen Sie?

The fill-in-the-blank format is also useful for *testing irregular verb forms in context*.

W21 (I and A) Write in the margin the correct form of the verb on the left, as indicated by the clues in the sentence.

1. können   Wir gehen heute, weil das Wetter gestern so   1. _____
             schlecht war, daß wir es nicht _____.
2. mögen   Ich _____ gern ein Pfund Äpfel haben.   2. _____

3. sitzen   Nachdem er zwei Stunden lang da _____,   3. _____
          kam sie endlich.
4. wissen   Ich habe eben etwas Interessantes erfahren.   4. _____
          Was? _____ du noch nicht, was morgen
          passiert?

Commentary

1. In a complete exercise more items would be given for each verb.

2. The format with blank in the right-hand margin provides for rapid correction of the test, since all the answers are in one column. As a class exercise, it would be preferable for students to write in the blanks within the sentences so that they could read over the complete sentence as they checked the appropriateness of their choice of tense and mood.

3. A set of such exercises, with alternative versions, covering all the common irregular verbs is useful in an individualized program. Students can then check regularly their control of this troublesome area.

The fill-in-the-blank exercise may take the form of a *connected passage* of prose. This is a common way of giving practice in, or testing, the use of modal auxiliaries.

W22 (A) Write out the following passage, supplying the most appropriate modal auxiliary in the tense which best fits the context. Underline each auxiliary in your answer.

"Herr Francke _____ hier sein, hat seine Frau gesagt. Stimmt das? Er _____ morgen wegfahren, das ist seine feste Absicht. Ich _____ ihn aber vorher dringend sprechen."

Die dicke Alte blieb lange stumm. Dann erhob sie sich langsam vom Stuhl und sah aus dem Fenster.

"Ist er hier?"

Die Alte setzte sich wieder und sprach, ohne meine Frage gehört zu haben. "_____ ich doch etwas dagegen machen _____! Der war doch lieb. Immer. So was erwartet man nicht. Ich _____ am liebsten vergessen, daß er je hier im Hause war."

Sie schaute mich plötzlich an, aufflammend und dann wieder dumpf. "Er _____ zu Hause bleiben _____, dann wäre es nicht passiert. Jetzt ist es zu spät. _____ Gott ihm helfen!"

Clearly, this format is also useful for other areas of grammar, e.g., the recurrent problem of how and when to use separable prefixes with different verbs. This is a more natural way to practice this feature than by writing out lists of verbs with various prefixes.

W23 (E or I) Complete the following passage by inserting the appropriate separable prefixes.

Der Zug kommt langsam im Bahnhof _____. Ob Robert noch so jung _____ sieht? Ach, was fällt dir _____, er ist auch zehn Jahre älter. Jetzt steigt er _____ . . .

Uses for fill-in-the-blank exercises are limited only by the imagination of the instructor, as witness the following miscellany:

W24 (E or I) With English translation stimulus.

(what)   1. _____ willst du denn wissen?
(who)   2. Ich habe viele Freunde, _____ in die Planck-Schule gehen.
(which)   3. Er will jetzt den neuen Wagen verkaufen, _____ er letzte Woche gekauft hat.

Commentary

The indications in English are unnecessary for any of these items. In Item 1, the use of *wissen* precludes the possibility of anything but *was;* to make this more obvious to the student more context could be supplied, e.g., *Du hast eine Frage?* _____ *willst du denn wissen?*

W25 (E or I) With German paraphrase as stimulus.
Peter _____ heute abend ins Kino gehen.
(Peter hat die Erlaubnis, heute abend ins Kino zu gehen.)

Commentary

Presumably *darf* is sought. With this type of exercise care must be taken to see that the paraphrase is not in less familiar language than the item sought. The student could be distracted by *hat die Erlaubnis* into selecting the perfect tense, but should recognize his error upon observing the word order more closely.

W26 (I) With grammatical indications given.
Petra und Max _____.
(bleiben, Plusquamperfekt)

Commentary

This would be a more cognitive type of exercise if a suitable context were given for the item rather than the precise tense reference (see W13). In this example, only the form for the tense is being tested, not the use. Both would be tested in:

Petra und Max fuhren weiter nach Rom, nachdem sie zwei Wochen in Florenz _____. (bleiben)

W27 (E or I) With information given in associated sentences to show what is required.

1. Barbara spielt gut Geige. Franz spielt nicht sehr gut.
Barbara spielt _____ als Franz.
2. Hans ist groß. Paul hat die gleiche Größe.
Paul ist _____ groß _____ Hans.

The cloze procedure

If we combine the idea of W20 with the sequential format of W22, we arrive at the cloze procedure. Strictly speaking, the cloze procedure, as developed for native speakers, was a test of reading comprehension. It consisted of giving the student a passage to complete in which every *n*th word was deleted. In one passage it could be every fifth word, in another every tenth word or whatever the examiner chose. This will immediately recall the discussion in Chapter 3 of Cherry's uncertainties of a spoken message and Schlesinger's semantic-syntactic decoding. In a cloze test, the native speaker projects expectations about the development of the message. The foreign-language learner has also to think carefully about grammatical detail. For the foreign-language learner, then, the blanks need not be kept rigidly to a set pattern. The cloze procedure provides an interesting and thought-provoking exercise which trains the student to look carefully at all structural clues and to range around within a semantic field for related concepts. It is good preparation for careful reading and a useful overall written test.

W28 (E) Klaus und Regina sind _____ zwei Stunden in Stuttgart. _____ fahren mit dem Wagen _____ München, weil die Zugverbindungen _____ sind. Leider haben sie _____ vor Stuttgart eine Panne_____. In der Nähe war _____ Tankstelle zu sehen. Sie _____ also eine halbe Stunde _____ Fuß gehen, bevor sie _____ Telephon fanden. Das nennt _____ eine Vergnügungsreise!

Commentary

1. Any completion which makes sense in the context and fits into the grammatical structure is acceptable. Passages can be constructed which are more ambiguous than W28, thus allowing more scope for student ingenuity. (See also W47.)

2. (I and A) After a reading passage has been studied intensively, the students may do a cloze test on it to see how much of the vocabulary and grammatical structure they have retained.

* Prepare a cloze test from one of the passages in Chapters 6 or 7.

* Look at fill-in-the-blank exercises in various textbooks and suggest ways for making them more intellectually stimulating.

Beyond the elementary level

Inductive learning need not be limited to a few early lessons of patterned oral practice of the type discussed in Chapter 4. At the intermediate and advanced levels, the students' curiosity can be channeled into discovering for themselves quite complicated sets of rules which they tend to remember better because they themselves have worked them out.

The Rosetta procedure[11]

(I) The rules for the *agreement of relative pronouns* in German are not difficult to discover inductively from manifestations in written script.

The students express curiosity about differences they have observed in relative pronouns and hazard guesses as to the rules governing these divergencies. The teacher then gives them the following sets of sentences to study and asks that they develop from them coherent rules which will explain each form and its use (including punctuation).

W29

1. Kennst du Franz? Er ist der jüngere Bruder von Heinz Keller, den du neulich bei Hannelore kennengelernt hast. Franz ist der ganz tolle Schifahrer, von dem ich dir erzählt habe. Weißt du noch? Schifahren hat ihm ein Onkel beigebracht, der vor zwanzig Jahren bei den Olympiaden eine Medaille gewonnen hat. Dieser Onkel soll ein Sportler sein, dessen Form sich mit den Jahren sogar verbessert hat.

2. Kennst du Vreni? Sie ist die jüngere Schwester von Anna Keller, die du neulich bei Heinz kennengelernt hast. Vreni ist die tolle Schifahrerin, von der ich dir erzählt habe. Weißt du noch? Schifahren hat ihr eine Tante beigebracht, die vor zwanzig Jahren bei den Olympiaden eine

Medaille gewonnen hat. Diese Tante soll eine Sportlerin sein, deren Form sich mit den Jahren sogar verbessert hat.

3. Kennst du Uschi Keller? Das ist die kleine Schwester von dem Mädchen, das du neulich im Fernsehen gesehen hast. Uschi ist das ganz tolle Kind, von dem ich dir erzählt habe. Weißt du noch? Das kleine Wesen, das mit drei Jahren schon Schifahren konnte? Erstaunlich, nicht? So was lernt man am besten, wenn man noch klein ist. Das ist aber auch ein Kind, dessen Begabung kaum zu glauben ist.

Learning from living language

Even at the advanced level, English-speaking students find the subtleties of the use of the modal auxiliaries difficult to grasp. Instead of telling students all over again, with demonstration sentences, about how the auxiliaries can be used to indicate probability, possibility, necessity, constraint, expectation, obligation, and so forth, the teacher may give advanced students extracts of living language in which the context clarifies the nuance expressed by the auxiliary, e.g., *mögen*. Through an exercise of this type, the students focus on the variable semantic contribution of this auxiliary and the formal indications of its role (that is, the tense in which it appears).

W 30 (A) Examine the following extracts carefully, and identify the *nuance of meaning* of *mögen* in each. Does it indicate some degree of possibility or probability, preference or desire, a wish or a polite command? Note the *tense used* in each case. From your answers, work out which tenses of *mögen* are used to convey very specific meanings. Which tenses of *mögen* seem to be ambiguous, that is, capable of bearing two different meanings?

1. Im hohen Grade freilich, hat sie doch nichts von dem Charakter der Einöde; vielmehr *mögen* wenige Landschaften so voll Grün, Nachtigallenschlag und Blumenflor *angetroffen werden.* . . . (A. von Droste-Hülshoff)
2. Da . . . der Direktor . . . vor dem großen Salto mortale das Orchester mit aufgehobenen Händen beschwört, es *möge schweigen,* . . . legt der Galeriebesucher das Gesicht auf die Brüstung. . . .   (F. Kafka)
3. Inzwischen war der Laut von oben körperlicher geworden, er schwoll an und drohte. Ich hatte mich einigemal gefragt, ob ich warnen solle; aber *mochte* ich oder ein anderer *getroffen werden,* ich wollte es nicht tun!   (R. Musil)
4. Aber dann sah ich, daß das fremde Kind gar nicht die Bücher ins Auge faßte, sondern seine Blicke auf dem Tablett ruhen ließ, auf dem mein

Tee und meine belegten Brote standen. Vielleicht *möchtest* du etwas *essen,* sagte ich schnell.   (M. L. Kaschnitz)

5. Willi sah an ihm vorbei auf die Frau. *"Mochtest* du sie nicht?" "Nein", sagte der Mann.   (W. Schnurre)

6. In unseren Statuten heißt es: Wir wollen nicht ruhen, bis daß rechts wie links ist.
Wie schön und kraftvoll dieser Satz auch sein *mag,* ist er doch lautester Unsinn.   (G. Grass)

7. Dann hat mich gefroren, aber ich *hab* noch nicht *heimgehen mögen.* Ich bin noch in der Stadt herumgelaufen, aber dann bin ich doch heimgegangen.   (L. Rinser)

8. Mein Projekt ist, mich nach dem Kap einzuschiffen, an der Südspitze von Afrika ein Jahr zu bleiben und mich mit den südlichen Strömen zu beschäftigen.... *Möge* die äußere Lage der Welt meine Pläne bald *begünstigen.*   (A. von Humboldt)

9. Wie sehr man auch zögerte und sich umsah, schließlich kam doch der Giebel hinauf. Das erste Fenster oben faßte einen ins Auge, es *mochte wohl* jemand dort *stehen.*   (R. M. Rilke)

Commentary

1. These examples are not sufficient to cover all aspects of this complex subject, but they provide enough material to alert students to the complications of meaning of *mögen,* to stimulate their curiosity to identify the nuances of *mögen* in what they are reading, and to help them to use it in a more versatile fashion in speech.

2. There is enough material in W30 to draw together the following information.[12]

Possibility	Present, sie *mögen,* no. 3;
	simple past, *ich mochte,* no. 1;
	(all indicative tenses) ;
and probability	present, *er mag,* no. 6;
	simple past, *es mochte.* no. 9;
	(all indicative tenses).
Liking or having the	Simple past, *du mochtest,* no. 5;
desire to do something	present perfect, *ich habe mögen,* no. 7;
	(all indicative tenses) ;
	subjunctive II, *du möchtest,* no. 4.

Wishes	Subjunctive I, *sie möge,* no. 8;
	(subjunctive II, *er möchte*);
and polite commands	subjunctive I, *es möge,* no. 2.

* Find sentences illustrating the most important uses of other modal auxiliaries, e.g., *dürfen* and *sollen.*

(I and A) German word order frequently poses a particular problem for English-speaking language-learners. Although they become accustomed to using "normal" German word order (subject-verb-object) rapidly, they remain under the influence of the more rigid patterns in English word order and unaware of the flat effect when these patterns are used without relief in German. Consider the following examples:

W31 a. Ich bin zufällig hier. Ich möchte meine Bekannte nicht treffen. Ich halte mich nur einen Tag lang auf. Ich habe keine Zeit. Wenn ich sie treffe, muß ich mich ihr widmen. Sie beschlagnahmt mich. Sie sagt, was machst DU denn hier . . .   (H. NOVAK)[13]

b. Ich bin zufällig hier, und meine Bekannte möchte ich nicht treffen. Nur einen Tag lang halte ich mich auf: Ich habe keine Zeit. Ihr muß ich mich widmen, wenn ich sie treffe, denn sie beschlagnahmt mich. Was machst DU denn hier, sagt sie . . .   (Adaptation)

Commentary

The first version of the text consists of a series of simple, at times apparently unrelated sentences with very little variety in order. In contrast an attempt is made in the second version to connect the sentences by rearranging the statements and by thus placing emphasis on particular segments. Of course the writer of (a) clearly seeks through the monotony of the statements to characterize the young woman who is represented. But most students learning to write German would prefer not to project unwittingly the same image of themselves.

Only through living language can we really assimilate differences like these which are fundamental to the effective use and understanding of German.

Teachers who wish to retain and improve upon the level of German they attained on graduating will seek opportunities to visit Germany and German-speaking countries. Meanwhile, they will read widely and constantly in German for pleasure. Material of the type used in W30 and W31 can be collected by teachers from their own reading of newspapers, magazines, plays, novels, or books of general information.

✱ Find material to clarify the uses of tenses in contemporary written German. Remember that there must be sufficient context in each item to establish the particular meaning conveyed by the use of one tense, rather than another.

Deductive learning also has its place at the advanced level. Because of the subtlety of the distinction and the paucity of comparable examples in any one text, it would be very time-consuming, for instance, to try to work out inductively the way the subjunctive mode[14] is used in German to convey a subjective assessment of the situation, as opposed to the objective observation of fact of the indicative.

In a particular context, the writer may have chosen to express his opinion, and to make it clear that this is his opinion, by using the subjunctive, whereas he might very well have used the indicative in an identical sequence of lexical items had he wished to convey a different impression. For instance, (a) *Sie glauben, daß er sich täuscht* and (b) *Sie glauben, daß er sich täusche* could occur in similar contexts without any clear contextual clues as to why the author selected one rather than the other. Yet the intention of the author in selecting (a) rather than (b) would be basic to the interpretation of the text.

For these reasons, the particular problems of the subjunctive would normally be explained deductively, with demonstrations in passages of living language of the various ways in which it is used (see R42–R44). Students would then be encouraged to explain why an author had used a subjunctive whenever an interesting example was encountered in texts for intensive study. They would also be expected to have a reason for using a subjunctive in their own writing.

✱ Begin a collection of suitable extracts for the advanced level demonstrating interesting uses of *conditional sentences* or *ellipsis* and share them with other members of the class.

GRAMMAR AND WRITING SKILL

However grammatical concepts are introduced and demonstrated, it is essential that the students' activity be directed as soon as possible to *the concept in use*. Understanding the operation of the grammar, observing its functioning, or practicing the effective use of it in exercises will not ensure that the student can use it efficiently in writing.

Experiments in the writing of English by native speakers have shown specifically that the formal study of grammar and of grammatical terminology does not improve skill in writing.[15] Native speakers who can control the grammar of their language in speech and have been taught in elementary and secondary school how it operates still write ungrammatical and incomplete sentences. Formal grammar is an abstract study. After foreign language students have been shown how the various parts of the language system operate, they seem to benefit more from discussion of the types of errors they are making in their writing in relation to what they were trying to say, with opportunity provided to correct their errors in context, than from a second (third, fourth, fifth?) exposition of the workings of the German pronoun system.[16] In this way they focus on the details they partly know or do not know, rather than having their attention dispersed over a wider area of abstract concepts.

9
Writing and written exercises II: flexibility and expression

III. Production: flexibility measures

Cognitive exercises of the types described, despite their usefulness in clarifying grammatical concepts, do not require students to construct their own sentences to express their personal meaning, nor to develop their ideas in logical and coherent paragraphs within a larger discourse. "Knowing about" is not "knowing how." *Practice is needed in actual sequential writing.* Having learned about the various parts of the machine, and parts of parts, and how these synchronize in action, the student needs to set the machine in motion with the different parts active in weaving the intricate pattern of meaning. Here guidance is helpful in learning which parts will operate together to form new patterns. Student aptitudes vary widely in writing. Some need considerable help in developing a smooth and effective operation; others seem intuitively to take off and create interesting patterns of their own. The teacher needs to distinguish these types early and *individualize writing activities* so that each benefits to the maximum, according to his preferred style of activity.

Although writing within a framework and expressive writing will now be discussed in sequence, it must be emphasized that opportunities for expressive writing should be provided as soon as possible. Even the elementary-level student should have opportunities to experiment with the potential for expression of his rudimentary knowledge of the language. Students should not, however, be left to sink or swim in such a difficult area. Most students need some guided practice in using new combinations and exploring possibilities of expression, if they are to go beyond simple, uncomplicated sentences; they need resources other than "gemischte pickles" when they wish to express more sophisticated ideas in the new medium.

Expressive writing experiments with all the possibilities of syntax and lexicon. If there is to be transfer from guided practice in using this potential, then the practice itself must be recognizably purposeful and applicable.

This section will concentrate on measures for developing flexibility in the construction of sentences and paragraphs within the shelter of a framework.

CONVERSIONS AND RESTATEMENTS

The problems of single-sentence conversions have been discussed at length in Chapter 4. Since they are to be found in any textbook, examples of all the different kinds will not be given here. Some will be examined in detail to show ways in which they can be made to serve the ultimate purpose of developing ability to write clearly, comprehensibly, and expressively.

Conversions are cognitive exercises in that they require the student to think through the rules and select the ones applicable to the particular case under consideration. Two of the commonest types are the following.

W32 (E) Rewrite the following sentences in the feminine, making all necessary adjustments.

> 1. Mein älterer Bruder fährt zu seinem französischen Freund.
>   (Expected conversion: Meine ältere Schwester fährt zu ihrer französischen Freundin.)

W33 (E) Answer the following questions according to the indication given, replacing the italicized words with appropriate pronouns.

> 1. Hat *Ihr Bruder den grünen Anzug* gekauft?
>   Ja, ...
>   (Expected conversion: Ja, er hat ihn gekauft.)
> 2. Hat *Heidi ihre Uhr* gefunden?
>   Nein, ...
>   (Expected conversion: Nein, sie hat sie nicht gefunden.)

Students may learn to complete exercises like W32 and W33 accurately, without there being any necessary transfer of what has been learned to expressive writing. Some items of this type may be useful for familiarizing students with the mechanics of these operations, but, as soon as the students seem to have grasped the idea, they should be given a more interesting and imaginative task like W34, which requires of them the same types of operations in a simulated, possible situation. (After completing the writing, they may act out the short scene they have created.)

W34 (E or I)

1. Sie gingen gestern in die Stadt und kauften einen Transistor, der jetzt nicht funktioniert. Sie gehen zum Geschäft zurück und verlangen einen neuen Apparat. Der Verkäufer glaubt nicht, daß Sie ihn bei diesem Geschäft gekauft hätten, und Sie bestreiten das. Geben Sie den Dialog wieder, der sich ergibt.

This subject should elicit sentences like the following:

KUNDE   Guten Tag. Ich bringe den Transistor zurück, den ich gestern bei Ihnen gekauft habe. Leider funktioniert er nicht besonders gut.

VERKÄUFER   Diesen Transistor haben Sie nicht hier gekauft. Wir führen diese Marke gar nicht. Ich kann ihn also nicht ersetzen. Sie müssen ihn zum Geschäft bringen, wo Sie ihn gekauft haben.

KUNDE   Ich habe ihn aber doch bei Ihnen gekauft. Hier ist die Quittung . . .

2. Sie haben bei einem Geschäft eine Sporthose gekauft, die auseinanderreißt. Gleiche Situation: Die Verkäuferin behauptet, sie hätte Ihnen diese Hose nicht verkauft. Geben Sie den Dialog wieder, der daraus erfolgt.

Possible dialogue:

KUNDE   Guten Tag, Fräulein. Ich bringe die Sporthose zurück, die ich am Montag gekauft habe. Ich habe sie nur zweimal angehabt, und die Nähte reißen schon auseinander.

VERKÄUFER   Diese Hose hätten Sie nicht bei uns kaufen können. Wir führen nur Hosen von der besten Qualität . . .

* Take from a textbook an exercise for converting conditional clauses from one tense to another (e.g., *Wenn ich ihn sehe, werde ich ihm die Nachricht geben* for conversion into *Wenn ich ihn je sähe, würde ich ihm die Nachricht geben* or *Wenn ich ihn gesehen hätte, hätte ich ihm die Nachricht gegeben*) and work out a more imaginative exercise which would elicit these types of conversions in a creative framework.

A conversion becomes a *restatement* when it retains the general form of the original, but the changes made are more than mere switches from tense to tense, gender to gender, or sentence type to sentence type. W35 below is a conversion and W36 a restatement using the same basic material.

W35 (I) Nach Daninos[1] schrieb ein englischer Lord seinem Chauffeur Zehn Gebote vor. Unter ihnen waren folgende:

—Die Kleidung soll immer tadellos und ordentlich sein;
—Die Mütze soll immer gerade auf dem Kopf sitzen;
—Es darf nie im Wagen geraucht werden;

Schreiben Sie diese Gebote durch den Gebrauch der Zukunftsform in direkte Rede um, wie zum Beispiel: "Sie werden immer ruhig fahren."

W36 (I) In *Snobissmo* zählt Daninos die Zehn Gebote auf, die ein englischer Lord seinem Chauffeur vorschrieb. Sechs davon folgen:

—Die Kleidung soll immer tadellos und ordentlich sein: blauer Anzug, kastanienbraune Handschuhe, schwarze Schuhe;
—Die Mütze soll gerade auf dem Kopf sitzen;
—Es darf nie im Wagen geraucht werden;
—Wenn man halten muß, soll man sich still wie ein Standbild halten;
—Bremsen, damit die Fußgänger über die Straße gehen können;
—Ganz anhalten und höfflich einen Wink geben, damit eine Kinderpflegerin mit Kinderwagen über die Straße gehen kann.

Sie sind eine alte Dame, die jeden Tag Sir Henry in seinem Rolls vorbeifahren sieht. Sie erzählen Ihre Jugenderinnerungen, und dabei machen Sie Bemerkungen über die Kleidung und das Benehmen seines Chauffeurs.

The restatement comes closer to *composition or expressive writing,* when W36 is followed by W37.

W37 (I) Verfassen Sie nach diesem Muster Zehn Gebote für den Fahrer eines Touristenautobuses oder für den Portier bei einem Hotel.

SENTENCE MODIFICATION

Flexibility in writing means being able to make a sentence say what you want it to say and to say it vividly, humorously, poignantly, obliquely, or succinctly.

W38 The simple notion *Ich begleite Sie* can be expressed with all kinds of nuances:

Ich werde Sie mit großem Vergnügen begleiten.
Natürlich werde ich Sie begleiten.
Ich begleite dich, komm!
Ich würde Sie begleiten, aber leider . . .
Ich möchte Sie gerne begleiten, aber leider . . .
Es ist nicht, daß ich Sie nicht begleiten möchte, aber . . .

Practice in types of sentences

Students should learn early to try to express similar ideas in different forms from various points of view. One amusing way to do this is to take a particular situation and ask the students to express the reactions of a number of people to it.

W39 (E or I) Ein junger Arzt, der eben aus dem Krankenhaus gekommen ist, läuft über die enge Straße, die mit den vielen Wagen der Hauptverkehrszeit verstopft ist. Sein unvorsichtiges Benehmen hat auf allen Seiten Aufsehen erregt. Geben Sie die Bemerkungen wieder, die die Reaktion folgender Leute darstellen:

Ein Polizist (Frage)
Ein Kind zu seiner Mutter (Frage, Bemerkung)
Ein Busfahrer (Ausruf)
Die Frau des Arztes (Ausruf, Frage)
Ein Fußgänger zum Polizisten (Ausruf, Frage)
Ein junger Mann auf seinem Motorrad (Ausruf)
Eine alte Frau zum Kind (negative Frage)
Ein Kaufmann an der Tür seines Geschäfts (Bemerkung)

Since what is written is intended to be read, students may copy down the comments in W39 as one side of a dialogue, exchange papers with other students, and complete the dialogues for acting out.

One side of the dialogue might read:

W40 Polizist: Wer ist der Verrückte, der über die Straße läuft?!

. . . .

Kind zu seiner Mutter: Gehen wir auch über die Straße, Mutti? Der hat's gemacht.

. . . .

Busfahrer: Schau mal, was der Idiot macht! Er hat nicht alle Tassen im
Schrank!

. . . .

Frau des Arztes: Peter, komm zurück! Willst du umkommen?

. . . .

Fußgänger zum Polizisten: Das verstößt gegen die Verkehrsordnung! Was
passierte, wenn alle sich solche Freiheiten er-
laubten?!

Combinations

If students are to write well they must be shaken out of the shelter of the
simple sentence and the compound sentence with *und* and *aber*. One way
of eliciting complex sentences from students has been the combination
exercise.

W 41 (E) Combine the following pairs of sentences into one by using relative
pronouns.

1. Ich war bei einem italienischen Sänger.
   Er hat sieben Kinder.
      (Expected combination: Ich war bei einem italienischen Sänger, der
      sieben Kinder hat.)
2. Meine Tante hat einen schönen Kuchen gebacken.
   Ich habe den schönen Kuchen aufgegessen.
      (Expected combination: Ich habe den schönen Kuchen aufgegessen,
      den meine Tante gebacken hat.)

or (E or I) Combine the following sets of sentences into one sentence
without using *und* or *aber*.

3. Da steht ein Polizist.
   Er hält die Wagen an.
   Er läßt eine alte Dame über die Straße gehen.
      (Expected combination: Da steht ein Polizist, der die Wagen anhält,
      um eine alte Dame über die Straße gehen zu lassen.)

Too many of these become busywork exercises. After a few examples,
the students know what is expected of them and their energies are taken up
with "completing the set."

A more interesting approach which challenges the students' ingenuity
is as follows:

W42 (E) Students are asked to think of simple sentences—any simple sentences. These are written on the chalkboard in the order in which they are supplied. Students are then given time, singly, in pairs, or in groups, to combine these sentences in any way they like to make a sensible paragraph. No simple sentences may be used and only one *und* and one *aber* for joining clauses are permissible in each paragraph. Adverbs, adjectives, and a few phrases may be added to improve the narrative.

Below is an example of how the procedure might work.

Sentences provided by students:

Der Mann verläßt das Haus.
Der Bäcker verkauft Brot.
Die Katze jagt nach einer Maus.
Der Hund bellt.
Die Mutter schimpft auf das Kind.
Das Kind läßt das Spielzeug fallen.
Der Weihnachtsmann grüßt die Kinder.

Possible paragraph:

Der Bäcker verkauft morgens Brot, aber am Nachmittag verkleidet er sich als Weihnachtsmann. Nachdem er sein Haus verlassen hat, geht er zu einem großen Kaufhaus, wo er die Kinder freundlich grüßt. Plötzlich bellt ein Hund, weil er eine Katze sieht, die nach einer Maus jagt. Ein kleines Kind läuft zur Tür, um zu sehen, was draußen los ist, und es läßt unterwegs sein Spielzeug fallen. Natürlich schimpft seine Mutter, auch wenn der Weihnachtsmann dabei ist.

Contractions

Writing in German can be made more concise and succinct if certain clauses are reduced to phrases (*bevor er abgefahren ist—vor seiner Abfahrt; weil sie Hunger haben—wegen ihres Hungers*) and some phrases reduced to single words (*der Mann, der die Fahrkarten kontrolliert—der Schaffner; einer, der einen Bus fährt—ein Busfahrer*). Instead of giving students a series of disconnected sentences to contract in specific ways, the teacher may provide a complete passage and ask students to use their ingenuity to reduce its length by at least a third.

Expansions

Students should have many opportunities to expand simple statements by using all the variations they have been learning—to flex their writing muscles as it were. Most textbooks provide a number of expansion exercises, but these are usually very dull affairs. Sometimes, a list of adjectives is set down beside a series of simple sentences and students are asked to insert before nouns appropriate adjectives from the list and to supply correct endings. In other cases, the student is given a series of adverbs or adverbial phrases and asked to expand a set of simple sentences by inserting these at the appropriate places. Students may complete these exercises dutifully, but it is doubtful whether they thereby improve their ability to write in the language, since they contribute nothing of their own to the task. Much of the cognitive learning involved in these tasks can be accomplished as effectively or at least more briskly in the types of oral exercises described in Chapter 4.

Even if staid exercises like those described above appear in an imposed textbook, teachers should be prepared to think up more imaginative ways of presenting the same material. Writing assignments should be interesting, amusing, or useful, never boring or trivial.

Below are some suggestions for creative approaches to the same problems.

Expanding with adjectives. Students can be handed part of a passage like C58 and asked to help the police identify the skyjacker.

W 43 (E or I) Zwei Männer entführten ein Flugzeug der Lufthansa auf der Strecke München–Berlin. Sie bedrohten den Piloten mit einem Gewehr und zwangen ihn dadurch, in Richtung Hamburg zu fliegen. Kurz vor der Landung in Hamburg verschwanden sie vom Flugzeug. Man glaubt, daß sie mit einem Fallschirm über den Feldern außerhalb der Stadt abgesprungen seien. Die Polizei sucht sie noch.

Nachdem die Passagiere aus dem Flugzeug ausgestiegen waren, wurden sie von der Polizei ausgefragt, die ein ungefähres Bild von den Luftpiraten zusammenstellen wollte. Leider stimmten die Beschreibungen der Passagiere nicht miteinander überein.

Verfassen Sie drei verschiedene Beschreibungen der Piraten. Benutzen Sie möglichst viele Eigenschaftswörter, um der Polizei behilflich zu sein.

Expanding with adverbs.

W 44 (E or I) Ihre Nachbarin singt immer sehr laut, wenn sie morgens badet, aber nicht alle freuen sich darüber. Jeder nach seinem Geschmack. Beschreiben Sie die Reaktion folgender Leute. (Als Ausgangsphrase nehmen Sie "sie singt" und unterscheiden Sie die verschiedenen Standpunkte durch Adverbialbestimmungen, die wo, wann, wie und warum angeben.)

1. Der Ehemann der Nachbarin spricht zu seinem Chef.
2. Ihr Sohn spricht zu seinem Spielkameraden.

3. Sie sprechen zu Ihrem Friseur (zu Ihrer Friseuse).
4. Die Putzfrau spricht zu ihrer Freundin.
5. Der Briefträger spricht zu seiner Frau.

Possible answer no. 5: Die Dame von der Schillerstraße 5 singt morgens in der Wanne so laut, daß ich sie auf der Straße hören kann. Das Schlimme dabei ist, daß sie immer falsch singt!

Expanding frames. Sometimes students are asked to expand what have been called *dehydrated sentences.*

W45 (E or I) Write out the following outline in the past tense in complete sentences, supplying any words missing and making all necessary changes. Double slashes indicate new sentences.

Sommerferien / anfangen / eben // früh am Morgen / wecken / Mutter / Ursula // müssen / eilen / weil / Eilzug / um sieben Uhr / abfahren / sollen // als / Ursula / Mantel / anziehen / hören / sie / draußen / Hupe // müssen / Taxi / sein / rufen / Mutter // sein / du / bereit /

W46 Unraveled, the passage reads as follows:

Die Sommerferien hatten eben angefangen. Früh am Morgen weckte die Mutter Ursula. Sie mußte eilen, weil der Eilzug um sieben Uhr abfahren sollte. Als Ursula den Mantel anzog, hörte sie draußen eine Hupe. Es muß das Taxi sein, rief die Mutter. Bist du bereit?

This format can be useful for testing ability to introduce grammatical features at required points in the sentence, although the same kinds of demands are made by the cloze procedure within a framework which is much closer to normal language. (Cf. W28.)

W47 Die Sommerferien _____ eben angefangen. _____ am Morgen weckte die Mutter Ursula. Sie _____ eilen, _____ der Eilzug _____ sieben Uhr abfahren _____. _____ Ursula den Mantel anzog, hörte sie _____ eine Hupe. Es _____ das Taxi sein, rief die Mutter. Bist du _____?

Commentary

A few more grammatical features are supplied for the student in W47 than in W45 and there are several places which allow for more than one possibility, but these are not necessarily undesirable features. In W45, students may become confused by the number of decisions they have to make.

Because of their artificiality, dehydrated sentences can become something of a chore, and therefore counterproductive. A note of reality is added if the dehydrated frame is presented in the form of *news headlines* or *telegrams* for expansion.

Fortunately, there is available in the real world a type of script which resembles the dehydrated sentence but which gives students authentic contact with many aspects of German life, namely, the *Anzeigen* in the daily newspapers (*Tageszeitungen*). One copy of almost any local German paper (the ads in these are most abbreviated) will supply the teacher with numerous items from which to draw dealing with everything from positions vacant, apartments to let, cars and animals for sale, lost property to vacation opportunities and eligible partners for marriage (*Ehewünsche*). The less abbreviated classified advertisements supply useful clues for the interpretation of the more abbreviated.

W 48 (I) Write out in full the following advertisements from the *Rhein-Neckar-Zeitung* for rooms to let. Study them and then write a letter in German to a friend telling her about the advantages of the apartments and why you decided to take one instead of the other.

1. 4 ZW, 95 qm, HASENLEISER, Balk., Bad, sep. WC, ZH u. wW-Vers., Fahrstuhl, Pkw-Abstellpl. in Tiefgar. m. Berechtigungsschein B sof. zu verm. monatl. Miete 397 DM zzgl. Umlagen u. Heizung. Angeb. Chiff. 18699 u. Tel. HD 2 71 36 Mo-Fr.

2. Schöne möbl. 2-ZW, ca. 70 qm in Bammental, Kü., Bad, gr. Abstellraum, Öl-ZH, Terrasse, sep. Eingang, Auto-Abstellpl., ab 1. 2. 74 für 380 DM incl. NK zu vermieten. Zuschriften u. 18411 an die RNZ.

At the advanced level, the *Anzeigen* can be used as a basis for a practical writing project. Students can learn a great deal from the advertisements for positions vacant.

W 49 Buchbindermeister von leistungsstarkem und finanzkräftigem Unternehmen als Abteilungsleiter zu besten Bedingungen gesucht. Sicher in Personalführung, kostenbewußt und mit Organisationsgeschick. Offerten unter Nr. 18651 erbeten.

From a number of such listings the students may make a list of the kinds of qualities and qualifications which seem to be sought (*sicher in Personalführung, kostenbewußt, Kenntnisse in Maschinenschreiben, selb-*

ständig arbeiten, Englischkenntnisse, gute Fachausbildung, and so on). They may then list in German the qualifications they feel they possess, select an advertisement, and write an application for the position advertised.

The *Ehewünsche* may also serve as the basis for a writing project. After collecting various terms for human qualities (*häuslich, Herzensbildung, sympathisch, seriös, temperamentvoll, sportlich-elegant,* and so forth), students write descriptive sketches of various persons, real or imaginary.

THE IDEA FRAME

Dehydrated sentences and cloze tests control the structure the students will use. Some experienced teachers feel that progress toward expressive writing is more rapid if content rather than structure is controlled.[2] The student, relieved of the complete responsibility for the development of the content, can concentrate his energies on vigorous writing and can experiment with various possibilities for expressing an idea. (In this sense, the *Anzeigen* of W48 and W49 can be considered idea frames.)

1. The idea frame may be related to current reading. For instance, the reading passage R49 may be taken as a basis for writing activities. Here we have the story of a war casualty whom officialdom wishes to place neatly in a niche.

W 50 (I) A questionnaire is developed in such a way that, when it is answered consecutively, it produces a coherent paragraph:

1. Warum ging der Mann zum Amt?
2. Wer hat ihn auf dem Amt empfangen?
3. Wozu hat man Fragen gestellt?
4. Was schlug man ihm vor?
5. Wie reagierte der Mann auf den Vorschlag?

A set of questions like this provides the student with a developing situation and some essential vocabulary. It should not, however, be the final stage. The student should then be asked to write creatively, thus reusing language material he has just acquired in new ways to express his own ideas.

W 51 (I) Hat der Mann eine Stelle angenommen? Erzählen Sie, was er Ihrer Meinung nach unternehmen sollte, nachdem er das Amt verläßt.

2. Stevick's *microtexts* can provide useful idea frames (see Chapter 2, p. 50). After a text has been discussed orally, students may be asked to

describe a similar situation in which they found themselves, the implications for this particular situation of the arguments in the text, the reasons why they could not agree with the writer of the text, and so on.

3. The land of make-believe. The students as a group invent an imaginary setting as a background for some of their writing activities.

W 52 (E, I, or A) The students *invent a country,* give it a name (e.g., *Abdera*), design its map, describe its history, its economy, its living conditions, and its problems with its neighbors. (If the class is working in small groups, each group has its own country and displays its map prominently on its section of the bulletin board.) From time to time, they write about events which affect *Abdera.*

—Abdera will eine neue Universität in der Provinz gründen. Erklären Sie, warum Abdera sie braucht. Beschreiben Sie den Plan, den man vorgeschlagen hat, und die Reaktion unter den Studenten der alten Universität von Abdera.

—Eine Krise in Abdera! Ein Bürgerkrieg bricht aus! Geben Sie die Nachrichten wieder, die Radio Abdera während der ersten Tage des Krieges sendet.

W 53 (E or I) The students *invent a family* and keep a copy of all the data: number of children and their names, ages, and interests, cousins, aunts, and uncles, where they live, what they do for a living and what they enjoy doing in their leisure, their friends, neighbors, and pets, some of their well-remembered joys and misfortunes, and their hopes and plans for the future. They occasionally tackle problems like the following:

—Tante Amalie, die auf einem kleinen Dorf in Schwaben wohnt, teilt ihrer Familie mit, daß sie ihren Nachbarn, einen achtzigjährigen Rentner, heiratet. Sie ist 78 Jahre alt. Geben Sie die Korrespondenz wieder, die sich ergibt (Briefe an ihre Nichte, an ihr Patenkind; Antworten darauf).

W 54 (E) For the elementary level, a treasure island (*Schatzinsel*) is a fruitful notion. The students themselves will provide plenty of ideas for bringing it into existence and for projects associated with it. If the class is divided into groups, each group may use the same island but have its own theories on where and how the treasure is hidden.[3]

INTEGRATED LANGUAGE ACTIVITIES WITHIN AN IDEA FRAME
Writing with Visual

1. (E or I) *Objects.* Students are shown some object and asked to write a *concise description* which would distinguish it from all other objects, e.g.,

a pencil, a book, an eraser, or a window. The descriptions are read out in class and other students try to show how the descriptions could apply to other objects. The written description is then further refined to meet these objections.

Variations. (E) An adaptation of *Kim's Game.* Students are shown briefly a tray of jumbled objects. Each student may look at the tray for one minute. Students then list as many objects as they can remember with a short descriptive comment, e.g., *ein blaues Taschentuch mit weißen Blümchen.* Students read out their lists with descriptions and discuss the objects they forgot.

2. (E or I) *Persons.* Students write descriptions of no more than two sentences in length of persons in the class, in school, in the news, on television, or pictured in the textbook. No names are given. The descriptions written by one group are circulated to other groups who try to guess who has been described.

3. (E or I) *Pictures.* Students bring to class pictures selected from magazines or newspapers. Photographs of unexpected situations are useful. These are distributed at random. Students write anecdotes, descriptions, or explanations about the pictures which are then read to the class. Each student may correct his version as he reads it and other students suggest improvements. The student then rewrites his version for grading. Students select by vote the most interesting compositions which will be posted, with the picture, on the bulletin board or reproduced in the class newspaper.

4. (E or I) *Cartoons.* Students working in pairs are given cartoon strips (*Bildstreifen*) without balloons (*Sprechblasen*) or captions (*ohne Bildtext*). Each student writes captions for his series of sketches (*geschriebene Sprache*), developing the story line. They then exchange cartoons and write balloon dialogue for each other's stories (*gesprochene Sprache*). Pairs work together in perfecting their cartoons which are later displayed on the bulletin board for the amusement of the rest of the class. (Note: single picture cartoons are more difficult since they require witty comments. These may be used at the advanced level.)

5. (I or A) *Films.* Short silent films and documentary sound films may be used to stimulate written composition.

Writing with speaking and listening

Many activities are listed in C67, under Writing. To these may be added the following:

1. (E or I) The composition is given orally and discussed with other students before being written in its final form. (See *Oral Reports* in Chapter 1.)

2. (E or I) After students have acted out dialogues they have studied, they write, singly or in groups, original dialogues which recombine the

material in new situations. They then act out their dialogues for the rest of the class.

3. (E or I) Students are given a partial dialogue, that is, with the utterances of one participant but not the other. They make up the other half of the dialogue so that it fits in with the half supplied. (See also *Situation Tapes* in Chapter 1.) They then act out their different versions. (Originality and whimsicality are encouraged.)

4. (E or I) Activities 1, 2, and 3 in the section *Writing with Visual,* p. 276, may be performed orally.

5. (E or I) *Klatsch.* This is an old party game which makes an amusing writing exercise for groups of eight or less. The eight questions below are typed on a sheet with plenty of space, not only for the written answer but also to allow the paper to be turned back to hide what has been written. Student A answers the first question, turns back the sheet to hide the answer, and passes the sheet to Student B, who does likewise with the second question. The paper is passed on for all eight questions. Each student in the group begins a sheet, so that up to eight sheets can be circulating at once. When the last questions have been answered, the papers are unfolded and the incongruous results are read to the group.

Questions:

1. Wer?
2. hat wen getroffen?
3. Wo?
4. Was hat er ihr gesagt?
5. Was hat sie geantwortet?
6. Was haben sie gemacht?
7. Was ist daraus geworden?
8. Und die Moral der Geschichte?

6. (I or A) *Erzähl weiter.* This is also played in groups. Each person is given a sheet of paper on which is written the opening sentence of a story. He reads what is written and adds a sentence of his own. The papers are then circulated around the group, with each student adding a sentence to each story. The last student in each case writes a concluding sentence and gives the story a title. The complete stories are then read aloud to the group.

7. (I or A) *Was meinen Sie?* Students bring in information on current controversial issues which they present to the class. After class discussion of the data and the problem, students write out their own opinions on the issue, with any supporting information they have been able to find. They then present this viewpoint orally to the class, or to a small group, as a basis for further discussion.

8. (E) Students listen to a story on tape or as told to them by the

teacher or an advanced student. They then write the story out in their own words, adding embellishments in keeping with the theme as they wish.

9. (I or A) Students take a story they have been reading, rewrite it in simple German, then tell the story to an elementary class.

10. (I or A) Students interview in German visiting native speakers or German-speaking local residents about their special interests and then write up the interview for the class newspaper or the bulletin board. If the school newspaper can be persuaded to print the interview in German, this will arouse the curiosity of other students about language study. (If no native speakers are available, a fellow German teacher agrees to be interviewed in German on some hobby or special interest.)

11. (E or I) Students are given a skeleton outline with blanks of a lecture, discussion, interview, story, or play they are to hear on tape. (At the elementary level, the outline may be like C57; at the intermediate level it will omit segments of vital information.) After listening, students either complete the outline or use it as a guide in writing up their own account of what they heard.

12. (I or A) Students listen to interviews with, or speeches by, political leaders, national figures, artists, or writers. They make notes on what they have heard; they complete their notes in group discussion with other listeners; finally, they use the material they have noted in a research project.

13. (I or A) Students complete a written research project on a leading German personality. After this has been presented to the class and discussed, the students listen to a speech by, or interview with, this personality.

14. (I or A) Students watch a German documentary film and use the information in it for a written research project.

15. (E) *Writing with listening at the beginning stage:* Postovsky[1] reports an experiment in which adult students of Russian performed written drills from spoken input, without speaking themselves, for one month of intensive study (six hours per day with additional homework). They heard only native speakers. At that stage, they were superior in morphology and also in pronunciation to the regular audiolingual group. This approach is not necessarily transferable to other age groups and other situations, but it has interesting implications.

Writing with reading

Some suggestions have already been given in the section *Integrating the Language Skills* in Chapter 7. To be able to write well, the student needs to read widely, thus familiarizing himself with the way recognized German writers write. He must, through much experience with written texts, develop his ability to assimilate information directly in German and to think in German, so that his writing acquires the rhythms and associations of the German writer.

1. (E or I) Students rework the linguistic material of a story by rewriting it from the viewpoint of a different character or from the changed perspective of one of the characters when writing in retrospect. R56 may be rewritten from the point of view of one of the guards at the prison or R49 as an experience told by the official to his wife.

2. (I or A) After careful reading of a text, students sum up its main thrust by giving it a title. They then identify the *main topics* and trace *the development of thought* through each paragraph. The processes associated with C52, C53, and C54 may be applied at this point. The students set down the main ideas in a logical sequence in simple active declarative sentences. This skeleton outline is then put away. Another day, the students take the outline and write a text of their own from it. They then compare their text with the original to see what they can learn linguistically from the comparison.

3. (I or A) The appropriate use of *logical connectives* is a problem in writing a foreign language, yet it is essential to the coherent development of ideas. This subject is discussed in Chapter 7, R50 and R51. The procedure in R51 can be applied to full paragraphs and to a reasoned argument of several paragraphs in length.

4. (I or A) An excellent intellectual and linguistic exercise is the *Zusammenfassung:* the gathering together of the main ideas of the text in succinct summary form. This is a useful art in this busy age. To do this well, the student has to understand the text fully and rethink it in concentrated terms which he expresses in German. Applied to sophisticated texts, this is certainly an advanced-level activity, but it can be practiced with less complicated texts at the intermediate level.

5. (I or A) Writing can be associated with *rapid reading.* Students need to learn to skim through informational material to draw from it the specific facts they require for some definite project. For this, they are given a set of questions beforehand and a specified period of time to find and write down the information from a long article or a chapter of a book.

(E) This approach can be used also with narrative material for *extensive reading* as soon as students begin to read longer passages for pleasure. It can also serve as a familiarization process before the students study sections of the material in detail.

6. (I or A) Where students are encouraged to read German articles and books of their own choice from an extensive reading library, they should be encouraged to write short *reactions* of a paragraph or two to what they have read. These brief communications should not be stereotyped book reports or summaries of the content, but quite personal, reflecting the concern of the student with some aspect of the reading material, information he gained from it, or imaginative ideas which came to him as he read it. The most interesting of these may, with the writer's permission, be posted

on the bulletin board to encourage or discourage other students from choosing the same reading material. (This moves beyond the frame to expressive writing.)

7. (I) The cloze procedure can be used for introductory courses in *literature* for developing sensitivity to the author's choice of a particular word in preference to other semantic alternatives. This process involves both structure and divergence from that structure. Structure is present when the context of the whole text makes it possible to fill in a missing element with little effort. Understanding the total organization is the main point. Divergence occurs when the gap is filled by an unexpected element of the author's choosing. And it is this divergence between what the reader expects and what the author says which provides a measure of the style.[5]

8. (A) Further sensitivity to literary style can be encouraged at the advanced level by attempts at writing short passages in imitation of the style and approach of particular authors.

9. Further suggestions will be found later in this chapter in *Normal Purposes of Writing*, 3 and 4.

PRACTICE IN STYLES OF WRITING (A)

Arapoff has suggested a format within which students may practice various styles of writing. Taking the content of a simple dialogue, students are encouraged to rewrite it in the form of direct address, narration, paraphrase, summary, factual analysis, assertion, in essay form, as argumentative analysis with evaluation of the argument, as a critical review which objectively examines the validity of the evidence, and as a term paper. This interesting approach should be studied in the original article, "Writing: A Thinking Process."[6]

Shortening Arapoff's sequence somewhat, the teacher would proceed as follows.

1. Students would be given a short dialogue like W55 as *foundational content*.

W55 PETER   Guten Tag, Anna.

     ANNA   Guten Tag, Peter.

     PETER   Wohin gehst du?

     ANNA   Ich gehe zum Strand. Komm mit!

     PETER   Aber es regnet gleich. Schau mal, wie dunkel die Wolken sind.

     ANNA   Gar nicht möglich! Es kann nicht wieder anfangen. Es hat die ganze Woche lang geregnet.

2. Next, students rewrite W55 as *direct address in a narrative framework*.

W 56 —Guten Tag, Anna, sagt Peter, als er sie auf der Straße trifft.
—Guten Tag, Peter, erwidert sie.
—Wohin gehst du jetzt? fragt er.
—Ich gehe zum Strand, antwortet sie mit Begeisterung. Komm mit!
—Aber es regnet gleich, wendet Peter ein, als er einen Blick zum Himmel wirft. Schau mal, wie dunkel die Wolken sind.
—Gar nicht möglich, protestiert Anna. Es kann nicht wieder anfangen. Es hat schon eine ganze Woche lang geregnet.

3. Students then write a paraphrase of W55 in *narrative form.*

W 57 Als Peter Anna auf der Straße trifft, erkennt er sie gleich und grüßt sie freundlich. Wenn er sie fragt, wo sie hingeht, antwortet sie, daß sie zum Strand geht, und lädt ihn ein mitzukommen. Peter wendet ein, daß es gleich regnet, und zeigt ihr die dunklen Wolken, die oben drohen. Aber Anna will nicht glauben, daß es wieder Regen geben kann, weil es eine Woche lang unaufhörlich geregnet hat.

4. This is followed by a *résumé,* written very concisely in one or two sentences.

W 58 Wenn Anna Peter einlädt, mit ihr zum Strand zu gehen, macht er die Bemerkung, daß es gleich regnet, aber sie will nicht glauben, daß es nach einer Woche Regen schon wieder anfangen könnte.

5. Next, the main argument of the passage is set out in the form of an *assertion.*

W 59 Peter und Anna haben entgegengesetzte Meinungen zum Thema Wetter. Er ist Pessimist und sie ist Optimist.

6. Finally, this analysis leads to a short *essay* on optimists and pessimists.

W 60 Schreiben Sie einen kurzen Aufsatz zum folgenden Thema: Der Optimist setzt sich dem Pessimisten entgegen.

7. The further steps proposed by Arapoff—*argumentative analysis, evaluation of the arguments, critical review of the essay,* and *term paper* would require a careful study of styles of writing. The complete project would be a very interesting undertaking for a German major, who must

learn at some stage to write various kinds of essays, seminar and term papers, and even critical reviews, for literature courses.

IV. Expressive writing or composition

If we wish students to write German spontaneously, we must give them opportunities to acquire confidence in their ability to write. We must, however, expect shavings on the floor in the process. Learning to write is not a natural development like learning to speak. As Arapoff has observed: "Everyone who is a native speaker is not necessarily a 'native writer.'"[7]

Our students will have varying degrees of interest in writing as a form of self-expression, even in their native language. If they are to submit willingly to the discipline of learning to write well in German, they will need to see some *purpose in the writing activity*. In this way writing is differently motivated from speaking, which is an activity in which most people readily and frequently engage every day of their lives. In speaking, a student without much to contribute can often adroitly involve others and support them enough, with his attention and interest, to free himself of the necessity to participate fully. (This support function is a normal form of communicative involvement which the student of a foreign language should also learn to fulfill acceptably.) Faced with a blank page, however, the unimaginative student does not have this alternative.

Personality plays an important role in writing, as it does in speaking. Some feel inhibited as soon as they take pen in hand, although they might have expressed themselves orally without inhibitions. These students need a clearly defined topic, often an opening sentence, or even a framework, to get them started. Just as some are terse in speech, others are incapable of being expansive in writing—they do not waste words and elaborate the obvious. These students find it hard to write a full paragraph, or a complete composition, on something as irrelevant to their preoccupations as "What I did last weekend" or "A day on a farm." We must not forget that there are also some students who are most reluctant to expose their real thoughts on paper, sometimes because, in their experience, teachers have never really cared what they thought. In speech they can be vague, whereas in writing this is rarely acceptable, except in poetry. For them also, writing as a class exercise is unappealing.

For these reasons among others, we cannot expect all of our students to achieve a high standard of expressive writing in our foreign-language class. For many, we will be satisfied if they are able to say what they want or need to say with clarity and precision.

There are students, of course, who enjoy writing, and these will want to write from the beginning. Many of them will have already acquired a style of writing in their native language which has been praised and encouraged. Such students often feel frustrated when they find they cannot express themselves in the foreign language at the same level of sophistication as they do in their native language. In their efforts to do so, they often load their writing with poorly disguised translations of their English thought. The enthusiasm of these students must be encouraged, while they are guided to see that writing well in another language means thinking in the forms of that other language. This does not mean just the adoption of its semantic distinctions and syntactic structures, but also its approach to logic and the development of an idea. Even in writing style, there are culturally acquired differences.[8] A student whose native culture encourages allusive and indirect rhetorical development finds it hard to be explicit, just as one who has learned to express his ideas by building logical step on logical step finds it difficult to indulge in what seem to him digressions from the line of thought. Even students who are natural writers need guidance in adapting to the rhetorical style of a new language.

WHAT WRITING MAY BE CALLED "EXPRESSIVE"?

"Expressive" writing does not necessarily mean imaginative or poetic writing. Not all students have the gift of imagination. Writing is expressive if it says what the student wants it to say in the situation. If writing is to be a natural, self-directed activity, the student must have the choice between writing for practical purposes or creating a work of imagination. Even where guidance is offered, that is, where the student is given a structure and facts on which to base his writing, he should always have the privilege of ignoring what is offered if he can write from his own inner inspiration.

What is needed is writing for the *normal purposes of writing,* not just as a self-contained language exercise. In a diversified foreign-language program,[9] students have the opportunity to concentrate on the use of German for specific purposes: the study of literature, the reading of contemporary informational materials, concentrated aural-oral development, translation or simultaneous interpretation, the learning of special skills through German (e.g., German cooking, German music or art), or the acquiring of certain subject matters taught in German (e.g., German history or political institutions). Clearly, then, what is "expressive" in such cases depends on the student's own goals.

Except in specialized programs, where students learn to write in the language in order to study in the same classes as native speakers, writing should not be a distinctive activity. It should, rather, be a natural ingredient in ongoing activities. Since one writes better in a language on a subject which one has experienced in that language, students more inclined to the practical should have experiences learning in German about practical things, while imaginative topics will spring naturally out of experiences (whether graphic, aural, or visual) with literature of the imagination.

These will be organized in six categories under two main headings: *Practical* (everyday living, social contact, getting and giving information, study purposes) and *Creative* (entertainment, self-expression).

actical use

1. *Everyday living.*

a. *Forms and applications.* Students learn to fill in customs declarations, passport applications, entry permits, identity information, and applications for posts abroad. (The student who wished to spend a year studying at the university of Tübingen may have impressed the administration with his good intentions but not with his command of German when he applied for admission as an *außerordentlicher Student,* instead of as a *Gasthörer.*) Where there are German-speaking communities nearby, students may go and help monolinguals fill in social security, medical benefit, or welfare claims.

b. *Arrangements and records.* Students should know how to write notes and notices setting out arrangements for travel, meetings, concerts, dances, weekend camps, or competitions. They should be able to write up short accounts of activities for German club records or for the class or school newspaper.

c. *Orders and complaints.* Students should know how to order goods and services, and how to protest errors in shipping or billing, shoddy quality of goods, or neglect of services. They should be able to write for hotel rooms, information on study abroad, or subscriptions to newspapers and magazines. They should know the correct formulas for commercial and official correspondence of various kinds.[10] These can all be given a realistic twist by basing them on information in newspapers and tourist pamphlets. Students may write, for instance, to the *Verkehrsamt* or the university in the town in which they are interested, and request information for friends and relatives, if not for themselves, or for use with a research project.

2. *Social contact.* Students should learn the correct formulas for congratulations and various greetings, and ways of notifying others of family events or changes of circumstances. They should be encouraged to use this knowledge by sending such greetings and announcements to friends and correspondents, or displaying them on the bulletin board.

Students should be encouraged to write to correspondents in Germany and German-speaking areas. Classes should be twinned with classes of a similar level abroad, so that they may exchange projects giving personal, local, and national information, youth trends and customs, ways of spending leisure time, and so on.

3. *Getting and giving information.* Students gather information for projects, collate it, and report it to others in written form. They prepare com-

ments in writing on controversial articles in newspapers and magazines for later presentation as oral reports or for circulation in the class as a basis for discussion. They may take articles reporting the same event from two German newspapers (or discussing the same topic from two magazines), and write *Zusammenfassungen* of the content for discussion in class. They may prepare items of international, national, local, or school news for wall, class, or school newspapers. They may take turns in preparing weekly bulletins of news from German newspapers, or newscasts, for their own class and for distribution to more junior classes. They distribute similarly reviews of German films which are being shown at school or in the local area.

4. *Study purposes.* Students who intend to make German a major study need practice in taking notes of lectures (*Vorträge*) and of reading material (*Lektüre*). They should know how the Germans develop a line of thought. They need to be able to write good summaries (*Zusammenfassungen*), reports (*Berichte*), essays (*Aufsätze*), and literary analyses (*Kommentare zu einem literarischen Text*).

Creative expression

5. *Entertainment.* Students write skits, one-act plays, or scripts for their own radio and television programs (which may be taped or shown on closed-circuit television for the entertainment of other classes). They write out program notes for a fashion parade, or captions for a display of students' baby pictures or unidentified photographs of famous people. They write parodies of well-known advertisements or radio and television commercials. They prepare puzzles and mystery stories for other members of the class to solve.

6. *Self-expression.* Students write stories, poems, nonsense rhymes, nursery rhymes, biographical sketches, and autobiographical narratives. They keep personal records of their thoughts and experiences as resources from which to draw material for creative writing. (A good starting-point for the inexperienced, or those lacking in confidence, is the writing of a story, poem, or autobiographical incident in the style of an author they have just been reading.)

WRITING AS A CRAFT

Even with motivation to express oneself in written form, coherent, readable material does not necessarily flow from the pen. Nor is such writing merely a matter of composing carefully constructed grammatical sentences. Lucid writing is only possible when the writer has clarified his own thinking on the subject and knows how he wishes to present his viewpoint or develop his argument. The idea may be obscure, even esoteric or hermetic, but the writer knows that this is what he wants to say and the reader tries to penetrate his thought. Muddled thinking, however, leaves the reader confused and frustrated.

Arapoff calls the process basic to writing "purposeful selection and organization of experience."[11] If one of the objectives of the German course is ability to write well and expressively in German, then the teacher must guide the student in developing his skills in analyzing his thoughts, shaping them into central and subordinate ideas, and developing a line of thought which carries the reader to the heart of the matter. The German teacher cannot presume that the students already know these things from some other course.

How can we interest students in the process of reflecting on what they really want to say and organizing it before starting to write? This initial stage becomes more attractive as a group experience. The students in the group pool their ideas, break off to gather more information if necessary, discuss various ways of organizing their ideas into a central line of thought, with major topics and subordinate ideas related to these major topics. They decide on a title to express the central theme, a way of introducing the material so that the reader's attention is caught, and the type of conclusion to which they will direct the development of thought. The actual writing is then done in small groups (or individually, if there are students who prefer to work alone). The draft elaboration of the theme is then discussed by the group; the choice of words is refined, and the syntactic structure is tightened up, with transitional elements supplied where these are still lacking. Finally the rhythm and flow of the writing receive special attention, as the completed text is read aloud. The group texts are then dittoed for presentation to and discussion by the class as a whole.

This type of group elaboration of a composition ensures some proofreading for inaccuracies of spelling and grammar. Valette[12] suggests that the group approach be used also to establish criteria for correcting and assessing the texts prepared by the groups. The students are asked to rank the compositions before them in order of preference. They then "describe which qualities they think characterize a good composition. The class might come up with categories such as: organization, good opening sentence, appropriate use of vocabulary, original imagery, etc." The class then looks over each composition and rates it on a scale decided on by themselves and weighted according to group decision. After the class has perfected its scale in relation to the actual compositions it is considering, this rating scale is adopted by the teacher for grading tests of writing. Valette's procedure has two advantages: the students consider the system fair since they participated in its design and modification, they also understand by what criteria their writing will be graded, and they have guidelines for improving their work in the future.

Some teachers will object that this system cannot ensure that all errors in the texts are corrected. This is true. The question arises: for expressive writing should all inaccuracies and errors be corrected in every composition? Most of us have ourselves experienced the discouragement of staring in horror at a veritable forest of red marks and comments on a piece of writing over which we had toiled in the belief that we were achieving something worthwhile. The place for fastidious correction is at the stage of cognition and production exercises. If students are making serious errors persistently, more practice exercises should be provided at the point of difficulty. When students are writing to express their ideas, corrections should focus on incomprehensibility, inapt word choice, and errors in grammatical form or syntactic structure which mislead the reader. The most serious mistakes must be those which native readers can tolerate the least, rather than those kinds of inaccuracies which native writers themselves commit. Students can be trained to proofread their work for blemishes, as suggested in the previous chapter, but penalizing students for sheer inaccuracy of surface detail at the expressive stage encourages the production of dull, unimaginative, simple sentences, with students taking refuge in the forms they have thoroughly mastered over a long period of study.

With expressive writing, students should learn to check their completed drafts for things other than commas and spelling errors. They should be looking at the way their thought falls naturally into paragraphs and their use of logical connectives and other transitional devices which show the development of thought and cement internal relationships. They should seek ways to eliminate repetitions, tighten the structure through judicious use of complex and compound sentences, and highlight ideas through nuances of word choices and their combinations.

The ever-present danger of anglicisms in structure and lexical choice cannot, of course, be ignored. Students should be sensitized to this problem, which is most likely to arise when they try to express a complex idea in the foreign language. Students should be encouraged to break down a complex idea into a series of simple active affirmative declarative sentences in German which represent the facets of its meaning, and then to rebuild them into a complex or compound sentence which responds to the rules of combination and modification in German as they know them. Francis Bacon has said: "Reading maketh a full man, conference a ready man, and writing an exact man."[13] It is when we try to express our meaning in writing that we discover where our ideas are fuzzy or incomplete. Trying to set down the elements of our meaning in simple form pinpoints areas of confusion and uncertainty and forces us to ask ourselves what we are really trying to say. Then, and then only, can we seek the best way to express our ideas in another language.

It cannot be emphasized too strongly that students learn to write well in German by doing all the planning and drafting of their compositions, and discussion of appropriate content, *in German.* The teacher must help the student from the beginning to acquire confidence in writing directly in the foreign language. Where students have done their initial planning and early writing in English and have then translated what they wanted to say into German, the writing is usually stilted and anglicized, lacking the feeling for the language and natural flow and rhythm toward which the student should be aiming. If the flexibility measures recommended earlier in this chapter are adopted, students will have experience, even at the elementary level, in trying to express their own ideas and imaginings in German. Where the writing program is associated with oral language activities of the creative type described in Chapter 2, students begin to think in German and to compose German sentences spontaneously without nervousness or inhibition.

Correcting and evaluating expressive writing

A number of systems for grading expressive writing have been proposed, each of which has merits for particular situations or students with specific aims.

The following guidelines have emerged from the experience of many teachers.

1. One learns to write sequential prose by writing sequential prose. Practice exercises are merely muscle-flexing. What one does correctly in structured practice, one does not necessarily observe when trying to express one's own meaning.

2. It is better to draw a student's attention to a few important faults in his writing at a time and to encourage him to improve these, rather than to confuse him with a multiplicity of detail which he cannot possibly assimilate immediately.

3. The persistent errors of a number of students lead to group discussions and practice. At the intermediate and advanced levels these errors provide a logical framework for a review of grammar based on existential frequency of commission.

4. Students should be encouraged to keep checklists of their own weaknesses, since these, as with errors in spoken language, will vary from individual to individual.

5. Time should be taken in class for students to check their work before submitting it for grading. Editing is a normal part of native-language writing and should be equally normal for foreign-language writing. Research has shown that students "can reduce their grammatical and mechanical errors —including spelling and capitalization—more than half by learning how to correct errors before submitting their papers."[14]

6. Similarly, class time should be given to the perusing and immediate

correction of a script in which the errors have been marked, so that the student may ask questions and receive explanations as he needs them.

7. An active correction process is more effective than the passive reading by the student of corrections written in by the instructor.

8. Several active correction processes have been proposed:

a. Errors are merely underlined. Students, alone or in groups, decide in what way their writing was inadequate and make changes.

b. Errors are underlined and marked with a symbol which acts as a guide to the kind of error made (e.g., T = tense, A = agreement, V = lexical choice, etc.).

c. Errors are underlined and given numbers which refer to sections of a brief review of grammar rules to which all students have access.

d. Errors are underlined, with no comments or symbols, but no grade is assigned until the student resubmits a corrected script.

e. Errors are not indicated specifically, but a check mark is placed in the margin opposite the line where the error occurs. The student must identify the actual error himself.

f. Knapp[15] adopts a positive, rather than a negative, approach to grading expressive writing. He establishes a Composition Check-List of items to which students should pay attention in writing compositions. While correcting, he assigns red pluses for all items successfully handled. Students try, from composition to composition, to increase the number of pluses on their individual checklist. Lack of pluses arouses student concern so that they seek help in overcoming specific weaknesses. (Careless mistakes are merely underlined.)

9. Writing in more felicitous expressions can be time-wasting for the teacher unless he makes few such suggestions, discusses these with the students, and encourages them to use the suggested expressions in later writing.

Scoring systems

The subjective nature of grades assigned to written expression has long been criticized. Where one teacher is involved and the students know what that teacher expects, the unreliability of the scoring and ranking is reduced. In allotting a grade, an experienced teacher is considering the interplay of a number of factors. If the number of scripts is not too great, and the teacher is not too tired or harassed, his grading will normally be reasonably consistent.

Inexperienced teachers would, however, do well to consider what qualities they are looking for and to assign grades according to some weighted system until they acquire more confidence. Where more than one corrector is involved with the ranking of one group or of parallel groups, agreement should be reached on the weighting they are assigning to different factors.

The following weighted checklist is proposed for discussion:

W 61 *Weighted assessment scheme for expressive writing in a foreign language*

1. Organization of content (focus, coherence, clarity, originality)

   20 per cent

2. Structure
   a. sentence structure (appropriateness and variety)
   b. morphology (accurate use of paradigms, adjective endings, forms of pronouns, etc.)
   c. use of verbs (forms, tenses, moods, sequence of tenses, agreements, etc.) 40 per cent

3. Variety and appropriateness of lexical choices 20 per cent

4. Idiomatic flavor (feeling for the language, fluency) 20 per cent

Commentary

1. At the advanced level, there will also be consideration of content in addition to organization of content. Further variation of this checklist will be developed where students have reached the stage of writing in German essays on literary, cultural, or other informational subjects.

2. Students should be aware of the criteria adopted for the assessment of their writing.

Research in native-language writing[16] has shown that for assessment of achievement two compositions on different subjects written on two separate occasions produce a more reliable evaluation than one composition. It has been found that the performance of good writers varies more than that of poor writers. The fairest procedure is to assess the student according to the grade of the more successful of the two compositions. Apart from the common factor of day-to-day variability in inspiration and energy, the finding seems intuitively transferable to the assessment of foreign-language writing, in that a particular student may find one composition topic unduly cramping from the point of view of content or vocabulary area.

Translation

Translation is both a skill and an art, of considerable practical and esthetic value in the modern world, as it has been down the ages. It provides access for millions to the scientific and technical knowledge, the great thoughts, the artistic achievements, and the societal needs and values of the speakers of many tongues.

In foreign-language teaching, it has been at different periods either an accepted or a controversial element, depending on prevailing objectives and teaching preferences. It was a keystone of the learning and testing process in the grammar-translation approach. Direct method theorists de-emphasized it as a learning device, excluding it from early instruction as much as possible while admitting it as an art at advanced stages. Audiolingual text-books usually printed English translations of the early German dialogues and included translation drills for practice. Translation of continuous passages from the native language into the foreign language was, however, considered an advanced exercise in this approach also.

Unfortunately, much of the discussion between proponents and opponents of translation in foreign-language learning has been at cross-purposes, since the kind of translation and its function in the learning process have not been specified. The following aspects of translation need to be differentiated in such discussion.

1. Translation may be from the foreign language into the native language or from the native language to the foreign language.

2. Translation may be *oral* or *written*.

3. Translation may be used as a *learning* or a *testing* device or it may be practiced for its intrinsic value as a *practical skill* or a *discriminating art*.

4. Translation may be *simultaneous,* as in oral interpretation, which draws on the interpreter's internalized knowledge of both languages, or carefully *edited* and re-edited after consultation of dictionaries and grammars, as in literary or technical translation.

5. *Oral translation* from the foreign language to the native language may be a classroom technique by which the teacher rapidly clarifies the meaning of an unfamiliar word or phrase in listening or reading exercises. It may be the way the student is required to demonstrate his aural or reading comprehension. It may also, at the advanced level, be a sophisticated activity like oral interpretation. (Since most professional oral interpreters translate only from the foreign language into their native, or dominant, language, this would also be the direction of any classroom practice of this demanding process.) Oral translation from the native to the foreign language may be used for practice or testing of the application of grammatical rules.

6. *Written translation,* as German to English, may be a device to test comprehension of factual detail. On the other hand, as English to German, it may be used to test application of the rules of grammar as in the translation of sample sentences, specially constructed passages (*nacherzählende*

Übersetzung), or passages of English constructed along the lines of W29. Whether as English to German or vice versa, it may be an advanced activity to test ability to transfer meaning comprehensively and elegantly from one language code to the other.

In view of these many ways in which the term "translation" is used, it is difficult to take a position for or against its use in the foreign-language class. Rather, one should consider the possible contributions to language learning of each of these activities at various levels and in relation to the objectives of the course.

The main objection to translation as a teaching device has been that it interposes an intermediate process between the concept and the way it is expressed in the foreign language, thus hindering the development of the ability to think in the new language. It may be argued that even when students are taught by direct methods, they often mentally interpose this intermediate translation process themselves in the early stages. Such mental translation usually disappears as a superfluous step when students become familiar with the language through continual exposure to it. Teachers will need to decide for themselves which position they will take in this controversy, whether to eschew all translation or use it judiciously for certain purposes. Here we will discuss such judicious use and also opportunities to engage in translation as an activity in its own right at the advanced level.

TRANSLATION AS A TEACHING/LEARNING DEVICE
Translation from the foreign to the native language

This process is useful for clarifying the meaning of certain abstract concepts, some function words and logical connectives, and some idiomatic expressions which context alone does not illuminate. Such translation, if used too frequently, can become a crutch, reducing the amount of effort given to inferencing[17]—a process which is of considerable importance in autonomous language use. Some teachers like to make quick oral checks of comprehension of reading and listening materials by asking for native-language equivalents of certain segments of the messages. In moderation, and in association with other checks of comprehension conducted in the foreign language itself, this procedure can pinpoint and eliminate some areas of vagueness for the student.

In the early stages, some judicious translation of common expressions can familiarize students with different levels of language. Such expressions will normally be presented through situations in which they would be used. Even then, however, it is not always perfectly obvious to the student that different relationships are expressed by the choice, for instance, of *Guten Tag, Peter. Wie geht es dir?* rather than *Tag, Peter. Wie geht's?*

Translation from the native to the foreign language

     1. *Translation of isolated sentences.* This process as a practice exercise has been brought into disrepute by its excesses. Sentences of improbable or infrequent occurrence, constructed so that they positively bristle with problems, have made language learning an ordeal for many students, without doing more than convincing them of their inadequacies. Such sentences may still be found in many contemporary textbooks.

     The process can be useful, however, when a set of short sentences which focus on a particular grammatical feature is used as a stimulus for eliciting formulations in German, as in the following examples.

W 62   For practicing the form and order of pronoun objects in the sentence.

Sagen Sie auf deutsch:
1. I give him the book.
2. I give her the book.
3. He gives her the book.
4. He gives me the book.
5. She gives it to me.
6. He gives it to her . . .

Commentary

W62 is a familiarization exercise. Conducted orally, it may be a chaining activity, with students proposing short sentences for each other to translate. It may appropriately be accompanied by action. See also G51.

     2. *Nacherzählende Übersetzung.* This is a specially constructed exercise which is useful for identifying student problems in grammatical and vocabulary usage in written German. The instructor extracts from a passage of German, which has been read and studied, useful features for the students to learn, and prepares for translation into German an English text which requires the use of these features. The students translate the passage without consulting the original on which it is based, and then examine the original to see where they can improve or correct their translation. Group discussion is useful at this stage.

W 63   *Nacherzählende Übersetzung* based on R38.

Übersetzen Sie ins Deutsche:

     Günther and Jochen have been friends for a long time because they have always been in the same class at school. They also enjoy visiting each other at home. Last October Günther started helping Jochen's younger sister Uschi with math after she had gotten some bad marks . . .

TRANSLATION AS A SPECIALIZED STUDY[18]

Once we go beyond the transposition into German of sentences and sequences of sentences that either parallel what the student has already encountered or test what he is learning at the time, we approach translation as a demanding, often frustrating, study in its own right. Genuine translation involves the exploration of the potential of two languages. It not only involves the student in serious consideration of the expressive possibilities of the foreign language, but also extends his appreciation of the semantic extensions and limitations of his own language, and the implications for meaning of its syntactic options. It is, then, an appropriate undertaking in an advanced course, or even at the intermediate level when a particular group of students is especially interested in attaining competence in it. It may be offered as an advanced option in an individualized or small-group program, or as a specialized course among diversified options.

Translation must be distinguished from the extracting of information from a text. Much information can be gleaned without exact translation, although readers may resort to translation at times to clarify important details. (See *Reading for Information* in Chapter 6, p. 169.)

Translation and meaning

The teacher will want to sensitize students interested in translation to the many facets of meaning with which they will have to deal. This provides an excellent context for familiarizing them with basic concepts of linguistics.

Translation involves careful analysis of the meaning of the source text. Students consider various aspects of the meaning they have extracted and rethink it in terms of the target language so that as little is added and as little is lost as possible. They learn a great deal as they discover that it is not always possible to attain exact equivalence and as they evaluate possible versions to see which most fully captures all the implications of the original. They will find that they need to look beyond single words, segments of sentences, or even complete sentences to whole stretches of discourse as they make their decisions. Much can be thrashed out in group working sessions as they ask themselves some searching questions[19] about the text they wish to translate.

1. What type of writing does the passage represent: descriptive, narrative, conversational, expository, argumentative, polemical, or some other? What are the features of this style in the target language?

2. What is the overall meaning of this passage in its context in a larger discourse? Is it a serious development of ideas or is it satirical? Is it deliberately vague? Is the original inaccurate or fallacious? Is it carelessly put together? (Any of these characteristics, and many others, must be faithfully reproduced.)

3. Is the tone of the passage assured, hesitant, dogmatic, humorous, solemn, neutral, or something else?

4. Is the passage boring, repetitive, exciting, laconic, provocative, mysterious . . .?

5. Is the general structure such that it can be reproduced in the translation, or would an equivalent in the other language require different sentence division or repositioning of segments, for emphasis or for other reasons?

6. How can the time relationships in the source text be most clearly expressed in the target language? (This is not always a question of which tenses to select.)

7. For which lexical items is the semantic content different from seemingly equivalent lexical items in the target language? Should additional lexical items be introduced to carry the meaning which would otherwise be lost, or can this extra meaning be carried by grammatical morphemes, or by implications from syntactic choices? Consider the following passage from James Joyce's *Ulysses:*

W 64 What special affinities appear to him to exist between the moon and woman?
Her antiquity in preceding and surviving successive tellurian generations: *her* nocturnal predominance: *her* . . .[20]

Commentary

The difficulty involved in rendering this passage without the loss of a fine nuance of meaning is not immediately apparent. At first it seems obvious that "her" can be translated simply as *ihr-*. But *ihr-* is ambiguous and in this context would take on the meaning "their" because the feminine singular possessive adjective could not refer to *Mond,* which is masculine. The use of "their," on the other hand, would alter the sense of the passage in two ways: neither the gender which forms the basis for comparison nor the unity implied by the singular would be emphatically expressed.

8. Do superficially equivalent expressions in the original and in the proposed translation have different denotative (referential) meaning or

connotative (emotive) meaning? (*Falsche Freunde*[21] fall into these categories.)

9. Are there sociolinguistic or emotional levels of language or specialized fields of knowledge implicit in the text which will need careful attention in the translation?

10. Are there culturally related items in the source text which will need to be rethought in relation to the cultural concepts of the speakers of the target language, or should literal translations be used for these to preserve in the translation the foreign flavor of the original?

11. Are there figurative, rhetorical, or specifically literary aspects of the language of the original which require careful transposition?

12. Are there any idiosyncratic features of the author's style observable in this passage? Are there any mechanisms in the target language which would convey the same impression?

Clearly such a task is formidable for a language learner. If students are not to become discouraged, they will need to be given much practice with translation graded in difficulty, with particular passages selected because they allow the student to focus on specific problems. Students will also derive considerable benefit from pooling ideas in group preparation of a final translation, and from discussion of the efficacy of published translations of passages they themselves have attempted to translate.

W 65 Compare the English translation with the original German from *Haus ohne Hüter* by Heinrich Böll.[22] Do you think the translator has captured the tone of the original and reproduced the full meaning?

A. Diese Schonung genoß Will sein Leben lang. "Ein bißchen schwach, ein bißchen nervös" — und Nachtschweiß, das wurde für ihn zu einer Rente, die seine Familie ihm auszuzahlen hatte. Martin und Brielach gewöhnten sich eine Zeitlang daran, morgens ihre Stirnen zu betasten, sich auf dem Schulweg das Ergebnis mitzuteilen, und sie stellten fest, daß auch ihre Stirnen manchmal etwas feucht waren. Besonders Brielach schwitzte nachts häufig und heftig, aber Brielach war von der Stunde seiner Geburt an nicht einen Tag lang geschont worden.

B. Will had enjoyed being coddled all his life. The night sweats had provided him with a permanent allowance from his family. For a while Martin and Brielach used to feel their foreheads on their way to school to persuade themselves that theirs, too, were sometimes quite damp. Brielach in fact often perspired heavily in the night, but no one had ever coddled *him*.

W 66 Discuss the decisions made by the translator of this passage from Thomas Mann's *Zauberberg*.[23] Do you consider them necessary and effective?

A. Dergleichen erfuhr auch Hans Castorp. Er hatte nicht beabsichtigt, diese Reise sonderlich wichtig zu nehmen, sich innerlich auf sie einzulassen. Seine Meinung vielmehr war gewesen, sie rasch abzutun, weil sie abgetan werden mußte, ganz als derselbe zurückzukehren, als der er abgefahren war, und sein Leben genau dort wieder aufzunehmen, wo er es für einen Augenblick hatte liegenlassen müssen. Noch gestern war er völlig in dem gewohnten Gedankenkreise befangen gewesen, hatte sich mit dem jüngst Zurückliegenden, seinem Examen, und dem unmittelbar Bevorstehenden, seinem Eintritt in die Praxis bei Tunder & Wilms (Schiffswerft, Maschinenfabrik und Kesselschmiede) beschäftigt, und über die nächsten drei Wochen mit soviel Ungeduld hinweggeblickt, als seine Gemütsart nur immer zuließ. Jetzt aber war ihm doch, als ob die Umstände seine volle Aufmerksamkeit erforderten und als ob es nicht angehe, sie auf die leichte Achsel zu nehmen.

B. Such was the experience of young Hans Castorp. He had not meant to take the journey seriously or to commit himself deeply to it; but to get it over quickly, since it had to be made, to return as he had gone, and to take up his life at the point where, for the moment, he had had to lay it down. Only yesterday he had been encompassed in the wonted circle of his thoughts, and entirely taken up by two matters: the examination he had just passed, and his approaching entrance into the firm of Tundor and Wilms, shipbuilders, smelters and machinists. With as much impatience as lay in his temperament to feel, he had discounted the next three weeks; but now it began to seem as though present circumstances required his entire attention, that it would not be at all the thing to take them too lightly.

German to English translations

As with other aspects of the foreign-language course, translation can begin with *useful things which are near at hand*.

1. Students translate German *labels, slogans,* and *advertisements,* trying to produce English versions which ring true to the commercial style to which they are accustomed. This activity can lead to interesting discussions of differences in approach to the consumer.

2. Students translate *instructions* for the use of products for local merchants (car salesmen or hair stylists, for instance) or for relatives, or *cooking recipes* for themselves or friends. Where necessary, they use specialized dictionaries to help them.

3. Students translate interesting sections of *letters from correspondents* to publish in the school newspaper or share with others in the geography or social studies class.

4. Students translate *historical documents,* such as Luther's *Von der Freiheit eines Christenmenschen* or Marx's *Manifest der kommunistischen Partei,* for use in their history class; selections from important *political speeches* (taken from newspapers or news magazines) for a political science or international relations class; *scientific articles* for their science class; or words of *songs* for the school choir.

5. Some students become interested in attempting the translation of passages in all kinds of styles and moods; others try to develop real proficiency in scientific or technical translation in specialized fields.

6. Some students, deeply interested in language and in literature, might work together (or individually) to produce an English *poem* which is a translation of a German poem. (A translation of a poem in poetic form is a new creation.) This would be submitted for publication in the school magazine.

Techniques for German to English translation. Early attempts at German to English translation often result in gibberish.

W 67 Übersetzen Sie ins Englische:

Es war in der geheimnisvollen Zeitspanne der rauhen Nacht, da ich diesen Artikel las. Nachdenklich ließ ich die *Süddeutsche Zeitung* sinken und griff zu der Zeitschrift *Paris Match.* Und was sah ich? Auch hier die Kunde, daß der Verkehr immer dichter wird. Nicht allein Amerika, wo die "Fliegenden Untertassen" an manchen Tagen so zahlreich zu sein scheinen, daß sich die Sonne verdunkelt, auch Frankreich werde letzthin mehr und mehr das Ziel des außerirdischen Tourismus.

Student translation: It was the secret time span of the raw night when I read this article. Thinking, I let the *Süddeutsche Zeitung* sink and grabbed for the magazine *Paris Match.* And what did I see? Also here the report that the traffic is always becoming thicker. Not alone America, where the "flying saucers" on many days seem to be so numerous that the sun darkens itself, also France is becoming lately more and more the goal of tourism from outside earth.

Commentary

1. Many a student has felt frustrated when this type of translation was rejected. He knew what most of the passage was about and could have

answered a comprehension test fairly adequately. This student does not understand what a translation should be like.

2. Many of the weaknesses of this type of response can be corrected by asking students to read their translations aloud. As they read, they become conscious of the odd quality of their English and often correct it as they proceed. Group discussion helps to refine the final version.

3. Group discussion before individual writing of the translation is also helpful in impressing on the student that the passage has a sensible, sequential meaning. Part of the translation may be written on the chalkboard or the overhead projector as the group works it over. The students then complete the translation individually, comparing their versions with each other to decide on the best possible translation.

4. Before considering their translation final, students should ask themselves the following six questions:

    a. Have I respected contrasts between German and English structure?

    b. Have I fallen for any *falsche Freunde?*

    c. Have I used my common sense with time relations?

    d. Have I used all the clues in the passage to help me translate unfamiliar words?

    e. Have I used the appropriate style and level of language?

    f. Is my final translation English or *gemischte pickles?*

English to German translation

We can place translation from the native language into the foreign language in perspective, as a student activity, by asking ourselves the question which has become one of the central preoccupations of this book: To what normal uses can such an activity be put? For German to English translations, we were able to find many uses. For English to German, the only one which springs immediately to mind is the translating of school brochures, local area information booklets, or articles from school magazines or newspapers for inclusion in a twinned schools exchange project, or for sending to a German-speaking correspondent who does not know English. Otherwise, it is difficult to think of possible occasions when a student would be called on to perform this task. In writing letters or preparing reports, students should be encouraged to write directly in German, not to translate scripts they have composed in English.

We should consider the production of an acceptable English to German translation as a means, not an end—a means for developing sensitivity to the meanings expressed in a stretch of discourse in one's own language and to the different linguistic mechanisms used by the two languages to convey these meanings. Students learn to translate ideas, not words. English to German translation is, therefore, an analytic activity. Through a comparative examination of the syntactic and semantic systems of English and German and the cultural contexts in which they operate, the student attempts to expand his own potential for expression in the German language.

Techniques for English to German translation. 1. If students are to gain the benefits from a comparative study of two language systems, teachers must avoid the types of passages one finds in some textbooks which distort English into near-German to make the translation process "easier" for the student, e.g., "After two minutes Ursula could push down her feelings no longer. 'Or should one perhaps call it friendly that one has no time any more for others?' "

2. Since English to German translation is an intellectual exercise—an active, conscious process of attacking linguistic problems—it is a suitable project for group discussion and preparation before the individual prepares his own draft.

3. Students will begin by analyzing certain basic stylistic factors which will affect the whole translation, e.g., is the passage informal and conversational in tone so that I should use particular tenses (perfect instead of simple past), a familiar level of vocabulary, and simple, parenthetical syntactical structures? Which form of address (*du* or *Sie*) best suits the relationship of the characters involved?

4. Students will learn to use monolingual and bilingual dictionaries and grammars efficiently to verify the appropriateness of their proposed translations.

5. Students will learn to check their own work for basic inaccuracies in writing (incorrect choice of auxiliaries, mistakes in agreement, wrong tense forms, mistakes in spelling and punctuation). This mechanical task should be the student's own responsibility. (Students may keep checklists of the types of mistakes to which they are prone.) Students may help each other by double-checking each other's work.

6. Group correction and discussion of the translations proposed by the students in relation to the model translation presented by the teacher is more effective than returning individually corrected scripts, since it focuses the student's attention on one thing at a time and gives him several opinions to consider.

7. English to German translations should be a *study of techniques.* Several variants may be tried.

a. Students may compare their translations with a professional translation of the same passage, discussing the merits and insufficiencies of the two versions.

b. Students may be given a translation of the passage which was made by a student in another class. They then discuss proposed corrections and improvements to this translation before attempting their own version.

c. Students may discuss the qualities of the translations of the same passage by two professional translators.

d. Students in one group may translate a German passage into English, then pass their translation to another group to translate into German. Subsequent discussion of the original German passage, the English translation, and the re-translation will illuminate many of the problems of conveying every aspect of meaning in a translation and the variety of ways in which a sentence may be interpreted.

EXPLORING THE DICTIONARY

We profess that one of our aims in teaching foreign language is to open up to our students the world of language itself. Part of this world is the wonder of words—their multiplicity, their variety, their elasticity, their chameleon-like quality of changing and merging in different environments. We know that different languages view reality from different perspectives and that many of these cultural differences are reflected in words and in their nuances of meaning. Yet frequently we keep our foreign-language learners impoverished in this area, depriving them of the opportunity to explore another world of words.

For this, the dictionary can be an invaluable friend. Instead of steering our students away from it, we should teach them to use it effectively. We should provide interesting opportunities for them to familiarize themselves with various kinds of dictionaries as aids in their pursuit of personal fluency in speech and writing.

Of course, the dictionary can mislead the neophyte. Until the student has learned how to consult a dictionary, there will be the inevitable crop of "die ersten Linien des Gedichts" and "ich gehe herunter die Straße." We must provide the kinds of experiences that will make these aberrations a passing phase.

Quite early, and certainly by the intermediate level, our students should have learned that there are two kinds of dictionaries available to them: the monolingual (the kind to which they are accustomed in their native language) and the bilingual (which they will certainly find in the attic or in the local bookshop if they do not find it in the classroom). Each of these, then, should be accessible to them and they should learn to use them purposefully.

A. *The monolingual dictionary.* The dictionary used by the students of German will depend on the type of information they are seeking. Wahrig's *Deutsches Wörterbuch* is the most satisfactory dictionary available at the moment. The *Sprach-Brockhaus* is known for pictorial presentation of specific vocabulary in a number of areas, and *Der kleine Brockhaus* contains general information.[24]

a. The students' interest in *Der kleine Brockhaus* can be stimulated by encouraging them to seek quick answers there to many questions which arise in history, geography, art, music, social studies, classical mythology and literature.

This initial interest can be quickened by a few competitive general knowledge quizzes which draw him into the dictionary, showing him that it is not difficult to extract information there, even though it is in German. (The clues to finding the answers in W68–69 will not appear in the students' quizzes.)

W68 (I or A)

1. Many Germans are given to punctuating their speech with Latin expressions, e.g., *mutatis mutandis* and *circulus vitiosus*. What do these expressions mean? (The answer is found under the terms.)

2. When did Immanuel Kant live? (Answer under *Kant.*)

3. Who was Carl Schurz and what was his significance for American history? (Answer under *Schurz.*)

Commentary

It may seem that questions like 3 could provide a great deal of information which might be broken down to form further questions, but this questionnaire is not intended as a test. Since its purpose is to arouse interest in searching for information in *Der kleine Brockhaus,* the questions should provide interesting reading in themselves. For intermediate and advanced students the questions may very well be written in German, so long as the general appearance of the quiz is not so forbidding as to be self-defeating.

b. Browsing through the plates in the *Sprach-Brockhaus* (or the *Duden Bildwörterbuch*) can greatly benefit the students' general vocabulary. Questions of the following sort will introduce them to various pictures:

W69 (E or I)

1. Where would you go in the railroad station if you wanted (a) to check your suitcase; (b) to purchase a ticket; (c) to know exactly when your train is leaving; (d) to buy some fruit for your trip. (Answers from plate B4: *Bahnhof.*)

2. Describe the organization of a German newspaper, e.g., what sections might you expect to find and what would probably appear on the front page? (Answer from plate Z6: *Zeitung.*)

3. You probably know the word *Heft* from the classroom. What is another meaning? (Answer from plate H16: *Heft.*)

Very soon, groups of students, or individuals, should be enthusiastic enough to make up their own questions to try out on each other.

c. Students sharpen their awareness of fine points in usage when they are sent off to consult Wahrig's *Deutsches Wörterbuch.*

W 70　(I) German borrows English words, just as the English language has borrowed words like *Angst, Bratwurst,* and *Hinterland.* Sometimes these English borrowings are used in ways rather different from their native usage. What is the meaning of: a. *der Autostopp;* b. *die Musikbox;* c. *der Ohrklipp;* d. *der Crack;* e. *hallo;* f. *der Twen.*

W 71　(I) How would you characterize the level of speech of the italicized words? Find synonyms on other levels.

   a. Das ist *prima!*
   b. Wir *verduften* gleich.
   c. Diesen *Fraß* kann kein Mensch essen.
   d. Die zwei Schwestern *schnattern* den ganzen Nachmittag.
   e. Mein Geld ist *alle!*
   f. Sie hat eine *miese* Stimmung.

d. Word formation is a fascinating study, already discussed in R4–5 and R69–72. Advanced students should pursue this area further for its intrinsic interest.

W 72　(A) From Wahrig's *Deutsches Wörterbuch,* comment on the relationships of the pairs (or sets) of words below. Write down a sentence showing the use of each.

   a. schließen　verschließen
      brauchen　verbrauchen
      achten　verachten . . .

   b. gehen　　Gang
      binden　　Band
      stechen　　Stich . . .

   c. fertig　　fertigen　abfertigen
      nötig　　nötigen　abnötigen . . .

B. *The bilingual (or German-English, English-German) dictionary.* It is this dictionary that most students have tucked away in their desks, usually in a very abbreviated paperback edition, and to which they refer to produce the howlers with which every teacher is familiar.

a. We should help our students by recommending a dependable, reasonably-priced bilingual dictionary which will be used consistently during their studies, so that they will know how to use it when they are on their own.[25]

b. A larger, more comprehensive bilingual dictionary will be available for reference in the classroom and in the library, alongside the monolingual German dictionaries discussed.

c. Students will be given practice exercises in dictionary search so that they become familiar with the various features—pronunciation guides; abbreviations for parts of speech (e.g., v.a. = transitive verb, v.r. = reflexive verb); levels of language and usage (e.g., dialect, vulgar, slang, student slang, colloquial, engineering); relationships with other words (i.e., how to find derivatives); grammatical indicators (e.g., with dative: *ich bin ihm gefolgt*); and sample sentences demonstrating general use and inclusion in specifically idiomatic expressions.

d. Finally, and most importantly, students will be trained to check meaning in both parts of the dictionary. The lady who, wishing to compliment a helpful salesgirl, looked in her pocket dictionary and said, "*Sie sind wählerisch,*" could have been saved much embarrassment had she checked the various German entries for "nice" in the German-English section before taking the plunge. Exercises like W73 and W74 are easy to construct and interesting to work out with the help of the dictionary.

W73 (I or A) Find out from a bilingual dictionary how to express in German the expressions italicized in the following sentences:

1. This is a *famous picture* by Dürer.
2. I can *picture* the look on her face.
3. She sent me a *picture-postcard* of Austria.
4. He loves to take *pictures* with his new camera.
5. She is the *picture of good health.*
6. His daughter is *pretty as a picture.*
7. I am very interested in *motion pictures.*
8. The *television picture* is never very clear.

W74 (I or A)

1. How would you interpret the following newspaper headline?
   Gute Mienen—böses Spiel.
2. What is the meaning of this wall poster: *Autofahrer!*
   Stoppt die Auspuff-Pest!
3. Waiting for the train you see the following sign:
   Überschreiten der Gleise strengstens verboten!
   What are you expected to do?

4. How do the meanings of *wohl* differ in these sentences:

Er fühlt sich *wohl.*

Er hat *wohl* sein Buch vergessen.

EXPLORING THE GRAMMAR

Students at the advanced level who wish to write well must learn to find answers to their own questions about written German. At this stage they should be given practice in formulating the questions they want answered in such a way that they can find the information they need in a German grammar book, like the *Grammatik der deutschen Sprache* of Schulz and Griesbach or the *Duden Grammatik.*[26] For this they need to know the basic grammatical terms in German so that they can make efficient use of the indexes to these grammars. If a student wishes to know whether he should write: "Er hat den Roman umgeschrieben," or "Er hat den Roman umschrieben," he will need to know that this is a question of whether the prefix is separable or inseparable, and that he will find the answer under *Präfix bei Verben* or *Verb, trennbare.*

Learning terms of this type is unexciting, but it can be made more appealing by giving the student interesting problems to solve through personal search in the grammar book. When he feels at home with it, he will enjoy finding his own answers instead of asking other people.

Questions like the following may be proposed. (The indications given here as to how this information might be obtained from the *Grammatik der deutschen Sprache* of Schulz and Griesbach would not be given to the students.)

W75 (A)

1. *ein noch zu lesendes Buch*

What is the meaning of this structure and how is it used in modern German?

(Answer: The name of the verb form can be found by looking at the verb tables, where one finds *Partizip Präsens. Partizip Präsens* is then found in the index, which indicates the section where the matter is discussed.)

2. What is the difference in meaning between

der Band	*and*	das Band;
der Gehalt	*and*	das Gehalt;
der Kunde	*and*	die Kunde;
der Tor	*and*	das Tor.

(Answer: The student looks for *Nomen* or *Geschlecht* in the index.)

3. Which form is correct:
    a. Er bedarf den Trost,
or b. Er bedarf des Trostes?

(Answer: The student looks in the index for *Objektsakkusativ* and *Objektsgenitiv*.)

4. Are *dieser* and *jener* still used to make distinctions in literary and spoken German?

(Answer: The student will find *dieser* and *jen-* in the index.)

Students can be asked to propose their own problems which will be worked into a *search questionnaire*.

III
ACROSS MODALITIES

10
Testing and assessment

This section of the book differs from earlier sections in that no examples are given. There will, however, be frequent reference to examples in other chapters, which illustrate (often with commentary) the types of tests being discussed. For easy reference, a table listing the letter-number indices of these examples for the different skill areas is appended to this chapter (pp. 332–34).

Testing as a learning experience

Tests should be a help, not a hindrance. They should act as a guide to both student and teacher as to progress made, level of proficiency attained, gaps to be filled, misinterpretations and misconceptions, and the need for further learning or further teaching. We must avoid tests that merely place hurdles or obstacles in the path of our students, upsetting and confusing them with no particular gain from the experience. It is this approach to testing that will be emphasized in this chapter.

A test should act like a thermostat. Students test themselves and, if they find they have met the criterion, they move on without further adjustment. If, however, the criterion is not met, the thermostat flips on — that is, the students return to review the work and, ideally, test themselves again.[1] Having students retake tests to see whether they are closer to the criterion will act as a valuable motivator and learning device. Since language learning is cumulative, what was learned in the first language class may be needed on any day afterwards. We want our students to learn; so, students' efforts to review what was only partially learned must be encouraged and applauded.

Opportunities to retake tests are not difficult to organize. It is sufficient to prepare alternative versions of the test (which are also useful for makeups) and to set a time, several days later, when students may retake the test, or whichever parts of the test they select, on their own out-of-class time. This practice reduces the tension and anxiety associated with the once-for-all type of test.

We must learn to write tests which are a means of growth. Such tests provide the students with another opportunity to develop control of the language through focused attention on, and synthesis of, aspects of inter-nalized knowledge, while drawing the student out in active creative language use. Students should be able to approach each test or quiz in anticipation of an interesting set of tasks, coming away exhilarated with, or at least pleasura-bly surprised at, the opportunities that were provided to demonstrate ability to use the language to express real meanings in possible situations of lan-guage use. Test items on which students can perform well are preferable to tricky, esoteric questions that students approach with apprehension. Tests should be rewarding, challenging experiences, rather than the punitive de-vices they so often seem to students. Testing and evaluation are too often discussed impersonally and abstractly, as though only pegs in a pegboard were involved instead of living human beings with their apprehensions and individual personality traits (boldness, timidity, caution, literal-mindedness, lack of confidence). Each test should be an enjoyable opportunity for learn-ing, for both student and teacher.

The influence of testing on the curriculum and classroom teaching

Serious consideration should be given to the form of the testing when a course is being developed. Ill-considered testing with an eye to easy correc-tion can ruin an otherwise well-designed course. Inevitably teachers will teach to the form of the test, and students will learn what will be tested to the neglect of other important elements of the course. We may wish it were otherwise, but realities must be faced. Hence, it is important to decide why one is testing at all. Is it to see whether students will have difficulty in studying a language and what kinds of difficulties they will experience (an *aptitude* test)?[2] to assign students for courses at particular levels (a *placement* test)?[3] to gauge the proficiency level attained in relation to work needs or across groups of students from different institutions (a *proficiency* test)? to provide parents and administrators with grades they expect or demand or to recommend students for certificates or diplomas (an *achievement* test)? or to assist learning by guiding students in review and development (a *diagnostic* test), perhaps in the form of a short quiz? Tests developed for any of these reasons may be very different indeed (or just the same old tests) and may have varying effects on teaching and learning.

In this discussion, *proficiency* has been used in the sense of levels of attainment expected of students after certain periods of study when the material in the test is not related specifically to what was taught in any particular course or what was presented in any set of materials. The TOEFL (Test of English as a Foreign Language, prepared by the Educational Testing Services for administration in all parts of the world) and the Modern Language Association Proficiency Tests for Teachers and Advanced Students (available for French, German, Italian, Russian, and Spanish) are proficiency tests in this sense. However, proficiency is now being used in a wider sense to mean "the ability to function effectively in the language in real-life contexts"[4] and is being recommended by the American Council on the Teaching of Foreign Languages (ACTFL) as the "'organizing principle' by which various . . . methods, approaches, materials, and curricula might begin to make collective sense."[5] We will refer to testing with this purpose in mind as *proficiency-oriented testing* and discuss it in depth in a separate section below. Proficiency-oriented testing can be the basis for any of the types of tests discussed above.

Testing and the objectives of the course

Before we choose materials and decide on the form of the testing, we must study the objectives of the course. Even a "general basic language course" will be oriented toward the acquisition of communication skills, reading literary or technical material, understanding another culture, or developing the four language skills, either consciously as a result of the teacher's day-to-day decisions or indirectly by the department's or school district's selection of teaching materials.[6] It is better for a reasoned decision on objectives to be reached by careful study of the student body and its needs in relation to future plans or possibilities,[7] rather than by happenstance. The decision on objectives will then affect the testing program.

If the course is to be specifically directed toward oral communication, then listening and speaking must play a dominant role from the early stages. This means that listening and speaking will both be tested, preferably in an interactive fashion (which we will discuss below under *Teaching Communication: The Oral Interview*). If the course is a short one for tourists going abroad or for students preparing for a school trip, then the tests should involve ability to read maps, schedules, and menus; understand information in different sections of the newspaper; fill in forms; use the telephone for hotel bookings, ticket requests, and other informational purposes; ask for help and comprehend responses (seeking directions, arranging for film de-

veloping and dry cleaning, shopping, negotiating with service station personnel and medical attendants); and so on.

If the course is preparing students for a specific career, then the instructor
must be well informed as to the language needs in particular professional
settings, whether for international business dealings, diplomatic services, fire
rescue operations, or day-to-day police affairs. Just as the course must deal
with the types of situations the student will encounter professionally, so must
the tests be developed as realistically as possible, providing opportunities for
students to display the particular interactional, reading, writing, or cultural
comprehension skills each student will eventually need.

If the course is directed specifically toward developing ability to read
scientific, technological, literary, or philosophical material with comprehension and then to extract information for incorporation in written reports
(usually in the native language), then both extraction of information and
ability to reorganize it in written form must be tested. There will be no need
for explicit testing of grammar or of ability to speak or write the language.
(See Chapter 6, *Reading for Information.*) Sometimes courses of this type
include listening comprehension, since much professional information at
present is communicated in oral form. For those who need it, listening to
specialized lectures and drawing information from them for specific tasks
will also be included in the testing.

The course may be designed to develop in students interactional skills in
multicultural settings. In this case, students will be tested on their understanding of the ways of thinking, acting, and reacting of native speakers and
on their ability to use the language acceptably in such settings without social
offensiveness and without suffering culture shock. For this, they will practice
with culture capsules[8] (in which component parts of the behavior of a native
speaker of the language in a particular situation are studied through visual
demonstration or action); these capsules will be gathered together into culture
clusters[9] (where acting out of scenes integrates what has been acquired in the
capsules). What has been learned of the culture may then be tested in cultural
assimilators,[10] minidramas, open scenarios,[11] or sociodramas.[12] In these
activities, culturally significant situations are described and the students are
required to write or act out a solution which would solve a dilemma or
resolve a problem within the other culture in a socially acceptable way. These
activities may be developed so that they involve listening, speaking, reading,
and writing, or any combination of these. They provide interesting problem-
solving tasks through which students demonstrate their understanding of the
other culture. Testing cultural understanding through problem-solving tasks,
rather than with multiple-choice or short answer factual quizzes, not only is
more interesting but also requires students to see the significance of cultural
facts and pay attention to the ways in which these facts contribute to attitudes

that affect everyday decisions. The students' ability to operate in the language will be further developed if their preparation has enabled them to reduce the social and psychological distance[13] between themselves and the speakers of the language, so that they are accepted by, and accept, them and can share endeavors with them. Teachers should seek out opportunities for students to interact with members of German-speaking communities in daycare and kindergarten centers, collecting songs and folklore from native speakers, developing telephone friendships not only with peers but also with the elderly and shut-ins. Testing may well take the form of assignments which require students to gather information from living sources for written and oral reports to be shared with the class or reported in student newspapers.

Is the course designed, as in so many places, for students to pass some outside required examination? In this case, teachers should teach language for use, reserving some time at the end of the course for intensive practice in the types of questions on the examination. The teacher's responsibility to the students is twofold: to see that they learn the language in usable ways, but also to prepare them for success on the examination, even if the latter is of a type the teacher would not choose and may not approve. Students' careers cannot be sacrificed to teachers' preferences, but neither should opportunities to learn the language for use be bypassed because of an outdated examination format. Students can both learn the language and prepare for the examination, while the teacher may want to work in cooperation with other colleagues to have the form of the examination changed.

* Select some subjects suitable for minidramas that pose a problem which would be solved in a distinctive way in the target culture.

SITUATIONS OF UTTERANCES[14]

When programs are designed to prepare students to interact in specific professional or vocational settings, research is required to determine the type of language that the language user will need. Research is being conducted, for instance, into the type of language used between doctors and patients, factory supervisors and operatives, social workers and persons in need of their assistance. Howatt points out that designing a course which prepares students to interact in specific roles in real-life situations requires that the course designer "first discover what activities the job entails and what part is played in these activities by language of different kinds. He must decide how much emphasis is to be placed on talking and how much on reading or writing. He must find out what topics come up often enough to be worth discussing in class and he must also bear in mind the kind of people the pupil will eventually have to deal with."[15]

The Council for Cultural Co-operation of the Council of Europe (CCC) has published "an analytical classification of the categories of adults needing to learn foreign languages" which is intended "to provide a starting-point for a description of linguistic situations" in which persons in these occupations will have to use English.[16]

The CCC classification breaks down the actual activities in which persons of specific occupations will need to employ, with varying degrees of proficiency, the skills of understanding, speaking, reading, and writing a foreign language. Actors, musicians, and dancers, for instance, will need, among other things, to be able to understand and give stage directions and instructions; office supervisors will need to be able to read written documents in the fields with which they are associated, to draft reports, and to write letters; guards, conductors, flight attendants, and guides will be required to understand a language of everyday communication in order to give information and attend to the comfort and security of the public; while waiters and bar personnel will be required to understand and speak, not only a language of everyday communication, but a quite specialized language as well.[17]

A breakdown of this type is equally applicable to adolescent students who have a specific career goal in mind. Obviously, persons in any occupational category will operate more efficiently if they have a greater command of the language. However, in many programs in adult basic education or in vocational training, students may have to settle for less than ideal proficiency. Analyses like that of the CCC can be very helpful in designing activities and simulated situations that focus on the needs of the students. Students can then extemporize and practice using what they know in a realistic and purposeful way.

As used by the contributing experts of the Council for Cultural Co-operation of the Council of Europe, "situation of utterance" is not a simple concept such as acting out the ordering of a meal in a restaurant or the buying of a ticket at an airport.[18] It includes "the sum of those extralinguistic elements that are present in the minds of speakers or in external physical reality at the moment of communication . . . [which] play a part in determining the form or the function of the linguistic elements"[19] and also the particular spatio-temporal situation in which speaker and hearer are interacting[20] in order to produce some result, whether purely psychological or concrete. The use of situations of utterance is intended to make language learning "a process of acquiring a new aid to action."[21] In this way, they have great potential for motivating students to engage in autonomous interaction.[22]

This systematic approach to teaching for specific purposes greatly facilitates the testing process. Students who are accustomed to using language in situations of utterance are ready for the integrative and proficiency-oriented types of testing discussed below.

Discrete-point and integrative testing

Language tests are frequently characterized as discrete-point or integrative tests. Discrete-point tests focus on specific details of syntax, morphology, or vocabulary, aural discrimination of individual sounds, or identification of isolated facts in reading or in the study of culture. (For examples, see in Chapter 4, G5–8; in Chapter 5, S15–22; in Chapter 8, W9–15; and in Chapter 7, R58.) They test details of the students' knowledge of the language. Integrative tests also draw on the students' knowledge of details but focus on students' control of the language, usually testing several aspects of that control at the same time, with attention focused on how well students communicate and receive meaning in functioning language. The following are examples of integrative tests.

1. *Dictation* (drawing together sound discrimination; listening comprehension; knowledge of details of structure, vocabulary, and spelling; and ability to write in the language, especially where there is a different alphabet or peculiarities of the written language not evident in the spoken language). For seven ways of giving a dictation test, see Chapter 8, *Reproduction*.

2. *Free composition* or *expressive writing* (drawing together knowledge of structure and vocabulary; ability to write in the language; ability to think coherently and compose cohesively in the language; and familiarity with logical connectives and the way native speakers develop their ideas in written form). Expressive writing tests overall control of written language for communication purposes. See Chapter 9, *Writing as a Craft* and *Correcting and Evaluating Expressive Writing*.

3. The *cloze test* (drawing together ability to read a text and extract information; knowledge of the structure of the language and of vocabulary and logical connectives; familiarity with the culture of the speakers of the language sufficient to permit interpretation of meaning and projection of expectations; and ability to write in the language and spell correctly). See Chapter 8, *The Cloze procedure* and in Chapter 9, W47.[23]

4. The *oral interview* (drawing together ability to pronounce the sounds of the language and approximate native-speaker intonation, stress, and grouping of words; knowledge of structure and vocabulary and the expressive choices these allow; ability to use these in fluent phrases that express personal meaning; knowledge of conversational gambits, pause fillers, and pragmatic conventions; ability to understand spoken language and marshal one's thoughts in the language; and ability to interact in culturally acceptable ways). The oral interview is discussed in detail below.

The distinction between discrete-point and integrative tests recalls the distinction in C1 between skill-getting and skill-using. Much of early language study must perforce be given over to acquiring elements of the language that can later be used in an integrated way in expressing personal meaning in a nuanced sophisticated manner. So that students may be able to assess their own progress and recognize where there are lacunae, we give simple tests on particular features. These discrete-point tests should be so constructed that they require thought and reflection on the part of the students. It should not be possible to complete an item in a multiple-choice or fill-in-the-blank test without understanding the context and recognizing the structure or word required as an essential element in the meaning, consistent with the clues in the parts of the sentence supplied. (See Chapter 8: *Cognitive Exercises,* W9–14, W19–22.) Careful construction of such tests so that they are challenging prepares the student to use these features in personally selected contexts and facilitates eventual skill-using in effective communicative exchanges. Discrete-point and integrative tests are thus complementary, each serving a useful purpose, with neither being sufficient without the other. Where only integrative tests are used, their evaluation often involves allotting credit for discrete features, as when accuracy of structure or precision of vocabulary choice are evaluated in written composition or oral expression. This, however, can distract attention from the holistic evaluation of effective communication, so that the focus is on the trees, even the branches and the leaves, instead of the all-important forest. Confusion of this type can be avoided if detail is tested as detail and written and oral communication are assessed for their effectiveness as acts of communication.

Proficiency-oriented testing

There has been much discontent in the past with the fact that students completing language courses have not been able to demonstrate much capacity for using the language, oral or written, in real-life situations. They seem to have acquired a certain amount of knowledge of the structure and vocabulary of the language, and these they can reproduce and manipulate sufficiently well to obtain good grades on discrete-point tests, but they appear to be stymied if expected to use the language for the functions of everyday communication.

Considerable research has gone into the question of the functions for which one uses language. From these studies has emerged what has come to be called the *functional-notional* approach.[24] Basically this parallels the emphasis on categories of language use for normal purposes of language in communication discussed in Chapter 2: *Autonomous Interaction.* The functions now being listed, however, are much more detailed and all-embracing. It is considered that students should be taught not structures but how to use the language for such functions as requesting, suggesting, apologizing, warning, approving, disapproving, persuading, dissuading, seeking and giving information, arguing, participating in social routines (greeting, introducing, taking leave, enquiring after people's health, paying compliments, etc.), narrating, expressing emotions (pleasure, disappointment, anger, and the like), promising, and expressing desires at various levels of intensity. The list of functions for which we use language becomes unmanageable.[25] Fortunately, teachers who follow this approach find the potential functions circumscribed by the limitations of the textbook and the choices the textbook writer has made. These functions are used in situations that vary according to participants and their relationships, settings, and topics. Again an infinite variety of possibilities and permutations presents itself.

We will not go here into a complete description of the functional-notional approach,[26] but concentrate on proficiency-oriented testing, which is particularly compatible with this approach since it requires students to demonstrate their ability to use language actively in situations of everyday or professional life.

On the basis of rating scales used for many years by U.S. Government language teaching agencies, such as the Foreign Service Institute and Defense Language Institutes (which are now sharing expertise as the Interagency Language Roundtable), the American Council on the Teaching of Foreign Languages (ACTFL) and the Educational Testing Services (ETS) have developed Provisional Proficiency Guidelines, which set out in pragmatic terms what a language learner should be able to do at different levels of proficiency. (The Provisional German Descriptions for speaking, listening, reading, writing, and culture are reprinted in the Appendix.) The levels for rating students according to the ACTFL Guidelines are termed novice-low, -mid, and -high; intermediate-low, -mid, and -high; advanced and advanced plus; and superior. The guidelines describe in general terms what language functions a student at each of these levels should be able to perform, with approximately what control of vocabulary, syntax, and pronunciation, and with what degree of fluency, accuracy, and acceptability. "A proficiency-oriented programme is one that trains students to use the language outside the classroom, independently of the materials and activities of the course."[27] Students can thus know the functions, content, and degree of accuracy expected of them when they present themselves for testing, and teachers can test them on their ability to perform these functions in certain contexts to a specified degree of language control. As this type of testing becomes more widespread, the expectation is that language learners will emerge who are able to use what they have learned at identifiable levels which are comparable across school districts and levels of instruction, the outcome being to facilitate student transfer and placement and eventually to prepare students more effectively for the needs of careers requiring language use. In this way, interaction or skill-using (C1) is being tested and the degree of skill-getting is gauged from this interaction.

*   Consult the guidelines in the Appendix. Discuss the types of spoken functions a novice-high should be able to perform. Think of several situations in which these functions would be exercised. Act out a scene in German in your training class at the level of expression you think a novice—high student would control. What types of errors would you expect from a student at this level? Which errors would make you reduce the rating to novice—mid?

The ACTFL guidelines should act as a yardstick so that individual students can see how far they have come in being able to use the language for real-life purposes. To be labeled "novice-mid" or "intermediate-high" has no meaning for students, who should rather know that they can now "operate . . . in a very limited capacity within very predictable areas of need," and that in a real-life situation they can "be understood only with difficulty, even by persons . . . used to speaking with non-native speakers," and that, therefore, they have still a long way to go. Those rated "intermediate-high" will be pleased to know that they can now "satisfy most survival needs and limited social demands," that they can be expected to "initiate and sustain a general conversation on factual topics beyond basic survival needs" and "be comprehensible to native speakers used to dealing with foreigners," but that they may still have "to repeat utterances frequently to be understood by the general public."[28]

If the guidelines are used as a *guide* to students and teachers as to the degrees of language to be set as goals, then proficiency-oriented testing becomes a form of *criterion-referenced* testing. Students know the requirements of the criterion they wish to reach at a particular level; they strive to reach it; if they fail, they try again and continue until that level is mastered, after which they set their sights on the next. If, however, the guidelines are not used as a guide, but rather as prescriptions for judges to rate students irrespective of preparation, the testing becomes *norm-referenced* proficiency testing (that is, a way of comparing student achievement across large populations and relating the achievement of the individual to the norm for a particular type of performance required in certain contexts). Norm-referenced testing has its use as a selection instrument. In this case, teachers teach, and students learn, with a view to achieving high scores on the rating instrument. Language learning, instead of being a stimulating educational experience, culminating in the exhilaration of being able to communicate (to comprehend and be comprehended), becomes another item to be checked off in a competitive race for college entrance, graduation, job placement, or some other goal extraneous to the learning process. This leads to conventional outer-directed teaching and a grade-grabbing attitude on the part of the students. In order for the guidelines to function as guidelines, teachers must study them and internalize their meaning, so that the pragmatic purpose of the guidelines pervades their teaching. In this way, the guidelines will influence the students' attitude to language, who will see it not as just another subject but as a valuable tool to use and continually burnish through life.

Furthermore, the continual use of the proficiency levels as testing criteria can lead to overtesting, which may result in students' developing a blasé attitude toward the ratings. Since the various levels are described in fairly broad terms, the rating scale, in many cases, will not be sensitive to the finer degrees of improvement from semester to semester. Consequently, remaining at the same level through several testings (even several semesters) may become discouraging to students and mislead them into believing they have not progressed when they actually have. The ratings, therefore, should not be used as promotion instruments and should never be entered on report cards without some explanation. The ratings should, in most cases, be accompanied by an achievement score to show how the student rates in relation to the work of the semester. Since students and parents lack the professional experience to interpret the ratings, their perception of the meaning of the categories may be different from the teacher's.

As a placement instrument where large numbers of students from different backgrounds need to be rapidly sorted into appropriate courses, testing for proficiency levels may be too time-consuming for the value of what will, at best, prove to be a rough sieve, because of students' varied educational experiences and gaps in their learning sequence. Judgment will have to enter into the picture so that adjustments in placement may be made once instruction begins. No system intended as a guide should be used to sort people into irrevocable categories that may seriously affect their educational near or distant future or their morale in relation to their immediate studies.

We have talked vaguely for too long about proficiency-oriented testing without details of how it is to be performed. We shall now consider how this orientation can be implemented in testing various areas—even in the familiar discrete-point testing.

Testing communication: the oral interview

The proficiency-oriented test most frequently cited is the oral interview. If courses are directed toward developing ability to communicate in real-life contexts, then the test should be such that we are able to see how the student communicates in a face-to-face situation. With careful preparation, the interviewer can steer the discussion into various topic areas and, through sequenced questions, can lead the student into utterances that reveal ability to talk about various matters in past, present, or future, in a conditional or hypothetical framework, with varying degrees of negation or emphasis, and so on, all in a smooth-flowing, naturalistic conversation which also reveals the student's breadth of vocabulary and control of compound and complex sentences. With an inexperienced or untrained interviewer, however, this approach can lead to a stereotyped, stilted version of authentic communication, since an interview situation is only one of many communicative possibilities.

Because the interview is not for purposes beyond evaluation (it is not a job interview or other real situation), elements of simulation or group interaction can broaden its scope. The communicative exchange can be steered toward normal functions of language by *group testing*. Two or three students who are being interviewed together may be asked to take up a problem in the other culture and either discuss in the language how it would be solved or act out an improvised scene into which particular functions would naturally enter. For instance, students may be asked to discuss from a German viewpoint the situation where a teenage girl living in a small town wishes to leave the family for work in a big city, taking an apartment on her own near her work in the center-city. Each student in the group identifies with a relevant figure (the father, the mother, the godmother who is a career woman, the girl herself, or a friend who did the same thing a year previously) and maintains a viewpoint in the discussion. Alternatively, the group may act out a family reunion, at which people greet each other, introduce friends they have brought, apologize for lateness, compliment certain people, ask conventional questions, avoid giving answers to certain questions, persuade or dissuade each other from specific actions, apologize for the absence of family members, argue about political developments, take their leave, and so on. Students may be given cards with particular functions they are to try to incorporate, being given a few minutes to study these before they begin the simulation.

The oral interview should not become a test of personality or temperament. Some oral interviews reward the assured and penalize the diffident or nervous student. The typical environment of the oral interview can be very intimidating. Students wait for their turn, mentally running through possible subjects that may be raised, asking others what happened to them in the interview, becoming more and more nervous as the appointed time draws closer, finally facing one or two interviewers who may or may not be known to the interviewee. They may start off on an unfortunate note or with an unintentional mistake, or may not understand the first remarks because of their emotional turmoil or an unfamiliar accent. Fortunately, ways have been devised to set students at their ease and help them to begin the interview with confidence and project an impression of success and fluency so that the occasion becomes stimulating and enjoyable for the one being tested.

1. Students may be encouraged to choose their own topics for starting the interview. In this way, they can begin confidently and in a relaxed mood, with the interviewer gradually leading the conversation in other directions by careful questions and comments. This approach brings out the quiet, reticent student who may otherwise be at a loss for something to say and thus be graded at a lower level than his or her communicative ability warrants.

2. Students may be given a series of possible topics to think about ahead of time, from among which the interviewer will select one to begin the interview.

3. The interview may begin with a discussion of pictures or objects, or with some concrete task for the student to perform, so that the interviewee has time to settle in comfortably before having to communicate one on one. (Interviewees in this case listen to and interpret instructions, and then explain what they are doing as they do it.)

4. The evaluation of communicative ability may be conducted indirectly by keeping a cumulative score of exchanges that have taken place in classroom simulations or during the acting out of roles in naturalistic situations, particularly while the class is working in small groups.

5. Students may be asked to role-play an incident in the culture with the interviewer, instead of being faced with an interrogation-type situation. In this case it is advisable to have an evaluator as well as an interviewer present, so that one person may concentrate on the quality and appropriateness of the linguistic responses, while the other is fully occupied with developing the situation for response. (For some suggestions, see Chapter 2, *Categories of Language Use,* category 11.)

6. The interview may be given a realistic twist by the use of air schedules, advertisements, menus, or bank or railway brochures setting out available services; the student is then asked to plan a trip, select a purchase, conduct business, or order a meal, thinking aloud as he or she uses the authentic materials. Students should be encouraged to involve the interviewer by asking questions about his or her experiences or preferences, or by seeking advice or comment.

7. Students may be put into a hypothetical problem situation. ("You are visiting Germany. On your departure from Bonn, you present yourself at the *Lufthansa* agent's desk, only to find that your passport was not stamped upon your arrival. You try to explain to the immigration official what happened and endeavor to get permission to leave on your scheduled flight.") The interviewer acts out the antagonist's role in this situation and judges how well the interviewee deals with the situation in German. All kinds of situations can be invented which require the candidates to "talk their way out of trouble" (see Chapter 2, *Categories of Language Use,* category 4; similar possibilities emerge from categories 1, 3, 6, 8, or 9).

* Discuss other ways in which normal communication can be stimulated in an evaluation setting.

It is well to remember that the oral interview or any other form of oral testing involves not just speaking but *communication,* which includes comprehension of what is said to one as well as the formulating of messages so that one is comprehended by another. It should also provide an opportunity for the interviewer, or evaluator accompanying the interviewer, to assess the degree of acceptability of pronunciation, intonation, and kinesics, as well as confidence in functioning within the parameters of a different cultural system. Above all, an oral assessment or rating should never be made on one occasion alone because of the number of elements (such as emotional stress, poor health, or unfamiliarity of setting), which can impair the student's performance on a particular day.[29]

Canale makes a very pertinent comment on oral testing when he says: "One must seek to focus on core rather than peripheral aspects of communication."[30] Some writers give the impression that all we wish to establish in oral testing is whether the student can communicate. So long as the person addressed "gets the message" or the person speaking "gets the meaning across" or obtains an appropriate response this is considered evidence of success in communication. It certainly is. We can "get meaning across" through gestures, actions, or even appealing, helpless, or angry looks. Cats and dogs communicate very effectively with their owners. We must remember that we are asking more of our students than this. We are asking them to communicate their meaning through the medium of another language. Each language provides a system whereby this may be done and the student is being asked to use this system for conveying meaning. To do this, the student must know at least the broad outlines of the system (details add precision) and the options it allows. We must be sure, in oral testing, that we are rewarding the communication of meaning through the system of the other language (phonological, syntactic, semantic and lexical, sociolinguistic, and pragmatic) and not just an improvised series of gestures and a natural quick-wittedness, which succeed in conveying meaning because of our experience in drawing inferences.

Listening comprehension

All forms of oral testing call into play the ability to comprehend aural messages, and this should be kept in mind in the assessment. However, we sometimes exercise our skills in listening apart from our ability to express ourselves orally. We listen to plays or radio and watch films or television programs. In some courses, listening comprehension is the primary aim (e.g., training air controllers or personnel whose task is to monitor foreign broadcasts). Whether listening is the sole objective or just part of a broader communication aim, it is well to remember that *authentic listening materials* differ considerably from artificially prepared scholastic materials (see Chapter 3, C35–37). For proficiency-oriented testing of listening comprehension, authentic spoken materials must be used, not only for testing but also for practice, from the early stages, whether in the language-learning laboratory, in the classroom, or in the natural context of contact with a local German-speaking community. Where such contact is available, listening to radio programs in German, participation in local activities with German-speaking neighbors, and conversing over the telephone in organized or student-initiated partnerships provide excellent material for realistic testing. Televised programs in German that are available via satellite may be used in videotaped form for learning and testing. In many areas, German-language films are shown regularly in local cinemas and can be incorporated into the study and assessment procedures. As part of the test, students may be asked to gather information or prepare comments from such activities, which they will discuss with the interviewer, convey to the class in an oral report (after which they will answer questions from other students), or use in acting out a role in a group interlude.

Note that in all the testing procedures proposed above, listening again becomes associated with oral production (talking on the telephone, oral reports, acting roles). It is difficult to test pure listening, except through action (filling in diagrams and maps or identifying features in them; drawing figures and schematic scenes or locales in conformity with aural input; performing actions; following an explanation while studying a picture, chart, or graph; making an object; and so on).

The traditional listening test, without oral response, has commonly required selection among multiple-choice or true-false items given to the student in aural or written form. (Guidance in developing valid tests of these types is given in Chapter 3: *Recirculating, Selecting, Recoding for Storage; Assessment of Micro-Language Learning,* C59–63; and *Designing Multiple-Choice Items for Listening Comprehension,* C64–66.) If the choices are given orally, we must see that listening to the choices does not become such a strain on the memory that the original material on which the choices were based slips from the mind. On the other hand, if the choices are given in printed form, we are testing reading *and* listening (which we may want to do) while inexpertly written choices may give the students unintentional clues to the meaning of the aural input.

In testing listening, we must be aware of the creative nature of the process: we constantly draw inferences and project expectations about the nature of the message. Much information is available on the ways in which information is selected, reduced to the gist for storage, and later retrieved (see Chapter 3). Knowledge of the process will prevent us, for instance, from constructing tests which require students to reproduce material in the exact form in which they originally heard it—something we do not do even in our own language.

Since much of what we are testing in listening is skill in drawing inferences, success depends to a large extent on one's background in the subject-matter of what is being heard and the ability to relate new information in the input to this existing knowledge. Anticipating meaning and drawing inferences can, therefore, be facilitated by knowing early in the test what the input is about. For this reason, titles are helpful to the listener, as are topic sentences which occur at the beginning and which do not use unusual, unexplained vocabulary. Sometimes the listening material may be closely related to something that was recently discussed and is still in the forefront of the student's thinking. Unfortunately, a student who does not recognize the central focus of a listening passage may be extracting information for retention other than that the teacher expected when writing the questions; once having extracted this information, the listener no longer has access to the original signal and can reconstruct it only partially by inference and probability. Furthermore, because of the inferential factor, it is difficult to categorize listening materials as being of successive levels of difficulty; the problems for the students do not lie entirely in complexity of syntax or breadth of vocabulary. For these reasons, several short passages are more effective testing instruments than one long passage. Students then have a second or even a third chance to show how well they comprehend if the organization of the material does not disconcert them.[31]

Proficiency-oriented tests will turn rather on the results of listening — what students can do with what they have heard, which is the normal way of using aural material. They may use it as background for reading or for supplementing cultural information. They may listen to speeches from people about whom they have been reading, to plays and poems they have studied, to interviews with writers or national leaders in various areas. They then use this material for written assignments or for discussion in oral testing. From a simpler, more elementary perspective, they may listen to the dramatization of a skit or an unfinished incident, which they then use as the basis for a written test — completing the story or incident, explaining a mystery in the skit, or resolving a cultural dilemma. Alternatively, the aural input may serve as the basis for a further group presentation or continuation, which becomes impossible if the input was not comprehended. Many of the activities suggested in Chapter 3, C67: *Chart of Listening Comprehension Activities,* can be transformed into tests of macro-language use that reflect the normal purposes of listening. Whichever approach we take, listening will be tested best in a larger communicative context.[32]

* Examine listening comprehension tests from several levels. On what basis do you think they were categorized elementary, intermediate, or advanced? Try them out on students at different levels and see if the tests clearly discriminate various levels of achievement. Finally, analyze your results. What suggestions can you draw from this study for preparing listening comprehension tests?

Reading comprehension

Reading comprehension shares many features with listening comprehension. Readers, as do listeners, extract a semantic message without undue attention to syntactic details. Using their knowledge of the world, they draw inferences and anticipate meaning by selecting elements related to what they see as the main topic and its subtopics.[33] Sometimes they err, in which case they check back to details they had not bothered with earlier and reorient their ideas about the material. As with listening, they reduce what they have read to the gist and recirculate this in relation to the developing meaning, finally storing what they consider to be the essentials in a way that augments existing knowledge. In testing reading, we must remember that too close attention to unimportant details can confuse the student as to the main thrust of the material. This can result from poorly conceived multiple-choice or true-false items, or persnickety questions (see Chapter 7: *Assisting and Assessing Reading Comprehension,* R57–67). Where necessary, students can always look back for anything important they missed, a possibility not open to the listener.

A proficiency-oriented approach to reading requires students to write reports or summaries of what they have read or to use reading material as the basis for some other activity: discussion of controversial subjects, updating the class on the news from overseas papers, acting out roles from novels, constructing new denouements, writing a different conclusion for a short story or a scene based on a short story, or debating the viewpoints of political figures from German-speaking countries. They may use sources of information in German for planning a trip or using a product. (Suggestions for integrating reading with writing, listening comprehension, speaking, or purposeful activity are to be found at the end of Chapter 7.)

Translation, which for centuries has been associated with reading, is a valid proficiency-oriented test where translation has been taught as a separate skill, usually at the advanced level. Translation may be oral, in the form of simultaneous or consecutive interpreting and, therefore, related to listening (see Chapter 4). Or it may be written, in which case students are being trained in a career skill, and tests will be prepared that reflect the type of translation students will later be called upon to perform, e.g., translation of instructions, forms or regulations; of literary or philosophical texts; or of scientific and technological reports or articles. (See Chapter 9: *Translation as a Specialized Study,* W65–67.)

Grammar and vocabulary

Grammar can be overemphasized and grammar can be underemphasized. Because it is easy to teach to large groups and easy to test and correct in discrete-point form, many teachers take the conventional and satisfying route of giving lucid, schematic explanations of structures in a carefully graded sequence and then testing features one by one. Grammar is not easy to learn, however, and teachers are often disappointed that what seemed to be "learned," according to test results, is "forgotten" or ignored in language use.

The real learning of grammar comes through using the grammar, not merely through intellectual understanding of a complicated abstract system, no matter how simplified the form in which it is presented and no matter how enlightening the explanations may be. Similarly, playing a musical instrument well requires much practice — much playing, which is, nonetheless, facilitated by understanding the language of music, rather than relying totally on playing by ear (although this can be done to a high degree of performance by a gifted few). A thorough knowledge of music theory contributes greatly to a high level of performance, but of itself does not ensure ability to perform. No one seems to be surprised that musicians must practice long hours, exercising their minds and fingers with more and more complicated exercises, as ballet dancers do in their domain, yet there is a tendency in some quarters to disparage similar practice in foreign-language learning. The answer is not to throw out all study of grammar, as some would suggest.

Understanding the language system and practicing how to express specific meanings in the language have their place. Language practice, however, needs to be of two kinds: practice of unfamiliar or complicated routines to develop accuracy and fluency in their use; and practice in using this material in unstructured situations for conveying one's personal meaning. The problem in many classrooms is that the first type of practice, skill-getting, takes most if not all of the time, and teachers feel that skill-using in real communication situations is a ''waste of time'' when there is ''so much to cover.'' As soon as students begin using the language independently, inevitably making mistakes as they concentrate on meaning, teachers tend to draw everyone back into the safety of structured practice that leads to correct responses. This is one of the root causes of the lack of confidence and facility in using the language that students who have studied a language for a number of years experience outside the classroom.

Since the form of the test affects the perceptions of both teacher and students as to the relative importance of language-related activities, a strong weighting of the test grade in favor of easily constructed and assessed discrete-point grammar tests will result in most of class time being devoted to point-by-point grammar teaching. A balance must be established between testing abstract understanding of grammar and testing ability to use grammar for one's own purposes, that is, between assessing language knowledge and assessing language control. Regular discrete-point quizzes of what is being learned at a particular time are useful indicators of the degree of comprehension of the workings of the language system for both student and teacher, but major assessments of progress should concentrate on how the student uses grammar in speaking, writing, and comprehension. This does not mean ''neglecting grammar,'' since use of grammar is basic to everything the student does with the language. Grammar is being tested through listening and reading, as well as in the more active modes of language use. The same applies to *vocabulary,* which may be tested separately in quizzes to encourage students to keep on acquiring new words for expressing meanings, but which is actually being tested every time a student uses the language.

Proficiency-oriented testing of grammar will ensure that grammar is always tested in the way in which it is used, never like a dead specimen on a pin. Even discrete-point testing of grammar will be affected by this approach. For instance, in Chapter 4, we discussed the difference between Type A and Type B grammar exercises and this difference applies equally to test items. Type A test items are strictly manipulative: students perform operations on specimens of language — substitutions, conversions, expansions, combinations, restatements — in a sterile, detached way as though taking apart and reassembling a mechanism. In Type B test items, students perform similar operations but through the creation of original sentences or imaginative completions and conversions of sentences; they are working with the mechanism and showing what it can do for them and, therefore, they are thinking their way through the operation. (For some applications of the Type A and B approach, see Chapter 4, G33–40.)

Proficiency-oriented testing of grammar will principally be in an implicit or indirect way through the testing of speaking and writing, which students cannot perform without using grammar. A direct evaluative grade for use of grammar may be assigned as part of the general assessment of these activities (as in W61 in Chapter 9),[35] or the assessment may be holistic (the student uses the language well, not badly, or poorly), in which case the knowledge of grammar is assessed as being an inseparable part of using the language.

The problems of *multiple-choice* and *fill-in-the-blank* tests are discussed in Chapter 8, W9–18, and W19–28.[36] *Expanding frames* is a useful technique for testing grammatical knowledge since it approaches real-life language use (see Chapter 9, W45–49). Grammatical features are elicited in a more creative, yet still controlled fashion, in tests along the lines of the *flexibility measures* demonstrated in Chapter 9, W34–44. These activities may look like guided composition, but they are centered on certain grammatical features or syntactic arrangements.

Grammar use, rather than knowledge of particular features, is also tested in the *cloze test,* discussed above. This test also assesses reading comprehension and knowledge of vocabulary. In the original form of the cloze test, every *n*th word is deleted (for instance, every fifth or seventh word) to avoid subjective choice of features by the examiner. The student then either writes in what seems to have been deleted or selects a suitable insertion from multiple-choice items. In a modification of the cloze test, specific types of words are deleted (for example, verbs, prepositions, or adjectives) so that the test is not unlike the fill-in-the-blank overall structure test of grammar knowledge (W20), but set in continuous discourse. This type of test can provide useful diagnostic information on students' control of particular features (uses of tenses, agreement, and so on), as can the dictation test, discussed above.

Vocabulary and common expressions may also be tested in multiple-choice or fill-in-the-blank form or, more creatively, in a kind of guided composition. Ideas can be gleaned from the exercises illustrated in Chapter 7, R66 and R72–82, and Chapter 8, W14–18.

* Look at example W13 in Chapter 8, in which students are tested on the present indicative tense, the conditional, and the subjunctive. Design a Type B test in which students would demonstrate this knowledge in a creative way.

Writing

Writing has been dealt with extensively in Chapters 8 and 9. As emphasized in those chapters, we must not confuse written tests (pencil-and-paper tests, as they are usually called) with testing ability to write in German. Pencil-and-paper tests usually concentrate on morphology, syntax, sentence structure, and vocabulary. These written tests of language knowledge have been discussed under *Grammar* above.

Writing is communicating meaning within the accepted written conventions of the language. It is a difficult art which few people succeed in doing well in their native language. As can be seen in Chapter 9: *Normal Purposes of Writing,* we write in a simple way for practical reasons: filling in forms; writing notes, short letters, and notices; ordering goods; lodging complaints; sending greetings; and so on. If we are students, we take notes on lectures and readings in an abbreviated form. Students can learn to do these things for their own convenience without paying attention to stylistic elegance. When, however, it is a question of creative expression, students have to be taught a craft, not a skill—a highly polished way of conveying meaning that requires much concentration and practice in writing and rewriting, as well as the ability to select and vary syntax and vocabulary to convey precise effects. Few students of German will need to write at this level. There will be a few who will go on to higher degrees where well-written papers and perhaps a dissertation are required, but these are the gifted ones who will have many years to develop their knowledge of the language and their control of the finer nuances that are basic to writing well. In considering the testing of writing, we will confine ourselves to less lofty reaches of expression in German.

Writing is a supportive and consolidating activity in language learning. Although written and spoken German differ in many ways, as was demonstrated in Chapter 1, C2, writing out what we would say is basic to note and letter writing, as well as diary keeping. In these activities, students can see what they can do with what they know, experimenting with language in a less threatening situation than speaking. Written material can be edited and reedited, and hidden from other eyes until a certain perfection has been reached. Dictionaries can be consulted, even grammars. The spoken utterance must come out "trippingly on the tongue," to quote Shakespeare.[37] It may be well formed and expressive but cause embarrassment, because of problems with pronunciation or intonation or because it is inappropriate in that particular setting or as a response to a previous utterance. Slips of the tongue can change it unintentionally. In writing the student is much more in control, even if writing is also more complicated, just because it requires a fuller, more redundant message to be constructed than when there is an interlocutor.

Properly presented, writing in German can be fun, even for those who do not particularly like writing in their native language. If students are allowed early in their studies to play with German, to write as they feel and about what interests them, then writing will become a natural way to test how well they control the language. Students should be allowed to take their own time with the writing assignment and edit and polish it before submitting it for assessment. With word processors, some of the labor will be taken out of this work.

All writing for assessment need not be done under test conditions. Quite early, students can submit short original poems or anecdotes. They may keep diaries which are regularly submitted for cumulative assessment. Dialogue journals are becoming popular. In these, students write as little or as much as they like about what they have been thinking or experiencing; the journals are then passed in to the teacher who writes a response: questioning, commenting, or sharing ideas, adding a few suggestions for improvement, or else rephrasing incorrect sentences as part of the response; the students then respond to the teacher's contribution in any way they please. Students may also work together to produce a weekly or monthly newspaper, writing the items in German. If a newspaper is not feasible, a section of the bulletin board may be allocated for students to conduct a "letters to the teacher or school administration" column, to which the teacher will add replies. In these ways writing is being used in a normal communicative way. This kind of writing, for pleasure, usually on a regular basis, provides quite enough material for assessing writing without a formal test. Better writing will also be obtained than in a conventional testing time-slot because of the importance of the communication to the student and the fact that it will be read for its message.

Should more formal tests of writing be required, the various *idea frames* in Chapter 9, W50–54, will provide some initial suggestions for imaginative and interesting writing projects. Within the idea frame, writing can be integrated with visuals, or with speaking, listening, and reading. At a more elementary level, the writing activities described in W39–44 will be useful. The variety of interesting writing projects available to the students will be limited only by the imagination of the teacher.

When students reach the stage of confident creative writing, they may submit short stories, poems, or one-act plays for assessment (the latter will be acted out and perhaps videotaped as part of the test). They may try their hand at biographical sketches or autobiographical reminiscences. The essential thing is that, whether assessed as a test item or not, such contributions should be distributed for reading by other members of the class. Sometimes this takes the form of a class anthology that is distributed to other classes, interested parents, and friends.

If we seem now to have progressed beyond formal testing to evaluation in naturalistic settings, this has been intentional. In the relaxed, interactional language learner's domain, the formal test should wither away, so that assessment, where necessary, becomes part of the developing process — something not to be feared, but to be appreciated for its intrinsic interest and for what can be learned from it.

Testing specific areas (reference list)

Refer to the chapters and pages listed below for more information on the topics at the left.

1. *Cloze Test*	Chapters 8, 9, and 10 pp. 258–59, W28; pp. 273–74, W47
2. *Culture*	Chapter 10
Culture capsules, clusters, and assimilators	p. 314
Open scenarios and sociodramas	pp. 314, 322–23
3. *Dictation*	Chapters 6 and 8
Seven procedures for	pp. 239–40
Spot	p. 189, R26; p. 238
4. *Grammar*	Chapters 4, 8, and 10
Conversions, combinations, and restatements	pp. 120–26, G23–32; pp. 266–68, W32–37
Expanding frames	pp. 273–75, W45–49
Fill-in-the-blank	pp. 108–9, G5–7; pp. 254–59, W19–28
In living language (advanced)	pp. 259–62, W29–30
Multiple-choice	pp. 248–54, W9–18

Epilogue

Consider the following statement in relation to the model C1 in the Prologue: *Communicating* (p. 4).

We may identify *two levels of language use* for which our students must be prepared. At the first level is the manipulation of language elements which occur in fixed relationships in clearly defined closed systems; (that is, relationships which will vary within very narrow limits). We need facility in correctly combining and varying these elements, in order to express our meaning comprehensibly according to the demands of the language system. At the second level is the expression of personal meaning, for which possible variations are infinite, depending on such factors as the type of message to be conveyed, the situation in which the utterance takes place, the relationship between speaker and hearer or hearers, and the degree of intensity with which the message is to be conveyed. At the second level, we have an intention to express, for which we select appropriate means, within our knowledge of the potentialities of the new language system; and through this selection we call into play the necessary first-level elements.[1]

In this book, we have looked carefully at various aspects of language use and ways of helping students acquire sufficient knowledge of phonological features, lexicon, and syntax (*skill-getting*) to be able to operate freely at the second level: expression of personal meaning (*skill-using*). Throughout our teaching, *interaction* should be central: as a goal and as a process for reaching that goal. This focus affects the way we view all large-group, small-group, and individual activities. It is the way we proceed that makes communicative interaction a normal and familiar undertaking, so that, when plunged into unstructured language use in the real world, students are not suddenly transferring to new ways of using their language knowledge but are expanding and consolidating what has been budding, leafing, and blooming from the beginning. We call this *interactive language teaching,* since all learning of language takes place in the context of interaction between teacher and student, student and student, student and community.[2]

To draw together the ideas you have been developing while reading this book, reflect on and discuss the following questions.

1. Which parts of the C1 model apply to the first level of language use and which parts to the second level? Do you see these levels as being developed consecutively or in parallel? In this regard, discuss the concepts of *bridging activities* (p. 43) and *flexibility measures* (p. 265). What is the place, if any, of formal learning in the acquiring of a second language? Is skill-using sufficient of itself to ensure an adequate control of a second language? Is skill-getting enough? As a group, develop your own short statement of what the teacher is trying to do in the language class. Now prepare a short statement on what the language learner is trying to do.

2. Draw together on one sheet, or on the chalkboard, the normal purposes served by the language skills of speaking, reading, writing, and listening, as set out in different chapters of this book. Upon reflection, can you add to this list? Discuss the pros and cons for each addition. Which of these normal purposes are most served and which least served in the typical foreign-language textbook? in the proceedings of a typical class lesson? Now consider ways in which those least served might be brought into focus. Would we need to take the language out of the classroom to serve some of these purposes better or could ways be devised within the classroom setting?

3. Observe a language class, keeping a careful diary of what took place. Form discussion groups and consider the following questions.

What kinds of activities were taking place in the classroom? What area of language learning was being served by each of these activities? Was each activity an effective way of achieving language control in the intended area? Did it move beyond language control into interaction? In what ways could you convert the activities you observed into more normal uses of language? Could you propose other approaches that might have served this purpose more directly?

4. In Chapter 9, there is extensive discussion of writing within an idea frame (p. 278). Is the concept of an idea frame useful for developing speaking and listening? Discuss in small groups imaginative idea frames for oral communication. What are their advantages and disadvantages in promoting normal use of language?

5. Discuss among yourselves the difference, if any, between using language for a normal purpose and ''natural'' use of language.[3] Can you

remember occasions in language classes when natural use of language prevailed? How frequent were these occasions? In what ways were these interludes different from dynamic classroom activity? What precipitated such a change in language use? Can occasions for natural use of language be stimulated by the teacher or does this *ipso facto* render them "unnatural"? What elements other than the phonological, syntactic, and lexical become important once natural language comes into play? List as many of these features as you can and discuss how they can be taught for German.

6. What resources are there in your community on which to draw to provide natural language input and opportunities for interaction? How can students be brought in touch with these resources so that such interaction is promoted in a natural, uninhibiting way? What kind of preparation and follow-up should there be to enable students to derive the greatest benefit from the experience? If there are no such resources in your area, what substitutes or vicarious experiences can you propose to ensure contact with authentic language and culture?

Suggested assignments and projects

Communicating (chapters 1–3)

1. Write a situational dialogue suitable for the second month of instruction. Write a critique of the first draft of your dialogue, then rewrite it if necessary. From your final dialogue write a spiral series and a situation tape. (You may find what you have written needs considerable adaptation for the situation tape. You should try the script for the tape out on several people to see if it is workable.) If you have the facilities available, record your tape as it would be used by students.

2. Choose a grammatical feature. Write a grammar-demonstration dialogue to display the various facets of this feature. Construct a unit showing how you would exploit this feature in guided oral practice, in student-directed practice, and then in some natural language activity. (Consult also chapter 4.)

3. Design a module for small-group activity which explores some facet of the everyday culture of West Germany, East Germany, Switzerland, or Austria. Include natural communicative activities and some culminating display for sharing the material with the whole class.

4. Take a unit or lesson from a direct method textbook and examine the types of activities proposed. Design a learning packet for individualized

338

instruction or a unit for small-group work using this material. (Remember that individualized instruction does not mean independent study. This distinction is important if communication skills are to be developed.)

5. Design in detail for fourth year high school, fourth semester of college, or advanced level college an aural-oral communication course based entirely on natural uses of language. Your course should supply ample opportunity for developing facility in listening to all kinds of German and for expressing oneself in different situations and styles of language. (Think of ways of stimulating genuinely self-directed activity by the students. Do not make the course dependent on expensive equipment and aids which you could not realistically expect to be available in the average foreign-language department.)

6. Take two textbooks designed specifically for conversation courses. Analyze and comment on the types of communicative activity they promote, using the following heads as an outline.

Situations. For what situation is practice provided? Are these adequate? useful? culturally illuminating? Could the material be adapted easily to other situations?

Normal uses of language. How do the types of activities proposed relate to the normal communicative categories of chapter 2? What other categories can you establish from this examination?

Strategies of communication. What techniques for expressing personal meaning within a limited knowledge of the language do these texts encourage? What other strategies do learners of a foreign language need to practice? How could these be incorporated into these texts?

7. Design two listening comprehension tests—one multiple-choice and the other based on natural language activities. Discuss for each of the tests the problems involved in assessment of the degree of listening skill and in administration in a practical teaching situation.

8. Design in detail a course for developing facility in listening along with facility in reading. State the level at which the course would be offered and give your reasons for offering it at that level. (See also chapters 6 and 7.)

Oral practice for the learning of grammar (chapter 4)

9. Take six Type A exercises from current textbooks and show how each could be developed as a Type B exercise.

10. Take a unit for grammatical practice from a current textbook, classify the types of exercises proposed, and design further exercises of the types described in chapter 4 which are not already included but which you would consider suitable for practicing this area of grammar.

11. Draft a series of oral exercises for teaching the use of the interrogative pronouns in German. Draw freely from the various types described in chapter 4, passing from teacher demonstration to student-directed application to autonomous student production.

12. Examine critically the oral exercises for the learning of grammar on a set of tapes accompanying a current textbook. What are their best features and their weaknesses? Propose types of exercises which would, in your opinion, make them more interesting and more useful for developing ability to use the language in interaction.

Teaching the sound system (chapter 5)

13. Make a tape of your own reading of the evaluation passage S44. Choose the four most striking weaknesses in your production (see S43) and work out articulatory descriptions, empirical recommendations, and remedial exercises which would help students to correct these same faults.

14. Work out some multiple-choice items to test aural discrimination of [ø/y]; [U/u]; [x/ç]; [əʁ/ə]; [ɔ/o] when they occur in context in normal word groups.

15. Make some tapes of your students conversing in German. From an analysis of these tapes, list in descending order of frequency the ten features of German pronunciation and intonation for which you consider they need the most remedial practice. Compare your list with those of other students or teachers and discuss the differences.

Reading (chapters 6 and 7)

16. Take a survey of interests in reading material in the class you are teaching (or in which you are practice teaching). Find suitable materials in German to meet these interests at different stages of reading development. List these (with complete bibliographic information) and explain the reasons for your selection.

17. a. Take a reading passage or story your students have found difficult to read and another they enjoyed but did not consider particularly difficult.

b. Compare the two texts according to: level of difficulty of vocabulary; structural complexity; interest of content; familiarity or unfamiliarity of content; and any other criteria you consider relevant.

c. Ask your students to write down why they found one passage difficult and the other accessible.

d. Compare (b) and (c) and give what seems to you the most reasonable explanation of the students' reactions to the two texts.

18. Undertake a survey of German-language newspapers and magazines available in your area (from West Germany, East Germany, Switzerland, or Austria). Examine various aspects of their content and rate them appropriate or inappropriate in content and language for Stages 4, 5, and 6.

19. The physical aspects of a reading text are important factors in readability. Examine a number of books for reading development in German from the point of view of: varieties of type (italic, bold face, etc.) and length of line; layout (spacing, headings and subheadings, breaks in the text); convenience and placing of supplementary helps (glosses, notes, etc.); usefulness and attractiveness of illustrative materials; general appearance of the body of the text; attractiveness and durability of the cover; any other physical features which have attracted your attention.

20. Find two textbooks which include the same reading selection. Compare the way the material has been presented and exploited in each (adaptation, if any, of the original text, layout, glosses and supplementary helps, types of questions and exercises, interest and usefulness of these for a particular stage of reading development, integration of reading with other skills).

21. Examine some German children's books and comic books from the point of view of vocabulary level, grammatical complexity, and content. Classify them as possibilities for supplementary reading at specific stages of reading development.

Writing (chapters 8 and 9)

22. On separate occasions within the same week, give your students three tests of one grammatical feature (e.g., form and position of pronoun objects): a multiple-choice test, a cloze test, and a set of stimulus sentences to translate into German. Make graphs of the number of errors made by the students on each test. Repeat the tests in a different order for another feature and examine these results as well. Give an analysis of what this informal experiment has revealed about the relative difficulty and discriminatory power of the three tests, and the most persistent problems for the students who are learning these features.

23. Examine a textbook for elementary language instruction. What part does writing play in this book? Are the writing activities integrated with the other skills? Are they imaginative and interesting for students of the age to which the book is directed? Are they purposeful? What suggestions can you make to improve their effectiveness?

24. Examine a manual for advanced German composition. Do the types of activities provided leave scope for personal initiative? Are they directed toward normal purposes of writing? What aspects of writing have been ignored? What suggestions would you make for a revised edition of the manual?

25. Examine a book (A) written for instruction in the writing of the native language (English or German). Compare it with a book (B) intended to improve foreign-language writing. What ideas can be gleaned from the study of A for the improvement of B, or vice versa?

Testing and assessment (chapter 10)

26. Your students have access to news broadcasts, either directly or through recordings in the language learning laboratory, as well as some newspapers in German. Design a unit in which students study the political developments in a particular area and reactions there to your own nation's foreign policy. Then design a proficiency-oriented test to cover this material.

27. Examine the materials and tests presently used for elementary German in your school. Do they reflect normal uses of language? In what ways would you propose adapting them so that students can demonstrate what they can do with the language in naturalistic situations?

28. Select two situations in which English native speakers and German-speaking students might misunderstand each other's reactions. Design two teaching units centered on these situations in which students study the potential clash

   a. through information search and discussion;
   b. through an open-ended minidrama in which students extemporize various possible solutions to the conflict.

Try these out on students. Then consider which one seemed to you to involve the students most and which one gave them the deepest insight into the problem. Why?

29. Examine the test that was last administered in the class you are teaching (or a class in which you are studying a language). What proportion

of the test was discrete-point and what proportion was integrative? Did the percentages of the final grade allotted to various sections of the test (listening, reading, vocabulary, etc.) reflect their relative importance in relation to the objectives of the course? How would you propose revising the test?

30. Study the German guidelines for listening and speaking in the Appendix. With a colleague conduct several oral interviews with students from different levels of instruction. See if you can arrive at a consensus as to the level on the ACTFL/ETS scale to which each student should be assigned (novice—mid, intermediate—low, etc.). What problems arose in reaching this consensus? What recommendations would you make to colleagues who wish to conduct oral interviews together?

Appendix

ACTFL Provisional Proficiency Guidelines

The experts appointed by the American Council on the Teaching of Foreign Languages (ACTFL) to develop guidelines for generic and language-specific goals for language skills were Dale Lange (coordinating consultant), Pardee Lowe (speaking and listening), Howard Nostrand (culture), Alice Omaggio (writing), and June Phillips (reading).[1]

The following correspondence was established with the Interagency Language Roundtable (ILR) scales for speaking proficiency (formerly the Foreign Service Institute, or FSI, scales[2]).

ILR Scale	*ACTFL/ETS* Scale*
0	Novice—Low
No practical proficiency	Novice—Mid
0+	Novice—High
1	Intermediate—Low
Elementary proficiency	Intermediate—Mid
1+	Intermediate—High
2 Limited working proficiency	Advanced
2+	Advanced plus
3 Professional proficiency	Superior
3+	
4 Distinguished proficiency	
4+	
5 Native or bilingual proficiency	

*American Council on the Teaching of Foreign Languages (Hastings-on-Hudson, N.Y.) and Educational Testing Services (Princeton, N.J.)

PROVISIONAL GERMAN DESCRIPTIONS — SPEAKING

Novice—Low — Unable to function in spoken German. Oral production is limited to occasional isolated words such as *ja, nein, ich, Sie, Fritz* (name), *Fräulein*. Essentially no communicative ability.

Novice—Mid — Able to operate only in a very limited capacity within very predictable areas of need. Vocabulary is limited to that necessary to express simple elementary needs and basic courtesy formulae such as *Guten Tag/Morgen; Auf Wiedersehen; Das ist . . .* (name); *Was ist das?; Wer ist das? Danke; Bitte; Grüß Gott*. Speakers at this level cannot create original sentences or cope with the simplest situations. Pronunciation is frequently unintelligible and is strongly influenced by the first language. Can be understood only with difficulty, even by persons such as teachers who are used to dealing with non-native speakers or in interactions where the context strongly supports the utterance.

Novice—High — Able to satisfy immediate needs using learned utterances. There is no consistent ability to create original sentences or cope with simple survival situations. Can ask questions or make statements with reasonable accuracy only where this involves short memorized utterances or formulae. Vocabulary is limited to common areas such as colors, days of the week, months of the year, names of basic objects, numbers, and names of immediate family members—*Vater, Mutter, Geschwister.* Grammar shows only a few parts of speech. Verbs are generally in the present tense. Errors are frequent and, in spite of repetition, may severely inhibit communication even with persons used to dealing with such learners. Unable to make one's needs known and communicate essential information in a simple survival situation.

Intermediate— Low — Able to satisfy basic survival needs and minimum courtesy requirements. In areas of immediate need or in very familiar topics, can ask and answer some simple questions and respond to and sometimes initiate simple statements. Can make one's needs known with great difficulty in a simple survival situation, such as ordering a meal, getting a hotel room, and asking for directions; vocabulary is adequate to talk simply about learning the target language and other academic studies. For example: *Wieviel kostet das? Wo ist der Bahnhof? Ich möchte zu . . . Wieviel Uhr ist es? Ich lerne hier Deutsch. Ich studiere schon 2 Jahre. Ich habe eine Wohnung.* Awareness of gender apparent (many mistakes). Word order is random. Verbs are generally in the present tense. Some correct use of predicate adjectives and personal pronouns (*ich, wir*). No clear distinction made between polite and familiar address forms (*Sie, du*). Awareness of case system sketchy. Frequent errors in all structures. Misunderstandings frequently arise from limited vocabulary and grammar and erroneous phonology, but, with repetition, can generally be understood by native speakers in regular contact with foreigners attempting to speak German. Little precision in information conveyed owing to tentative state of grammatical development and little or no use of modifiers.

Intermediate—
Mid

Able to satisfy most routine travel and survival needs and some limited social demands. Can ask and answer questions on very familiar topics and in areas of immediate need. Can initiate and respond to simple statements, and can maintain simple face-to-face conversation. Can ask and answer questions and carry on a conversation on topics beyond basic survival needs or involving the exchange of personal information, i.e., can talk simply about autobiographical information, leisure-time activities, academic subjects. Can handle simple transactions at the post office, bank, drugstore, etc. Misunderstandings arise because of limited vocabulary, frequent grammatical errors, and poor pronunciation and intonation, although speakers at this level have broader vocabulary and/or greater grammatical and phonological control than speakers at Intermediate—Low. Speech is often characterized by long pauses. Some grammatical accuracy in some basic structures, i.e., subject/verb agreement, word order in simple statements (excluding adverbs) and interrogative forms, present tense of irregular verbs, and imperative of separable prefix verbs (*Kommen Sie mit!*). Fluency is still strained, but language use may be quite natural while within familiar territory. Is generally understood by persons used to dealing with foreigners.

Intermediate—
High

Able to satisfy most survival needs and limited social demands. Developing flexibility in language production although fluency is still uneven. Can initiate and sustain a general conversation on factual topics beyond basic survival needs. Can give autobiographical information and discuss leisure-time activities. Most verbs are still in the present tense, more common past participles appear (*gegangen, gesehen, geschlafen*). Many mistakes in choice of auxiliary (**habe gegangen* with the present perfect). Past tense is attempted also with common imperfect forms (*sagte, hatte, war*). Several high-frequency separable prefix verbs appear in the indicative (*ich gehe mit*). There is inconsistent coding of proper dative and accusative cases following prepositions in singular and plural. Attempts to expand discourse, which is accurate only in short sentences. Frequently gropes for words. Comprehensible to native speakers used to dealing with foreigners, but still has to repeat utterances frequently to be understood by the general public.

*Denotes an error characteristic of speakers at this level.

Advanced   Able to satisfy routine social demands and limited school and work requirements. Can handle with confidence, but not with facility, most social and general conversations. Can narrate, describe, and explain in past, present, and future time. Can communicate facts — what, who, when, where, how much — and can explain a point of view, in an uncomplicated fashion, but cannot conjecture or coherently support an opinion. Can talk in a general way about topics of current public interest (e.g., current events, student rules and regulations), as well as personal interest (work, leisure-time activities) and can give autobiographical information. Can make factual comparisons (e.g., life in a city vs. life in a rural area). Can handle work-related requirements, needing help in handling any complications or difficulties. Can make a point forcefully and communicate needs and thoughts in a situation with a complication (e.g., calling a mechanic for help with a stalled car, losing traveler's checks). Has a speaking vocabulary sufficient to respond simply with some circumlocutions. Can be understood by native speakers not used to dealing with foreigners, in spite of some pronunciation difficulties. Good control of all verbs in present tense, past participles of most verbs, simple past tense of most irregular verbs, modal auxiliaries, most separable verbs and some reflexives. Double infinitives in main clauses may be attempted (mistakes are expected). Genders of high frequency words are mostly correct. Some inaccuracy in choice of prepositions as well as in distinctions between position and motion. Speaker is hesitant at times and gropes for words, uses paraphrases and fillers. Uses uncomplicated dependent clauses (*daß, weil*), but mistakes are expected when sentences are joined in limited discourse.

Advanced Plus   Able to satisfy most school and work requirements and show some ability to communicate on concrete topics relating to particular interests and special fields of competence. Can narrate, describe, and explain in past, present, and future time. Can consistently communicate facts and explain points of view in an uncomplicated fashion. Shows some ability to support opinions, explain in detail, and hypothesize, although only sporadically. Can discuss topics of current and personal interest. Can handle most situations that arise in everyday life (see Advanced Level examples) but will have difficulty with unfamiliar situations (e.g., losing a contact lens in a sink drain and going to a neighbor to borrow a wrench). Normally controls general vocabulary with some groping still evident. Speaking performance is often uneven (e.g., strong in either grammar or vocabulary but not in both). Good control of most verbs in present and past tense and most imperative forms. Irregular control of infinitive clauses with *zu,* conditional sentences (with *würde* plus infinitive, *hätte, wäre, könnte,* and *da(r)-* and *wo(r)-* compounds). Better control of prepositions and adjective endings but mistakes will occur. Control of dependent clauses. Distinguishes between subordinating and coordinating conjunctions and how they affect word order (*denn, weil*). Good control of limited discourse, but many errors in all more complicated structures. Often shows remarkable fluency and ease of speech, but under tension or pressure language may break down.

Superior

Able to speak the language with sufficient structural accuracy and vocabulary to participate in most formal and informal conversations on practical, social, and professional topics. Can discuss particular interests and special fields of competence with reasonable ease. Can support opinions, hypothesize, and conjecture. May not be able to tailor language to fit various audiences or discuss highly abstract topics in depth. Vocabulary is broad enough that speaker rarely has to grope for a word; good use of circumlocution. Pronunciation may still be obviously foreign. Control of grammar is good. Sporadic errors but no patterns of error in tenses, cases, attributive adjectives, pronouns, most verbs plus preposition, dependent clauses, subjunctive II (present and past). Control less consistent in low-frequency structures such as passive plus modals, the *lassen* construction, verbs plus specific prepositions (*achten auf, sich halten an, sich irren in*), directional adverbs (*hinauf, hinunter, herüber*), double infinitives in dependent clauses (*daß er das nicht hat machen sollen*). Varying degrees of competence in usage of idiomatic expression and slang. Errors never interfere with understanding and rarely disturb the native speaker.

PROVISIONAL GERMAN DESCRIPTIONS — LISTENING

Novice—Low

No practical understanding of spoken German. Understanding is limited to cognates, borrowed words, high frequency social conventions, and occasional isolated words, such as *Tag, Auto, Haus, heute, morgen, schön.* Essentially no ability to comprehend even short utterances.

Novice—Mid

Sufficient comprehension to understand some memorized words within predictable areas of need. Vocabulary for comprehension is limited to simple elementary needs, basic courtesy formulae, such as *Guten Tag, Wie geht's?, Auf Wiedersehen, Bis morgen, Danke,* and very simple memorized material relating to everyday objects and situations. Utterances understood rarely exceed more than two or three words at a time, and ability to understand is characterized by long pauses for assimilation and by repeated requests on the listener's part for repetition, and/or a slower rate of speech. Confuses words that sound similar, such as *fährt/ Fahrt,* and pronouns, *er/ihr.*

Novice—High	Sufficient comprehension to understand a number of memorized utterances in areas of immediate need. Comprehends slightly longer utterances in situations where the context aids understanding, such as at the table, in a restaurant/store, in a train/bus. Phrases recognized have for the most part been memorized: *Die Milch/Marmelade, bitte. Die Fahrkarten, bitte.* Comprehends vocabulary common to daily needs. Comprehends simple questions/statements about family members, age, address, weather, time, daily activities and interests: *Wie viele Brüder/Schwester haben Sie? Wie alt sind Sie? Wie ist das Wetter heute?* Misunderstandings arise from failure to perceive critical sounds or endings. Understands even tailored speech with difficulty but gets some main ideas. Often requires repetition and/or slowed rate of speed for comprehension, even when listening to persons such as teachers who are used to speaking with non-natives.
Intermediate—Low	Sufficient comprehension to understand utterances about basic survival needs, minimum courtesy and travel requirements. In areas of immediate need or on very familiar topics, can understand non-memorized material, such as simple questions in German. Comprehension areas include basic needs: meals, lodging, transportation, time, simple instructions (e.g., route directions, such as *Gehen Sie geradeaus! Sie müssen links abgehen.*) and routine commands (e.g., from customs officials, police, such as *Darf ich Ihren Paß sehen? Machen Sie die Koffer auf, bitte!*). Understands main ideas. Misunderstandings frequently arise from lack of vocabulary or from faulty processing of syntactic information often caused by strong interference from the native language or by the imperfect or partial acquisition of the target grammar (e.g., *er/ihr, -er/-en*).
Intermediate—Mid	Sufficient comprehension to understand simple conversations about some survival needs and some limited social conventions. Vocabulary permits understanding on topics beyond basic survival needs (e.g., personal history and leisure-time activities), such as *Wo sind Sie geboren? Was tun Sie während der Freizeit? Was machen Sie gerne am Wochenende?* Evidence of understanding basic constructions, e.g., subject-verb and noun-adjective agreement; some inflection is understood. Understanding of grammatical structure allows recognition of future and past references either by verb forms, such as the constructed future (*Ich werde in die Stadt gehen*), the present perfect (*Ich bin in die Stadt gegangen*), and the simple past (*Als ich in die Stadt ging . . .*), or with adverbs of time, such as *morgen, heute, gestern.*
Intermediate—High	Sufficient comprehension to understand short conversations about most survival needs and limited social conventions. Increasingly able to understand topics beyond immediate survival

needs, such as biographical information (*Geburtsort, Geburtsdatum, Mädchenname der Mutter/Frau, Heimatstadt, Kindheits-/Jugenderlebnisse, Urlaubspläne/-erlebnisse/-ziele*). Able to comprehend most sentences, including those which use *daß, wenn, weil* constructions and which feature vocabulary and familiar situations (home, office, school, and daily activities; simple purchases; directions). Most of the time is able to comprehend the semantic differences between utterances, such as *Er war einen Monat in Köln. Er ist seit einem Monat in Köln. Sie sind nur eine Woche hier.* Shows spontaneity in understanding, but speed and consistency of understanding uneven. Understands more common tense forms and some word order patterns. Can get the gist of conversations, but cannot sustain comprehension in longer utterances or in unfamiliar situations. Understanding of descriptions and detailed information is limited. Aware of basic cohesive features, e.g., pronouns, verb inflections, but may misunderstand, especially if other material intervenes. Still has to ask for utterances to be repeated.

Advanced

Sufficient comprehension to understand conversations about routine social conventions and limited school or work requirements. Able to understand face-to-face speech in standard German spoken at a normal rate, with some repetition and rewording, by a native speaker not used to dealing with foreigners. Able to get the gist of some radio broadcasts. Understands everyday topics, common personal and family news, well-known current events, and routine matters involving school or work; descriptions and narration about current, past, and future events; the essential points of a discussion or speech at an elementary level on topics in special fields of interest. For example: *Wer hat die hiesige Wahl gewonnen? Wie reagierten die Deutschen auf den Bau neuer Kernkraftwerke? Zu welchem Grad leidet der Mittelstand unter der Inflation? Wurde die Kaufkraft durch die Inflation eingeschränkt?*

Advanced Plus

Sufficient comprehension to understand most routine social conventions, conversations on school or work requirements, and discussions on concrete topics related to particular interests and special fields of competence. Often shows remarkable ability and ease of understanding, but comprehension may break down under tension or pressure (including unfavorable listening conditions). May display weakness or deficiency due to inadequate vocabulary base or less than secure knowledge of grammar and syntax. May be deficient or uneven in completely comprehending conversations or discussions by educated native speakers due to a less-than-adequate knowledge of more complex syntactic structures (tense usage in simple and complex statements, passive voice and extended adjective constructions, relative clauses, word order, subject-object relationships). Still has some difficulty following radio broadcasts. Can sometimes detect emotional overtones. Increasing ability to understand "between the lines" (i.e., to make inferences).

Superior Sufficient comprehension to understand the essentials of all speech in standard dialects, including technical discussions within a special field. Has sufficient understanding of face-to-face speech, delivered with normal clarity and speed in standard dialects, on general topics and areas of special interest; understands hypothesizing and supported opinions. Has broad enough vocabulary so that rarely has to ask for paraphrasing or explanation. Can follow accurately the essentials of conversations between educated native speakers, reasonably clear telephone calls, radio broadcasts, standard news items, oral reports, some oral technical reports, and public addresses on non-technical subjects. May not understand native speakers if they speak very quickly or use some slang or unfamiliar dialect. Can often detect emotional overtones. Can understand "between the lines" (i.e., make inferences).

PROVISIONAL GERMAN DESCRIPTIONS — READING

Novice—Low No functional ability in reading German.

Novice—Mid Sufficient understanding of written German to interpret highly contextualized words or cognates within predictable areas. Vocabulary for comprehension limited to simple elementary needs, such as names, addresses, dates, signs indicating names of streets and avenues (*Straße, Weg*), building names (*Hotel, Restaurant, Apotheke*), short informative signs (*Eingang, Ausgang, Rauchverbot, Taxi, Fernsprecher, Flughafen, Straßenbahn*). Material understood rarely exceeds a single phrase and comprehension requires successive rereading and checking.

Novice—High Sufficient comprehension of written language to interpret set expressions in areas of immediate need. Can recognize all letters of German (including umlauted ones and *ß*). Where vocabulary has been mastered, can read for instructional and directional purposes standardized messages, phrases, or expressions, such as some items on menus (*Tagessuppe, Getränke, Salat*), schedules, timetables, maps, signs indicating hours of operation, social codes (*Rauchen verboten*), and street signs (*Haltestelle*). Vocabulary and grammar limited to the most common nouns, adjectives, question words, and a few verb forms. Material is read for essential information. Detail is overlooked or misunderstood.

Intermediate—
Low

Sufficient comprehension to understand in printed form the simplest connected material, either authentic or especially prepared, dealing with basic survival and social needs. Able to understand previously mastered material and recombinations of mastered elements kept to the same level. Understands main ideas in material when structure and syntax parallel the native language. Can read simple handwritten telephone messages, personal notes, or simple letters, all of which may contain social amenities, such as simple forms of address, closure, queries about family and friends. Understands simple language with high-frequency grammatical, semantic, and syntactical items such as NP + VP of most frequent regular verbs (such as *arbeiten, bleiben, glauben, tun*), irregular verbs (such as *haben, sein, wissen, werden*), and modals (*müssen, wollen, können, sollen, mögen, dürfen*) in the present tense. Familiar with idioms relating to weather, age, personal well-being, and time (such as *Wie ist das Wetter? Er ist sechs Jahre alt. Wie geht's? Wie spät ist es?*). Adverbs of time will be used more frequently to determine the tense or time of what is being read than the actual verb tenses. Past meaning of specific verbs might be missed quite frequently. Misunderstandings may arise when syntax diverges from that of the native language (such as the verb in second position) or when grammatical cues are overlooked (such as article and adjective declensions).

Intermediate—
Mid

Sufficient comprehension to understand, in printed form, simple discourse for informative or social purposes. In response to perceived needs, can read public announcements to determine *who, what, when, where, why,* and *how much* regarding such subjects as sporting events, concerts, parades, and celebrations. Can also identify products, prices, and some conditions of sale in popular, illustrated advertising for everyday items, such as food, clothing, work or school supplies, and travel. Can comprehend a note or letter in which a writer used to dealing with non-native readers describes self and family, ages, occupations, residence, personality traits, and common preferences when high-frequency vocabulary or cognates and simple structures are used. Understands the general content of headlines in newspapers, such as *Die Welt,* or article titles in popular magazines such as *Der Spiegel* and *Illustrierten,* if the content is familiar or of high interest. Understands facts and follows events of simple narration in either authentic or especially prepared texts when syntax is related to simple NP + VP + NP constructions. Recognizes negation (*nein, nicht, kein*) and interrogative forms. Generally consistent in interpreting the present, the future as expressed by adverbs of time with the present tenses, but recognizes only the most common strong and weak verbs in the present perfect and simple past tenses. Understands adjective declensions and the use of other determiners such as definite and indefinite articles, demonstratives, possessives, and interrogatives. Has some difficulty matching pronouns to referents and with the use of relative pronouns. Uses guessing strategies to interpret vocabulary consisting of regular cognate patterns, and highly contextualized items. May have to read several times before understanding.

Intermediate—High

Sufficient comprehension to understand a simple paragraph for personal communication, informational, or recreational purposes. Can read with understanding invitations, social notes, personal letters, and some simple business letters on familiar topics. Can identify main ideas from topic and summary paragraphs of simple articles in popular magazines (such as fashions, gardening, furniture, homes), news publications (national, regional, and local), or other informational sources (travel and tourist brochures, guides). Appreciates descriptive material on daily life and routines, and biographical information. Can read for pleasure some uncomplicated, yet authentic prose and a limited amount of poetry (Kästner, for example). Guesses at meaning from the context of a fictional narrative description or from cultural information. Begins to rely on a dictionary or glossary to check meaning and expand vocabulary. Is able to recognize present and past tenses in a widening variety of strong and weak verbs. Recognizes, but does not fully comprehend, connected discourse with coordinating conjunctions (*aber, oder, denn, und*) and relative pronouns and other relative connectors which result in dependent word order. Also recognizes reflexive verbal constructions. Interprets expressions of quantity quite accurately. Is beginning to understand the use of particles (such as *noch, doch, gar, ja, also*) in strengthening meaning. Begins to connect sentences in the discourse and to attach advance meaning to them, but cannot sustain understanding of longer discourse on unfamiliar topics. Misinterpretation occurs with more complex patterns (such as dependent word order and most idiomatic expressions).

Advanced

Sufficient comprehension to read simple authentic printed material or edited textual material within a familiar context. Can read uncomplicated, authentic prose on familiar subjects (sports, travel, movies, theater, food, music, current events), news items in newspapers and popular magazines, biographical information in personal letters on family topics. Reads within the limits of identifiable vocabulary some unedited texts, such as prose fiction, from carefully chosen authors, usually contemporary. Such selections might appear in Sunday newspaper supplements, other daily papers, or special anthologies on modern culture.

The constructed future and the subjunctive are appreciated as different from the present, simple past, and present perfect. Conditions contrary to fact are recognized with more than average difficulty. The ability to guess at compounded vocabulary, nouns in specific, within context is becoming more accurate, but still some confusion over grammar and vocabulary not yet assimilated. As far as total comprehension is concerned, is able to read facts, but cannot extend them or put them together to draw inferences.

Advanced Plus   Sufficient comprehension to understand most factual information in non-technical prose as well as some discussions on concrete topics related to special interests. Able to read for information and description, to follow sequence of events, and to react to information read. Can separate main ideas from lesser ones and use that division to advance understanding. In major newspapers and magazines, can read international items and social and cultural news. Understanding of specialized items depends upon individual interests and background. At this level can read material in own areas of interest. Within literary fields of interest, can read non-esoteric prose, including critical articles and books. Can read signs, posters, advertisements, and public announcements. Can follow simple printed directions for cooking and other projects within areas of expertise. Guesses logically at new words by using linguistic and non-linguistic contexts and prior knowledge. Is able to comprehend most high-frequency idiomatic expressions, but will still have difficulty with figurative meanings. Even though the subjunctive and conditional are better recognized and understood, the reader still has difficulty in detecting subjective attitudes, values, and judgments in what is read.

Superior   Able to read standard newspaper items addressed to the general reader, routine correspondence reports, and technical material in a field of interest at a normal rate of speed (at least 220 WPM). Can gain new knowledge from material in a variety of publications on a wide range of unfamiliar topics related to fields of interest. Can interpret hypotheses, supported opinions, and documented facts, as well as figurative devices, stylistic differences, and humor. Can read most literary genres in the original: novels, essays, poetry, short stories, and most literature written for the general public. Reading ability is not subject dependent. Broad general vocabulary, knowledge of most structures, and development of strategies for logical guessing allow for successful interpretation of unfamiliar words, idioms, or structures. Verb tenses and moods have been largely mastered. Interpretation of the subjunctive and conditional forms and passive constructions in indirect discourse of formal writing is generally complete, and with few errors. Able to achieve overall comprehension of material, even though there may be some gaps in detail. Is generally able to comprehend facts, although misinterpretation may still occur. Can draw inferences, but may be unable to appreciate nuances or stylistics.

Novice — Low   No functional ability in writing German.

Novice — Mid   No practical communicative writing skills. Able to copy isolated words and short phrases. Able to transcribe previously studied words or phrases. Able to write name, address, dates and other numbers, as well as common expressions such as those used in greetings and leave-takings.

Novice — High   Able to write simple fixed expressions and limited memorized material. Can supply information when requested on forms such as hotel reservations and travel documents. Can write names, write out numbers from 1 to 20, dates (days of the week, months of the year), own nationality as well as other common adjectives of nationality, addresses, and other simple biographic information. Can write limited learned vocabulary for common objects, short phrases, and simple lists. Can write such expressions as *Guten Tag! Ich heiße . . . Wie geht es Dir? Wie geht es Ihnen?* and other fixed social formulae. Can name some common objects; knows some common adjectives and adverbs; can use the present tense of some common regular verbs, such as forms of the present tense of *haben* and *sein;* can write simple negative sentences using *nicht* (but often in wrong place) and interrogative sentences with words such as *wo, wie, warum, wann,* etc. Writes simple yes-no or information questions using limited memorized or very familiar sentence patterns, with frequent misspellings and inaccuracies. Usually forgets umlauts. Sometimes uses infinitives for conjugated verbs. Has a concept of gender, and can produce definite and indefinite articles, though often inappropriately. Often forgets to make adjectives agree with nouns. Generally cannot create own sentences in the language, but uses memorized material or transformations of familiar patterns.

Intermediate — Low   Has sufficient control of the writing system to meet limited practical needs. Can write short messages, such as simple questions or notes, postcards, phone messages, and the like. Can take simple notes on material dealing with very familiar topics within the scope of limited language experience. Can create statements or questions, in the present tense using negative and interrogative constructions, within the scope of limited language experience. Material produced consists of recombinations of learned vocabulary and structures into simple sentences. Can express present and future by using the present tense and adverbs of time such as *morgen, heute, nächste Woche, nächstes Jahr*. For example: *Ich schriebe heute eine Prüfung. Wir fahren nächste Woche nach Berlin*. Generally cannot express past time by past tenses, but may incorrectly use the present tense and an adverb of time such as *gestern, gestern abend, heute morgen* to convey past meaning. Awareness of gender apparent (many mistakes). Awareness of case system sketchy. Some correct use of predicate adjectives and personal pronouns (*ich, wir*). Vocabulary is limited to common objects and cognates, and is inadequate to express anything but elementary needs. Can express numbers from 1 to 100 with some misspellings. Often inserts native-language vocabulary for unknown words, and is generally not capable of circumlocution to get meaning across. Writing tends to be a loose collection of sentences or sentence fragments on very familiar topics (likes and dislikes, general routine, everyday events or situations). Makes continual errors in spelling (*ei* vs. *ie*, often omits umlauts), grammar (incorrect adjective endings, incorrect subject-verb agreement), and punctuation. Word order is random, but writing can be read and understood by a native reader used to dealing with foreigners. Able to produce appropriately some fundamental sociolinguistic distinctions in formal and familiar style (*Herr, Frau, Fräulein*), but no clear distinction between polite and familiar address forms (*Sie, du*), such as appropriate subject pronouns, titles of address, and basic social formulae.

Intermediate— Mid

Sufficient control of writing system to meet some survival needs and some limited social demands. Able to compose short paragraphs or take simple notes on very familiar topics grounded in personal experiences. Can discuss likes and dislikes, daily routines, give dates and times, discuss everyday events, describe immediate surroundings (home, work, school), narrate simple events, and the like. Can use correctly the present tense of most regular verbs and some common irregular verbs, such as *haben, sein, tun, wollen, können, wissen, verstehen*, and *möchten*, with occasional production errors. Can use *werden* plus infinitive to express future time. Has sporadic control of high-frequency verbs in the compound past but may not attend to correct auxiliary verb or past participle agreement. Can use definite, indefinite, and partitive articles, but often uses them inappropriately; usually gets cases wrong. Frequent errors in gender-adjective agreement and cases may occur. Shows some ability to use some determiners other than articles, such as possessive adjectives or interrogative adjectives, but may make errors in appropriate choice of form. Tends not to use object pronouns, relative constructions, or their cohesive elements of discourse, rendering the written style somewhat stilted and simplistic. Generally good control of basic constructions and inflections, such as subject-verb agreement, noun-adjective agreement, and straightforward syntactic constructions in present and future time. Grammatical accuracy in some structures solidifies, e.g., word order in simple statements (excluding adverbs), interrogative forms, and imperative of separable prefix verbs (*Kommen Sie mit!*). May make frequent errors when venturing beyond current level of linguistic competence (such as when expressing opinions or emotions, where non-memorized conditionals, subjunctives, and other advanced concepts of grammar may come into play). When resorting to a dictionary, often is unable to identify appropriate vocabulary, or uses dictionary entry in uninflected form.

Intermediate—
High

Sufficient control of writing system to meet most survival needs and limited social demands. Can take notes in some detail on familiar topics (autobiographical information, preferences, daily routine, simple descriptions and narration of everyday events and situations) and respond to personal questions on such topics using elementary vocabulary and common structures. Can write simple letters, brief synopses and paraphrases, summaries of biographical data and work experience, and short compositions on familiar topics. Can create sentences and short paragraphs relating to most survival needs (food, lodging, transportation, immediate surroundings and situations) and limited social demands. Can express fairly accurately present and future time, using the future and present tense of most common regular and irregular verbs, including reflexive verbs. Can use the compound past with both *haben* and *sein* auxiliaries, but does not always use it correctly or appropriately. Past tense is also attempted with common simple past forms (*sagte, hatte, war*). Several high-frequency separable prefix verbs appear in the indicative (*ich gehe mit*). There is inconsistent coding of proper dative and accusative cases following prepositions in singular and plural. Shows good control of elementary vocabulary and some control of basic syntactic patterns (some object pronouns and determiners, usually use of negative in past tenses and future with correct placement, etc.). Still has problems in inverted word order and in proper placement of time, place, and manner phrases. Major errors still occur when expressing more complex thoughts. Dictionary usage may still yield incorrect vocabulary or forms, although can use a dictionary to advantage to express simple ideas. Generally does not use basic cohesive elements of discourse to advantage (relative constructions, object pronouns, connectors, and the like). Writing, though faulty, is comprehensible to native speakers used to reading German written by non-natives. Is able to express a few thoughts for which vocabulary is unknown via circumlocution, but may insert native-language equivalents for unknown words or use native language syntactic patterns when expressing ideas beyond current level of linguistic competence.

Advanced

Able to write routine social correspondence and simple discourse of at least several paragraphs on familiar topics. Can write simple social correspondence, take notes, and write cohesive summaries, résumés, and short narratives and descriptions on factual topics. Able to write about everyday topics by using adjectives, with mostly correct gender and case. Genders of high-frequency words are mostly correct. Able to narrate events using present, compound past, some simple past, and future forms, although the contrast between uses of the two past tenses may not be consistently accurate. Occasional use of some subjunctive forms to express politeness and preference. Has sufficient writing vocabulary to express oneself simply with some circumlocutions. Can write about a very limited number of current events or daily situations and express personal preferences and observations in some detail using basic structures. Is able to recycle new but meaningful phrases whether lexical or structural, i.e., lifts phrases appropriately, writing appears more sophisticated. When writing own thoughts, is more likely to paraphrase according to native language at times. Controls many separable and reflexive verbs and double infinitive construction in main clauses. Good control of morphology in verb tenses; correct endings for regular and irregular verbs in tenses mentioned above. Often uses correct endings for adjectives. Controls frequently used structures such as interrogatives, negatives (but still not always correctly placed), prepositions with some rest/motion distinction but not always proper cases for the distinction, and choice of determiners (*der* vs. *ein*). Preposition use after verbs or adjectives is often inaccurate. Writing is understandable by a native speaker not used to reading German written by nonnatives. Writer uses a limited number of cohesive devices such as a single object pronoun (direct or indirect). Some use of relative pronouns to combine sentences and some common conjunctions are used (*denn, weil, wann, wo,* etc.). Mistakes in subordinate clause auxiliary verb placement and double infinitive order. Able to join sentences in limited discourse, but has difficulty and makes frequent errors producing complex sentences. Paragraphs are reasonably unified and coherent.

Advanced Plus

Shows ability to write about most common topics with precision and in some detail. Can write fairly detailed résumés and summaries and take accurate notes. Can handle most informal and business correspondence. Can describe and narrate personal experiences and explain simply point of view in prose discourse by using introductory phrases (e.g., *meiner Meinung nach, ich glaube, daß . . . , ich bin sicher, daß . . .*). Can write about concrete topics relating to particular interests and special fields of competence. Normally controls general vocabulary with circumlocution or modification where necessary, e.g., may use negation plus lexical item for an unknown antonym, or modify words with *sehr, viel,* etc., if a more specific term is unknown, or resort to a category label for unknown components. Often shows remarkable fluency or ease of expression, but under time constraints (e.g., no opportunity to rewrite) and pressure (e.g., testing), language may be inaccurate and/or incomprehensible, especially if important lexical items are missing or if inaccurate tense usage interferes with meaning. Generally strong in either grammar or vocabulary, but not in both. Weaknesses and unevenness in one of the foregoing or in spelling result in occasional miscommunication. Areas of weakness may involve detail in the use of simple constructions: irregular plurals of nouns, adjectives; determiners (usage rather than form); prepositions (after verbs or adjectives); negatives (still has problems with subtleties of placement and form, *nicht ein* vs. *kein*). Weaknesses are also observed in more complex structures: tense usage; compound past vs. simple past after *als;* avoidance where possible of *würde* in *wenn* clauses; passive constructions (rarely uses *man* or reflexive but tends to parallel English with consequent use of *sein*); statal and real passive confused; word order still a problem, sometimes with inversion, reflexive and auxiliary placement in dependent word order. Good control of simple dependent word order, subordinating and coordinating conjunctions (*denn* vs. *weil*), and relative pronouns. Irregular control of infinitive clauses with *zu.* Uses wide range of tenses as time indicators including hypothetical subjunctive (with *würde* plus infinitive, *hätte, wäre, könnte*). Uses *da(r)-* and *wo(r)-* compounds. Better control of prepositions, adjectives and case endings, but mistakes still occur. Some misuse of vocabulary still evident, especially when using dictionary for words with multiple meanings or where related words carry various functions, but does use a dictionary to advantage where a fairly direct bilingual translation and no intralingual ambiguity exist. Shows ability to use circumlocution. Writing is understandable to native speakers not used to reading material written by non-natives, though the style is still obviously foreign.

Superior   Able to use written German effectively in most formal and informal exchanges on practical, social, and professional topics. Can write most types of correspondence, such as memos, social and business letters (with appropriate formulaic introductions and closings), short research papers, and statements of position. Can express hypotheses and conjectures, and present arguments or points of view accurately and effectively. Can write about areas of special interest and handle topics in special fields. Has good control of a full range of structures so that time, description, and narration can be used to expand upon ideas. Errors in basic structures are sporadic and not indicative of communicative control. In addition to simple tenses, can use compound tenses to show time relationships among events and to express coordinate and subordinate ideas clearly and coherently. Has lexical control of subordinate conjunctions. Controls dependent word order with auxiliary and reflexive placement such as *ich weiß, daß er hatte gestern kommen sollen,* and *er sagte, daß sich der mann umzog.* Able to use quotative subjunctive (subjunctive I) consistently, as well as passives plus modals. Can use hypothetical subjunctive (subjunctive II) correctly, as well as directional adverbs (*hinauf, hinunter, herüber,* etc.) and the *lassen* construction. Has a wide enough vocabulary to convey the message accurately, though style may be foreign. Uses dictionary to a high degree of accuracy to supplement specialized vocabulary or to improve content or style. Although sensitive to differences in formal and informal style, still may not tailor writing precisely or accurately to a variety of audiences (except for personal vs. business correspondence) or styles.

PROVISIONAL GERMAN DESCRIPTIONS — CULTURE

Novice

Limited interaction. Behaves with considerateness. Is resourceful in nonverbal communication, but does not interpret reliably gestures or culturally specific behavior, such as physical contacts with greetings. Is limited in language (see listening/speaking guidelines) but may be able to use short phrases of courtesy (*Danke, Danke schön, Bitte, Bitte schön, Entschuldigung, Verzeihung*) and basic titles of respect (*Herr, Frau, Fräulein*). Lacks generally the knowledge of culture patterns requisite for survival situations.

Intermediate

Survival competence. Can deal with familiar survival situations and interact with a culture bearer accustomed to foreigners. Is able to use conventional phrases when being introduced, such as *Es freut mich* or *Sehr erfreut,* as well as proper greetings at different times of day, such as *Guten Tag, Guten Abend, Grüß Gott* (in Bavaria) and leave-taking, *Auf Wiedersehen, Bis bald.* Shows comprehension of distinction between *Sie* and *du* form of address. Can provide background material in the standard form of the culture, such as a personal address (street name followed by number — *Leopoldstraße 30,* zip code preceding name of city, zone within large city following name of city — *8000 Mün-*

chen 23) and telephone number (in many areas in groups of two—*23 23 67*). Is able to express wants in routine situations with simple phrases, such as *Ein Zimmer ohne Bad, bitte. Ein Bier, bitte. Wieviel kostete eine Postkarte nach U.S.A. per Luftpost?* and to ask directions such as *Wo ist hier die Schellingstraße?* Understands the need to go to specialty shops such as *die Metzergerei, die Bäckerei, die Konditorei* to buy certain foods but is also aware of the offerings in supermarkets and department stores. Is aware of the use of the metric system and can function in it, using such phrases as *Ein Kilo Orangen* and *200 Gramm Leberwurst*. Is aware of different meal schedules as well as the usual content of each: breakfast, light, without either warm cooked meats or eggs other than boiled; noon meal, the main meal of the day, heavy, but usually without a rich dessert; often, late in the afternoon, coffee and a pastry; evening meal, light, usually consisting of cold meats, salads, and cheese. Knows how to use public transportation systems, whether to buy a ticket from an automat, a ticket agent, or a conductor. Is generally aware that small tips are expected in addition to the tip and service charge that have been added to the bill in restaurants and cafes. Is generally aware that tips are expected in other service areas such as hotels and bars. May make errors as the result of misunderstanding or misapplying assumptions about the culture, such as not tipping a gas station attendant or arriving too early for a dinner invitation.

Advanced

Limited social competence. Handles routine situations successfully with a culture bearer accustomed to foreigners. Though home culture predominates, shows comprehension of common rules of etiquette, of titles of respect, of importance of dressing according to the occasion in more formal society. Is aware of taboos and sensitive areas of the culture and avoids them. Shows comprehension of guest etiquette, such as bringing the hostess a small gift (chocolates or flowers), keeping both hands on the table while dining, holding the knife in the right hand, understanding that the kitchen is off-limits unless invited, offering food and cigarettes to others before taking them oneself. Knows how to use the phrases commonly used at table, such as *Guten Appetit;* and while drinking, such as *Zum Wohl* and *Prosit*. Is aware of gifts as expression of friendship, personal esteem, or gratitude. Knows appropriate gift for various occasions; knows the basic guidelines for presenting flowers. Knows how to accept gifts graciously. Knows conventional phrases for accepting invitations, such as *Sehr gern,* as well as for refusing them, such as *Vielen Dank für die Einladung, aber ich kann leider nicht kommen*. Knows how to apologize with such phrases as *Pardon; Entschuldigen Sie, bitte, vielmals;* or *Das tut mir furchtbar leid*. Can make introductions and can introduce self in both informal and formal situations. Knows how to use the telephone. Answers by giving the last name, calls by saying *Hier ist* . . . Knows how to ask for a third party: *Ich möchte, bitte,* . . . *sprechen.* Knows how to leave a message: *Könnten Sie, bitte,* . . . *ausrichten, daß* . . . Is able to shop in both large and small stores and to ask for specific items, using such expressions as *Ich hätte gern ein Sporthemd, Größe 38. Der Schnitt gefällt mir schon, aber die Farbe nicht. Haben Sie vielleicht etwas in einer niedrigeren Preislage?* Is able to do routine banking, using such phrases as *Ich möchte, bitte, Dollarreiseschecks in DM wechseln. Wie steht der Dollar heute? Ich möchte, bitte, einzahlen. Ich möchte, bitte, abheben. Ich möchte, bitte, ein Scheck einlösen.* Knows how to handle routine business at the post office, including telephone and monetary service provided there, using such phrases as *Geben Sie mir zehn Neunziger, bitte. Einschreiben, bitte. Ich möchte ein Personengespräch mit Herrn Bianco in Italien führen. Ich möchte bitte Geld überweisen.* Is not competent to take part in a formal meeting or in a group where several persons are speaking informally at the same time.

Superior   Working social and professional competence. Can participate in almost all social situations and those within one vocation. Handles unfamiliar situations with ease and sensitivity, including some involving common taboos, or some that are otherwise emotionally charged. Comprehends most non-verbal responses. Laughs at some culture-related humor, such as imitation of substandard speech, imitation of foreign accents, and references to stereotypes within the culture. In productive skills, neither culture dominates, nevertheless makes appropriate use of cultural references and expressions, such as colloquial phrases (*gottseidank, Mein Gott*) and idiomatic phrases (*Er hat sie nicht alle. Ich drücke dir die Daumen.*). Understands more colloquial and idiomatic phrases than can use, such as *Gute Miene zum bösen Spiel machen* and *Der langen Rede kurzer Sinn.* Generally able to distinguish between formal and informal registers of speech, such as *Ich war wie aus den Wolken gefallen* vs. *Mir blieb die spucke weg.* Uses titles of respect correctly. Discusses abstract ideas relating to foreign and native culture and is aware of areas of difference. Has some awareness and understanding of typical German characteristics and expressions such as *Gemütlichkeit, Wanderlust, Sehnsucht, ein schönes Gesprach* vs. small talk. Has some understanding of the role that German history, literature, folklore, and music play in the everyday life and attitudes of the people. Is aware of differing attitudes toward religion and the church in various parts of German-speaking areas. Is aware of various social classes and of the feelings of members of a given social class toward members of other social classes. Can discuss current events as well as fields of personal interest and can support opinions, but is generally limited in handling abstractions. Is aware that people do not generally accept criticism of their country from foreigners although they may be quite free to criticize aspects of their own country themselves. Minor inaccuracies occur in perception of meaning and in the expression of the intended representation but do not result in serious misunderstandings, even by a culture bearer unaccustomed to foreigners.

Near-Native
Competence

Full social and professional competence. Has internalized the concept that culture is relative and is always on the lookout to do the appropriate thing; no longer assumes that own culture is "the way it is." Fits behavior to audience. Can counsel, persuade, negotiate, represent a point of view, describe and compare features of the native and target cultures. In such comparisons, can discuss geography, history, institutions, customs and behavior patterns, current events and national policies. Perceives almost all unverbalized responses (gestures, emotional reaction) and recognizes almost all allusions, including historical (*Der alte Fritz* or *Der Lotse geht von Bord*) and literary commonplaces (*die Gretchenfrage; Es irrt der Mensch, solang er strebt*). Laughs at most culture-related humor, such as imitations of regional dialects and allusions to popular figures in public life and in the media. Uses low-frequency idiomatic expressions (*Das geht auf keine Kuhhaut*), sayings (*Er säuft wie ein Besenbinder*), and proverbs (*Was Hänschen nicht lernt, lernt Hans nimmermehr*). Controls formal and informal register of the language. Knows when and how to offer the *du* form of address and understands the implications of doing so. Has lived in the culture for a long time and has studied it extensively. Is inferior to the culture bearer only in background information related to the culture such as childhood experiences, detailed regional geography, and past events of significance.

Native
Competence

Native competence. Examinee is indistinguishable from a person raised and educated in the culture.

Notes

Abbreviations used in notes and bibliography

AATG	American Association of Teachers of German
ACTFL	American Council on the Teaching of Foreign Languages (Hastings-on-Hudson, New York)
ADFL	*Bulletin of the Association of Departments of Foreign Languages* (MLA, New York)
AFLT	*American Foreign Language Teacher* (Detroit, Michigan)
ESL	English as a Second Language
ETS	Educational Testing Services (Princeton, New Jersey)
FLA	*Foreign Language Annals* (ACTFL)
IJAL	*International Journal of American Linguistics*
IRAL	*International Review of Applied Linguistics*
LL	*Language Learning* (University of Michigan, Ann Arbor)
LTLA	*Language Teaching and Linguistics:* Abstracts (Cambridge University Press) now called *Language Teaching: The International Abstracting Journal for Language Teachers and Applied Linguists*
MLA	Modern Language Association
MLJ	*Modern Language Journal* (National Federation of Modern Language Teachers' Associations)
NEC	Reports of the Working Committees of the Northeast Conference on the Teaching of Foreign Languages
TQ	*TESOL Quarterly* (Teachers of English to Speakers of Other Languages)
UP	*Unterrichtspraxis* (American Association of Teachers of German)

365

I Communicating

1. The terms "skill-getting" and "skill-using" have been borrowed from Don H. Parker, "When Should I Individualize Instruction?" in Virgil M. Howes, ed., *Individualization of Instruction: A Teaching Strategy* (New York: Macmillan, 1970), p. 176.

2. The rationale for interaction activities of this type is set out in "Talking Off the Tops of Their Heads," in Wilga M. Rivers, *Communicating Naturally in a Second Language* (Cambridge, Eng.: Cambridge University Press, 1983a), pp. 41–53.

1. STRUCTURED INTERACTION

1. How this can be done is discussed fully in W. M. Rivers, "Bridging the Gap to Autonomous Interaction," in W. M. Rivers (1983a), pp. 55–64.

2. In *Lange Schatten* (Hamburg: Claasen, 1960), p. 144.

3. *Phonetik der deutschen Sprache* (Munich: Hueber, 1961), pp. 230–47.

4. In *Ein Bündel weißer Narzissen* (Frankfurt am Main: Fischer, 1956), p. 163.

5. Wahrig, *Deutsches Wörterbuch,* special ed. (Gütersloh: Bertelsmann, 1968). A more extensive work (as yet unfinished) which indicates a broad range of language levels in its definitions is the *Wörterbuch der deutschen Gegenwartssprache,* compiled by Ruth Klappenbach and Wolfgang Steinitz (Berlin: Akademie Verlag, 1964ff). The *Duden Grammatik der deutschen Gegenwartssprache,* ed. Paul Grebe, 2d ed., Der Große Duden, vol. 4 (Mannheim: Bibliographisches Institut des Duden-verlags, 1966) provides some scattered notes on colloquial syntax, but German grammars in general tend to emphasize the structures of the written *Hochsprache* rather than those of the spoken language.

6. M. Joos, *The Five Clocks* (New York: Harcourt, Brace and World, 1961). For a more detailed analysis of the conversational register from the point of view of Transactional Engineering Analysis, see L. Jakobovits and B. Gordon, *The Context of Foreign Language Teaching* (Rowley, Mass.: Newbury House, 1974), Chapter 3.

7. In *Eine Rechnung, die nicht aufgeht. Erzählungen.* (Freiburg in Breisgau: Walter-Verlag, 1958), pp. 37–38.

8. John R. Searle, *Speech Acts: An Essay in the Philosophy of Language* (Cambridge, Eng.: Cambridge University Press, 1969), p. 16.

9. Ibid.

10. "Semantics plays a central role in syntax," George Lakoff in "On Generative Semantics," in D. D. Steinberg and L. A. Jakobovits, eds., *Semantics* (Cambridge, Eng.: Cambridge University Press, 1971), p. 232, footnote *a*.

11. Discussed more fully in W. M. Rivers, *Teaching Foreign-Language Skills.* 2d ed. (Chicago: The University of Chicago Press, 1981), p. 95.

12. C. Gattegno, *Teaching Foreign Languages in Schools: The Silent Way* (Reading, Eng.: Educational Explorers Ltd., 1963). The Silent Way is described in more detail in two articles in *ADFL* 5 (1973–74): C. Dominice, "The Silent Way: A Student Looks at Teaching" (pp. 23–24), and C. Perrault, "The Silent Way: An Experienced User Speaks" (pp. 25–26).

13. Ibid., p. 39.

14. Ibid., p. 21.

15. Ibid., p. 40.

16. Ibid., p. 24.

17. The Gouin series is described in detail, with class procedure, in R. Titone, *Teaching Foreign Languages. An Historical Sketch* (Washington, D.C.: Georgetown University Press, 1968), pp. 33–37. A similar approach to the beginning stages was taken by M. D. Berlitz, the founder of the Berlitz schools.

18. This has a contemporary ring. The Berkeley linguist Wallace Chafe considers the verb to be central in semantics. In *Meaning and the Structure of Language* (Chicago: The University of Chicago Press, 1970) he suggests as "a general principle that semantic influence radiates from a verb" (p. 190) and in his work he considers the verb central and the noun peripheral (p. 96). This quotation is from François Gouin, *The Art of Teaching and Studying Languages,* trans. H. Swan and V. Bétis, (London: George Philip and Son; New York: Charles Scribner's Sons, 1892), p. 131.

19. Gouin, *Art of Teaching*, p. 162.

20. Ibid., p. 173.

21. The use of the *Sie* or *du* form in this case will depend on the age of the students and the approach the teacher has decided to take to this aspect of the language. Many teachers use *Sie* to older students and expect *siezen* in return, while encouraging students to use *du* to each other. In this way students have regular practice in switching from one to the other.

22. See J. J. Asher, "The Learning Strategy of the Total Physical Response: A Review," *MLJ* 50 (1966), 79–84. Asher claims that the association of action and sound results in longer retention, at least for listening comprehension.

23. Developed by the Institute of Modern Languages in Washington, D.C., and described in John Schumann, "Communication Techniques," *TQ* 6 (1972), 143–46.

24. E. B. de Sauzé's approach is described in *The Cleveland Plan for the Teaching of Modern Languages with Special Reference to French* (Philadelphia: The John C. Winston Company, 1929). Ralph Hester, ed., in *Teaching a Living Language* (New York: Harper and Row, 1970), p. x, claims that the verbal-active method, a "rationalist direct method," derives from de Sauzé. Franz J. Pfister acknowledges the influence of the ideas of Yvone Lenard, herself a follower of Emile de Sauzé, on his textbook *Deutsch durch Deutsch. Eine Moderne Sprachlehre* (New York: Harper and Row, 1968).

25. Y. Lenard, "Methods and Materials, Techniques and the Teacher," in Hester, ed., *Teaching a Living Language,* p. 37.

26. Karl C. Diller, "Linguistic Theories of Language Acquisition," in Hester, ed., *Teaching a Living Language,* pp. 16–17, 18; and also K. C. Diller, *Generative Grammar, Structural Linguistics, and Language Teaching* (Rowley, Mass.: Newbury House, 1971), pp. 25, 27.

27. Lenard in Hester, ed., *Teaching a Living Language,* p. 36.

28. Ibid., p. 50.

29. Ibid., p. 55.

30. Pfister, *Deutsch durch Deutsch,* pp. 170–71.

31. L. G. Kelly in *25 Centuries of Language Teaching* (Rowley, Mass.: Newbury House, 1969), p. 120, traces the use of the dialogue in foreign-language teaching back to the *colloquium* of the Middle Ages.

32. In a description of direct method techniques in *Méthodologie des langues vivantes* (Paris: Armand Colin, 1921, originally published 1902), C. Schweitzer and E. Simonnot refer to the dramatized dialogue as recreational (pp. 242–43).

33. Dialogue in Lesson 5 of W. P. Lehmann, Thomas J. O'Hare, and Christoph Cobet, *German: Language and Culture* (New York: Holt, Rinehart and Winston, 1972), p. 65.

34. There seems to be a misconception among some foreign-language teachers that only learning grammar rules and working deductively and analytically can be called "cognitive." Actually, from the point of view of cognitive psychology any process which requires students to think, to extract meaning from any symbolic behavior (action, strange utterance, pictorial representation), to work out generalizations from examples or instances (induction), is a cognitive operation. See "The Second Language Teacher and Cognitive Psychology," in Rivers (1983b), pp. 86–102.

35. Earl W. Stevick of the Foreign Service Institute, Washington, D.C., originated the "microwave cycle" which he described in "UHF and Microwaves in Transmitting Language Skills," in E. W. Najam and Carleton T. Hodge, eds., *Language Learning: The Individual and the Process, IJAL* 32, 1, Part 2 (1966), Publication 40 of the Indiana University Research Center in Anthropology, Folklore, and Linguistics, pp. 84–94. In *Adapting and Writing Language Lessons* (Washington, D.C.: Foreign Service Institute, 1971), pp. 310–15, Stevick explains that he developed this device from the question-answer technique of Thomas F. Cummings in *How to Learn a Language* (New York: privately published, 1916), and that he now prefers the term "Cummings device." The device has been used with good results in Peace Corps and Foreign Service Institute materials in a variety of languages. Chapter 6 and Appendices P, Q, and R of Stevick (1971) give detailed examples of the device in languages as diverse as English, French, Lao, Bini, Kikuyu, and Ponapean.

36. Stevick, *Adapting and Writing,* p. 311.

37. Ibid., pp. 312–13.

38. Stevick, "UHF and Microwaves," p. 92.

39. Stevick, *Adapting and Writing,* p. 314.

40. Ibid., p. 37.

41. Lenard in Hester, ed., *Teaching a Living Language,* p. 50, says "There should be [an oral composition] for every lesson, to be followed the next day by a written one. The oral composition becomes, in fact, the most important exercise of the verbal-active method in building the elements of which fluency is composed: the ability to speak at length, aloud, clearly and confidently, in front of other people, and to use the words and structures that you know freely and correctly in order to say what you mean."

42. This is a German rendition of Lenard's words. Ibid., p. 50.

43. Ibid., p. 56.

44. Francis A. Cartier reports that a team of programmers under his direction

at the Defense Language Institute English Language Branch has developed a series of situational conversations on tape along these lines for individual learning and practice. These tapes seek to elicit certain structures. It was found that students experienced a definite feeling of rapport with the speakers and would work through the tapes several times to try to improve their efforts.

2. AUTONOMOUS INTERACTION

1. Rivers (1981), p. 239.
2. Emma M. Birkmaier, "The Meaning of Creativity in Foreign Language Teaching," *MLJ* 55 (1971), p. 350.
3. Abraham H. Maslow, *Motivation and Personality,* 2d ed. (New York: Harper and Row, 1970), Chapter 4: "A Theory of Human Motivation" sets out this hierarchy. Its importance in communication in the foreign-language classroom is discussed in Earl W. Stevick, "Before Linguistics and Beneath Method," in Kurt Jankowsky, ed., *Language and International Studies,* Georgetown University Round Table on Languages and Linguistics 1973 (Washington, D.C.: Georgetown University Press, 1973), pp. 99–106.
4. Christina Bratt Paulston and Howard R. Selekman, "Interaction Activities in the Foreign Language Classroom or How to Grow a Tulip-Rose," to appear in *FLA* 9 (1976), pp. 248–54.
5. Paulston and Selekman, "Interaction Activities," tell of the shock and disappointment experienced by one of his students when he discovered that the ostensibly monolingual person to whom he was speaking spoke perfect English.
6. Described fully in Paulston and Selekman, "Interaction Activities."
7. Alexander Lipson, "Some New Strategies for Teaching Oral Skills," in Robert C. Lugton, ed., *Toward a Cognitive Approach to Second Language Acquisition* (Philadelphia: Center for Curriculum Development, 1971), pp. 231–44.
8. Paulston and Selekman, "Interaction Activities."
9. Lipson, "Some New Strategies," p. 240.
10. Stevick, *Adapting and Writing,* pp. 365–90.
11. The passage, which is taken from the transcription of a taped interview with a Rhine river pilot, has been simplified with regard to punctuation. Printed in *Texte gesprochener deutscher Standardsprache I,* erarbeitet im Institut für deutsche Sprache Forschungsstelle Freiburg i. Br., Heutiges Deutsch, Series II, vol. I (Munich: Hueber; Düsseldorf: Schwann, 1971), pp. 122–23.
12. Stevick, "Before Linguistics," p. 100.
13. Ibid.

3. LISTENING

1. P. T. Rankin, "Listening Ability: Its Importance, Measurement, and Development," *Chicago Schools Journal* 12, pp. 177–79, quoted in D. Spearritt, *Listening Comprehension—A Factorial Analysis* (Melbourne: Australian Council for Educational Research, 1962), p. 2.
2. Spearritt, *Listening Comprehension,* pp. 92–93. Spearritt adds "There is some evidence that performance on listening comprehension tests is related to

performance on inductive reasoning, verbal comprehension and certain types of memory tests.''

3. R. E. Troike, "Receptive Competence, Productive Competence, and Performance," in J. E. Alatis, ed., *Linguistics and the Teaching of Standard English to Speakers of Other Languages or Dialects,* Report of the Twentieth Annual Round Table Meeting on Linguistics and Language Studies, Monograph No. 22 (Washington, D.C.: Georgetown University Press, 1969), pp. 63–73.

4. See T. Bever, "The Cognitive Basis for Linguistic Structures," in J. R. Hayes, ed., *Cognition and the Development of Language* (New York: John Wiley and Sons, 1970), and "Linguistic and Psychological Factors in Speech Perception and Their Implications for Listening and Reading Materials," in Rivers (1983b), pp. 78–90.

5. These two levels, the recognition and selection levels, are discussed fully in relation to listening comprehension in Rivers, *Teaching Foreign-Language Skills* (1981), pp. 168–72.

6. N. Chomsky in *Aspects of the Theory of Syntax* (Cambridge, Mass.: The MIT Press, 1965), p. 9, says that "a generative grammar is not a model for a speaker or a hearer. It attempts to characterize in the most neutral possible terms the knowledge of the language that provides the basis for actual use of language by a speaker-hearer."

7. For some perceptual strategies, see Bever, in Hayes, ed., *Cognition and Development,* pp. 287–312.

8. Colin Cherry, *On Human Communication: A Review, A Survey, and A Criticism,* 3d ed. (Cambridge, Mass.: MIT Press, 1978), p. 279.

9. Ibid.

10. *Texte gesprochener deutscher Standardsprache I,* vol. 1, pp. 83–84.

11. The system for transcription employed in *Texte gesprochener deutscher Standardsprache* has been simplified here. A sentence or syntactic unit is defined as a sequence of words which are governed by a finite verb and in which a subject is generally required. See Karl-Heinz Bausch, "Zur Umschrift gesprochener Hochsprache," *Texte,* vol. 1, p. 36.

12. For a detailed discussion of hearing as a stochastic process, that is, based on expectations, see Charles F. Hockett, "Grammar for the Hearer," in R. Jakobson, ed., *On the Structure of Language and its Mathematical Aspects* (Providence, R.I.: American Mathematical Society, 1961), pp. 220–36.

13. For a survey of work in this area, see Jerald R. Green, "A Focus Report: Kinesics in the Foreign-Language Classroom," *FLA* 5 (1971–72), pp. 62–68.

14. For a discussion of some aspects of student unrest in Berlin see Harold von Hofe, *Im Wandel der Jahre,* 5th ed. (New York: Holt, Rinehart and Winston, 1974).

15. *Duden Grammatik,* no. 980, p. 119. Explanations of many nuances of syntax which help with interpretation can usually be found easily in this book because of its detailed index.

16. *Deutsche Welle* broadcast, February 12, 1974.

17. Most geographical names can be located in *Siebs Deutsche Aussprache: Reine und gemäßigte Hochlautung mit Aussprachewörterbuch,* ed. H. de Boor, H. Moser, C. Winkler, 19th ed. (Berlin: de Gruyter, 1969). Proper names are

usually pronounced according to the usual German sound-symbol correspondences, but the teacher should listen to the news broadcasts first and prepare the students for idiosyncrasies.

18. *Deutsche Welle* broadcast, January 24, 1974.

19. A detailed description of these stages is given in Rivers (1983b), pp. 81–84. See also U. Neisser, *Cognitive Psychology* (New York: Appleton-Century-Crofts, 1967), Chapter 7: Speech Perception.

20. Asher, "The Learning Strategy," pp. 79–80.

21. Ibid., pp. 80–82.

22. G. A. Miller's term in "The Magical Number Seven, Plus or Minus Two: Some Limits on Our Capacity for Processing Information," *Psychological Review* 63 (1956), pp. 81–96. Reprinted in G. A. Miller, *The Psychology of Communication: Seven Essays* (New York: Basic Books, 1967).

23. The pros and cons of the backward buildup technique are discussed in detail in Rivers (1981), p. 204.

24. Other structural features which students should learn to recognize rapidly are listed in Rivers (1983b), p. 87.

25. Processes involved in fluent reading are compared with processes of listening in Rivers (1983b), pp. 88–90.

26. From Robin T. Hammond, *Fortbildung in der deutschen Sprache,* transcriptions (Oxford: Oxford University Press, 1972), pp. 18–19.

27. This example is from Manfred Bierwisch, *Grammatik des deutschen Verbs,* Studia grammatica II, 7th ed. (Berlin: Akademie Verlag, 1971), pp. 16–17.

28. The information in this paragraph and the quotation are from "Research in Listening Comprehension," by Andrew Wilkinson, *Educational Research* 12 (1970), pp. 140–41.

29. The text as presented here was adapted from *Texte gesprochener deutscher Standardsprache I* by K. Braun, "Probleme der Verschriftlichung gesprochener Texte als Basis für deren Verwendung im Fremdsprachenunterricht," *Forschungen zur gesprochenen Sprache und Möglichkeiten ihrer Didaktisierung,* ed. Goethe-Institut (Munich, 1971), pp. 261–63.

30. Bever in Hayes, ed., *Cognition and Development,* p. 291.

31. This is basic to the controversy between the transformational-generative grammarians who support the standard theory and the generative semanticists. Chomsky has stated that "there must be, represented in the mind, a fixed system of generative principles that characterize and associate deep and surface structures in some definite way—a grammar, in other words, that is used in some fashion as discourse is produced or interpreted" (*Language and Mind,* 1st ed., 1968, p. 16). According to G. Lakoff, "the theory of generative semantics claims that the linguistic elements used in grammar have an independent natural basis in the human conceptual system. . . . Generative semantics takes grammar as being based on the independently given natural logical categories, . . . and on natural logical classes. . . ." (from "The Arbitrary Basis of Transformational Grammar," in *Language* 48 (1972): 77–78).

32. These are basic to Charles Fillmore's Case Grammar. Fillmore adds other functions such as instrument and experiencer.

33. Bever in Hayes, ed., *Cognition and Development,* pp. 286–99. The

strategies are described as follows: Strategy A p. 290, Strategy B p. 294, Strategy C p. 296, Strategy D p. 298.

34. In transformational-generative grammar each clause is considered a sentence and assigned the symbol S.

35. I. M. Schlesinger, *Sentence Structure and the Reading Process* (The Hague: Mouton, 1968), pp. 122–41.

36. *Deutsche Welle* broadcast, January 21, 1974.

37. For advanced level, see T. B. Kalivoda, "Developing Advanced Listening Comprehension Skill in a Foreign Language: Problems and Possibilities," *Hispania* 64 (1981): 80–85.

38. Short-term retention, as used in this chart, is not synonymous with short-term memory. Echoic memory is useful for only a few seconds, during which the listener still has recourse to the raw data. Active verbal memory (immediate memory or short-term memory) can hold from five to nine cognitive chunks (e.g., short phrases or groups of digits) created by the listener. This material is then recoded for storage in long-term memory. The expression "short-term retention," as used in this chart, is a pragmatic one, referring to the short interval that elapses before what the student has heard is put to some active use. Students are not expected to hold the material in their memory for use at a later stage, as they are for the long-term retention of Stage D.

39. *Geheime Mission* (St. Paul, Minn.: EMC Corporation) is described as "a suspense thriller in 25 episodes." Recorded by professional actors, this tape program maintains the interest of the students by involving them in an intrigue between Austrian and German cosmetic firms. More material along these lines for German would be useful.

40. A similar technique is described and discussed by S. Belasco in "C'est la Guerre? or Can Cognition and Verbal Behavior Co-exist in Second-Language Learning," in R. C. Lugton, ed., *Toward a Cognitive Approach,* pp. 191–230. In Belasco's approach, the student is provided from the beginning with a text with visual hints to deviations from standard style of language. Here, at the advanced level, we suggest a purely listening and writing task.

4. ORAL PRACTICE FOR THE LEARNING OF GRAMMAR

1. These five possibilities are not an exhaustive list of uses of the dative, but five common uses to which the student is usually introduced in early lessons.

2. The use of substitution tables has been traced back to Erasmus in the sixteenth century. See L. Kelly, *25 Centuries,* p. 101. Harold Palmer gives examples of substitution tables and advocates their use in *The Scientific Study and Teaching of Languages* (London: Harrap, 1917).

3. An interesting analysis of drills into mechanical, meaningful, and communication categories is made in C. B. Paulston, "The Sequencing of Structural Pattern Drills," *TQ* 5 (1971), pp. 197–208. The subject is also discussed in "Talking Off the Tops of Their Heads," in Rivers (1983b), pp. 41–53.

4. The concept of Type A and Type B exercises is developed more fully in W. M. Rivers, "Bridging the Gap to Autonomous Production," in Rivers (1983a), pp. 55–64.

5. The observations made here are derived from Ulrich Engel's analysis of rules for word order, "Regeln zur 'Satzgliedfolge': Zur Stellung der Elemente im einfachen Verbalsatz," *Linguistische Studien I,* Sprache der Gegenwart XIX (Düsseldorf: Päd. Verlag Schwann, 1972), pp. 17–75.

6. News value refers to the principle for ordering elements in the middle field of the sentence. Items of more informational value tend to move towards the end of the middle field. If the speaker wants to give a particular element greater stress, that unit of the sentence will be shifted from its basic position towards the end of the middle field. For further discussion of informational value and word order see Herbert Lederer, *Reference Grammar of the German Language* (New York: Charles Scribner's Sons, 1969), pp. 571–85, and Walter F. W. Lohnes and F. W. Strothmann, *German, A Structural Approach,* 2d ed., (New York: Norton, 1973), pp. 98–100.

5. TEACHING THE SOUND SYSTEM

1. It is presumed that most trainee teachers and practicing teachers have at some time studied the German sound system. This very sketchy introduction to terminology is included for the benefit of the occasional student to whom it is new. It is customary to use square brackets [k] for phonetic representations (emphasizing as many features as possible of any given sound) and slashes /k/ for phonemic representations (emphasizing the distinctive features of a sound within one particular sound system).

2. For further information on this subject, see S. A. Schane, *Generative Phonology* (Englewood Cliffs, N. J.: Prentice-Hall, 1973).

3. The nineteenth edition of *Siebs Deutsche Aussprache* (1969) includes comments on *gemäßigte Hochlautung.* The controversies surrounding the separate vowels and consonants are briefly outlined by H. Penzl in "Zu Problemen der neuhochdeutschen Phonologie," *Jahrbuch für Internationale Germanistik* IV, 1 (1972), pp. 9–17.

4. Even before the revised *Siebs* (1969), the *Duden Grammatik der deutschen Gegenwartssprache,* pp. 38–63, compared sound features that vary on three levels: *Hochlautung, gemäßigte Hochlautung,* and *Nichthochlautung.*

5. For a short summary of dialect peculiarities see *Siebs* (1969), pp. 145–48. Teachers who are interested in detailed information on dialects and texts which could be recorded for presentation in class should consult R. E. Keller, *German Dialects. Phonology and Morphology with Selected Texts* (Manchester: Manchester University Press, 1961).

6. P. Delattre, *Comparing the Phonetic Features of English, French, German and Spanish* (London: Harrap, 1965), p. 55–56. For students who have not completed a course in German phonetics, the terms used by Delattre in this quotation may seem mysterious. Such students would do well to acquire clear explanatory texts like W. Moulton, *The Sounds of English and German* (Chicago and London: The University of Chicago Press, 1962), and H.-H. Wängler, *Instruction in German Pronunciation,* 3rd ed. (St. Paul, Minn.: EMC Corporation, 1972) as teaching references. An explanation of the terms in German is contained in H.-H. Wängler, *Grundriß einer Phonetik des Deutschen. Mit einer*

allgemeinen Einführung in die Phonetik, 2d ed. (Marburg: Elwert, 1967). The expressions *high-low* refer to the highest position of the tongue-hump during articulation and are visually approximated by their position on a vowel triangle or quadrilateral. The higher a vowel the more *geschlossen* (*close*) it is, and the lower it is the more *offen* (*open*) it is. Students should also know the *front-back* (*hinteres-vorderes*) and *rounded-unrounded* (*gerundet-nicht gerundet*) distinctions. In addition to the works just mentioned, instructors are referred to Delattre, *Comparing the Phonetic Features,* p. 47, for further information. They will also find useful the comparative charts of the vowel systems of English, French, German, and Spanish in Delattre, *Comparing the Phonetic Features,* pp. 50–51.

7. Teachers will find clearly presented articulatory information, with diagrams and exercises, in Wängler, *Instruction in German Pronunciation.* Tapes are available.

8. Sometimes a student will succeed in making the correct sound in a somewhat different way, but most students will need the teacher's help and will profit from precise instructions.

9. C. H. Prator, Jr., *Manual of American English Pronunciation,* rev. ed. (New York: Holt, Rinehart and Winston, 1957), p. 83.

10. L. E. Armstrong, *The Phonetics of French* (London: Bell, 1959), p. 110. First published 1932.

11. Wängler, *Grundriß einer Phonetik des Deutschen,* p. 89.

12. Moulton, *The Sounds of English and German,* p. 37.

13. The tense/lax feature as well as the short/long feature is discussed in Moulton, *The Sounds of English and German,* pp. 61–64.

14. Stress was touched upon in Chapter 1, and is treated by Moulton, *The Sounds of English and German,* pp. 113–28. *Intonation,* which generally does not cause students severe problems, is not dealt with here. The work by Otto von Essen, *Grundzüge der hochdeutschen Satzintonation* (Ratingen bei Düsseldorf: Henn, 1956) is limited because it is based on literary rather than spoken models. The subject is discussed in a comparative context by Moulton, *The Sounds of English and German,* pp. 129–38. Correct intonation is best taught early through imitation of the teacher or tape model. Exercises for both stress and intonation are provided by H.-H. Wängler, *Patterns in German Stress and Intonation* (St. Paul, Minn.: EMC Corporation, 1966). Tapes available.

15. Discussed in Chapter 6.

16. Juncture and glottal stops are outlined by Moulton, *The Sounds of English and German,* pp. 139–45. See also *Siebs* (1969), pp. 51–52.

17. Used in C. Martens and P. Martens, *Phonetik der deutschen Sprache* (Munich: Hueber, 1961), pp. 145, 198.

II *The Written Word*
6. READING I: PURPOSES AND PROCEDURES

1. More research is needed to determine which basic grammatical relations in German are essential to enable a person to read German with comprehension.

2. J. McGlathery describes such a course in "A New Program of Substitute and Supplementary German Language Courses," in W. M. Rivers, L. H. Allen, et al., eds., *Changing Patterns in Foreign Language Programs* (Rowley, Mass.: Newbury House, 1972), pp. 248–53.

3. For detailed information on the formation of compounds see Joseph B. Voyles, "German Noun and Adjective Compounds," *LL* XVII (1967), pp. 9–19.

4. Carl Hammer provides a useful discussion on teaching cognate recognition in "Stress the German-English Cognates!" *MLJ* 41 (1957), pp. 177–82.

5. From Viola Herms Drath and Otto G. Graf, *Typisch Deutsch?* (New York, Toronto, London: Holt, Rinehart and Winston, 1969), p. 63.

6. Some students are able to reach this stage more rapidly through the experience of living for a time in a German community — unfortunately many are not.

7. By Heinz Held in *Westermanns Monatshefte,* August, 1973, p. 24.

8. The methods of establishing the frequency lists of *Grunddeutsch* are described by Pfeffer in the introductions to the *Grundstufe* and the *Mittelstufe.*

9. Kaeding's work was originally to be used for the development of a new system of shorthand notation. The fields from which the words were derived are listed on page vii of Morgan, *German Frequency Word Book.*

10. The expansion of the list to include derivatives from one stem is intended to help students become familiar with the German system of "word families."

11. In *Kindergeschichten* (Neuwied and Berlin: Luchterhand, 1969), pp. 21–22.

12. N. Brooks, *Language and Language Learning. Theory and Practice,* 2d ed. (New York: Harcourt, Brace and World, 1964), pp. 120–25.

13. This concept is explained more fully in the article, "Linguistic and Psychological Factors in Speech Perception with Their Implications for Listening and Reading Materials," in Rivers (1983b), pp. 78–90.

14. Helmut Rehder, Ursula Thomas, and Freeman Twaddell, *Verstehen und Sprechen,* rev. ed. (New York: Holt, Rinehart and Winston, 1970), p. 18.

15. Edda Weiß, *Deutsch: Entdecken wir es!* (New York: McGraw-Hill, 1973), pp. 2–4.

16. Rehder, Thomas, and Twaddell, *Verstehen und Sprechen,* p. 40.

17. Weiß, *Deutsch: Entdecken wir es!,* p. 95.

18. Bichsel, *Kindergeschichten,* pp. 26–27.

19. George Winkler, Alfred Hayes, Betty Robertson, Pierre Capretz, and Nelson Brooks, *A-LM German. Level One,* 2d ed. (New York: Harcourt Brace Jovanovich, 1974), p. 109.

20. In *Sagen Sie nicht: beim Geld hört der Spaß auf* (Zürich: Benziger, 1971), p. 35.

21. As in the reading method described in Rivers (1981), pp. 35–38.

22. Kimberly Sparks and Edith Reichmann, *So ist es! A Contemporary Reader* (New York: Harcourt Brace Jovanovich, 1972), pp. 28–29.

23. *Lektüre. A-LM 2,* ed. Cecilie Raht Courtright and Gisela Triesch (New York: Harcourt Brace Jovanovich, 1972), p. 14.

7. READING II: FROM DEPENDENCE TO INDEPENDENCE

1. The matter of systems and subsystems of language is discussed in W. M. Rivers, "Contrastive Linguistics in Textbook and Classroom," in J. A. Alatis, ed., *Contrastive Linguistics and Its Pedagogical Implications* (Washington, D.C.: Georgetown University Press, 1968), pp. 151–58.

2. The many uses of the subjunctive are discussed in the *Duden Grammatik,* pp. 576–602, and in a detailed study by Siegfried Jäger, *Empfehlungen zum Gebrauch des Konjunktivs,* Sprache der Gegenwart, vol. x (Düsseldorf: Schwann, 1970).

3. In *Gesammelte Dichtungen,* vol. 4 (n.p.: Suhrkamp, 1952), p. 498.

4. *Krautgärten* (Neuwied and Berlin: Luchterhand, 1970), p. 9.

5. We are distinguishing here between (1) How (manner)? questions like *Wie hat er die Tür geöffnet? Er hat die Tür mit dem Schlüssel geöffnet* (directly quoted from the text), and (2) How (explanation)? questions like *Wie hat sie wissen können, daß ihre Nachbarin nicht zu Hause war? Weil die Fenster geschlossen waren und weil ihre Freundin sie immer offen läßt* (drawn from several parts of the text).

6. This slightly simplified version is from E. S. Joynes, *A German Reader for Beginners in School or College* (Boston: D. C. Heath, 1897), pp. 97–98.

7. G. A. C. Scherer, "Programming Second Language Reading," in G. Mathieu, ed., *Advances in the Teaching of Modern Languages,* vol. 2 (London: Pergamon, 1966), p. 113.

8. Ibid., pp. 114–15.

9. Ibid., p. 120.

10. From "Mein teures Bein" in *Wanderer, kommst du nach Spa . . .* (Frankfurt am Main and Berlin: Ullstein, 1963), p. 126.

11. From "Abschied" in Böll, *Wanderer, kommst du nach Spa,* p. 69.

12. In *Sämmtliche Schriften,* Part 11 (Stuttgart: Cotta, 1871), p. 264. The orthography of the text has been modernized in the example.

13. Techniques for using concrete poetry in teaching are proposed by Joyce Rollinson in "Concrete Poetry in the Beginning Foreign Language Class," *FLA* 6 (1972), pp. 214–19.

14. In *Seventeen Modern German Poets,* ed. Siegbert Prawer (London: Oxford University Press, 1971), pp. 69–70.

15. In *Erzählungen* (n.p.: Fischer, 1959), p. 291.

16. W. Borchert, "Die Hundeblume" in *Draussen vor der Tür und ausgewählte Erzählungen* (Reinbeck bei Hamburg: Rowohlt, 1962), pp. 105–6.

17. Scherer, *Programming Second Language Reading,* p. 123.

18. In *Als Vaters Bart noch rot war* (Frankfurt am Main: Ullstein, 1971), pp. 20–21.

19. Stuart Hoffman, quoted in *Glamour,* August, 1972, p. 39.

20. By Marian Podkowinski in *Spiegel der Zeit,* ed. Gertrud Seidmann (New York: David McKay, 1969), p. 2.

21. W. G. Moulton, *A Linguistic Guide to Language Learning* (New York: MLA, 1966), p. 18.

22. For further discussion along these lines see "Linguistic and Psychological Factors in Speech Perception . . ." in Rivers (1983b), pp. 78–90.

8. WRITING AND WRITTEN EXERCISES I: THE NUTS AND BOLTS

1. L. S. Vygotsky, *Thought and Language,* trans. E. Hanfmann and G. Vakar (Cambridge, Mass.: The MIT Press, 1962), p. 97.

2. Some differences between spoken and written language have been discussed in Chapter 1 (C2–6). More thorough research on the subject would be of great assistance to language teachers.

3. This example is based on the model presented by M. Aupècle, "La langue française écrite en milieu étranger à l'école primaire," in *FM* No. 99 (1973), p. 26. Even more elaborate combination tables from R. Moody and N. Arapoff are reproduced in C. B. Paulston, "Teaching Writing in the ESOL Classroom: Techniques of Controlled Composition," *TQ* 6 (1972), pp. 43–44, where they are called "correlative substitution exercises."

4. Of great assistance in questions concerning orthography is the *Duden Rechtschreibung der deutschen Sprache und der Fremdwörter,* ed. Dudenredaktion, 17th ed., Der Große Duden, vol. 1 (Mannheim: Bibliographisches Institut des Dudenverlags, 1973).

5. The future teacher should familiarize himself with the common usage regarding capitalization and commas in a work such as *Duden Rechtschreibung,* pp. 38–42. The controversy surrounding capitalization, a central issue of spelling reform, is discussed in detail by Leo Weisgerber in *Die Verantwortung für die Schrift,* Duden Beiträge, 18 (Mannheim: Bibliographisches Institut des Dudenverlags, 1964), pp. 121ff. The use of commas and other punctuation marks is outlined with examples in *Duden Komma, Punkt und alle anderen Satzzeichen,* Dudentaschenbücher, 1 (Mannheim and Zürich: Bibliographisches Institut des Dudenverlags, 1968).

6. Clearly there are many exceptions to nearly all the categories one might set up in this area. Some are more dependable than others, e.g., *-ismus* m.: *der Kommunismus, der Chauvinismus,* etc. One generalization to be avoided is that nouns ending in *e* are always feminine: that is not so and the students will produce *der Name* and *der Russe* which they know already. On the other hand, *-heit* (and *-keit*) f. is predictable, e.g., *schön, die Schönheit; frei, die Freiheit.*

7. Deduction and induction are discussed at the beginning of Chapter 4.

8. According to Piaget's theory of cognitive development, it is not until somewhere between twelve and fifteen years that the average child reaches the stage of "formal operations," where he is able to use freely verbal, symbolic forms of reasoning. See J. S. Bruner, R. R. Olver, et al., *Studies in Cognitive Growth* (New York: John Wiley & Sons, 1966).

9. The terminology used for subjunctive forms varies a great deal and tends to be confusing. Here, "subjunctive I" refers to the forms based on the stem of the present tense and "subjunctive II" to the forms derived from the simple past.

10. It is difficult to randomize deliberately the positions of the correct answers in a pattern of A's, B's, and C's. One way of ensuring that one is not subconsciously arranging them in some way is to allot numbers to the letters and then arrange the correct choices according to a set of telephone numbers selected at random from the telephone book. If $A = 1$; $B = 2$; $C = 3$; $D = 4$;

E = 5; the phone numbers are 352-1808; 463-7496; 359-1990. The pattern of correct answers for ten questions will be C E B A D C D C E A.

11. The whimsicality of the extrapolation in this title is admitted. It was by comparison with the same inscription in demotic and classical Greek that Champollion was able to decipher the hieroglyphics on the Rosetta Stone.

12. We have included the most important areas of meaning (but not all tenses) which students may encounter. For a more comprehensive grasp of the full complexities of the subject teachers should consult an advanced grammar. Note that almost all of the tenses are ambiguous, even the tenses in the subjunctive mood, which tend to be more limited and specific in meaning. The tenses in the subjunctive mood can, of course, also be used (particularly in conditional sentences) to express possibility which is increasingly tentative or remote.

13. "Kräftig essen" in *Geselliges Beisammensein* (Neuwied and Berlin: Luchterhand, 1968), p. 105.

14. Some modern textbooks prefer to use the term *mode* for the indicative, subjunctive, and imperative, because the older term *mood* has misleading connotations.

15. R. Braddock, R. Lloyd-Jones, and L. Schoer, *Research in Written Composition* (Champaign, Ill.: National Council of Teachers of English, 1963), p. 83.

16. This was the finding also for native English writers in the Buxton Study, reported in Braddock et al., *Research in Written Composition,* pp. 58–70.

9. WRITING AND WRITTEN EXERCISES II: FLEXIBILITY AND EXPRESSION

1. The material for W35 and W36 is based on P. Daninos, *Snobissimo* (Paris: Hachette, 1964), p. 109.

2. M. Bracy, "Controlled Writing vs: Free Composition," *TQ* 5 (1971), p. 244.

3. For further suggestions along these lines, see K. Sandburg's "writing laboratories," quoted in Paulston, "Teaching Writing," pp. 57–58.

4. V. Postovsky, "Effects of Delay in Oral Practice at the Beginning of Second Language Learning," dissertation written at the University of California, Berkeley, in 1970, and reported by S. Ervin-Tripp, "Structure and Process in Language Acquisition," in J. E. Alatis, ed., *Bilingualism and Language Contact: Anthropological, Linguistic, Psychological, and Sociological Aspects,* Report of the Twenty-first Annual Round Table Meeting on Linguistics and Language Studies, Monograph No. 23 (Washington, D.C.: Georgetown University Press, 1970), p. 340.

5. Paraphrase of M. Benamou, *Pour une nouvelle pédagogie du texte littéraire* (Paris: Hachette/Larousse, 1971), pp. 12–13. Other useful references for the teaching of literature are: T. E. Bird, ed., *Foreign Languages: Reading, Literature, and Requirements* (1967 *NEC*); *UP* IV, 2 (1971), on the teaching of German literature (special ed., K. Schaum); and *MLJ* 56 (1972), of which the theme is "The Teaching of Foreign Literatures" (special ed., W. Lohnes). A reference work on literary concepts, genres, periods, and textual interpretation for teachers and advanced students has been provided recently by W.

Ruttkowski and E. Reichmann, eds., *Das Studium der deutschen Literatur* (Philadelphia: National Carl Schurz Association, 1974).

6. N. Arapoff, "Writing: a Thinking Process," *TQ* 1 (1967), pp. 33–39. Reprinted in H. B. Allen and R. N. Campbell, eds., *Teaching English as a Second Language: A Book of Readings,* 2d ed. (New York: McGraw-Hill, 1972), pp. 199–207.

7. N. Arapoff, "Discover and Transform: A Method of Teaching Writing to Foreign Students," *TQ* 3 (1969), p. 298.

8. This subject is discussed in an interesting article by R. B. Kaplan, "Cultural Thought Patterns in Inter-Cultural Education," *LL* 16 (1966), pp. 1–20, reprinted in K. Croft, ed., *Readings on English as a Second Language for Teachers and Teacher-Trainees,* 2d ed. (Cambridge, Mass.: Winthrop, 1980).

9. A number of possibilities for diversification are described in W. M. Rivers, L. H. Allen, et al., eds., *Changing Patterns in Foreign Language Programs* (Rowley, Mass.: Newbury House, 1972).

10. Formulas for beginning and ending all kinds of letters are set out in Ludwig Reiners, *Stilfibel. Der sichere Weg zum guten Deutsch* (Munich: Deutscher Taschenbuch Verlag, 1964), p. 230.

11. Arapoff, "Writing," in Allen and Campbell, eds., *Teaching English,* p. 200.

12. R. M. Valette in "Developing and Evaluating Communication Skills in the Classroom," *TQ* 7 (1973), pp. 417–18.

13. Francis Bacon, *Of Studies.*

14. R. L. Lyman, "A Co-operative Experiment in Junior High School Composition" (1931), quoted in Braddock et al., *Research in Written Composition,* p. 35.

15. D. Knapp, "A Focused, Efficient Method to Relate Composition Correction to Teaching Aims," in Allen and Campbell, eds., *Teaching English,* pp. 213–21.

16. See "The Writer Variable" in Braddock et al., *Research in Written Composition,* pp. 6–7, where the research of G. L. Kincaid and C. C. Anderson is reported.

17. For more information on inferencing, see Aaron S. Carton, "Inferencing: a Process in Using and Learning Language," in Pimsleur and Quinn, eds., *The Psychology of Second Language Learning* (Cambridge, Eng.: Cambridge University Press, 1971), pp. 45–58.

18. Teachers interested in translation should be familiar with books like E. A. Nida and C. R. Taber, *Theory and Practice of Translating* (Leiden: E. J. Brill, 1969) and H. J. Störig, ed., *Das Problem des Übersetzens,* 2d ed. (Darmstadt: Wissenschaftliche Buchgesellschaft, 1969). See also W. M. Rivers, "Contrastive Linguistics in Textbook and Classroom," in Alatis, ed. (1968), pp. 151–58.

19. Note that, since these questions apply to both German/English and English/German, the expression "source text" refers to a text in either German or English, and the "target language" is the one into which the passage is being translated.

20. *Ulysses* (London, Sydney, Toronto: The Bodley Head, 1967), p. 823.

21. *Falsche Freunde* are discussed in *Reading for Information* in Chapter 6.

22. A is from *Haus ohne Hüter* (Cologne and Berlin: Kiepenheuer und Witsch, 1954), pp. 16–17, and B is from *tomorrow and yesterday* (New York: Criterion Books, 1957), p. 9.

23. A is from *Der Zauberberg* (Frankfurt am Main: Fischer, 1960), pp. 12–13, and B is from *The Magic Mountain,* translated from the German by H. T. Lowe-Porter (New York: Knopf, 1968), p. 4.

24. *Der Sprach-Brockhaus* (Wiesbaden: Brockhaus, 1961); *Der kleine Brockhaus in zwei Bänden* (Wiesbaden: Brockhaus, 1962). German dictionaries in general tend to be more specialized in the type of information they contain than *Le Petit Larousse.*

25. J. Eichhoff weighs the relative merits of the bilingual dictionaries available in "German Dictionaries for Students: Which One is Better?" *UP* III, 2 (1970), pp. 12–17.

26. Schulz/Griesbach, *Grammatik der deutschen Sprache,* 3d ed. (Munich: Hueber, 1965). Herbert Lederer's *Reference Grammar of the German Language,* a useful German grammar in English with an excellent index, is based on the Schulz/Griesbach grammar.

III *Across Modalities*
10. TESTING AND ASSESSMENT

1. For a further elucidation of this view of testing, see "Testing and Student Learning," Chapter 10 of Rivers (1983b), pp. 141–53.

2. For a discussion of aptitude tests with full details of the Carroll-Sapon Modern Language Aptitude Test (MLAT) and the Pimsleur Language Aptitude Battery (LAB), see Rivers (1981), pp. 347–50.

3. A placement test is a specialized form of proficiency test, normed to correspond with the requirements of particular institutions or courses, and it is usually a rough sieve, sufficiently accurate for administrative purposes. In a humane approach to testing, the results of the placement test are checked against student performance in the early days of the course and adjustments made in student placement.

4. J. E. Liskin-Gasparro, "The ACTFL Proficiency Guidelines: A Historical Perspective" in T. V. Higgs, ed., *Teaching for Proficiency, the Organizing Principle* (Lincolnwood, Illinois: National Textbook Co., in conjunction with ACTFL, 1984), p. 12.

5. Ibid.

6. Often, unfortunately, teaching materials are selected because of their attractive presentation or because of teachers' and administrators' familiarity with them, without conscious attention to their appropriateness for a particular teaching situation or the needs of the students. These materials then determine the orientation of the course and often of the testing, particularly if tests are supplied with the materials. Teachers should be trained in evaluating textbooks. See "The Textbook" in Rivers (1981), pp. 475–83.

7. See "Educational Goals: The Foreign Language Teacher's Response," in Rivers (1983b), pp. 13–55, for a thorough discussion of ten directions foreign-language programs can take and how to go about determining the objectives of particular groups of students.

8. H. D. Taylor and J. L. Sorensen, "Culture Capsules," *MLJ* 45 (1961): 350–54.

9. B. Meade and G. Morain, "The Culture Cluster," *FLA* 6 (1973): 331–38.

10. F. E. Fiedler, T. Mitchell, and H. C. Triandis, "The Culture Assimilator: An Approach to Cross-Cultural Training," *Journal of Applied Psychology* 55 (1971): 95–102.

11. R. J. DiPietro, "Discourse and Real-Life Roles in the ESL Classroom," *TQ* 15 (1981): 27–33, and "The Open-Ended Scenario: A New Approach to Conversation," *TQ* 16 (1982): 15–20. In the open scenario, new information is introduced into a fully described situation and students acting roles in a minidrama have to adapt to the unpredictable responses of the other players.

12. R. C. Scarcella, "Socio-Drama for Social Interaction," *TQ* 12 (1978): 41–46. The socio-drama involves listening, speaking, reading, and writing. There is a clearly definable problem and a dilemma point from which students proceed with improvisational acting to solve the problem in a culturally acceptable way.

13. J. H. Schumann, "Social and Psychological Distance as Factors in Second Language Acquisition," Chapter 7 of J. H. Schumann, *The Pidginization Process: A Model for Second Language Acquisition* (Rowley, Mass.: Newbury House, 1978).

14. We have adopted this term from the work of the Committee for Out-of-School Education and Cultural Development of the Council for Cultural Co-operation (CCC) of the Council of Europe. See *Systems Development in Adult Language Learning* (Strasbourg: CCC, Council of Europe, 1973), pp. 67–68. Republished as J. L. M. Trim, R. Richterich, J. A. van Ek, and D. A. Wilkins, *Systems Development in Adult Language Learning* (Oxford: Pergamon Press, for the Council of Europe, 1980).

15. A. Howatt, "The Background to Course Design," in J. P. B. Allen and S. Pit Corder, eds., *Techniques in Applied Linguistics. The Edinburgh Course in Applied Linguistics,* vol. 3 (London: Oxford University Press, 1974), p. 7.

16. CCC (1973), p. 63. The authors state that their classification is intended as "a working hypothesis designed to clear the ground for future research." Those particularly interested in the teaching of languages to adults should consult the survey article, "Languages for Adult Learners," by J. L. M. Trim, *LTLA* 9, No. 2 (April, 1976), pp. 73–92, which concludes with an extensive Classified Bibliography on Adult Language Learning.

17. For the breakdown of some forty-four occupational categories, see CCC (1973), p. 68.

18. CCC (1973), p. 68.

19. F. François, "Contexte et Situation," *Linguistique. Guide alphabétique* (Paris: Denoël, 1969), p. 65. Quoted in CCC (1973), p. 68.

20. Paraphrased from J. Lyons, *Introduction to Theoretical Linguistics* (Cambridge, Eng.: Cambridge University Press, 1969), p. 413, as quoted in CCC (1973), p. 68.

21. CCC (1973), p. 68.

22. The very detailed description of how this approach was used at the Administrative College of Papua New Guinea may help others to develop similar courses. See S. Copland, "A Communicative Skills Course for Administrators in Papua New Guinea," *ELT* 30 (1976): 245–53.

23. For seven ways in which the cloze test can be designed and administered, see Rivers (1981), pp. 377–79.

24. The functional-notional approach evolved from the work of the CCC experts (n. 14 above) who initially were studying the problems of workers moving around within the European Community. See D. A. Wilkins, *Notional Syllabuses* (Oxford: Oxford University Press, 1976); J. A. van Ek, *The Threshold Level for Modern Language Learning in Schools* (London: Longman, 1977); J. A. van Ek, L. G. Alexander, and M. A. Fitzpatrick, *Waystage* (Oxford: Pergamon Press, 1980); and M. Finocchiaro and C. Brumfit, *The Functional-Notional Approach: From Theory to Practice* (Oxford: Oxford University Press, 1983).

25. Finocchiaro and Brumfit (1983), pp. 61–66, give categories of functions proposed by Wilkins (1976), van Ek (1980), and Finocchiaro.

26. For more details, see Rivers (1981), Chapter 8, subsection: "The Functional-Notional Communicative Approach," pp. 232–37.

27. Liskin-Gasparro, "The ACTFL Proficiency Guidelines . . ." in Higgs, ed. (1984), p. 316.

28. Quotations in this paragraph from ACTFL Provisional German Descriptions in the Appendix.

29. For more details on conducting and assessing the oral interview, see Rivers (1981), pp. 366–74.

30. M. Canale, "Testing in a Communicative Approach," in G. A. Jarvis, ed., *The Challenge for Excellence in Foreign Language Education* (Middlebury, Vt.: NEC, 1984), pp. 79–80.

31. See Rivers (1981), Chapter 6, "Hearing and Comprehending," pp. 160–67 for more information on listening as a creative activity.

32. For useful suggestions for proficiency-oriented testing of listening, see J. W. Larson and R. L. Jones, "Proficiency Testing for the Other Language Modalities," in Higgs, ed. (1984), pp. 118–23.

33. For reading as a "psycholinguistic guessing game," see "Reading Fluently: Extracting Meaning for Pleasure and Profit," in Rivers (1983b), pp. 92–106.

34. For a study of reading, with descriptions of many types of tests, see Larson and Jones, "Proficiency Testing . . . ," in Higgs, ed. (1984), pp. 124–32.

35. For a simple chart for assessing the oral interview, which includes a segment for assessing grammar, see Rivers (1981), p. 373.

36. For a discussion of the construction of objective tests and problems to be avoided, see Rivers (1981), pp. 387–93.

37. *Hamlet* III, 2.

EPILOGUE

1. Rivers (1981), p. 95.

2. For many interesting ideas on teaching interactively, see W. M. Rivers, ed., *Interactive Language Teaching* (Cambridge, Eng.: Cambridge University Press, 1987).

3. See also "The Natural and the Normal in Language Learning," in Rivers (1983a), pp. 104–113.

APPENDIX

1. The project for establishing the guidelines, entitled "A Design for Measuring and Communicating Foreign Language Proficiency," was funded by a grant (No. G008 103203) from the International Research and Studies Program of the U.S. Department of Education.

2. For the original Foreign Service Institute (FSI) scales for speaking and reading, with full descriptions of expectations at each level, see *Absolute Language Proficiency Ratings,* reprinted in Appendix A of W. M. Rivers, *Teaching Foreign-Language Skills,* 2d ed. (Chicago: University of Chicago Press, 1981), pp. 497–99.

General bibliography

Ahmad, K., Corbett, C., Rogers, M., and Sussex, R. 1985. *Computers, Language Learning, and Language Teaching*. Cambridge, Eng.: Cambridge University Press.

Alatis, J. E., ed. 1968. *Contrastive Linguistics and Its Pedagogical Implications*. Georgetown Round Table on Languages and Linguistics. Washington, D.C.: Georgetown University Press.

———, ed. 1969. *Linguistics and the Teaching of Standard English to Speakers of Other Languages or Dialects*. Georgetown University Round Table on Languages and Linguistics. Washington, D.C.: Georgetown University Press.

———, ed. 1970. *Bilingualism and Language Contact: Anthropological, Linguistic, Psychological, and Sociological Aspects*. Georgetown University Round Table on Languages and Linguistics. Washington, D.C.: Georgetown University Press.

Allen, E. D., and Valette, R. M. 1977. *Classroom Techniques: Foreign Languages and English as a Second Language*. New York: Harcourt Brace Jovanovich.

Allen, H. B., and Campbell, R. N., eds. 1972. *Teaching English as a Second Language: A Book of Readings*. 2d ed. New York: McGraw-Hill.

Allen, J. P. B., and Corder, S. P., eds. 1974. *Techniques in Applied Linguistics. The Edinburgh Course in Applied Linguistics*, Vol. 3. Oxford: Oxford University Press.

Allen, V. F. 1983. *Techniques in Teaching Vocabulary*. New York: Oxford University Press.

Alter, M. P. 1970. *A Modern Case for German*. Philadelphia: AATG.

Altman, H. B., ed. 1972. *Individualizing the Foreign Language Classroom: Perspectives for Teachers*. Rowley, Mass.: Newbury House.

────── and Politzer, R. L., eds. 1971. *Individualizing Foreign Language Instruction*. Rowley, Mass.: Newbury House.

Ashworth, M. 1985. *Beyond Methodology: Second Language Teaching and the Community*. Cambridge, Eng.: Cambridge University Press.

Benamou, M. 1971. *Pour une nouvelle pédagogie du texte littéraire*. Paris: Hachette/Larousse.

Birkmaier, E. M., ed. 1968. *Foreign Language Education: An Overview*. Britannica Review of Foreign Language Education, Vol. 1. Chicago: Encyclopaedia Britannica.

Braddock, R., Lloyd-Jones, R., and Schoer, L. 1963. *Research in Written Composition*. Champaign, Ill.: National Council of Teachers of English.

Brooks, N. 1964. *Language and Language Learning: Theory and Practice*. 2d ed. New York: Harcourt, Brace & World.

Brumfit, C. J. 1984. *Communicative Methodology in Language Teaching: the Roles of Fluency and Accuracy*. Cambridge, Eng.: Cambridge University Press.

────── , and Carter, R. A., eds. 1986. *Literature and Language Teaching*. Oxford: Oxford University Press.

Byrnes, H., and Canale, M., eds. 1987. *Defining and Developing Proficiency: Guidelines, Implementations and Concepts*. Lincolnwood, Ill.: National Textbook Co.

Catford, J. C. 1965. *A Linguistic Theory of Translation*. London: Oxford University Press.

Chastain, K. 1971. *The Development of Modern Language Skills: Theory to Practice*. Philadelphia: Center for Curriculum Development.

Clyne, M. 1984. *Language and Society in the German-Speaking Countries*. Cambridge, Eng.: Cambridge University Press.

Croft, K., ed. 1980. *Readings on English as a Second Language for Teachers and Teacher Trainees*. 2d ed. Cambridge, Mass.: Winthrop.

Dakin, J. 1973. *The Language Laboratory and Language Learning*. London: Longman.

Delattre, P. 1965. *Comparing the Phonetic Features of English, French, German, and Spanish*. London: Harrap.

Diller, K. C. 1971. *Generative Grammar, Structural Linguistics, and Language Teaching*. Rowley, Mass.: Newbury House.

DiPietro, R. 1987. *Strategic Interaction: Learning Languages through Scenarios*. Cambridge, Eng.: Cambridge University Press.

Duden Grammatik der deutschen Gegenwartssprache. 1966. 2d ed. Der Große Duden, Vol. 4. Mannheim: Bibliographisches Institut des Dudenverlags.

Duden Rechtschreibung der deutschen Sprache und der Fremdwörter. 1973. 17th ed. Der Große Duden, Vol. 1. Mannheim: Bibliographisches Institut des Dudenverlags.

Duff, A. 1981. *The Third Language: Recurrent Problems of Translation into English*. Oxford: Pergamon Press.

Finocchiaro, M., and Bonomo, M. 1973. *The Foreign Language Learner: A Guide for Teachers*. New York: Regents Publishing Co.

————, and Brumfit, C. J. 1983. *The Functional-Notional Approach: From Theory to Practice*. Oxford: Oxford University Press.

Freedman, A., Pringle, I., and Yalden, J., eds. 1983. *Learning to Write: First Language/Second Language*. London: Longman.

Fries, C. C. 1945. *Teaching and Learning English as a Foreign Language*. Ann Arbor, Mich.: University of Michigan Press.

Gattegno, C. 1963. *Teaching Foreign Languages in Schools: The Silent Way*. Reading: Educational Explorers Ltd. (2d ed. 1972. New York: Educational Solutions.)

Gaudiani, C. 1981. *Teaching Writing in the Foreign Language Curriculum*. Washington, D.C.: Center for Applied Linguistics.

Gouin, F. 1892. *The Art of Teaching and Studying Languages*. Trans. H. Swan and V. Bétis. London: George Philip and Son; New York: Charles Scribner's Sons.

Grellet, F. 1981. *Developing Reading Skills: A Practical Guide to Reading Comprehension Exercises*. Cambridge, Eng.: Cambridge University Press.

Grittner, F. M. 1969. *Teaching Foreign Languages*. New York: Harper and Row.

————, ed. 1974. *Student Motivation and the Foreign Language Teacher*. Lincolnwood, Ill.: National Textbook Co.

————, and LaLeike, F. H. 1972. *Individualized Foreign Language Instruction*. Lincolnwood, Ill.: National Textbook Co.

Hagboldt, P. 1940. *The Teaching of German*. Boston: D. C. Heath.

Hester, R., ed. 1970. *Teaching a Living Language*. New York: Harper and Row.

Higgins, J., and Johns, T. 1984. *Computers in Language Learning*. Reading, Mass.: Addison-Wesley.

Higgs, T. V., ed. 1982. *Curriculum, Competence, and the Foreign Language Teacher*. Lincolnwood, Ill.: National Textbook Co.

————, ed. 1984. *Teaching for Proficiency, the Organizing Principle*. Lincolnwood, Ill.: National Textbook Co., in conjunction with ACTFL.

Howes, V. M., ed. 1970. *Individualization of Instruction: A Teaching Strategy*. New York: Macmillan.

James, C. J., ed. 1983. *Practical Applications of Research in Foreign Language Teaching*. Lincolnwood, Ill.: National Textbook Co.

————, ed. 1985. *Foreign Language Proficiency in the Classroom and Beyond*. Lincolnwood, Ill.: National Textbook Co.

Jarvis, G. A., ed. 1974. *Responding to New Realities*. ACTFL Review of Foreign Language Education, Vol. 5. Lincolnwood, Ill.: National Textbook Co.

————, ed. 1974. *The Challenge of Communication*. ACTFL Review of Foreign Language Education, Vol. 6. Lincolnwood, Ill.: National Textbook Co.

————, ed. 1976. *An Integrative Approach to Foreign Language Teaching: Choosing Among the Options*. ACTFL Review of Foreign Language Education, Vol. 8. Lincolnwood, Ill.: National Textbook Co.

Jespersen, O. 1904. *How to Teach a Foreign Language*. London: George Allen & Unwin Ltd. Reissued, 1961.

Jones, K. 1982. *Simulations in Language Teaching*. Cambridge, Eng.: Cambridge University Press.

Kellermann, M. 1981. *The Forgotten Third Skill: Reading a Foreign Language*. Oxford: Pergamon Press.

Kelly, L. G. 1969. *25 Centuries of Language Teaching*. Rowley, Mass.: Newbury House.

Kenning, M. J., and M-M. 1983. *An Introduction to Computer-Assisted Language Teaching*. Oxford: Oxford University Press.

Klappenbach, R., and Steinitz, W., eds. 1964ff. *Wörterbuch der deutschen Gegenwartssprache*. Berlin: Akademie Verlag.

Kramsch, C. J. 1981. *Discourse Analysis and Second Language Teaching*. Washington, D.C.: Center for Applied Linguistics.

Krashen, S. D., and Terrell, T. D. 1983. *The Natural Approach: Language Acquisition in the Classroom*. Hayward, Calif.: Alemany Press.

Lambert, W. E., and Tucker, R. 1972. *The Bilingual Education of Children*. Rowley, Mass.: Newbury House.

Lange, D. L., ed. 1970. *Individualization of Instruction*. Britannica Review of Foreign Language Education, Vol. 2. Chicago: Encyclopaedia Britannica.

————, ed. 1971. *Pluralism in Foreign Language Education*. Britannica Review of Foreign Language Education, Vol. 3. Chicago: Encyclopaedia Britannica.

————, and James, C. J., eds. 1972. *Foreign Language Education: A Reappraisal*. ACTFL Review of Foreign Language Education, vol. 4. Lincolnwood, Ill.: National Textbook Co.

Lederer, H. 1969. *Reference Grammar of the German Language*. New York: Charles Scribner's Sons.

Logan, G. E. 1973. *Individualized Foreign Language Learning: An Organic Process*. Rowley, Mass.: Newbury House.

Lonergan, J. 1984. *Video in Language Teaching*. Cambridge, Eng.: Cambridge University Press.

Lugton, R. C., ed. 1971. *Toward a Cognitive Approach to Second Language Acquisition*. Philadelphia: Center for Curriculum Development.

Mackay, R., Barkman, B., and Jordan, R. R., eds. 1979. *Reading in a Second Language: Hypotheses, Organization, and Practice*. Rowley, Mass.: Newbury House.

Madsen, H. S. 1983. *Techniques in Testing*. New York: Oxford University Press.

Maley, A., and Duff, A. 1982. *Drama Techniques in Language Learning*. 2d ed. Cambridge, Eng.: Cambridge University Press.

Marchand, J. W. 1961. *Applied Linguistics: German, A Guide for Teachers*. Boston: D. C. Heath.

Martens, C., and P. 1961. *Phonetik der deutschen Sprache*. Munich: Hueber.

Morgan, B. Q. 1929. *German Frequency Word Book*. Publications of the American and Canadian Committees on Modern Languages, IX. New York: Macmillan.

————, and Wadepuhl, W. 1934. *Minimum Standard German Vocabulary*. New York: F. S. Crofts & Co.

Morgan, J., and Rinvolucri, M. 1983. *Once upon a Time: Using Stories in the Language Classroom*. Cambridge, Eng.: Cambridge University Press.

Moskowitz, G. 1978. *Caring and Sharing in the Foreign Language Class: A Source-book on Humanistic Techniques*. Rowley, Mass.: Newbury House.

Moulton, W. 1962. *The Sounds of English and German*. Chicago: The University of Chicago Press.

————. 1966. *A Linguistic Guide to Language Learning*. New York: Modern Language Association.

Newmark, P. P. 1981. *Aspects of Translation*. Oxford: Pergamon Press.

Nida, E. A., and Taber, C. R. 1969. *The Theory and Practice of Translating*. Leiden: E. J. Brill.

Northeast Conference (1959): F. D. Eddy, ed. *The Language Learner*. Middlebury, Vt.: NEC.

Northeast Conference (1960): G. R. Bishop, ed. *Culture in Language Learning*. Middlebury, Vt.: NEC.

Northeast Conference (1961): S. L. Flaxman, ed. *Modern Language Teaching in School and College*. Middlebury, Vt.: NEC.

Northeast Conference (1962): W. F. Bottiglia, ed. *Current Issues in Language Teaching*. Middlebury, Vt.: NEC.

Northeast Conference (1963): W. F. Bottiglia, ed. *Language Learning: The Intermediate Phase*. Middlebury, Vt.: NEC.

Northeast Conference (1964): G. F. Jones, ed. *Foreign Language Teaching: Ideals and Practices*. Middlebury, Vt.: NEC.

Northeast Conference (1965): G. R. Bishop, ed. *Foreign Language Teaching: Challenges to the Profession*. Middlebury, Vt.: NEC.

Northeast Conference (1966): R. G. Mead, Jr., ed. *Language Teaching: Broader Contexts*. Middlebury, Vt.: NEC.

Northeast Conference (1967): T. E. Bird, ed. *Foreign Languages: Reading, Literature, and Requirements*. Middlebury, Vt.: NEC.

Northeast Conference (1968): T. E. Bird, ed. *Foreign Language Learning: Research and Development*. Middlebury, Vt.: NEC.

Northeast Conference (1969): M. F. Edgerton, Jr., ed. *Sight and Sound: The Sensible and Sensitive Use of Audio-Visual Aids*. Middlebury, Vt.: NEC.

Northeast Conference (1970): J. Tursi, ed. *Foreign Languages and the "New" Student*. Middlebury, Vt.: NEC.

Northeast Conference (1971): J. W. Dodge, ed. *Leadership for Continuing Development*. Middlebury, Vt.: NEC.

Northeast Conference (1972): J. W. Dodge, ed. *Other Words, Other Worlds: Language-in-Culture*. Middlebury, Vt.: NEC.

Northeast Conference (1973): J. W. Dodge, ed. *Sensitivity in the Foreign-Language Classroom*. Middlebury, Vt.: NEC.

Northeast Conference (1974): W. C. Born, ed. *Toward Student-Centered Foreign-Language Programs*. Middlebury, Vt.: NEC.

Northeast Conference (1975): W. C. Born, ed. *Goals Clarification: Curriculum, Teaching, Evaluation*. Middlebury, Vt.: NEC.

Northeast Conference (1976): W. C. Born, ed. *Language and Culture: Heritage and Horizons*. Middlebury, Vt.: NEC.

Northeast Conference (1977): W. C. Born, ed. *Language: Acquisition, Application, Appreciation*. Middlebury, Vt.: NEC.

Northeast Conference (1978): W. C. Born, ed. *New Contents, New Teachers, New Publics.* Middlebury, Vt.: NEC.

Northeast Conference (1979): W. C. Born, ed. *The Foreign Language Learner in Today's Classroom Environment.* Middlebury, Vt.: NEC.

Northeast Conference (1980): T. H. Geno, ed. *Our Profession: Present Status and Future Directions.* Middlebury, Vt.: NEC.

Northeast Conference (1981): T. H. Geno, ed. *Foreign Language and International Studies: Toward Cooperation and Integration.* Middlebury, Vt.: NEC.

Northeast Conference (1982): R. G. Mead, Jr., ed. *The Foreign Language Teacher: The Lifelong Learner.* Middlebury, Vt.: NEC.

Northeast Conference (1983): R. G. Mead, Jr., ed. *Foreign Language: Key Links in the Chains of Learning.* Middlebury, Vt.: NEC.

Northeast Conference (1984): G. A. Jarvis, ed. *The Challenge for Excellence in Foreign-Language Education.* Middlebury, Vt.: NEC.

Northeast Conference (1985): A. C. Omaggio, ed. *Proficiency, Curriculum, Articulation: The Ties That Bind.* Middlebury, Vt.: NEC.

Northeast Conference (1986): B. H. Wing, ed. *Listening, Reading, and Writing: Analysis and Application.* Middlebury, Vt.: NEC.

Northeast Conference (1987): J. M. Darcey, ed. *The Language Teacher: Commitment and Collaboration.* Middlebury, Vt.: NEC.

Oller, J. W., Jr. 1979. *Language Tests at School: A Pragmatic Approach.* London: Longman.

———, and Richard-Amato, P. A., eds. 1983. *Methods That Work: A Smorgasbord of Ideas for Language Teachers.* Rowley, Mass.: Newbury House.

Omaggio, A. C. 1986. *Teaching Language in Context: Proficiency-Oriented Instruction.* Boston, Mass.: Heinle and Heinle.

Palmer, H. 1917. *The Scientific Study and Teaching of Languages.* London: Harrap.

Paulston, C. B. 1980. *Bilingual Education: Theories and Issues.* Rowley, Mass.: Newbury House.

Pfeffer, J. A. 1964. *Grunddeutsch. Basic (Spoken) German Word List. Grundstufe.* Englewood Cliffs, N.J.: Prentice-Hall.

———. 1970. *Grunddeutsch. Basic (Spoken) German Dictionary for Everyday Usage.* Englewood Cliffs, N.J.: Prentice-Hall.

———. 1970. *Mittelstufe,* Preliminary Edition. Pittsburgh: University of Pittsburgh Institute for Basic German.

Phillips, J. K., ed. 1977. *The Language Connection.* Lincolnwood, Ill.: National Textbook Co.

———, ed. 1979. *Building on Experience—Building for Success.* Lincolnwood, Ill.: National Textbook Co.

———, ed. 1980. *The New Imperative: Expanding the Horizons of Foreign Language Education.* Lincolnwood, Ill.: National Textbook Co.

———, ed. 1981a. *Action for the 80s: A Political, Professional, and Public Program for Foreign Language Education.* Lincolnwood, Ill.: National Textbook Co.

———, ed. 1981b. *New Cases for Foreign Language Study.* Middlebury, Vt.: NEC.

Politzer, R. L. 1968. *Teaching German: A Linguistic Orientation*. Waltham, Mass.: Blaisdell.

Prator, C. H., Jr., and Robinett, B. W. 1972. *Manual of American English Pronunciation*. 3d ed. New York: Holt, Rinehart and Winston.

Raimes, A. 1983. *Techniques in Teaching Writing*. New York: Oxford University Press.

Reichmann, E., ed. 1970. *The Teaching of German: Problems and Methods*. Philadelphia: National Carl Schurz Association.

Reiners, L. 1964. *Stilfibel: Der sichere Weg zum guten Deutsch*. Munich: Deutscher Taschenbuch Verlag.

Richards, J. C. 1985. *The Context of Language Teaching*. Cambridge, Eng.: Cambridge University Press.

———— and Schmidt, R. W., eds. 1983. *Language and Communication*. London: Longman.

Rivers, W. M. 1964. *The Psychologist and the Foreign-Language Teacher*. Chicago: The University of Chicago Press.

————. 1981. *Teaching Foreign-Language Skills*. 2d ed. Chicago: The University of Chicago Press.

————. 1983a. *Communicating Naturally in a Second Language: Theory and Practice in Language Teaching*. Cambridge, Eng.: Cambridge University Press.

————. 1983b. *Speaking in Many Tongues. Essays in Foreign-Language Teaching*. 3d ed. Cambridge, Eng.: Cambridge University Press.

————, ed. 1987. *Interactive Language Teaching*. Cambridge, Eng.: Cambridge University Press.

Robinson, G. L. N. 1985. *Crosscultural Understanding: Processes and Approaches for ESL, FL, and Bilingual Educators*. Oxford: Pergamon Press.

Russo, G. M. 1983. *Expanding Communication: Teaching Modern Languages at the College Level*. New York: Harcourt Brace Jovanovich.

Ruttkowski, W., and Reichmann, E., eds. 1974. *Das Studium der deutschen Literatur*. Philadelphia: National Carl Schurz Association.

Sadow, S. A. 1982. *Idea Bank: Creative Activities for the Language Class*. Rowley, Mass.: Newbury House.

Sauzé, E. B. de. 1920. *The Cleveland Plan for the Teaching of Modern Languages with Special Reference to French*. Philadelphia: The John C. Winston Co.

Savignon, S. J. 1983. *Communicative Competence: Theory and Classroom Practice. Texts and Contexts in Second Language Learning*. Reading, Mass.: Addison-Wesley.

Schaum, K., spec. ed. 1971. Theme: *Focus on Literature. UP* IV, 2.

Schmidt, E. 1970. *Let's Play Games in German*. Lincolnwood, Ill.: National Textbook Co.

Schulz, D., and Griesbach, H. 1965. *Grammatik der deutschen Sprache*. 3d ed. Munich: Hueber.

Schweitzer, C., and Simonnot, E. 1921. *Méthodologie des langues vivantes*. Paris: Armand Colin. Originally published 1902.

Seelye, H. N. 1984. *Teaching Culture: Strategies for Intercultural Communication*. 2d ed. Lincolnwood, Ill.: National Textbook Co.

Siebs, T. 1969. *Deutsche Aussprache: Reine und gemäßigte Hochlautung mit Aus-*

sprachewörterbuch. Ed. by H. de Boor, H. Moser, and C. Winkler. 19th ed. Berlin: De Gruyter.

Smith, E. C., and Luce, L. F., eds. 1979. *Toward Internationalism: Readings in Cross-Cultural Communication.* Rowley, Mass.: Newbury House.

Smith, S. M. 1984. *The Theater Arts and the Teaching of Second Languages.* Boston: Addison-Wesley.

Spolsky, B., ed. 1972. *The Language Education of Minority Children.* Rowley, Mass.: Newbury House.

Stack, E. M. 1971. *The Language Laboratory and Modern Language Teaching.* 3d ed. New York: Oxford University Press.

Stern, H. H. 1983. *Fundamental Concepts of Language Teaching.* Oxford: Oxford University Press.

Stevick, E. W. 1971. *Adapting and Writing Language Lessons.* Washington, D.C.: Foreign Service Institute.

———. 1976. *Memory, Meaning, and Method: Some Psychological Perspectives on Language Learning.* Rowley, Mass.: Newbury House.

———. 1980. *Teaching Languages: A Way and Ways.* Rowley, Mass.: Newbury House.

———. 1982. *Teaching and Learning Languages.* Cambridge, Eng.: Cambridge University Press.

Störig, H. J., ed. 1969. *Das Problem des Übersetzens.* 2d ed. Darmstadt: Wissenschaftliche Buchgesellschaft.

Sweet, H. 1899. *The Practical Study of Languages.* London: Dent. Reprinted 1964. London: Oxford University Press.

Titone, R. 1968. *Teaching Foreign Languages: An Historical Sketch.* Washington, D.C.: Georgetown University Press.

Trim, J. L. M., Richterich, R., van Ek, J. A., and Wilkins, D. A. 1980. *Systems Development in Adult Language Learning: A European Unit-Credit System for Modern Language Learning by Adults.* Oxford: Pergamon Press, for the Council of Europe.

Underwood, J. H. 1983. *Linguistics, Computers, and the Language Teacher: A Communicative Approach.* Rowley, Mass.: Newbury House.

Ur, P. 1984. *Discussions That Work: Task-Centred Fluency Practice.* Cambridge, Eng.: Cambridge University Press.

———. 1984. *Teaching Listening Comprehension.* Cambridge, Eng.: Cambridge University Press.

Valdes, J. M., ed. 1986. *Culture Bound: Bridging the Cultural Gap in Language Teaching.* Cambridge, Eng.: Cambridge University Press.

Valette, R. M. 1977. *Modern Language Testing.* 2d ed. New York: Harcourt Brace Jovanovich.

———, and Disick, R. S. 1972. *Modern Language Performance Objectives and Individualization: A Handbook.* New York: Harcourt Brace Jovanovich.

Van Ek, J. A. 1977. *The Threshold Level for Modern Language Learning in Schools.* London: Longman.

———. 1980. *The Threshold Level.* Oxford: Pergamon Press.

———, Alexander, L. G., and Fitzpatrick, M. A. 1980. *Waystage English.* London: Longman.

Ventriglia, L. 1982. *Conversations of Miguel and Maria: How Children Learn a Second Language*. Reading, Mass.: Addison-Wesley.

Wahrig, G. 1968. *Deutsches Wörterbuch*. Special ed. Gütersloh: Bertelsmann.

Wallerstein, N. 1983. *Language and Culture in Conflict*. Reading, Mass.: Addison-Wesley.

Wängler, H.-H. 1966. *Patterns in German Sress and Intonation*. St. Paul, Minn.: EMC Corporation.

————. 1967. *Grundriß einer Phonetik des Deutschen. Mit einer allgemeinen Einführung in die Phonetik*. 2d ed. Marburg: Elwert.

————. 1972. *Instruction in German Pronunciation*. 3d ed. St. Paul, Minn.: EMC Corporation.

West, M. 1941. *Learning to Read a Foreign Language and Other Essays on Language-Teaching*. London: Longman.

Widdowson, H. G. 1975. *Stylistics and the Teaching of Literature*. London: Longman.

————. 1978. *Teaching Language as Communication*. Oxford: Oxford University Press.

Wilkins, D. A. 1976. *Notional Syllabuses*. Oxford: Oxford University Press.

Wright, A., Betteridge, D., and Buckby, M. 1979. *Games for Language Learning*. Cambridge, Eng.: Cambridge University Press.

Supplemental bibliography

SOME INTRODUCTORY READINGS IN LINGUISTICS AND PSYCHOLOGY
OF LANGUAGE LEARNING

Admoni, W. 1970. *Der deutsche Sprachbau.* 3d ed. Munich: C. H. Beck.

Anderson, R. W., ed. 1984. *Second Languages: A Cross-Linguistic Perspective.* Rowley, Mass.: Newbury House.

Baddeley, A. D. 1976. *The Psychology of Memory.* New York: Basic Books.

Bailey, K., Long, M. H., and Peck, S., eds. 1983. *Second Language Acquisition Studies.* Rowley, Mass.: Newbury House.

Bierwisch, M. 1971. *Grammatik des deutschen Verbs.* Studia grammatica II, 7th ed. Berlin: Akademie Verlag.

Bloom, L. 1970. *Language Development: Form and Function in Emerging Grammars.* Cambridge, Mass.: MIT Press.

Boettcher, W., and Sitta, H. 1972. *Deutsche Grammatik III.* Frankfurt am Main: Athenäum.

Bolinger, D., and Sears, D. A. 1981. *Aspects of Language.* 3d ed. New York: Harcourt Brace Jovanovich.

Brown, R. 1973. *A First Language: The Early Stages.* Cambridge, Mass.: Harvard University Press.

Bruner, J. S., Olver, R. R., et al. 1966. *Studies in Cognitive Growth.* New York: Wiley.

Chafe, W. 1970. *Meaning and the Structure of Language.* Chicago: The University of Chicago Press.

Chall, J. S. 1983. *Stages of Reading Development.* New York: McGraw-Hill.

Cherry, C. 1978. *On Human Communication: A Review, A Survey, and a Criticism.* 3d ed. New York: Wiley.

Chomsky, N. 1957. *Syntactic Structures.* The Hague: Mouton.

———. 1965. *Aspects of the Theory of Syntax.* Cambridge, Mass.: MIT Press.

393

————. 1972. *Language and Mind*. Enlarged ed. New York: Harcourt Brace Jovanovich. Original ed. 1968.

————. 1980. *Rules and Representations*. New York: Columbia University Press.

Corder, S. P. 1973. *Introducing Applied Linguistics*. Harmondsworth, Middlesex, Eng.: Penguin Books.

Coulthard, M. 1985. *An Introduction to Discourse Analysis*. New ed. London: Longman.

Cummins, J., and Swain, M. 1986. *Bilingualism in Education: Aspects of Theory, Research, and Practice*. London: Longman.

Eckman, F. R., Bell, L. H., and Nelson, D., eds. 1984. *Universals of Second Language Acquisition*. Rowley, Mass.: Newbury House.

Ellis, A., and Beattie, G. 1986. *The Psychology of Language and Communication*. New York: Guilford Press.

Engel, U. 1972. "Regeln zur 'Satzgliedfolge': Zur Stellung der Elemente im einfachen Verbalsatz." In *Linguistische Studien I*, Sprache der Gegenwart 19. Düsseldorf: Pädagogischer Verlag Schwann.

Erben, J. 1960. *Abriß der deutschen Grammatik*. 3d ed. Berlin: Akademie Verlag.

————. 1968. *Deutsche Grammatik: Ein Leitfaden*. Frankfurt am Main: Fischer.

Essen, O. von. 1956. *Grundzüge der hochdeutschen Satzintonation*. Ratingen bei Düsseldorf: Henn.

Ferguson, C. A., and Slobin, D. I., eds. 1973. *Studies of Child Language Development*. New York: Holt, Rinehart and Winston.

Fodor, J. A., Bever, T. G., and Garrett, M. F. 1974. *The Psychology of Language: An Introduction to Psycholinguistics and Generative Grammar*. New York: McGraw-Hill.

Furth, Hans G. 1969. *Piaget and Knowledge: Theoretical Foundations*. Englewood Cliffs, N.J.: Prentice-Hall.

Gardner, H. 1985. *The Mind's New Science: A History of the Cognitive Revolution*. New York: Basic Books.

Gardner, R. C., and Lambert, W. E. 1972. *Attitudes and Motivation in Second-Language Learning*. Rowley, Mass.: Newbury House.

Gass, S., and Selinker, L., eds. 1983. *Language Transfer in Language Learning*. Rowley, Mass.: Newbury House.

Genesee, F. 1987. *Learning through Two Languages: Studies of Immersion and Bilingual Education*. Cambridge, Mass.: Newbury House.

Giglioli, P. P. 1972. *Language and Social Context*. Harmondsworth, Middlesex, Eng.: Penguin Books.

Glinz, H. 1970. *Deutsche Grammatik I*. Bad Homburg: Athenäum.

————. 1971. *Deutsche Grammatik II*. Frankfurt am Main: Athenäum.

Grosjean, F. 1982. *Life with Two Languages: An Introduction to Bilingualism*. Cambridge, Mass.: Harvard University Press.

Hakuta, K. 1986. *Mirror of Language: The Debate on Bilingualism*. New York: Basic Books.

Hall, E. T. 1959. *The Silent Language*. Garden City, N.Y.: Doubleday.

————. 1966. *The Hidden Dimension*. Garden City, N.Y.: Doubleday.

————. 1976. *Beyond Culture*. Garden City, N.Y.: Doubleday.

Halliday, M. A. K. 1973. *Explorations in the Functions of Language*. London: Edward Arnold.

———. 1978. *Language as Social Semiotic: The Social Interpretation of Language and Meaning*. London: Edward Arnold; Baltimore, Md.: University Park Press.

Hatch, E., ed. 1978. *Second Language Acquisition: A Book of Readings*. Rowley, Mass.: Newbury House.

Hayes, J. R., ed. 1970. *Cognition and the Development of Language*. New York: John Wiley and Sons.

Hymes, D. 1974. *Foundations in Sociolinguistics: An Ethnographic Approach*. Philadelphia: University of Pennsylvania Press.

Jäger, S. 1970. *Empfehlungen zum Gebrauch des Konjunktivs*. Sprache der Gegenwart, Vol. 10. Düsseldorf: Pädagogischer Verlag Schwann.

Johnson-Laird, P. N., and Wason, P. C., eds. 1977. *Thinking: Readings in Cognitive Science*. Cambridge, Eng.: Cambridge University Press.

Joos, M. 1961. *The Five Clocks*. New York: Harcourt, Brace & World.

Keller, R. E. 1961. *German Dialects: Phonology and Morphology with Selected Texts*. Manchester: Manchester University Press.

Krashen, S. D., Scarcella, R. C., and Long, M. H., eds. 1982. *Child-Adult Differences in Second Language Acquisition*. Rowley, Mass.: Newbury House.

Laforge, P. G. 1983. *Counseling and Culture in Second Language Acquisition*. Oxford: Pergamon Press.

Lambert, R. D., and Freed, B. F., eds. 1982. *The Loss of Language Skills*. Rowley, Mass.: Newbury House.

Lyons, J. 1968. *Introduction to Theoretical Linguistics*. Cambridge, Eng.: Cambridge University Press.

———. 1977. *Semantics*. Vols. 1 and 2. Cambridge, Eng.: Cambridge University Press.

———. 1981. *Language and Linguistics: An Introduction*. Cambridge, Eng.: Cambridge University Press.

Macnamara, J., ed. 1977. *Language Learning and Thought*. New York: Academic Press.

———. 1982. *Names for Things: A Study of Human Learning*. Cambridge, Mass.: MIT Press.

Maslow, A. H. 1970. *Motivation and Personality*. 2d ed. New York: Harper and Row.

McLaughlin, B. 1985. *Second Language Acquisition in Childhood*. 2d ed. Vols. 1 and 2. Hillsdale, N.J.: Lawrence Erlbaum Associates.

Miller, G. A. 1967. *The Psychology of Communication: Seven Essays*. New York: Basic Books. Published 1969 as *Psychology and Communication*. London: Pelican.

———, ed. 1973. *Communication, Language, and Meaning: Psychological Perspectives*. New York: Basic Books.

———. 1981. *Language and Speech*. San Francisco: W. H. Freeman.

Neisser, U. 1967. *Cognitive Psychology*. New York: Appleton-Century-Crofts.

———. 1982. *Memory Observed: Remembering in Natural Contexts*. San Francisco: W. H. Freeman.

Newmeyer, F. 1980. *Linguistic Theory in America: The First Quarter-Century of Transformational Generative Grammar*. New York: Academic Press.

Penzl, H. 1972. "Zu Problemen der neuhochdeutschen Phonologie," *Jahrbuch für Internationale Germanistik* IV, 1: 9–17.

Perdue, C., ed. 1984. *Second Language Acquisition by Adult Immigrants: A Field Manual*. Rowley, Mass.: Newbury House.

Pinker, S. 1984. *Language Learnability and Language Development*. Cambridge, Mass.: Harvard University Press.

Radford, Q. 1981. *Transformational Syntax: A Student's Guide to Chomsky's Extended Standard Theory*. Cambridge, Eng.: Cambridge University Press.

Schane, S. A. 1973. *Generative Phonology*. Englewood Cliffs, N.J.: Prentice-Hall.

Schlesinger, I. M. 1968. *Sentence Structure and the Reading Process*. The Hague: Mouton.

————. 1977. *Production and Comprehension of Utterances*. Hillsdale, N.J.: Lawrence Erlbaum Associates.

————. 1982. *Steps to Language: Toward a Theory of Native Language Acquisition*. Hillsdale, N.J.: Lawrence Erlbaum Associates.

Schumann, J. H. 1978. *The Pidginization Process: A Model for Second Language Acquisition*. Rowley, Mass.: Newbury House.

Searle, J. R. 1969. *Speech Acts: An Essay in the Philosophy of Language*. Cambridge, Eng.: Cambridge University Press.

Segalowitz, S. J. 1983. *Two Sides of the Brain: Brain Lateralization Explored*. Englewood Cliffs, N.J.: Prentice-Hall.

Slobin, D. I. 1979. *Psycholinguistics*. 2d ed. Glenview, Ill.: Scott, Foresman.

Smith, F., ed. 1973. *Psycholinguistics and Reading*. New York: Holt, Rinehart and Winston.

————. 1982. *Understanding Reading*. 3d ed. New York: Holt, Rinehart and Winston.

Smith, W. F., ed. 1987. *Modern Media in Foreign Language Education: Theory and Implementation*. Lincolnwood, Ill.: National Textbook Co.

Snow, C. E., and Ferguson, C. A., eds. 1977. *Talking to Children: Language Input and Acquisition*. Cambridge, Eng.: Cambridge University Press.

Sprache und Gesellschaft: Beiträge zur soziolinguistischen Beschreibung der deutschen Gegenwartssprache: Jahrbuch 1970. 1971. Sprache der Gegenwart, vol. 13. Düsseldorf: Pädagogischer Verlag Schwann.

Steinberg, D. D. 1982. *Psycholinguistics: Language, Mind, and World*. London: Longman.

Terrance, H. S. 1979. *Nim: A Chimpanzee Who Learned Sign Language*. New York: Washington Square Press Pocket Books.

Texte gesprochener deutscher Standardsprache I. 1971. Erarbeitet im Institut für deutsche Sprache Forschungsstelle Freiburg im Breisgau. Düsseldorf: Pädagogischer Verlag Schwann, and Munich: Hueber.

Thorne, B., Kramarae, C., and Henley, N. 1983. *Language, Gender, and Society*. Rowley, Mass.: Newbury House.

Trueba, H. T., ed. 1987. *Success or Failure: Learning and the Language Minority Student*. Cambridge, Mass.: Newbury House.

Van Patten, B., Dvorak, T. R., and Lee, J. F. 1987. *Foreign Language Learning: A Research Perspective*. New York: Newbury House.

Villiers de, J. G., and P. A. 1978. *Language Acquisition*. Cambridge, Mass.: Harvard University Press.

Vygotsky, L. S. 1962. *Thought and Language*. Trans. E. Hanfmann and G. Vakar. Cambridge, Mass.: MIT Press.

Wanner, E., and Gleitman, L. R., eds. 1982. *Language Acquisition: The State of the Art*. Cambridge, Eng.: Cambridge University Press.

Wells, G., et al. 1981. *Learning Through Interaction: The Study of Language Development*. Cambridge, Eng.: Cambridge University Press.

Wolfson, N., and Judd, E. 1983. *Sociolinguistics and Language Acquisition*. Rowley, Mass.: Newbury House.

Index

NTC PROFESSIONAL MATERIALS

ACTFL Review

Published annually in conjunction with the American Council on the Teaching of Foreign Languages

NEW PERSPECTIVES, NEW DIRECTIONS IN FOREIGN LANGUAGE EDUCATION, ed. Birckbichler, Vol. 20 (1990)

MODERN TECHNOLOGY IN FOREIGN LANGUAGE EDUCATION: APPLICATIONS AND PROJECTS, ed. Smith, Vol. 19 (1989)

MODERN MEDIA IN FOREIGN LANGUAGE EDUCATION: THEORY AND IMPLEMENTATION, ed. Smith, Vol. 18 (1987)

DEFINING AND DEVELOPING PROFICIENCY: GUIDELINES, IMPLEMENTATIONS, AND CONCEPTS, ed. Byrnes, Vol. 17 (1986)

FOREIGN LANGUAGE PROFICIENCY IN THE CLASSROOM AND BEYOND, ed. James, Vol. 16 (1984)

TEACHING FOR PROFICIENCY, THE ORGANIZING PRINCIPLE, ed. Higgs, Vol. 15 (1983)

PRACTICAL APPLICATIONS OF RESEARCH IN FOREIGN LANGUAGE TEACHING, ed. James, Vol. 14 (1982)

CURRICULUM, COMPETENCE, AND THE FOREIGN LANGUAGE TEACHER, ed. Higgs, Vol. 13 (1981)

ACTION FOR THE '80s: A POLITICAL, PROFESSIONAL, AND PUBLIC PROGRAM FOR FOREIGN LANGUAGE EDUCATION, ed. Phillips, Vol. 12 (1980)

THE NEW IMPERATIVE: EXPANDING THE HORIZONS OF FOREIGN LANGUAGE EDUCATION, ed. Phillips, Vol. 11 (1979)

BUILDING ON EXPERIENCE—BUILDING FOR SUCCESS, ed. Phillips, Vol. 10 (1978)

THE LANGUAGE CONNECTION: FROM THE CLASSROOM TO THE WORLD, ed. Phillips, Vol. 9 (1977)

AN INTEGRATIVE APPROACH TO FOREIGN LANGUAGE TEACHING: CHOOSING AMONG THE OPTIONS, eds. Jarvis and Omaggio, Vol. 8 (1976)

PERSPECTIVE: A NEW FREEDOM, ed. Jarvis, Vol. 7 (1975)

THE CHALLENGE OF COMMUNICATION, ed. Jarvis, Vol. 6 (1974)

FOREIGN LANGUAGE EDUCATION: A REAPPRAISAL, eds. Lange and James, Vol. 4 (1972)

Professional Resources

A TESOL PROFESSIONAL ANTHOLOGY: CULTURE

A TESOL PROFESSIONAL ANTHOLOGY: GRAMMAR AND COMPOSITION

A TESOL PROFESSIONAL ANTHOLOGY: LISTENING, SPEAKING, AND READING

THE COMPLETE ESL/EFL RESOURCE BOOK, Scheraga

ABC'S OF LANGUAGES AND LINGUISTICS, Hayes, et al.

AWARD-WINNING FOREIGN LANGUAGE PROGRAMS: PRESCRIPTIONS FOR SUCCESS, Sims and Hammond

PUZZLES AND GAMES IN LANGUAGE TEACHING, Danesi

COMPLETE GUIDE TO EXPLORATORY FOREIGN LANGUAGE PROGRAMS, Kennedy and DeLorenzo

INDIVIDUALIZED FOREIGN LANGUAGE INSTRUCTION, Grittner and LaLeike

LIVING IN LATIN AMERICA: A CASE STUDY IN CROSS-CULTURAL COMMUNICATION, Gorden

ORAL COMMUNICATION TESTING, Linder

PRACTICAL HANDBOOK TO ELEMENTARY FOREIGN LANGUAGE PROGRAMS, Lipton

SPEAK WITH A PURPOSE! Urzua, et al.

TEACHING CULTURE: STRATEGIES FOR INTERCULTURAL COMMUNICATION, Seelye

TEACHING FRENCH: A PRACTICE GUIDE, Rivers

TEACHING GERMAN: A PRACTICAL GUIDE, Rivers, et al.

TEACHING SPANISH: A PRACTICAL GUIDE, Rivers, et al.

TRANSCRIPTION AND TRANSLITERATION, Wellisch

YES! YOU CAN LEARN A FOREIGN LANGUAGE, Goldin, et al.

For further information or a current catalog, write:
National Textbook Company
a division of *NTC Publishing Group*
4255 West Touhy Avenue
Lincolnwood, Illinois 60646-1975 U.S.A.